The Raptors of Europe and the Middle East

A Handbook of Field Identification

The Raptors of Europe and the Middle East

A Handbook of Field Identification

DICK FORSMAN

Covering: Albania, Andorra, Armenia, Austria, Azerbaijan, Belgium, Bosnia, Bulgaria, Belarus, Czech Republic, Croatia, Cyprus, Denmark, Egypt, Estonia, Georgia, Germany, Great Britain, Greece, Hungary, Finland, France, Iceland, Ireland, Israel, Italy, Jordan, Latvia, Lebanon, Liechtenstein, Lithuania, Luxembourg, Macedonia, Malta, Monaco, Moldova, Norway, Poland, Portugal, Romania, Russia (European part), Serbia, Slovak Republic, Slovenia, Spain, Sweden, Switzerland, Syria, Turkey and Ukraine.

T & AD POYSER
London

First published in 1999 by T & A D Poyser Ltd
24–28 Oval Road, London NW1 7DX

ISBN 0-85661-098-4

This book is printed on acid-free paper

A catalogue record for this book is available from the British Library

Library of Congress Cataloging-in-Publication Data

Forsman, Dick.
    The Raptors of Europe and the Middle East : A Handbook of Field
Identification / by Dick Forsman.
       p. cm. — (Birds series)
    Includes bibliographical references (p.) and index.
    ISBN 0-85661-098-4 (alk. paper)
    1. Falconiformes—Europe—Identification.   2. Falconiformes
—Middle East—Identification. I. Title. II. Series.
QL696.F3F67 1997
598.9'094—dc21   96-37929
                                               CIP

Typeset by Wyvern 21, Bristol
Colour Separation by Tenon & Polert Colour Scanning Ltd.
Printed and bound in Milan by Rotilito

Contents

PREFACE

This book is a guide to the *field identification* of raptors, and it should be seen only as such, although it incorporates other sides of raptor biology as well. It does not deal with vagrant species to the area, such as the Crested Honey Buzzard *Pernis ptilorhyncus*, Bald Eagle *Haliaeetus leucocephalus* or Swainson's Hawk *Buteo swainsoni*, nor does it cover the rarest breeding species, such as the Black Eagle *Aquila verreauxii* or Shikra *Accipiter badius*, which mostly have an extralimital distribution.

Most of the findings on the species of N and C Europe have been published before in my earlier books *Suomen Päiväpetolinnut* 1980 (in Finnish), *Rovfågelsguiden* 1984 (in Swedish) and *Roofvogels* 1993 (in Dutch), but this material has never been published before in English, except for those species covered by Baker (1993), who, however, fails to present his original source. The data on S European and Middle Eastern species is largely built on personal first-hand knowledge and these findings are largely unpublished.

The data for this book come from various sources. The study of museum collections has played an integral part of the work, especially regarding the understanding of moult and plumage development. For the same reason also free-living live birds have been trapped and studied, mostly in Finland but also in Israel. Over the last 25 years most of my time in the field has been devoted to raptor-watching, in one way or another. During this time I have made some 40 trips to S Europe, N Africa and the Middle East in search of birds of prey, with more than 20 trips to Israel alone. Most of the findings and interpretations in this book spring from a combination of field studies and museum work, the working method largely being to cross-check field observations with museum specimens and to check the validity of in-hand characters in the field. Finally, I have looked through thousands and thousands of photographs for information on plumage characters and moult.

To keep the text as short as possible it has been important to focus on things important to field identification. Throughout the book the emphasis has been on relevant field characters, not on detailed plumage descriptions. The photographs have been chosen, whenever possible, to show relevant plumage characters and characteristic shapes of the species in question. However technically excellent a photograph may be, it rarely conveys the field impression of the bird. Therefore the photographs should be used only as a reliable source of reference regarding plumage characters and moult, while characters such as flight and the field impression of more distant birds should be checked from the text.

Despite the increasing photographic interest towards free-flying raptors many species and many plumages are still inadequately documented. I hope that this book helps to pinpoint the gaps, so that future editions may benefit from an even more complete selection of photographs.

All correspondence and any new photographic material is kindly requested to be sent through the publisher.

DICK FORSMAN

ACKNOWLEDGEMENTS

Producing a book like this is not possible without the help of other people. Some of them are mentioned hereafter, but over the years many have passed without leaving a name. To all these unknown people involved in the creation of this book I would like to express my sincere gratitude for their help in different ways.

This book would not have been possible without the help of all the photographers who generously lent me their best photographs. For this I am greatly indebted to Antti Arjava, Heikki Assinen, Alberto Badami, Salvatore Baglieri, Peter Barthel, Antti Below, Arnoud van den Berg, Klaus Bjerre, Jan-Michael Breider, Bertil Breife, Pierandrea Brichetti, Jan-Erik Bruun, Jens B. Bruun, Sampsa Cairenius, John F. Carlyon, Claudio Chini, Andrea Ciaccio, William S. Clark, Andrea Corso, David Cottridge, Paul Dernjatin, Paul Doherty, Björn Ehrnstén, Tommy Ekmark, Göran Ekström, Kari Engelbarth, Patrik Engström, Hanne and Jens Eriksen, Björn Forsberg, Annika Forstén, Hans Gebuis, Roberto Gildi, Jouko Hakala, Mikko Hakanen, Axel Halley, Hannu Hautala, Brian Hawkes, Jyri Heino, Pekka Helo, Teuvo Hietajärvi, Paul Holt, Markku Huhta-Koivisto, Johan Huldén, Hans Hästbacka, Björn Johansson, Lars Jonsson, Timo Jokela, Hannu Jännes, Pekka Kankaanpää, Matti Kapanen, Seppo Keränen, Hannu Kettunen, Juhani Koivu, Pekka Kokko, Pekka Komi, Jari Kostet, Lasse J. Laine, Tino Laine, Seppo Lammi, Olli Lamminsalo, John Larsen, Harry J. Lehto, Henry Lehto, Jyrki Lehto, Antti Leinonen, Mauri Leivo, Alfred Limbrunner, Antti J. Lind, Tom Lindroos, Jan Lontkowski, Jorma Luhta, Bruce Mactavish, Gabor Magyar, Juha Markkola, Jyrki Matikainen, Karel Mauer, David McAdams, Anthony McGeehan, Penny Meakin, Antti Mikala, Erkki Mikkola, Markku Mikkola, Krister Mild, Jussi Murtosaari, Harri Muukkonen, Tomi Muukkonen, Erik Mølgaard, Rishad Naoroji, Pekka J. Nikander, Andreas Noeske, Sven Nordqvist, Tapani Numminen, Klaus Malling Olsen, Urban Olsson, Jörgen Palmgren, Jari Peltomäki, Risto Petäjämäki, Mikko Pöllänen, Visa Rauste, Matti Rekilä, Martti Rikkonen, Staffan Rodebrand, Asko Rokala, Pentti Runko, Pekka Rusanen, Jouni Ruuskanen, Jukka Rysä, Hans Ryttman, Tapani Räsänen, Markku O. Saarinen, Otso Salmi, Veikko Salo, Hadoram Shirihai, Martti Siponen, Kari Soilevaara, Esa Sojamo, Ray Tipper, Jorma Turunen, Magnus Ullman, Tomi Valtonen, Markus Varesvuo, Timo-Heikki Varis, Hannu Virtanen, Heikki Willamo, Mikko Ylitalo and Dan Zetterström.

I am most grateful to the staff at the following museums for letting me study the collections in their custody: Risto A. Väisänen and Ann Forstén at the Zoological Museum in Helsinki, Carl Edelstam, Bengt-Olov Stolt and Göran Frisk at Naturhistoriska Riksmuseet in Stockholm, Jon Fjeldså at Universitetets Zoologiske Museum in Copenhagen and Peter Colston at British Museum (Natural History) in Tring.

The following persons helped me in various ways during the field-work, for which I owe them a special debt: Esko Aikio, Mauro Bailo, Juan J. Ferrer, Isabel and Jesus Garzón, Edward Gavrilov, Gerard Gorman, Vassilis Hatzirvassanis, Hannu and Irma Hautala, Graham Hearl, Jouko Högmander, Heikki and Sinikka Karhu, Juhani Koivu, Henry Laine, Pekka Paarman, Francisco Purroy, Jarmo Ruoho and Hadoram and Lilly Shirihai.

I am grateful to William S. Clark, who kindly gave me his data on measurements from live raptors and for letting me look through his photographs on trapped birds, while Hadoram Shirihai kindly handed me all his raptor photographs to choose from for the photo-collection. Per Alström, Björn Johansson, Lars Jonsson, Hannu Jännes and Jari Kostet sent me field-sketches on various raptors, for which I am grateful. I also want to express my gratitude to Steve Madge and Göran Frisk, who provided me with details on the occurrence of dark morph Rough-legged Buzzards in Europe, and to Killian Mullarney for his information on the occurrence of American Goshawks in Ireland and Britain.

My sincere thanks goes to my friends Jan-Erik Bruun, Björn Ehrnstén and Marcus Wikman for their great company over the many years trapping live raptors together in Finland, and to William S. Clark and his staff for letting me take part in their trapping projects in Israel.

I would also like to thank all the people at T & AD Poyser for a smooth co-operation during the production of the book. I am especially indebted to Dr Andrew Richford for his encouragement and support throughout the work, and to Manjula Goonawardena and Samantha Richardson for their important roles during the various stages of production. I am most grateful to Angela Turner, who, as a copy editor, did a great job, commenting on and clarifying my text in many ways.

Finally, I want to express my sincere gratitude to two Swedes for their inspiring work in the field. I am grateful to Carl Edelstam for introducing me to the basics of raptor moult over a Rough-legged Buzzard specimen some 23 years ago, and to Lars Svensson for his outstanding identification articles, which at the time set new standards to the whole approach of field-identification.

ABBREVIATIONS AND TERMINOLOGY

adult (ad; plumage)   The final plumage of a bird

anterior   Towards the front or the head of the bird

ascendant moult (moulting sequence)   When the moult wave in the wing progresses towards the body (away from the tip)

auricular (spot or patch)   Plumage mark on the ear coverts, sometimes including part of the cheeks as well

axillaries   The elongated feathers of the armpit

bare parts   The parts of a bird not covered with feathers (usually cere, bill, eyes, eye-rings and feet)

BMNH   British Museum of Natural History (Tring)

body plumage   All contour feathers of a bird except for the remiges and the rectrices

carpal (carpal-patch, area, comma, etc.)   The underwing primary coverts or the area close to it

centre (moult c.)   The position from where the moult of the flight-feathers starts

centrifugal (c. moult)   Moult of tail-feathers starting from the central pair and progressing outwards

cere   The unfeathered, waxy skin covering the base of the upper mandible in birds of prey

cheek   The side of the head below the eye

cm   centimetre

collar   Specially shaped feathers surrounding the facial disk of harriers *Circus*

contour feathers   All (visible) feathers covering the bird, as opposed to down

cy (calendar year)   A bird is in its 1st cy from its birth until 31 of Dec of that same year, when it over night becomes 2nd cy, and so on. The 'birthday' is thus on 1 of Jan every year.

descendant moult (moulting sequence)   When a moult wave progresses away from the body (towards the tip)

dimorphic   A bird showing two distinct morphs

distal   Towards the periphery; away from the bird's body; opposite of proximal

divergent (d. moult)   Wing-moult starting from a focus but progressing simultaneously inwards and outwards; typical of remex-moult in falcons

dorsal   Towards the upper surface (upperparts) of a bird

eye-line Usually a dark line in front of and/or behind the eye

eye-ring The bare skin around the eye, rather prominent e.g. in falcons *Falco*

feather tract The feathers of a bird that grow together, wear and are moulted at roughly the same time

fingers The emarginated tips of the longest primaries

flight-feathers The remiges and rectrices

focus (pl. foci) The point where a moult wave starts, indicating the first feather to be shed in a given sequence

gular (stripe) A longitudinal streak on the throat

immature (imm; plumage) In this book given the meaning 'not mature' or 'non-adult' and includes all the plumages except for the adult plumage (also the juvenile if not specified more exactly)

juvenile A young bird in its first year of life still carrying its juvenile remiges

juvenile (juv; plumage) The first complete plumage acquired in the nest and during the fledging stage. Most raptor species have this plumage until their first complete moult in 2nd cy spring, but some (smaller) species undergo a partial moult of the body feathers during the first winter

km kilometre

leading edge of wing The anterior edge of the wing

lores The area between the eyes and the cere. Usually covered in bristles, but in Honey Buzzard covered in scale-like feathers

malar stripe Usually a dark stripe running from the gape along the lower edge of the cheeks

mantle The feather tract between and in front of the scapulars, sometimes also given the meaning of the upperparts more generally, including the scapulars

monotypic Species with only one (the nominate) subspecies

morph A distinct (plumage) variant of a species

moustache A prominent dark mark below the eye, usually in falcons

n sample size

nape The upper hindneck

p Primary (pp. = primaries)   In this book numbered descendantly, unless otherwise stated

patagium   The fold of skin between the wrist and the body (often equal to forearm)

phase   A (colour) form of a species, but with more gradual changes between the different forms than in 'morph'

plumage   In this book used in the sense of 'aspect', i.e. all the feathers a bird has at any given time

polymorphic   A species showing a variety of plumage forms

polytypic   A species with geographical subspecies

primaries   The flight-feathers of the wing attached to the metacarpus and digits forming the 'hand'

primary projection   Part of primaries visible beyond the tertials on a closed wing

proximal   Towards the base of a structure (tail, feather, etc.); opposite to distal

rectrix (pl. rectrices)   Tail-feather(s)

remex (pl. remiges)   Wing-feather(s), used for primaries and secondaries together

ruff   The elongated neck feathers in some vultures

s Secondary (ss = secondaries)   In this book numbered ascendantly

scapulars   Dorsal feathers on each side of the mantle covering most of the upperparts on a perched bird

SD   Standard deviation

secondaries   The flight feathers of the wing attached to the ulna (and humerus)

serially descendant   About moult, when e.g. primaries are moulted descendantly in independent groups

sp.   Species (plural spp.)

ssp.   Subspecies

subadult (subad; – plumage)   The plumage(s) preceding the adult plumage

subterminal band (on feather)   Mostly a dark band just inside the tip of the feather

supercilium   Mostly a pale line running above the eye

suspended moult   When the moult is interrupted e.g. for the migration or during breeding, but resumed at the point of interruption shortly after

terminal band   A band at the tip of a feather

tertial   The innermost secondaries, varying in number between two and three in raptors

trousers   The elongated feathers of the thighs

underbody (plumage)   The feathering of the underparts of the body

underparts   The feathering of the underbody and the underwing coverts

underwing   The lower surface of the wing

upperparts   The feathering of the entire upperparts including body, wings and tail
upperwing   The upper surface of the wing

ventral   The underparts or lower surface of the bird or a structure; opposite to dorsal

wing-formula   The relative distances between the primary tips forming the wing-tip; mostly compared with the tip of the longest primary
wing-span   The measurement between the extended wing-tips
wrist   The joint between the hand and the arm in the wing. Also called the carpal bend

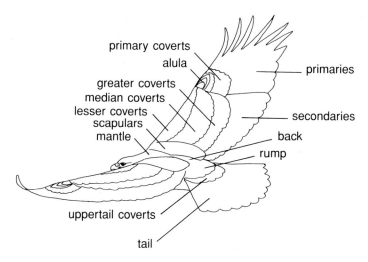

Fig 1   *Feather tracts of upperparts in flight.*

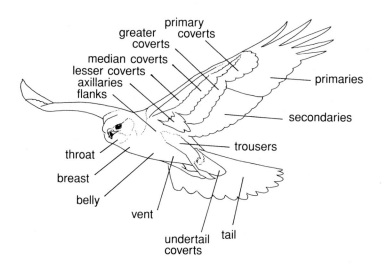

Fig 2   *Feather tracts of underparts in flight.*

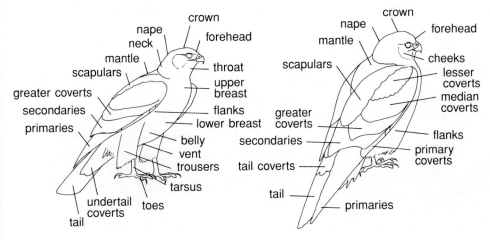

Fig 3 *Feather tracts of a perched raptor.*

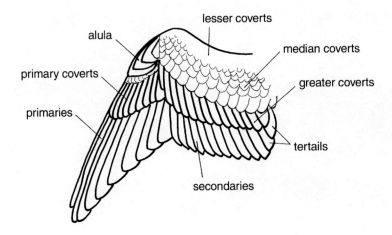

Fig 4 *Upperwing.*

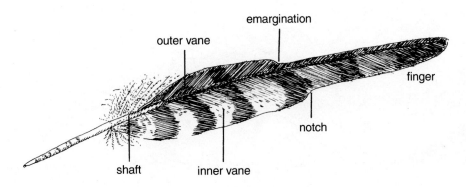

Fig 5 *A fingered primary.*

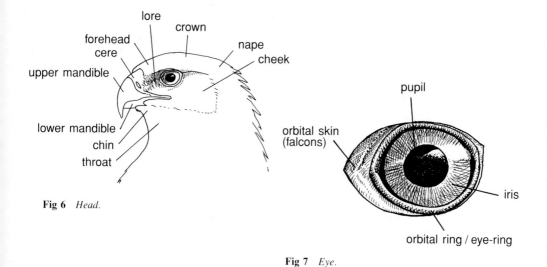

Fig 6 *Head.*

Fig 7 *Eye.*

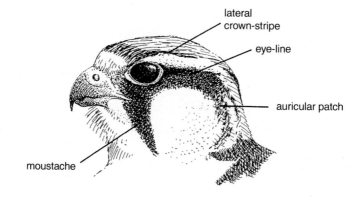

Fig 8 *Head-markings.*

HOW TO USE THE BOOK

To make the information more easily accessible, the species accounts are divided into smaller sections.

Species name: the most widely accepted English name has been used. Recently proposed names (e.g. Beaman 1994) have been avoided, except for a few cases, when regarding names of subspecies.

Latin name: this book follows the taxonomy and nomenclature adopted by *The Handbook to the Birds of the World* (Arroyo *et al.* 1995).

Subspecies: see above under Latin names.

Distribution: the distribution is given roughly just to indicate in which parts of the region a species is likely to occur.

Habitat: a short description of the habitat preferences is given, with emphasis on those habitats where the bird is most likely to be encountered.

Population: the population estimates are treated rather superficially unless recent drastic changes have occurred. The population figures are mainly based on Gensbøl (1995) and Tucker & Heath (1995).

Movements: the presentation aims to give the basic information about the migrational status of the species, peak migration times, passage routes and numbers, and wintering areas.

Hunting and prey: describes the hunting methods and mentions the usual prey taken, with emphasis on factors that may be of importance for identification.

SPECIES IDENTIFICATION

Total length and wing-span are given, based on recent measurements of live birds, or, when this has not been possible, on published material.

Note: gives a few important points with regard to the species identification.

Identification summary: gives the main points for identification and for separating from similar species. Reading this section is often enough to clinch the identification.

In flight, distant: present characters that are important when identifying the species of distant birds in flight, by describing the silhouette and flight, and focusing on the plumage patterns visible over greater distances.

In flight, closer: gives detailed description of the species in flight, with emphasis on the important plumage details, which can only be seen close up.

Perched: gives the main characters on how to identify the species when perched.

Bare parts: gives the color of the bare parts, with an emphasis on the differences between the species, age groups and the sexes.

Confusion species: tells which species are most likely to cause confusion and how to differentiate between the species.

Variation/subspecific identification: describes any distinctive plumage variants, or morphs, or additional subspecies, that may be identified in the field.

Moult: gives the moulting period and describes the annual moult, and relates this to the changes in the plumage. Also gives examples of moulting individuals, to show progression of moult with time.

AGEING AND SEXING

Note: raises a few points about the possible difficulties with regard to ageing.

Ageing summary: gives the main ageing features and describes the age classes briefly.

Plumages: describes all the plumages that are possible to identify in the field, with descriptions for distant and close-up of birds in flight, as well as for perched birds. Also mentions any notable changes in plumage due to wear.

Sexing: gives the differences between males and females, including plumage, unless these are already dealt with under the Ageing section.

INTRODUCTION TO THE FIELD IDENTIFICATION OF RAPTORS

MOULT

The bird's plumage consists of feathers, which wear in use and therefore have to be replaced regularly in a process called moult. The plumage (plumage is here defined as the entire feathering of a bird at any one time and is equivalent to the terms 'aspect' used by Humphrey & Parkes (1959) and 'feathering' used by Palmer (1972)) is moulted feather by feather. Basic knowledge about moult is vital for the birder who wants to be able to age raptors in the field. Indeed, in some of the larger eagles and vultures the moult pattern provides the only reliable clue for correct ageing.

The duration of the moult cycle (the time between the first and the last moulted feather of the same feather generation) seems to depend mainly on the size of the bird and its migration habits. The moult in most raptors is a prolonged process, lasting from 4 months in the smaller species to almost the whole year, apart from the migration periods, in the Osprey, while some of the larger eagles retain some juvenile feathers for up to 4 years before they are moulted!

Actively moulting birds are easily recognized by their symmetrical gaps in the wings and tail. Accidents may also result in lost or broken feathers, but these gaps are rarely symmetrical. The moult of species with an interrupted or incomplete moult can be studied even between the moulting periods by checking the condition of the flight-feathers: both fresh and worn feathers will be present in the same wing. This section summarizes the basic information needed to understand the different moult patterns in raptors and the mechanisms behind them.

Timing of moult

Different raptor species moult at different times of the year depending on their lifestyles. A general rule is that resident species and short-distance migrants moult during the breeding season, while long-distance migrants have a post-breeding moult in the winter quarters. In most species, females start to moult before the males, while young birds (2nd cy) moulting for the first time tend to start before the adults, although this varies from species to species.

In short-distance migrants the females usually start to shed their primaries during egg-laying or incubation, while the females of long-distance migrants, such as Honey Buzzard, Hobby and Eleonora's Falcon, either start during the late fledgling period or in the winter quarters. In both groups the males usually start some weeks to a month later than females, and in the tropical migrants the males often do not start until they have reached the wintering grounds.

The moult is not necessarily a continuous process even in those species that replace the entire plumage during the breeding season. Sparrowhawks suspend primary moult when their nestlings are half-grown (Newton & Marquiss 1982b) and a similar strategy seems to apply to other species as well. Breeding Goshawks, Marsh Harriers, Peregrines and Gyrfalcons studied in Finland also suspend their moult during the late nestling period (pers. obs.).

As regards timing of moult, it is important to remember that different subspecies, and indeed various populations of the same subspecies, may moult at different times. The White-tailed Eagles of Greenland moult more slowly than Scandinavian birds, which in turn are slower than S European and Caspian birds (Edelstam 1984) and a similar difference in moulting speed seems to apply to Golden Eagles from Fennoscandia and S Europe (pers. obs.). The Steppe Buzzard, which is a long-distance migrant, has a different moult strategy altogether from the nominate subspecies (Forsman 1980, 1984, 1993b), and a similar difference in moult strategy and timing can be noted between the N European migratory populations of Peregrine and populations from C and S Europe (Stresemann & Stresemann 1966; pers. obs.).

Partial and complete moult

A moult that includes the remiges is called a complete moult. This is the basic type of moult and every species has a complete moult annually. Some larger species, however, are not capable of replacing all their flight-feathers during one season, but suspend the moult until the start of the next moulting season. Although the moult is in a sense incomplete, as it does not comprise all the flight-feathers, it is nevertheless called complete moult. In addition to the complete moult some species have a partial moult that comprises variable parts of the body plumage, but never the remiges. In raptors the partial body moult typically occurs in juveniles during the first winter, but it varies in extent from species to species, and individual differences even within a species may be considerable. The small falcons all have a partial body moult during the first winter. Hobbies and Merlins usually moult only a few feathers of the upperparts, whereas Lesser Kestrels and Red-footed Falcons often replace most of their body plumage, often even including some tail-feathers, but not the juvenile remiges. The Levant Sparrowhawk also moults most of its juvenile body plumage before returning to Europe in the spring. The large falcons regularly moult the head and upper breast during the first winter but only a few feathers of the upperparts. Some juvenile Pallid and Montagu's Harriers replace most of their body plumage during their first winter, while others moult hardly any feathers.

Moulting sequence

In different groups of raptors different moulting strategies, as well as different moulting sequences, have evolved. The falcons (*Falconidae*) have a unique moulting sequence among the raptors, while the various eagles and hawks (*Accipitridae*) show a multitude of variations on the same theme, the variations mostly depending on the size of the bird and its migration habits. The Osprey (*Pandionidae*), although closely related to the accipitrids, has a moulting strategy of its own.

Hawks and eagles *Accipitridae* The primaries are basically moulted descendantly, starting from p1 and ending at p10. The secondaries are moulted from four different foci. The outermost focus is at s1, from which the front proceeds towards s4. The second focus is at s5, from which the wave progresses (ascendantly) towards the body until it meets the third wave, which has started from the innermost secondary (e.g. s11) and progressed outwards. The tertials are moulted as an independent group before the secondary moult is completed.

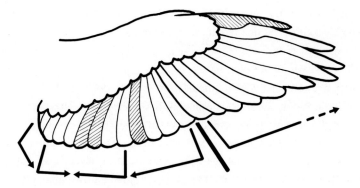

Fig 9 *Remex moult in hawks* Accipitridae. *Each arrow starts at a moulting centre (focus) and indicates the progression of the moult-front. The shaded feathers (p10, s4 and s7–8) are the last in a sequence to be moulted and are consequently the ones most often left unmoulted.*

Smaller species, such as accipiters, harriers, kites and buzzards, moult, as a rule, all of their primaries in one moult. However, *Buteo*s (and Red Kite?) moulting for the first time (2nd cy) regularly retain a few outermost juvenile primaries until the next moult in 3rd cy summer, when they develop a serial moult (see below). The greater primary coverts are moulted at roughly the same time as their corresponding primary. The secondaries are, as a rule, moulted completely, but some feathers (usually the last ones of a wave to be moulted, especially s4 and/or some of the median secondaries, mostly s7 and/or s8) may be retained in any moult, possibly indicating adverse conditions such as food shortage during moult. *Buteo*s seem to retain some of their secondaries unmoulted more often than other medium-sized accipitrids, which causes irregularities in the subsequent secondary moults and may be seen as a step towards the serial moult. In species such as accipiters and harriers the greater upperwing coverts are usually moulted rather simultaneously as a group at some stage during the secondary moult, while the more slowly moulting *Buteos* moult them at roughly the same time as the corresponding secondary.

Larger species, such as the larger eagles (*Aquila, Haliaeetus, Circaetus*) and all the vultures, have a different and very complex moulting strategy. The sequence from the beginning is the same as for the smaller *Accipitridae*, but the longer quills require up to 2 months to grow, and hence the big birds are not capable of replacing the entire set of flight-feathers in one season. The feather replacement is very slow at the beginning, and birds in their first and second moults replace only a relatively small number of flight-feathers. However, during the subsequent moults they gradually build up a so-called serial or serially step-wise moult (*Staffelmauser* Stresemann & Stresemann 1966), which allows them to replace the flight-feathers at a much faster rate than the younger birds and hence enables them to moult a greater proportion of the flight-feathers annually. The greater primary coverts are moulted with the corresponding primary.

The development of the serial moult is easiest to follow in the primaries, which are all moulted descendantly. The first moult starts in 2nd cy spring with the innermost primary but it is interrupted in the autumn, when only some inner primaries have been moulted. The moult is resumed, depending on the species, either in the winter quarters or in the following spring, when the dormant moult front is activated. Before the first moult cycle is completed (i.e. before all juvenile primaries have been replaced) a second moult wave starts from the innermost primary and begins to 'chase' the first moult front. In some species the second moult commences in the bird's 3rd cy summer, while larger species do not show a second moult front until in their 4th cy summer. Because the longer outer primaries grow out more slowly than the shorter inner primaries, the later moult front slowly

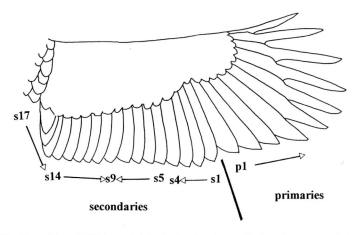

Fig 10   *Wing of juvenile White-tailed Eagle showing the numbering of remiges and the directions of the moult-waves (redrawn after Forsman 1981).*

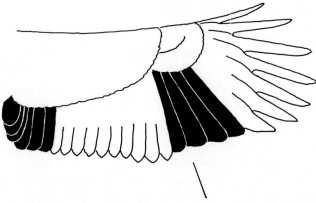

(a)   After first moult (second plumage). Has moulted p1–3, s1 and s17–12, while the other remiges are juvenile feathers.

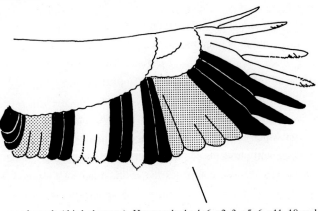

(b)   After second moult (third plumage). Has moulted p4–6, s2–3, s5–6, s11–10 and s17–14, while p7–10, s4 and s7–9 are retained juvenile feathers. Note the protruding juvenile secondaries.

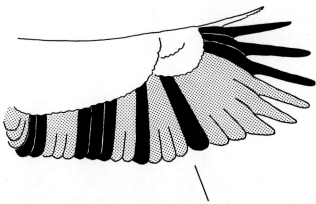

(c)   After third moult (fourth plumage). Usually only the outermost primary is a retained juvenile feather, while all the others have been replaced at least once, some, like s1 and the innermost secondaries, twice.

Fig 11 *Moulting sequence in the three first moults of White-tailed Eagle, where white feathers are juvenile remiges, black feathers are remiges replaced in the last moult and grey feathers are remiges replaced in an earlier moult (after Forsman 1981).*

catches up with the first. After another 1–2 years a third moult front starts again from p1, then a fourth and so on. This explains why adult birds of the largest species may show up to four simultaneously active moult fronts in the primaries, which all proceed outwards with just a few feathers separating them from each other. For a long time, adults of large raptors were thought to have an irregular primary moult, as their very complex moulting pattern was impossible to understand without the knowledge of the preceding moults.

The secondaries of large species are moulted in a similar fashion, but the moult pattern is slightly more complex because of numerous moult foci and both descendantly and ascendantly moulting groups at the same time. The larger eagles and vultures moult their greater upperwing coverts at roughly the same time as the corresponding secondary.

Osprey *Pandionidae* The moulting sequence in the Osprey is basically similar to that of the Accipitridae, but the moult is more or less continuous, except for moulting pauses during the migration periods. Juvenile Ospreys start their complete moult towards the end of their 1st cy, whereas all other species do not start until their 2nd cy spring.

Falcons *Falconidae* The falcons moult their primaries divergently, starting with p4 (sometimes with p5), from which the moult waves proceed simultaneously both descendantly towards p10 and ascendantly towards p1. The outermost primary (p10) is the last primary to be replaced and it usually also completes the entire moult of the flight-feathers. The greater coverts are moulted in pace with their corresponding primary.

The secondaries are moulted from three different foci. An outer, divergent moult focus is situated at s5 (sometimes s4), from which waves progress both outwards and inwards. A second focus is at the innermost true secondary, from where the moult wave proceeds

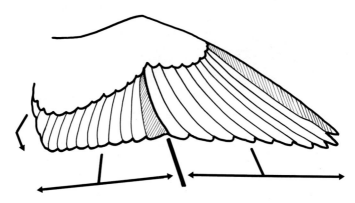

Fig 12   *Remex moult in falcons* Falconidae. *The arrows give the moult centres and the directions of the moult-fronts. The shaded feathers (p10 and s1) are the last ones to be replaced in each moult.*

outwards and meets with the ascendant wave from s4 halfway between the two foci. The third focus is in the tertials, which are replaced independently before the moult of the secondaries is completed. The greater upperwing coverts are moulted from the same foci as the secondaries, but their moult proceeds faster and is usually completed before the moult of the secondaries, which is normally completed with the replacement of s1.

Moult and field identification

Moulting birds often show strange looking plumages, which do not occur in the field guides, but which make sense if you have some basic knowledge about moulting sequences and timing of moult for the different species. In the first edition of the *Flight Identification Guide to European Raptors* (Porter et al. 1974) the very distinct plumage of the 2nd cy male Red-footed Falcon in autumn was thought to be an old adult male. Similarly, many transitional plumages, which result from partial and suspended moults, were either completely overlooked or poorly understood at the time.

Birds in active primary moult may also cause identification problems. When the primary moult reaches the wing-tip it changes the wing-formula, which is a reliable identification character between some difficult species pairs (e.g. Kestrel versus Lesser Kestrel, Hen Harrier versus Pallid and Montagu's Harriers, Greater versus Lesser Spotted Eagle, etc.). It is therefore important to note whether the bird is moulting before trying to assess its wing-formula. Actively moulting birds, with missing and/or growing remiges, may also fly differently from birds with complete wings, which is another factor worth keeping in mind.

Moult and ageing

A simple and important rule is that juveniles do not moult their remiges during their first autumn, with the exception of the Osprey, which commences its primary moult in 1st cy Nov–Dec. *Thus all birds showing active or suspended wing moult in late summer or autumn are at least 1 year old.* In the largest species, which develop a serial moult, the ageing can be taken a step further. Birds moulting for the first time show only one moult front in the primaries, while adult birds may show anything between one and four moult fronts in the hand at the same time depending on the species and the bird's age.

In most raptor species the remiges (and rectrices) differ markedly in length between adults and juveniles (see page 14). This can be of importance when trying to age larger species such as buzzards, eagles and vultures, which have a suspended remex moult. In the first moult these species always retain a number of juvenile feathers, which, depending on the species, will stand out as being shorter or longer than the freshly moulted feathers. In most species the second and subsequent feather generations are longer than the juvenile feathers, and are thus easy to pick out. The ageing of some larger species is largely based on the tracking of retained juvenile remiges, which may act as markers for

Plate 1   *Rough-legged Buzzard, 2nd cy male after first moult. Note retained juvenile p7–10, s3–4 and s7–9 differing from second generation remiges by size, shape, colour and pattern. 11 Oct 1995, Finland (Dick Forsman).*

Plate 2   *Long-legged Buzzard. The differences in wear between retained juvenile feathers and moulted second generation feathers are often more obvious on the upperparts, as shown by this 2nd cy bird at end of first moult. 13 Oct 1987, Finland (Dick Forsman).*

up to 4 years in slowly moulting species such as Golden and White-tailed Eagles and Bearded, Griffon and Black Vultures.

Not only the dimensions of feathers but also their pattern and colour vary between juvenile and later generations in most species. With a good knowledge of the juvenile plumage and its feather-patterns, these feathers can be used as markers for the bird's age. An adult male Hen Harrier in spring showing a dark retained secondary will tell the observer that the bird is a 3rd cy male. Similarly a spring *Buteo*-buzzard with a few median secondaries that show a faint subterminal band (and are short) is a 3rd cy bird.

Moult and sexing

Moult can only rarely be used for sexing, but the moulting stage may give an indication of a bird's sex. In breeding pairs the males show a less advanced moult than their mates at any given date, but the differences are more marked during the early stages of breeding as the males tend to catch up with their mates before the moult is completed.

PLUMAGE WEAR

After moult, plumage wear is the second factor most affecting a bird's plumage and appearance. As with moult, plumage wear follows certain principles, which are important to know in order to understand why plumages sometimes look as they do.

The plumage is constantly exposed to wear. Strong sun, dry climate, winds, sandstorms and abrasion from vegetation all have an adverse effect on the plumage, but even everyday activity such as flying, preening, etc. wear down the feather structure with time.

It is important to note that the juvenile plumage and that of the adults resist wear differently. The juvenile plumage is a mass product and grows while the bird is in the nest, hence the feathers are softer and of considerably poorer quality than those of the adult, which are replaced in a moult, one by one, over a longer period of time. Consequently, the juvenile plumage is uniform with respect to wear, while the feathers of adults show different degrees of wear (and age), although this can be difficult to see in the smaller species with a rather short moult cycle. Also, adult feathers never wear as badly as juvenile feathers, because they are of better quality from the beginning. A bird with a uniformly and heavily worn plumage is usually a juvenile, similarly a bleached and extremely worn remex is most likely to be a juvenile feather. The older birds of larger species always show feathers of different age and wear, most notably among the upperwing coverts and the remiges.

Wear does not affect the plumage uniformly, but certain tracts are more affected than others. This can best be seen on a worn juvenile (cf. plates 169 and 728). The crown, the scapulars, the tertials, the inner upperwing coverts and the central tail-feathers are more worn than neighbouring tracts, and so are the tips of the longest primaries. The underbody and the underwing coverts are more sheltered and hence better preserved, while on the upperparts the inner primaries and outer secondaries remain fresher than their neighbours.

Although all colours change through wear, different colours are affected differently. The darker the colour the more resistant it is against fading and abrasion. This is nicely shown in the barred tertials and central tail-feathers of buzzards or falcons in 2nd cy late spring, when the paler bands have almost worn away, while the darker bands remain. Similarly, most of the pale fringes and tips shown by juveniles on the upperparts disappear through wear by next spring, and yet the rest of the upperparts look quite well preserved. Even the darkest colours fade with time. The originally black fingered primary of a Golden Eagle or a Griffon Vulture becomes faded brown before it is eventually shed after 3–4 years.

Plumage wear can also affect the silhouette of birds. Since most juveniles have pale tips to their flight-feathers, and since the pale areas wear off first, the wings become narrower and the tails shorter during the first year of life. The difference is particularly striking in, for example, juvenile Steppe and Imperial Eagles, which have broad white trailing edges in fresh plumage. Another example is the tail of the Lesser Kestrel, which, through wear, adopts the 'classical shape' with protruding central feathers, not because these feathers are originally longer, but because they have narrower pale tips than their neighbours, and hence shorten less.

Different species show a different degree of plumage wear depending on their habits and biology. Plumage deteriorates quickly in strong sunlight and by abrasion from grass and sand, hence species living in deserts and grasslands are more worn than related species in other habitats. Juvenile Barbary Falcons, Marsh Harriers, Pallid and Montagu's Harriers and Lesser Kestrels all show extensively worn plumages in spring, which can be explained by their habitat preferences and lifestyles. Differences in plumage wear can be notable even within the species depending on different habitat choice. Juvenile Hen Harriers wintering in the Middle East and N Africa become extremely bleached and pale by spring, while their relatives wintering in C Europe retain their plumage colours much better.

IDENTIFICATION BY PLUMAGE CHARACTERS

Plumage characters still remain the most reliable feature on which to base identification. It is possible to identify any bird of prey if the plumage is seen well, and indeed the identification of most birds can be confirmed by looking at just a few crucial plumage characters. These important features vary from species to species and knowing what to look for is actually half the game.

Raptors are known for their extensive plumage variation even within a species. It is therefore important to focus on those parts of the plumage that vary less and remain rather constant. Generally, the pattern of the flight-feathers remains the same even in otherwise highly variable species, such as buzzards, eagles and harriers and the extensive plumage variation refers mostly to the body plumage.

Plate 3 *Change of iris-colour with age in Buteo-buzzards. Juvenile Common Buzzard (left) has a pale iris, while the adult (right) has a dark iris. The iris colour of first-adults (below) is rather juvenile-like, whereas the plumage is like an adult's. From left to right: 31 Aug 1980, 2 Jun 1981 and 23 Aug 1980, Finland (Dick Forsman).*

Plate 4   *In Montagu's Harrier the iris-colour differs between the sexes as early as from late nestling period. Males (left) have a grey iris, which turns yellow over the next few months, while juvenile females (right) have dark brown irides, which they retain for at least one year. The same applies to Hen and Pallid Harrier as well. 29 Jul 1991, Finland (Dick Forsman).*

LOOKING AT BARE PARTS

When a raptor provides good and prolonged views one should not miss the opportunity to check the coloration of the bare parts. In most species the bare parts change colour with age and hence are useful as ageing criteria, while in other cases they can be used for sexing or even for species identification.

The iris colour is very important for both ageing and sexing, especially in situations where plumage characters are difficult to assess, as on perched birds. In all buzzards (including Honey Buzzard) juveniles and adults are immediately separated by the iris colour, and in the *Buteo*s a third subadult age-class can often be separated. Sexing juvenile Hen, Pallid and Montagu's Harriers is usually only possible by the iris colour, which differs between males and females from the late nestling period. In most of the species studied the iris colour changes with age, the most notable exception being the falcons, which retain their dark brown irides for life.

The colour of the feet is especially important when ageing large falcons, but it can also be helpful when separating juvenile Red-footed Falcons and Hobbies or Ospreys/Short-toed Eagles and pale buzzards. Not only the colour but also the structure of the feet are worth noting. The toes of Sparrowhawk and Levant Sparrowhawk are very different, while the dimensions of the tarsus differ greatly between e.g. Marsh Harrier, Black Kite and dark buzzards. The *Hieraaetus* and *Aquila* eagles have feathered tarsi down to the toes, while all the other raptors (except for the Rough-legged Buzzard) have bare tarsi.

IDENTIFICATION BY SIZE, SHAPE AND STRUCTURE

Assessing the absolute size of a bird in the field is extremely difficult. The impression of size is often gained by comparing the bird with something of known size, be it a plant, a rock or another bird familiar from before. Raptors are, however, mostly seen in the sky, where there is usually nothing with which to compare it. The difficulties become even greater when moving away from familiar surroundings, e.g. when travelling abroad. In conclusion, size estimates are mostly of very little value for raptor identification. Using size-classes, like small for small falcons and accipiters, medium-sized for buzzards and large falcons and large for larger eagles and vultures, is mostly as far as one can reliably venture.

Mostly, the impression of size comes from the combined impression of the shape and the movements of a bird, which are more easily assessed than size and should therefore be given priority. It is possible for experienced birders to separate most of the species covered in this book just by shape and movements, and in many cases it is even possible to age the bird just by the silhouette!

The variable silhouette

It is important to understand that, even if it is possible to identify a species solely by the silhouette, the silhouette is a highly variable shape. Just look at any bird gliding overhead and you realize that the silhouette changes within seconds because of the constantly changing angle of view. Furthermore, the silhouette changes depending on the purpose of the flight. Powered flight, soaring, shallow gliding, steep gliding, diving and stooping all have their own series of gradually changing silhouettes. Only by careful studies of flying raptors can one learn to know the shapes of the different species in all these different situations. There is no easy way out.

Differences between species Some closely related species or difficult species pairs are, with experience, quite easily separated by the shape alone. Black Kites and Red Kites and Levant Sparrowhawks and Sparrowhawks show different proportions and wing-shapes, while distant adult female Pallid and Hen Harriers and adult Golden and Imperial Eagles are often easier to separate by silhouette than by plumage. There are, however, species pairs where the silhouettes are so similar that the identification always has to rely on plumage characters. Greater and Lesser Spotted and Steppe Eagles can be more or less identical in shape, as can juvenile Lanners and Sakers and juvenile Pallid and Montagu's Harriers. *No identification should ever be solely based on silhouette and shape*, but for the experienced birder they provide a helpful means of assessing distant birds.

Differences between age-groups In many species the juveniles show a distinctly different silhouette to the adults. This is because the juvenile remiges and rectrices differ in length from those of the adults, being longer in some species and shorter in others. In the White-tailed Eagle both remiges and rectrices are longer in juveniles than in adults resulting in distinctly longer tail and broader wings. The Honey Buzzard shows the opposite, with juveniles having clearly shorter remiges and rectrices than the adults, hence showing a 'smaller' and slightly differently shaped silhouette to the adults, being closer to the shape of the Common Buzzard. The Common Buzzard shows a third pattern, where the juveniles have distinctly longer rectrices but shorter remiges than the adults, being more harrier-like in silhouette than the more compact adults. In Marsh Harrier (Zuppke 1987), Sparrowhawk (Newton & Marquiss 1982b) and Lesser Spotted Eagle (pers. obs.) the length of the remiges continues to grow even after the first moult, suggesting small changes in the outline of the silhouette even at a later age.

A general trend among the accipitrids is for the juveniles to show shorter inner primaries than adults, which gives them a nicely S-curved trailing edge to the wing, while the adults show more rectangular wings with a straighter trailing edge. This difference in wing-shape between adults and juveniles is pronounced in the genera *Pernis, Circus, Accipiter, Buteo, Aquila* and *Hieraaetus.*

In the small falcons the juveniles often appear broader winged and longer tailed than the adults, which makes e.g. the juvenile Hobby more similar to a juvenile Red-footed Falcon than one would imagine judging from the silhouettes of the adults.

Differences between sexes Although adult males and females may differ slightly in silhouette, in many species this is often difficult to use without seeing the pair together, allowing a direct comparison. The males tend to be narrower winged and slimmer tailed and the body is lighter and slimmer with a proportionately bigger head. In powered flight they tend to give a lighter impression compared with the heavier females.

Head-on silhouettes
The head-on silhouette is another important identification character needing a lot of experience and practice before it can be used succesfully. Important points to note are the width of the body in relation to the wing-span, how the wings are held and what shape each wing has. Also here it is important to note whether the bird is gliding, soaring or diving, since the wing-attitude normally changes dramatically between these different flight modes. Strong winds also affect the wing-attitude. As a rule the wings are kept highest during soaring, rather level when gliding, and distinctly drooped when diving or gliding fast.

For the experienced observer the head-on silhouette is of great help during the first steps of trying to identify distant approaching birds. It is not enough to know the head-on silhouettes of the birds, one also has to know how they change with changing flight modes and wind conditions. Harriers, the Long- and Rough-legged Buzzards and the Golden Eagle, for example, are known to soar with their wings lifted above the horizontal, but when they go into a steep glide they will all fly with drooping wings! The head-on silhouette of the Honey Buzzard is usually depicted with horizontal or slightly arched wings, but when it soars in a good thermal the wings are often lifted slightly. It will, however, differ from a Common or Steppe Buzzard in the same thermal by its flat wings, lacking the elbow kink of the *Buteo*, and by the smaller body in relation to the wing-span. Similarly the Gyrfalcon looks a lot heavier than the Saker, because the body looks huge in frontal views compared with the wing-span, while the Saker gives the impression of being slim and long-winged.

The wing-formula

The wing-formula, or the spacing of the primary tips in relation to each other, is known to be an important tool for identifying passerines (Svensson 1992), but it is equally important when studying raptors. Another related character equally important for raptor identification is the number of the fingered primaries in the wing-tip. This is another character that requires experience to assess, but one can always start practising on photographs.

The Booted Eagle is often confused with dark buzzards, but it is easily told from all buzzards by its sixth finger alone, even without consulting plumage details. Similarly, Pallid and Montagu's Harriers are easily told from Hen Harriers in the field by the difference in the wing-tip, and Black Kites and Red Kites also show different wing-formulae. Peregrines and Barbarys are immediately separated from Gyrfalcon, Lanner and Saker by the wing-formula and also Kestrel and Lesser Kestrel show distinct differences in the spacing of the tips of the longest primaries.

In some species juveniles and adults have distinctly different wing-formulae, but in most species the differences are too slight for field use. The general trend seems to be that juveniles have more pointed wing-tips than adults, with fewer and/or shorter fingers.

The adult Lesser Spotted Eagle mostly shows seven-fingered primaries, whereas juveniles show only six fingers as a rule. Some juveniles may show a short seventh finger as well, but this is usually distinctly shorter than the adult's and not as prominent in the field. In this case the juvenile wing-formula also aids species identification, since the juvenile Lesser Spotted Eagle is the only *Aquila*-species treated in this book with only six fingers. All the others have seven. In the Bearded Vulture the adults have a narrower and more pointed wing than the juveniles, the difference coming from the different spacing of the primaries. In adults the outermost primary is distinctly longer than the sixth (counted inwards), while the juveniles show the opposite.

Even different populations of the same species may show different wing-formulae, probably reflecting different migratory habits. Common Buzzards from Scandinavia, showing nominate subspecies characters, have a more rounded wing-tip than birds showing Steppe Buzzard characters from the same area (unpubl. data). Also, some of the Black Kites migrating through the Middle East in spring show a more pointed wing than the wintering birds of that area, suggesting a difference between long-distance and short-distance migrants.

Age-dependent feather-shapes

The shapes of individual feathers differ between juveniles and adults. In juveniles the feathers are narrower and the tips are more pointed, while adults have broader feathers with blunt or rounded tips. In the Griffon Vulture, the difference can be seen even in the body plumage, where the upperwing coverts are narrow and pointed in juveniles and broader with rounded tips in adults.

The shape of the tips of the secondaries is often important to note, since they form the trailing edge of the wing. Juveniles in many species show a distinctly serrated or indented trailing edge, because of the pointed secondary tips, while adults show a straighter line. This difference is especially pronounced in, for example, the White-tailed Eagle and Bearded, Griffon and Egyptian Vultures.

The tips of the fingered primaries differ between juveniles and adults in the same way. The retained sharply pointed juvenile fingers are important ageing characters in larger species such as kites, buzzards, eagles and vultures, when they can be compared with moulted fingers of adult type.

Sexing by proportions of head and bill

In most species it is possible to sex a perched bird by the proportions of the head, bill and eye. Males have a larger head relative to their body, the head appears rounder, the face 'flatter', the bill smaller and the eye bigger than in the female. (The eye appears to be of roughly equal size in both sexes, but because of the bigger bill and head it appears *comparatively* smaller in the female.) This difference seems to work for most species tested so far including harriers, buzzards, eagles, accipiters, osprey and all falcons. It can even be used for the tentative sexing of half-grown nestlings.

IDENTIFICATION BY CHARACTERS OF FLIGHT AND MOVEMENT

Many species have a characteristic way of moving in the air, which may be used for identification once one is familiar with the bird. For instance, the Honey and Common Buzzards may, in certain plumages, resemble each other greatly and may from a distance be difficult to separate. After some practice, however, it is quite easy to see the difference in their powered flight: the Common Buzzard moves its wings quite rapidly and almost as much above as below the horizontal plane, while the Honey Buzzard moves its wings more slowly with an emphasis on the upstroke. There are, however, several factors affecting the flight of birds, which should be taken into consideration when trying to identify birds by the way they fly.

One of the most important factors is the wind, its force and direction in relation to the bird's flight-path. Birds flap and glide differently in strong winds and calm conditions and a head-wind affects the flight in a different way to tail-winds and side-winds. The head-on silhouette, which is diagnostic for many species and may hence be used as a supplementary identification character, is also strongly affected by the wind. Birds that normally glide on lifted wings, such as harriers, Golden Eagle and Long- and Rough-legged Buzzards, glide with wings drooped in a strong head-wind, often showing a prominent kink between the arm and the hand.

The purpose of the flight also makes a difference. A Sparrowhawk looks very different when displaying in the air, hunting low over the fields, migrating in a steady powered flight, soaring in the air or when stooping at prey. Quite understandably the flight of moulting birds with missing feathers in the wings, or of birds with damaged wings or birds carrying something in their talons, differs from the normal flight of the species.

THE VARIABLE LIGHT

Light is a prerequisite to all visual observations. However, the lighting conditions vary tremendously between different situations. Understanding the light, which more than anything else determines what we see and how we interpret what we see, is an integral part of field identification. In serious birding the lighting conditions should always be taken into consideration when assessing important or difficult observations.

Underlit or not

In some situations flying raptors appear just dark below, while the same bird somewhere else may show every plumage detail. The difference is largely due to the variable amount of light that is reflected from the ground. If the bird flies over a forest most of the light from the sky is absorbed by the foliage and very little is reflected back into the sky: the birds will then appear dark. Other light-absorbing surfaces are green and ploughed fields, all types of woodlands, dark rocks, etc. The best lighting conditions are when the sun is shining and the ground is covered in snow. These extreme conditions can create almost unrealistic impressions and colours, which are good for photographic purposes and plumage studies, but can easily give a false picture about the average impression of a bird in the field. Desert conditions can provide almost the same lighting conditions, with the light-coloured sand reflecting most of the light back into the sky.

In the afternoon and morning very little light is reflected back into the sky, even on a clear day, because of the low sun. This is well illustrated on a gliding raptor showing a strongly lit head and underbody, which catch the direct sunlight from the side, while the underwings remain in shadow and hence appear almost black.

Even if the underparts of a bird in flight vary enormously according to changing lighting conditions the upperparts mostly remain well lit, because they always catch the direct light from the sky. The identification characters of the upperparts are therefore, in most cases, much easier to assess than those of the underparts, especially in difficult lighting conditions or when looking at distant birds. This is worth keeping in mind, despite the fact that raptor identification was traditionally built on the plumage characters of the underparts.

Different backgrounds

Almost as important as knowledge of the lighting is knowing how the background affects what we see. This is clearly demonstrated by a bird flying across a partially cloudy sky. When the bird is seen against the cloud it appears almost black, and it is very difficult to see any plumage details, but when it crosses a clear patch of blue sky the colours suddenly break through and the conditions may appear quite good. On a dull overcast day even the palest birds, such as male harriers or Black-shouldered Kites, appear all-dark from below against the sky, and it is practically impossible to pick out any plumage characters from the underparts of dark birds such as spotted eagles or Black Vultures, even if they are reasonably close. Similarly, the pale feather-tips that many juveniles show in their wings and tail are completely lost against a cloud or an overcast sky, but are usually very prominent when seen against a clear blue sky, or when viewed against a dark background.

HYBRIDS

In recent years hybrids have been a constant matter of discussion because of the artificial hybrids between different species of large falcons that falconers have produced, and that have escaped from time to time (Gantlett & Millington 1992). Hybridization in the wild has so far been proved between only a few species and the chances of meeting with naturally born hybrids must be negligible. Red Kites and Black Kites have hybridized in both Sweden and Germany several times, and their offspring have successfully reared young together with a Red Kite (Sylvén 1977, 1987). In 1993 a male Pallid Harrier and a female Montagu's Harrier produced three hybrid young in Finland (Forsman 1993d, 1995c), while Newton (1979) mentions a case of hybridization from Britain between a Common Buzzard and an escaped Red-tailed Hawk. Considering the vast intraspecific variation in raptors and the several morphologically and ecologically closely related species, it would be very difficult to prove some hybridizations, for example, between Lesser and Greater Spotted Eagles.

The artificial hybrids are a true problem in W and C Europe, where falconry is widespread and artifical crossings are frequent. Birders just have to face the fact that these hybrids occur and that they can escape like any bird kept for falconry. Most hybrids will be difficult to identify as hybrids, except for those (rare) cases where the hybrid is a cross between two distinctly different species, and shows some diagnostic characters of both parents. Others are not possible to tell from the parental species, and are most likely to be misidentified as either of them. This is especially the case with hybrids between morphologically similar species and in the case of second or third generation back-crossings with either of the parental species.

POINTS TO REMEMBER

When faced with a strange raptor it is important to know what to do and where to focus your main interest, as time may be limited. Below is a list of points to remember for these situations.

(1) Try to get good views of the pattern of the flight-feathers, which is often diagnostic. This may be enough to clinch the identification.
(2) Try to work out the wing-formula.
(3) Note whether the bird is moulting. Active moult indicates a non-juvenile, which may be a helpful detail for the identification.
(4) Take notes or make a sketch of the wing-tip to tail-tip ratio on perched birds.
(5) Note the colour of the bare parts, especially those of the iris and feet.
(6) Try to get photographs of the bird. Even bad ones may prove helpful and are certainly better than nothing.

OSPREY   *Pandion haliaetus*
Plates 5–14

Subspecies: Four subspecies recognized. Nominate *haliaetus* in the Old World from W Europe and parts of N Africa to Kamtchatka and Japan. Extralimital *carolinensis* in N America, *ridgwayi* in the Caribbean and *cristatus* in SE Asia and Australia.

Distribution: A cosmopolitan found on all continents except for the Antarctic. In S America only as a migrant visitor.

Habitat: Always occurs close to water because of specialized diet. Northern populations nest in trees, often far from fishing waters, elsewhere also on sea cliffs or on ground on small islets. On migration crosses all kinds of habitats, stopping over at fish farms, lakes and rivers.

Population: European poulation estimated at 7100–8900 pairs, with majority in Sweden (3000–3500), Finland (900–1000) and Russia (2500–3000). Small populations also in Norway, around the Baltic basin, in Scotland, Portugal and on some of the Mediterranean islands.

Movements: Migratory, wintering throughout Africa, mainly south of Sahara. Migrates on a broad front and does not concentrate along traditional routes. Usually seen singly on migration, sometimes a few together. Leaves northern breeding grounds in Aug–Sep, with peak at Falsterbo, S Sweden in late Aug, with highest autumn total there 335 in 1993, with 53 passing on peak day 21 Aug 1991. Reaches wintering grounds by Nov–Dec.

   Leaves wintering grounds from Mar and appears at Nordic nest-sites by mid-Apr. Spring migration peaks at Eilat, S Israel between end of Mar and mid-Apr, with 130 in spring 1977, with 23 passing on 8 Apr. First-summer birds (2nd cy) do not return to breeding grounds and most spend the summer in Africa.

Hunting and prey: Feeds almost exclusively on fish. Hovers over shallow waters to locate prey and plunge-dives into the water with legs stretched out. Average prey size about 250 g. Often seen carrying fish in talons on migration.

SPECIES IDENTIFICATION

Length 55–60 cm

wing-span 146–173 cm (*n*=18; Finnish birds; D. Forsman, unpubl.)

Identification mostly straightforward thanks to diagnostic plumage and silhouette.

> **Identification summary:** Typical silhouette with long and narrow wings and short tail. Upperparts uniformly dark with white crown, underparts with white body and forearm and darker flight-feathers. At closer range white forearm, black greater coverts band and dark carpal-patch diagnostic. Soars and glides on typically arched wings, similar to a large gull, with prominently angled carpal during active flight and gliding.

In flight, distant A long- and narrow-winged and rather short-tailed raptor. In flapping flight, arms are pressed forward and hand kinked back, creating distinct angle at carpal, and with wings working mostly below the horizontal plane. When soaring, the long wings taper gradually towards the tips, because of slightly narrower hand than arm, and in head-on views the wings are held clearly arched, as in large gull. When gliding, wings are even more distinctly bowed.

Plumage characterized by rather uniformly dark brown upperparts and largely white underparts and head. Upperwings appear uniformly brown, sometimes (depending on light) with faintly paler arm or just a paler area diagonally across the coverts. When fanned, tail often shows a 'wheatear-pattern' above, with darker outer tail and central tail-feathers and paler, barred sides to tail. From below, identified, even from a distance, by whitish head and underbody, whereas the white forearm is often shadowed and the underwings appear dark.

Fig 13 *Osprey gliding. Head-on profile diagnostic with clearly arched wings and drooping hands.*

In flight, closer In closer views forearm and body uniformly white, latter with variable dark band across upper breast. Greater underwing coverts largely dark forming a black wing-band merging with dark carpal-patch. Paler window of inner hand contrasts with extensively dark wing-tips and darker secondaries. Remiges with rather dense barring, often with a broad, dark trailing edge to the arm (cf. Ageing and Sexing). Head white with dark eye-mask continuing down sides of neck.

Perched Dark brown above with contrastingly white underparts and head. Prominent dark eye-mask and darker band across upper breast (see, however, Sexing below). In side-views the long wings cover most of the body including the tail. Shows tight white 'stockings' instead of bushy 'trousers' and the feet are bluish.

Bare parts Feet pale bluish, bill dark with paler grey base and cere. Iris bright yellow in adults, more orange in juveniles.

Confusion species: Possible to confuse with other medium-sized raptors with largely pale underparts. Unlike true eagles, which show at least six fingered primaries, Ospreys show only five, with a rather short inner fifth.

Short-toed Eagle (page 156) Identified by distinctly paler greyish upperwing coverts and by much plainer underwing, lacking Osprey's black wing-bar, carpal-patch and dark secondaries.

Bonelli's Eagle (page 404) Adult has broad and rounded wings, a long greyish tail with a dark subterminal band, a white mantle-patch and a dark crown.

Booted Eagle (page 416) Pale form has very distinctly patterned upperwings and white uppertail coverts; the underwing is diagnostic with white coverts and very dark remiges.

Common Buzzards (page 266) and Honey Buzzards (page 30) Pale forms have whitish underparts, usually show less uniformly coloured upperparts and have diagnostic under-wing pattern, with distinct dark trailing edge. They are also proportionately shorter- and broader-winged birds than Ospreys.

MOULT

Moult is practically continuous, with stops for migration periods only (males suspend moult for part of nesting period?).

Juveniles (first moult) Start to moult their remiges in Nov–Dec, when only about 6 months old, with innermost primary from which the moult wave proceeds descendantly towards the tip. Secondary moult is initiated 1–3 months later. The moult continues without inter-ruptions until the first northbound migration at the age of either nearly 2 or nearly 3 years (3rd cy spring or 4th cy spring, respectively).

The juvenile primaries are moulted in *c.* 12 months. Before this, a second moult wave starts from the innermost primary, gradually building up the serial moult typical of older Ospreys, which show at least two, sometimes up to four, simultaneous moult waves in the primaries.

Adults (subsequent moults) Adults moult more or less throughout the year suspending the moult for the migration periods. The primary moult is serially descendant, with two to four simultaneous moult waves in each hand. This moult strategy enables the adults to replace the remiges annually and yet retain maximal flight abilities.

AGEING AND SEXING

Usually not difficult to separate adults and fresh juveniles when seen close. Transitional plumage possible to tell from adult by retained juvenile remiges.

Ageing summary: Juvenile has prominent pale tips to flight-feathers and upperparts, forming distinct trailing edge to wings and tail and pale scaling to upperparts. Greater underwing coverts are barred and form a less conspicuous and a narrower greater coverts band than in adults, while the barring of the secondaries is regular and more distinct. Underbody and underwing coverts show an ochre stain instead of being pure white. Adults appear uniformly dark brown above and lack juvenile's pale trailing edge of wings and tail. The greater coverts bar of the underwing is darker and more solid and the secondaries are darker and less distinctly barred, often with broadly darker tips. Owing to extensive wear of pale fringes and tips, juveniles become more difficult to age by 1st cy winter. Pattern of remiges and of greater coverts of underwing remain reliable until they are moulted.

Juvenile (1st cy – 2nd cy spring)   Plates 5–8

Easy to age in fresh plumage by regular buffish fringes to upperparts and distinct pale tips to flight-feathers. The pale tips of the greater coverts form a thin line across the upperwing, and seen against a darker background the pale trailing edge of wings and tail are prominent. From a distance the pale feather-tips of inner arm (elbow) appear as a distinct pale spot, lacking in older birds.

Underparts tinged buffish, especially on forearm and armpit. Crown streaked. Greater underwing coverts are barred and form a less distinct band than in adults. Secondaries are distinctly barred from base to tip lacking the broad dark subterminal band of the adults.

In spring, upperparts appear rather uniformly brown from wear, and ageing should therefore be based on characters of underwing, such as pattern of greater coverts and flight-feathers and pattern of moult.

Transitional plumage (2nd cy spring – 2nd cy autumn)   Plates 9–10

Possible to tell from adult only when plumage and moult can be studied in detail. Identified by retained extremely worn and faded juvenile secondaries, showing the juvenile pattern with distinct barring and lack of broad dark subterminal band. Also shows a hint of pale scaling to tips of moulted feathers on upperparts.

Adult (after completed first moult in late 2nd cy autumn)   **Plates 11–14**

Compared with juvenile appears uniformly dark brown above. Crown whiter, with darker forecrown and vestigial lateral crown-stripes. The fanned tail from above shows dark central feathers and a broad dark subterminal band contrasting with barred and paler sides to tail. Adults appear pure white below on body and forearm. The greater coverts band is darker and more solid than in juveniles. From below, the secondaries and rectrices show a dusky and wide subterminal band with finer and regular barring basally. The barring is more diffuse than in juveniles and the secondaries appear generally darker, contrasting more with pale inner hand. Some individuals show uniformly dark secondaries.

Sexing: Males have narrower wings and a slimmer body, particularly around belly and vent, than females, but this can be difficult to judge for the inexperienced without direct comparison. The majority of individuals (but not all!) are possible to sex by combining the following plumage characters. Females show, on average, a broader, darker and more heavily patterned breast-band, whereas males show either a faint band or no breast-band at all (some males have a rather prominent female-type breast-band). Males also show more uniformly white lesser and median underwing coverts than females, which often show more patterned forearm, with several rows of dark spots to their lesser and median coverts. The sexes are usually easily told in a breeding pair, but sexing birds away from the nest is often difficult.

Nothing is known about sexing juveniles by plumage.

References: Edelstam 1969; Forsman 1980, 1984, 1993b; Kjellén 1992b, 1994; Prevost 1982, 1983; Saurola & Koivu 1987; Shirihai & Christie 1992; Tucker & Heath 1995

Plate 5 *Juvenile. Note pale tips and regular barring to flight-feathers and narrower wings than in adult. Dec, Israel (Markku Huhta-Koivisto).*

Plate 6 *Juvenile. Ochre stain to underwing coverts typical of juvenile, as well as uniformly barred secondaries. Aug, Sweden (Jens B. Bruun).*

Plate 7 *Juvenile showing typically scaly upperparts. Diagnostic pale patch on inner median coverts (elbow) visible also in flight over great distances. Aug, Sweden (Jens B. Bruun).*

Plate 8 *Juvenile in slightly more worn plumage with reduced scaling above, but retaining diagnostic pale elbow-patch. Sep 1989, Israel (Markus Varesvuo).*

Plate 9   *Juvenile (2nd cy spring) in midst of first moult. Note extremely worn and faded juvenile outermost three primaries and median secondaries. 27 Feb 1990, UAE (Annika Forsten).*

Plate 10   *Juvenile in moult showing faded and worn juvenile outer primaries and median secondaries. The advanced moult may indicate that the bird originates from the earlier breeding resident Red Sea population. 23 Nov 1995, Oman (Hanne & Jens Eriksen).*

Plate 11 *Adult. Whiter underbody, broad dark trailing edge to wing and uniformly black mid-wing-band differ from juvenile. Apr 1992, Finland (Esa Sojamo).*

Plate 12 *Adult showing typically patterned underparts and diagnostic long-winged and short-tailed shape of the species. Aug, Finland (Mikko Pöllänen).*

Plate 13 *Adult. 14 Oct 1988, Israel (Dick Forsman).*

Plate 14 *Adult. Crown whiter than juvenile's and upperparts more uniform. 14 Oct 1988, Israel (Dick Forsman).*

HONEY BUZZARD *Pernis apivorus*

Plates 15–36

Subspecies: Monotypic. Crested Honey Buzzard *P. ptilorhyncus* of Siberia and SE Asia earlier considered conspecific but now given species status; rare vagrant to the W Palearctic (for identification of this see Forsman 1994, Morioka et al. 1995).

Distribution: Throughout Europe, but rare in the maritime areas in the west.

Habitat: Prefers woodlands with edges and openings, often close to glades and meadows.

Population: One of the more common raptor species of Europe, with an estimated total of *c.* 108 000–148 000 breeding pairs in the W Palearctic. European population considered fairly stable.

Movements: A long-distance migrant wintering in tropical and S Africa. In autumn adults migrate before juveniles, leaving northern breeding grounds at the end of Aug, whereas juveniles peak in mid-Sep. Concentrates along major flyways at Strait of Gibraltar (117 000 in autumn 1972, with peak in early Sep) and the Levant route (26 000 at Bosporus in 1971, 138 000 in E Turkey in 1976 and 417 000 at Kfar Kasem, Israel in autumn of 1986). At Falsterbo, S Sweden, recent numbers show a declining trend with 2738–7357 counted on passage in autumns of 1986–1994.

Spring migration at Eilat between mid-Apr and early Jun, concentrated in first 2 weeks of May; all-time peak on 7 May 1985, when 227 799 Honey Buzzards passed Eilat, with a spring total of 850 000. Adults reach northern breeding grounds at the end of May; majority of 2nd cy birds spend the summer in Africa.

Hunting and prey: Specialized on larvae and full-grown wasps and bees, dug out from underground nests. Also eats frogs and nestlings and fledglings of passerines, especially during cold and wet spells. Very elusive, sitting mostly hidden on low perches when looking for prey. Mostly seen on the wing, covering huge areas when looking for suitable hunting grounds.

SPECIES IDENTIFICATION

Length 51–57 cm

wing-span 113–136 cm. (*n*=24; Israeli spring migrants; W.S. Clark, unpubl.)

Adult and juvenile Honey Buzzards are rather different in plumage and proportions, almost like two different species. Adults are usually not difficult to identify if seen well, but juveniles are highly variable in plumage and are probably the most often misidentified raptors in Europe.

Since Honey Buzzards are extremely variable, identification should preferably be based on the least variable characters, such as pattern of flight-feathers, but also on diagnostic flight and typical wing-attitude when gliding/soaring.

Identification summary: Active flight with high and slow wing-beats compared with e.g. Common Buzzard. When gliding shows flat appearance in head-on views with slightly arched wings. Appears small-headed and rather long and narrow-tailed. Adults identified from below by characteristic barring of tail and underwings, with broad dark trailing edge and sparse barring to bases only of flight-feathers. Eyes are yellow. Juveniles from below have darkish secondaries and broadly dark wing-tips with pale centre to hand and the greater coverts appear pale; uppertail coverts are pale in most individuals and the bill and gape are extensively yellow.

In flight, distant In active flight the wing-beats are slower and the amplitude is greater, with emphasis on the upstroke, compared with Common Buzzard, the most common confusion species. The flight thus resembles more the flight of Booted Eagle or

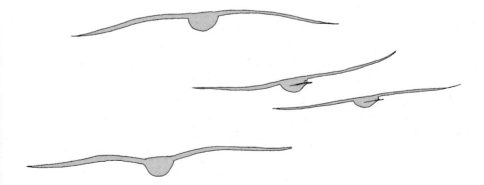

Fig 14 *Honey Buzzard. Wings barely arched when gliding (upper and lower image), flat or with upturned hand when soaring (middle two). Note also small body in relation to wing-span and compare with Common and Steppe Buzzard.*

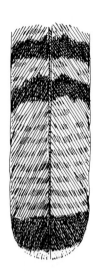

Fig 15   *Honey Buzzard. Central tail-feather from above of juvenile (left), adult male and adult female (right). Note different spacing of main barring and difference in coloration and feather-shape between juvenile and adult (after Forsman 1980).*

Egyptian Vulture, even bearing some resemblance to Short-eared Owl *Asio flammeus*. Honey Buzzards soar on horizontal, flat wings, and, even if the wings are slightly lifted at times, they maintain the flat appearance. When gliding, the wings are held only slightly and smoothly arched. In frontal view the wing always lacks the angled kink at the elbow, typical of *Buteo*s, and the fingered primaries do not bend up to form a small 'broom' as in the *Buteo*s. Adult Honey Buzzards have a smaller body in relation to the wing-span than the *Buteo*s, although this is less prominent on the shorter-winged juveniles.

The silhouette recalls other buzzards, but the Honey Buzzard soars on wings pressed more forward. The wings are clearly pinched in at the base (especially in juveniles) and more rounded at the tip, while the arm appears bulging and wider than the hand on a soaring bird. The tail is longer and when fanned shows more rounded corners than in *Buteo*s. When folded it appears to taper towards the tip and to have slightly convex sides and a slit at the tip. The head is typically small and slim, often held slightly lifted in active flight, the long neck adding to the cuckoo- or pigeon-like impression.

Distant Honey Buzzards appear similar in plumage to other buzzards if the pattern of the underwing is not seen. The greyish upperparts of adult males are characteristic, and also the whitish uppertail coverts of many juveniles. Adult females and some juveniles show typically translucent bases to inner primaries. With practice the wing-action in active flight, as well as the way of keeping the wings when soaring and gliding, can be used tentatively for separating Honey Buzzards from similar species, but it is important to remember that adults and juveniles differ considerably in silhouette.

In flight, closer In flight, best identified by typical pattern of the remiges and rectrices. Adults show dark finger-tips and the remiges are sparsely barred, with a broad black subterminal bar and a few additional bars proximally. The same pattern is repeated in the tail. Underwing coverts are boldly barred in most birds (rather uniform in dark individuals) and the darker carpal-patch is typically oval-shaped, not roundish as in the *Buteo*s. Bill and cere are darkish and the iris bright yellow.

Juveniles are much more similar to *Buteo*s, but show more extensively black wing-tips, reaching inside the fingers, whereas the primaries are paler basally with bold and sparse barring (cf. *Buteo*s). Secondaries appear dark with sparse and evenly spaced barring and often contrast markedly with paler hand. Greater coverts are mostly paler forming a broad wing-bar to the underwing, while the median and lesser underwing coverts are mostly rather uniformly coloured, either dark or pale depending on the colour phase of the bird. In juveniles the darker carpal-patch is also more elongated than in *Buteo*s. Tail shows three or four widely spaced dark bars, which are often difficult to see from above. Upperwings usually appear uniformly dark brown from a distance, but may show slightly paler inner primaries with sparse barring visible at closer range. Some individuals also show distinctly white-tipped coverts, forming a pale patch on the mid-arm. Many juveniles, regardless of colour morph, have distinctly paler uppertail coverts than the rest of the upperparts and many birds have a pale head with dark 'sun-glasses' excluding otherwise similar Common Buzzards. Eyes dark but the bill is diagnostic with extensively yellow base and a restricted black tip.

Perched The Honey Buzzard is a skulking species and is rarely seen perched in the open. Generally it resembles any buzzard in structure, but the head is diagnostic, small and slim with a rather fine bill, almost resembling a pigeon or a Cuckoo *Cuculus canorus*. Adults have yellow eyes and a dark cere, which is unique among European buzzards. Juveniles have dark brown eyes, like many other species, but the bill is diagnostic: cere and base are bright yellow with black only at the very tip. The juvenile Honey Buzzard shows much more yellow and less black in the bill than any other species—a useful character also on flying birds. Compared with *Buteo*s appears to 'sit low' when perched because of shorter tarsi.

Bare parts Feet yellow at all ages. Adults have a dark bill and a greyish cere and the iris is bright yellow, on average more orange in males than in females. Juveniles have a yellow cere, bill and gape and only the tip of the bill is dark; the iris is dark brown. Captive birds in 2nd cy summer had a yellow cere with darker spots and the eyes were turning yellow, appearing pale from a distance.

Variation: Although the pattern of the flight-feathers is rather constant, the body plumage varies individually. All-dark underbody and underwing coverts are rather rare in adults but predominate in juveniles. Regardless of sex most adults, but few juveniles, have boldly barred underwing coverts. Adult males are mostly whitish underneath with variable, bold cross-barring on breast and flanks, whereas females tend to be less distinctly marked and are more blotchy below, appearing more uniformly brownish at a distance (boldly barred females, however, are not rare).

Juveniles are mostly rather uniformly rufous brown underneath (appear dark from a distance) and do not show the three-coloured underbody typical of the *Buteos*; only a small percentage are whitish underneath, with or without fine dark streaks, often concentrated on the upper breast. Out of 283 juveniles studied on autumn migration in Turkey and Israel 28 (10%) were classified as 'pale', all the others being 'dark' (unpubl. data). Pale juveniles can be told from other similarly pale raptor species by diagnostic pattern of flight-feathers, dark eye-mask and oval dark carpal-patch. The largely yellow bill with narrow black tip is another good character at close quarters.

Confusion species: Often confused with other medium-sized raptors, especially the juveniles, which are probably the most often misidentified raptors in Europe. Underwing pattern is always a reliable identification character.

Common Buzzard (page 266) Underwing more finely barred, remiges generally paler, the lesser coverts are dark and the median coverts are paler. Also shows distinct paler breast-band between patterned upper breast and belly.

Booted Eagle (page 416) Conspicuously patterned upperwings whereas remiges appear very dark below with barring usually impossible to see in the field. Tail appears pale and unbarred and wings are more rectangular with six fingers.

Short-toed Eagle (page 156) Always a very pale underwing lacking dark carpal-patch and prominent black trailing edge. Upperwing shows distinctly paler coverts than remiges. Wing-tips are broad with six fingers.

Black Kite (page 65) Appears mostly uniformly dark. Longer and more rectangular wings with six fingers and the underwing, especially the arm, appears dark with hardly any discernible barring. Upperwing shows a pale diagonal area across the coverts and the tail is forked.

Marsh Harrier (page 167) Female-type birds are mostly dark, with conspicuous pale markings on head and wing coverts. Remiges are uniformly dark below, sometimes with broad bars on inner hand. Silhouette slimmer, with narrower wings and longer tail.

MOULT

Annually complete starting in the breeding season, but suspended for the autumn migration. Completed in the winter quarters just prior to spring migration.

Juveniles (first moult) Very little is known about the first complete moult, since most birds remain on the wintering grounds in Africa for the 2nd cy summer. In 2nd cy Feb one individual (BMNH) still largely in juvenile plumage although extremely worn; head, upper breast and mantle already moulted as well as some outer median and lesser upperwing coverts. Another individual from Cameroon (6 Jun; BMNH) in a rather similar stage of body moult, just starting to moult its remiges (tertials growing) and with heavily moulting tail-feathers. Probably moults remiges during late summer and autumn of 2nd cy. Based on studies of captive birds the species seems to moult straight into adult plumage (Forsman 1980).

Adults (subsequent moults) Moult of remiges commences in females during breeding in late Jun or Jul, and usually three or four primaries are moulted before moult is suspended for the autumn migration. Males start later and moult no more than one or two primaries and many migrate south with old set of remiges (Liberia 15 Sep moult not yet started; BMNH). Moult is resumed in the winter quarters and completed just prior to spring migration (adult females from Africa from 2, 9 and 11 Mar all still growing their outermost primary, whereas an adult female from Zimbabwe on 26 Mar had completed its remex moult but still showed sheets at base of outermost primaries. Two other adult females from 4 Mar and 20 Feb showed completed moult; all specimens from BMNH). Occasionally some median secondaries (mostly s4 and s7) may be left unmoulted.

AGEING AND SEXING

The ageing of Honey Buzzards and the sexing of adults is usually not difficult if the bird is seen relatively close and in good light, but some adult females may appear similar to juveniles. For ageing, the underwing pattern and details of the head are important. Sexing adults is mainly based on differences in pattern of flight-feathers below and on colour of head and upperparts. Note also different flight silhouette of juveniles and adults. See also under 'Variation' above.

Ageing and sexing summary: Juveniles from below show all-black fingers and darkish secondaries, while the greater underwing coverts form a broad, pale wing-band. Eye dark and bill extensively yellow, except for the narrowly black tip.

Adults show only black tips to fingers, a broad black trailing edge to wing and typical, sparse Honey Buzzard bars basally on the remiges. Eye yellow and bill appears all-dark in the field.

Adult males are uniformly greyish above with distinct black bars on the upperwing and tail and the head is predominantly grey. Females are darker and browner above, lacking distinct upperwing bars, and the head is brownish, often mixed with white. In males the ground-colour of the underwing is purer and paler with the proximal wing-bars closer to the coverts. In females the secondaries often appear smudgier and darker than the translucent hand and the proximal wing-bars are more evenly spaced between the coverts and trailing edge of the wing. On average, the tail-barring differs between the sexes with the inner bars running closer to the bases in males and further out in females.

Juvenile (1st cy – 2nd cy spring)   Plates 15–22

The juvenile has a dark iris and a predominantly yellow bill with a narrow black tip.

In flight from below, juveniles show a largely black wing-tip with pale primary-bases, which contrast with largely dark secondaries with paler bases. Remiges show *c.* three or four broad and evenly spaced dark bars. Greater underwing coverts are pale, forming a broad wing-band, which merges with the pale inner hand.

Upperparts are more variable, but normally show a dark tail and dark secondaries (barring usually not discernible), with pale tips, and with pale uppertail coverts forming a U at the tail-base. If the tail-barring can be seen it may either resemble the adults' or show three or four sparsely but regularly spaced dark bars. Upperwing coverts may either be uniformly dark or show distinct pale tips and fringes, sometimes making the median covert area appear paler from a distance. As in adult females, the inner primaries often form a paler, barred area on the upperwing, which is translucent from below.

Seen from above, distant juveniles are usually picked out by their distinctly pale uppertail coverts and rather uniformly dark upperwing, while other individuals additionally show paler bases to inner primaries, a paler area in the median wing coverts and a pale head. From below, the dark secondaries, the extensively dark wing-tip with contrasting pale area on the inner hand and the uniformly darkish body and underwing coverts of most birds are diagnostic against *Buteos*.

Transitional plumage (2nd cy spring – 2nd cy autumn)   Not depicted

These birds are not expected to occur in N Europe, as most of them spend the summer in Africa. (A published record of an alleged breeding first-summer female from Austria [Gamauf 1984] is incorrect, as it shows a bird with adult female characters.) This plumage is still poorly known and the description is based on just a few available museum specimens.

Iris already dull yellow and cere showing dark spots by 2nd cy Feb. In early summer birds are still mostly in juvenile plumage, although head, mantle and upper breast are largely moulted, latter already showing distinct cross-bars in males. Moult of juvenile remiges commences in Jun. Autumn birds should still show partly juvenile, partly adult-type flight-feathers, making ageing rather straightforward if seen properly. (See also under 'Moult'.)

Adult male (3rd cy spring and older)   Plates 24–29, 36

Adult males show largely greyish head; the sides of the head especially are uniformly bluish grey. From above, males appear typically uniformly grey, with distinct black tips to remiges and greater coverts and additional black bars on the inner hand. Tail also grey-ish above with prominent barring.

From below, the remiges look clean, uniform and pale with distinct bars. Finger-tips are black with a clear-cut inner margin and the black trailing edge is broad and distinct. The inner wing-bars run just outside the coverts, leaving a wide and uniformly pale and unbarred space inside the subterminal band. The tail-barring is similar, with the inner bars mainly hidden under the undertail coverts, followed by a long and plain gap before the dark subterminal band.

Underbody of adult males is mostly white, with distinct, transverse spots or bars especially on the upper breast and flanks. Some individuals are very sparsely barred and even all-white birds occur save for the dark, oval-shaped carpal-patch.

Adult female (3rd cy spring and older)   Plates 30–36

Adult females show less grey in the head than males, usually restricted to the lores and around the eye, the rest of the head being brownish, often with some white showing on nape. Upperparts are darker, browner and less uniform than in adult males and lack the prominent wing-bars. Inner primaries are often clearly paler than the rest of the upper-wing, with sparse but bold barring, forming a wide pale patch on the inner hand which contrasts sharply with the darker secondaries.

Underwings are less distinctly patterned than those of adult males, and may sometimes even resemble the pattern seen in juveniles. The fingers show more dark at the tips and a gradual and more diffuse border against the pale inner parts. Inner primaries are translucent, a character not found in males, and visible from afar in suitable lighting conditions (back-lit). The barring on the secondaries runs further out, leaving a less obvious gap between the proximal bars and the dark trailing edge than in males. On the primaries the outermost bar usually runs as far out as the notches of the fingers. Secondaries are slightly darker than the primaries, with less distinct barring than in males, adding to a somewhat juvenile-like appearance. The tail-bands are more evenly spaced than in males, with the outer narrow band running about halfway out on the tail, often well clear of the undertail coverts.

Underbody of adult females is usually darker and less distinctly patterned than in adult males and appears either uniformly brownish or blotchy, whereas the underwing coverts may be distinctly barred.

Sexing: The size difference between male and female is small and rarely of use in the field. In adults, males appear slimmer in flight than females, with narrower wings and longer and narrower tail. Plumages differ significantly between adults (see above); juveniles not possible to sex in the field.

References: Bernis 1975; Cramp & Simmons 1980; Forsman 1980, 1984, 1993b, 1994; Forsman & Shirihai 1997; Gamauf 1984; Gensböl 1995; Kjellén 1992b, 1995; Morioka et al. 1995; Shirihai & Christie 1992; Svensson 1976, 1981; Tjernberg 1989

Plate 15   *Juvenile of the commonest, uniformly warm brown colour morph. Note darkish secondaries, sparsely barred primaries with all-dark fingers and paler greater coverts band. 14 Sep 1993, Kazakhstan (Dick Forsman).*

Plate 16   *Black morph juvenile. Note sparse barring to underwings and tail and extensively yellow base to bill. 22 Sep 1996, Turkey (Dick Forsman).*

Plate 17   *Pale juvenile. Note sparsely barred flight-feathers with all-dark fingers and oval-shaped carpal-patch. 28 Sep 1997, Israel (Dick Forsman).*

Plate 18   *Dark mottled juvenile. Note diagnostic sparse and bold barring to remiges and tail and extensively yellow bill. Sep, Sweden (John Larsen).*

Plate 19   *Brown juvenile showing typically smaller pale area on outer hand than Common or Steppe Buzzard. Sep, Sweden (Jens B. Bruun).*

Plate 20   *A rather pale but mottled juvenile showing typically darkish secondaries and restricted pale area on outer hand owing to extensively dark wing-tip. Note also oval-shaped carpal-patch. Sep 1996, Sweden (Jens B. Bruun).*

Plate 21   *Juvenile. Note extensively yellow base of bill and short tarsi as well as white spotting to head and upperparts and dark eye-mask diagnostic of paler birds. Sep, Sweden (Jens B. Bruun).*

Plate 22   *Heavily mottled juvenile showing diagnostic underwings and head. Sep, Sweden (Jens B. Bruun).*

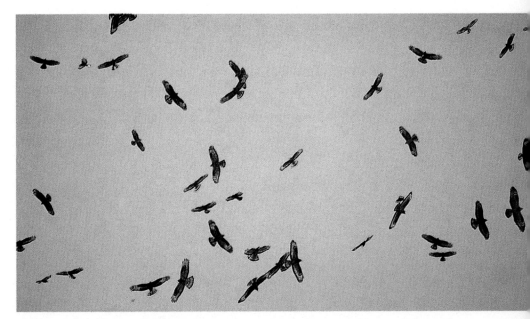

Plate 23 *Flock of migrating adults showing variation in body plumage. May 1994, Israel (Hadoram Shirihai).*

Plate 24 *Adult male. Note 'clean-looking' and distinctly marked remiges, distinct black finger-tips and all-grey head. May 1989, Israel (Paul Doherty).*

Plate 25   *Black morph adult male, showing typical distinctly marked remiges. May 1987, Israel (Hadoram Shirihai).*

Plate 26   *Adult male with distinctly barred body and underwing coverts. May, Israel (Hadoram Shirihai).*

Plate 27 *Adult male showing diagnostic underwings and grey head. May 1987, Israel (Hadoram Shirihai).*

Plate 28 *Adult male from above showing diagnostic grey head and greyish upperwings with distinct black trailing edge. May 1994, Israel (Hadoram Shirihai).*

Plate 29 *Adult male. Note yellow eye, grey bill and cere and short legs all typical characters for the species. The grey head and the uniform upperparts characterize a male. May, Israel (Hadoram Shirihai).*

Plate 30 *Adult female of common brownish type. Note less distinctly patterned underwing with different spacing of wing-bands compared with adult male. Told from similar looking juveniles by more distinct dark trailing edge to underwing, finer, more distinct and differently spaced barring of flight-feathers and by greyer fingers with dark tips only. May 1994, Israel (Hadoram Shirihai).*

Plate 31 *Adult female of common barred type. May 1994, Israel (Hadoram Shirihai).*

Plate 32 *Black morph adult female. Rather similar to black morph adult male, but trailing edge narrower and spacing of wing-bands different. May 1994, Israel (Hadoram Shirihai).*

Plate 33 *Some adult females show dark fingers, darkish secondaries and boldly barred remiges and may hence greatly resemble juveniles. Note, however, prominent dark trailing edge to underwing as well as yellow iris. May 1994, Israel (Hadoram Shirihai).*

Plate 34 *Adult female resembling juvenile due to largely dark fingers and darkish secondaries. Possible to age by typical barring of remiges of underwing. May 1994, Israel (Hadoram Shirihai).*

Plate 35 *Typical adult female from above. Browner and more varied above than adult male with darker and less distinctly patterned secondaries and coverts. Also lacks distinctly bluish grey head. May 1994, Israel (Hadoram Shirihai).*

Plate 36 *Adult female (left) and male on the nest. Note more uniform upperparts and grey sides of head in male compared with more variegated female. 28 Jul 1979, Finland (Dick Forsman).*

BLACK-SHOULDERED KITE *Elanus caeruleus*

Plates 37–44

Subspecies: Four subspecies, with nominate *caeruleus* in SW Europe, Africa and SW Arabia. Extralimitally three subspecies (*vociferus, hypoleucus* and *wahgiensis*) in SE Asia.

Distribution: In Europe, in Spain and Portugal, mostly in SW parts of Iberian peninsula. Also in NW and NE Africa, birds from latter sometimes reaching the Middle East.

Habitat: In Europe prefers open country with scattered trees or loose stands of oaks, olive-trees, etc. Hunts over open areas such as pastures and farmland but nearby trees or woodlots essential as vantage posts and nest-sites.

Population: The Spanish population has increased since 1960 from *c.* 50 to *c.* 1000 pairs (1993), whereas the Portuguese population is estimated to be between 100 and 1000 pairs. Cutting of oak woods to increase farmland poses a threat to the species.

Movements: Resident, but juveniles disperse and turn up as vagrants outside the breeding range. Has reached as far as W and C Europe and has recently bred in France. Occasionally crosses Strait of Gibraltar.

Hunting and prey: Hunts either from elevated perch or from flight. Perches prominently like Kestrel on telegraph poles, wires, dead tree-tops, etc. When hunting on the wing, stops frequently to hover, and drops or parachutes down on prey with wings stretched up in high V. Feeds mainly on small rodents and birds but also takes reptiles and insects.

Species identification

Length 31–35 cm

wing-span 75–87 cm (Cramp & Simmons 1980)

Unmistakable, with diagnostic plumage, flight silhouette and active flight.

> **Identification summary:** Easy to identify by diagnostic plumage: upperparts pale grey with whitish head and black forearm; underparts white with greyer wing-tips. In flight shows fairly broad but pointed wings, extremely short tail and big head. Active flight on soft rolling wing-beats; glides and soars on V-held wings.

In flight, distant Small, unmistakable raptor, plumage appearing white and black. Flight silhouette characterized by longish and rather broad, triangular wings, large head and stubby tail, creating unique shape among European raptors. Active flight quite fast and rolling, reminiscent of Roller *Coracias* or even Lapwing *Vanellus*; at higher speed, wing-action reminiscent of large falcon. When hunting low over ground the somewhat harrier-like flight is fast and pouncing but interspersed by short glides with wings held in deep V, very different to any other raptor. Every now and then makes long descending glides like a paper-swallow and stops frequently to hover like Kestrel at 10–30 m height, when short tail (only slightly more protruding than head) and comparatively broad wings become even more apparent. When hovering, wing-beats slightly slower than in Kestrel with greater amplitude, looking more elaborate. Descends from hovering with wings held almost upright in deep V before final plunge.

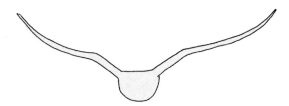

Fig 16   *Black-shouldered Kites glide on wings held in diagnostic deep-V. Note also comparatively big body in relation to wing-span.*

In flight, closer Easily identified by characteristic silhouette and plumage. Upperparts are grey with a black forearm formed by black lesser and median coverts. The short tail is shallowly forked, grey in the middle becoming white towards the edges. Underparts are largely white but the outer hand is diffusely darker grey. The black eye-brow is a promi-nent feature in the otherwise very pale head; the deep red eyes appear dark in the field.

Perched Likes to perch prominently on top of telegraph pole or dead tree. Small and compact in shape, appearing white from a distance, with large head and very short tail concealed under the relatively long wings. Wing-tips reach well beyond tail-tip. Black wing coverts and black eye-line also diagnostic at close range. Sits low because of short tarsi.

Bare parts Cere and feet yellow and bill black. Iris deep red in adults, pale brown or orange in juveniles, but usually appears all-dark in the field.

Confusion species: Unlikely to be confused with any other raptor of the region, owing to striking plumage and diagnostic flight and behaviour.

Pallid Harrier (page 196) Adult male similarly pale but has longer, narrower and less triangular wings and a considerably slimmer body and longer tail. It also shows a distinct black wedge in the wing-tip, both below and above.

MOULT

Complete annually. Since African populations may breed at any time of year moulting juveniles may be found in any month. Information below relates to European population.

Juveniles (first moult) Juveniles start to replace their body plumage some months after fledging and over the next few months attain a plumage very similar to the adult. Data on free-living European birds scanty, but Cramp & Simmons (1980) state that moult starts 3.5 months after fledging and lasts for 3 months. Complete moult, including flight-feathers, probably as in adult.

Adults (subsequent moults) Complete moult between Apr (Spain, p1 missing) and Oct (Spain, Sep, p9–10 still growing; BMNH).

AGEING AND SEXING

Two age-classes, separable in the field in ideal conditions. Juveniles moult their body-feathers comparatively soon, making ageing difficult from an early stage. After partial body moult of juvenile focus on feather-tips of upperparts and on tail.

> **Ageing summary:** Fresh juveniles have streaked crown and upper breast and pale feather-tips to grey brown upperparts. After partial body moult identified by greyer tail with faint dark subterminal band, by dusky not black lesser primary coverts and by pale tips to greater coverts of upperwing. Adults have a whiter tail with no subterminal band, the lesser primary coverts are black and the greater coverts lack pale tips.

Juvenile (first months of life in 1st cy)   **Plates 37–39**

In fresh plumage juveniles are streaked on crown and breast, but individuals vary in both the extent and the conspicuousness of the streaking. The mantle feathers are dark greyish brown with fine whitish tips when fresh, fading to bleached brown and pale tips wearing off at later stages. The dark area on the upper forewing is browner than in adults. This, together with the slightly darker grey upperparts, creates a less contrasting appearance than in adults. Also, the dark grey lesser primary coverts of the upperwing are not as contrasting as on adult birds. The tail feathers are grey on the outer webs, making the folded tail look all-grey from above. When fanned, the tail looks paler but shows a diagnostic darker subterminal band. From below, the tail appears whitish with a diffuse and narrow dusky subterminal band. The remiges and the greater secondary and primary coverts of the upperwing are tipped white, latter forming a narrow wing-band well visible in the field in fresh plumage.

Transitional plumage (1st cy late summer/autumn – 2nd cy spring)   **Plate 40**

In the partial body moult, commencing only some months after fledging, the streaked feathers of the underparts and head are replaced with uniformly white to pale-grey feathers and the pale-tipped feathers of the mantle and upperwing give place to paler and uniformly grey feathers. After the moult juveniles become increasingly difficult to separate from adults, but can still be aged under favourable circumstances by their juvenile rectrices and their dark grey, not black, lesser primary coverts and white tips of the retained juvenile remiges and greater primary coverts of the upperwing. They also show a less contrasting dark forearm than the adults.

Adult (2nd cy autumn and older)   **Plates 41–44**

Upperparts pale silvery or ashy grey with paler head and tail, latter appearing whitish from a distance. Adults can be told from juveniles at close range by their deep black upper forearm, their contrasting black lesser primary coverts of the upperwing and their predominantly white tail-feathers except for the grey central pair. Adults also have paler and more silvery remiges and greater coverts above, which lack the pale tips of the juveniles.

Sexing: Male and female similar in plumage and not possible to sex in the field.

References: Brown et al. 1982; Cramp & Simmons 1980; Tucker & Heath 1995; Underhill 1986

Plate 37 *Juvenile plumage. Note rufous streaking on upper breast and head. 24 Jan 1997, South Africa (Annika Forsten).*

Plate 38 *Juvenile plumage showing rufous collar, pale tips to primaries and brownish iris. 24 Jan 1997, South Africa (Dick Forsman).*

Plate 39 *Juvenile plumage. Note distinct pale tips to brownish scapulars and to greater upperwing coverts, as well as darker crown and greyish tail with faintly darker subterminal markings. 24 Jan 1997, South Africa (Tomi Muukkonen).*

Plate 40 *Juvenile after partial body moult showing adult-like body-plumage but retaining pale-tipped primaries and their coverts (visible on far wing) and juvenile tail-feathers with darker smudges near tip. 24 Jan 1997, South Africa (Dick Forsman).*

Plate 41 *Adult showing diagnostic silhouette and underwing pattern for the species, while the all-white and translucent outer tail-feathers separate it from juveniles. Apr, Morocco (Göran Ekström).*

Plate 42 *Adult. Note diagnostic large head and short tail in flight. Jan 1995, Morocco (Markus Varesvuo).*

Plate 43   *Moulting adult. Note difference in colour of wing-tip above and below and also colour difference between new and old remiges on upperwing. 24 Jan 1997, South Africa (Dick Forsman).*

Plate 44   *Adult. The wing-tips protrude well beyond the tail-tip. Note red eyes of adult and lack of pale tips to primaries and greater coverts. 27 Nov 1996, Ethiopia (Dick Forsman).*

RED KITE   *Milvus milvus*

Plates 45–54

Subspecies: Nominate *M. m. milvus* in Europe, extralimital *M. m. fasciicauda* on Cape Verde Islands, being smaller and somewhat intermediate in plumage between Black Kite and Red Kite.

Distribution: A European species breeding from Spain to C Sweden and from W Europe to the Black Sea. Distribution uneven with majority of population in SW and C Europe.

Habitat: Mostly seen in open, cultivated areas with low vegetation and scattered woods. Also on higher and more forested ground in the Alps and the Pyrenees, where it patrols meadows and slopes, often close to villages.

Population: Total population estimated at 19 000–37 000 pairs, with most breeding in Germany (12 000–25 000), France (2300–2900) and Spain (3000–7000 pairs). The Swedish population of about 500 pairs is showing a steady increase.

Movements: Birds of S Europe resident, but C and N European birds partly migratory, wintering in France, Spain (60 000 wintering birds) and Portugal. Some winter as far north as S Sweden, where 300 winter regularly. Autumn migration at Falsterbo, S Sweden starts in Aug and peaks in late Sep–Oct, with last migrants in Nov. Highest autumn total 829 in 1994, with highest daily of 151 on 28 Sep 1993; autumn numbers at Falsterbo show steady increase. Juveniles and subadults make up 80% of Swedish migrants but only 10% of the wintering birds. Only small numbers cross the Strait of Gibraltar to Africa. Very rare along the eastern flyway and in winter in the Middle East. Returns from late Feb, majority during Mar.

Hunting and prey: Scans for prey either in low harrier-like flapping flight or when soaring high in the air. Swoops down on prey from low searching flight and tries to seize the prey in flight rather than alighting on the ground. Feeds on carrion of all kinds but also takes live prey such as rodents, small birds, insects and fish, latter to a lesser extent than Black Kite.

SPECIES IDENTIFICATION

Length 55–60 cm

wing-span 160–180 cm (Cramp & Simmons 1980) wing-span 154–170 cm (Noakes 1990)

Red Kites are rather easy to identify thanks to extremely graceful flight and diagnostic plumage and silhouette. The problems in separating Black and Red Kites have been exaggerated, the only truly difficult birds being some extensively rufous and narrow-winged Black Kites occurring during spring migration in the Middle East.

> **Identification summary:** Red Kites are extremely long-winged and long-tailed, graceful fliers, although juveniles show less extreme proportions than adults. Upperparts characterized by the distinct pale area diagonally across the arm and the cinnamon coloured, deeply forked tail, which is clearly paler than the upperparts generally. Head very pale, almost whitish. Underwings show a distinct white and translucent window on the inner hand contrasting with dark wing-tips and secondaries. Soaring birds show only five-fingered primaries.

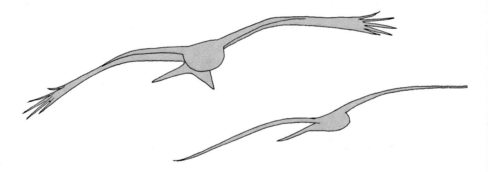

Fig 17 *Red Kite. Long and arched wings, small body and long, deeply forked and hanging tail make the head-on profile unmistakable.*

In flight, distant Red Kites belong to the most graceful fliers among raptors, with slow and elastic wing-beats. Despite the size of the bird the flight is magnificently light, almost tern-like and the extremely long tail waves in time with the wing-beats. The silhouette is characterized by the long and narrow wings, and by the long and deeply forked tail, which is very narrow at the base. On soaring birds the hand is somewhat narrower than the arm (cf. Black Kite) as Red Kites show only five-fingered primaries compared with six distinct fingers in most Black Kite populations. Red Kites soar on flat but slightly arched wings and glide on arched wings. From a distance the tail shines distinctly paler than the rest of the upperparts and the upperwing coverts are usually paler than the remiges, with a distinct pale diagonal bar from the tertials to the carpal. Underparts appear generally rather dark from a distance contrasting with the translucent primary window.

In flight, closer From above, the plumage appears rather contrasting, with a distinct pale diagonal upperwing patch and a pale cinnamon tail. Median and greater upperwing coverts have contrasting dark feather-centres. Head pale and, depending on the light, looks either whitish or greyish. From below, the Red Kite is characterized by the large whitish window on the inner hand contrasting sharply with the black wing-tips and very dark secondaries. The window is only faintly barred on the inner primaries and lacks a dark trailing edge. Underwing coverts typically bi-coloured, more clearly so in juveniles, with rufous or tawny forearm and a wide black wing-bar through the median and greater coverts.

Perched Perched Red Kites are extremely short-legged, with feet placed rather to the front, and with a long stern. Tail comparatively longer than in Black Kite and the wing-tips reach only to the base of the tail-fork (cf. Black Kite; the juveniles have a shorter tail and are thus closer to Black Kite in proportions). Bill longer and stronger than the Black Kite's and often yellowish (darker in juveniles), lacking Black Kite's marked contrast between black bill and yellow cere. Except for the pale head the plumage is largely rufous and the pale diagonal wing-patch on the upperwing is paler and more distinct with contrasting

Fig 18 *Distant perched Red Kites and Black Kites can be separated by different wing-tip to tail-tip ratio and different upperwing coverts. Red Kites (left) have a proportionately longer tail, with wing-tips reaching to base of tail-fork, while in Black Kite wing-tips reach tail-tip. The distinct pattern of the median upperwing coverts in Red Kite are visible from afar, while the upperwing in Black Kite appears uniform.*

dark feather centres, compared with Black Kite's rather uniform upperwing (although richly spotted in juvenile Black Kite).

Bare parts Cere and feet yellow. Bill in juvenile grey with dark tip and yellow base and gape; bill paler in adult, often largely yellow with diffuse grey tip in many (old?) adults. Iris grey or brownish grey in juveniles, although often appearing dark in the field, pale yellow to whitish in adult.

Confusion species: Mostly unmistakable, but distant birds possible to mistake for Black Kite, especially in bad light.

Black Kite (page 65) More uniform above, duller brown with less contrasting upperwing coverts and with tail and upperparts concolorous. Underparts darker and less rufous and underwing coverts appear uniformly dark. Inner hand never shows completely white and translucent window with fine barring as in Red Kite, but is either pale grey, or partly white (often near the leading edge) with bold barring. The silhouette is also different with more parallel-edged wings with a fuller tip (six fingers instead of five) and the shorter tail has only a shallow fork, which is lost when the tail is fanned.

MOULT

Annually complete. Starts in Apr–May and is completed in late autumn after the migration.

Juveniles (first moult) Juveniles undergo a variable partial body moult in winter, some starting as early as 1st cy Sep/Oct, while others still appear in complete juvenile plumage in 2nd cy Apr. Remiges moulted from 2nd cy Apr–May, starting with the innermost primary. Primaries are still in moult when the birds migrate south, and the moult is completed in the winter quarters. One or two juvenile outermost primaries are frequently retained until the next moult, being faded brown and pointed.

Adults (subsequent moults) Start to moult their primaries in (Apr–) May, on average slightly later than juveniles. Females start earlier than males. By the time of autumn migration some outer primaries and median secondaries are still unmoulted. These are replaced in late autumn in the winter quarters, although occasionally some median secondaries are retained until the next moult.

AGEING AND SEXING

Three age-classes separable in autumn, two and sometimes three in the spring. Juveniles have a shorter tail with a shallower fork resulting in a less extreme silhouette than adults, instead showing proportions closer to Black Kite.

Ageing summary: Fresh juveniles are extensively pale-spotted and pale-fringed above, with distinctly paler upperwing coverts than remiges, pale streaks on breast and marked contrast on underwings between tawny forearm and dark median/greater coverts. Adults are generally darker rufous brown with less marked upperwing contrast, black streaks on breast and darker rufous forearm. Juveniles also show a brighter and wider upperwing patch and diagnostic pale tips to greater coverts on both upper- and underwing. Second-winter birds may be told from full adults by retained juvenile feathers, but ideal conditions are required.

Juvenile (1st cy – 2nd cy spring)   Plates 45–50

Juvenile Red Kites appear paler than adults because of pale fringes of upperparts and extensive pale streaking of head and underbody. Whole head looks pale buff and individual streaks are difficult to discern. Bill appears more contrasting than in adult, with dark tip and yellow cere; iris grey or brown, appearing dark in the field.

In flight, upperparts paler and more contrasting, with a wider and brighter diagonal wing-patch than in adults. A reliable ageing character is the pale, fine line on the upperwing formed by pale tips to greater primary and secondary coverts. Underbody paler than in adults with bold buffish streaks and uniformly buffish vent and undertail coverts. Tail shorter than in adults and, when fanned, shows a faint dark subterminal bar instead of dark corners only. Greater coverts have pale tips, forming a regular band to the underwing.

Distant juveniles may be difficult to age but the paler upperwing coverts, the pale tips to the greater coverts above, and the pale vent and undertail coverts, which in colour merge with the undertail, are usually visible from afar.

During the winter juveniles start to attain adult-type breast feathers and the pale fringes of the upperparts wear narrower, but the general appearance remains the same.

Transitional plumage (2nd cy autumn – 3rd cy spring)   Plate 51

Like adult and possible to identify by retained juvenile feathers, best seen in flight. From above shows faded brown and more pointed outermost fingers contrasting with newly moulted inner, which are black with a rounded tip. Most individuals still show pale streaks on belly and partly pale vent and undertail coverts, as well as pale tips to greater underwing coverts, forming a complete or broken pale wing-band.

Adult (2nd cy autumn and older (cf. Transitional plumage))   Plates 52–54

Perched adults are darker rufous than juveniles, with prominent blackish streaking on breast and upperparts. Head whitish grey and finely streaked black. Bill largely yellow and just diffusely dark at the tip, appearing all-yellow from a distance. Iris pale yellow or whitish.

In flight from above, adults show distinct black centres to median and greater upperwing coverts and the diagonal patch on the upper arm is smaller and less contrasting than in juveniles. Adults also lack the pale fine line along the tips of the greater primary and secondary coverts. Underbody darker, deeper rufous than in juveniles, with bold black streaks especially on upper breast. In most adults the rufous vent and undertail coverts appear darker than the undertail, while others are paler and lack the contrast. Tail more deeply forked and lacks the subterminal band of the juveniles, showing only darker corners. In adults the underwing coverts are darker, with a deep rufous forearm contrasting only slightly with the black bar of the mid-wing. Adults also lack the pale tips to the greater coverts, while the secondaries show broad dark tips forming a dark trailing edge to the wing, although this can be difficult to see in the field.

Distant adults from above are best identified by darker upperwing coverts, with less conspicuous pale upperwing patch, by longer and brighter cinnamon tail and by lack of pale tips to greater coverts; from below by darker rufous forearm and body, latter contrasting with paler undertail with dark corners.

Sexing: Red Kites cannot be sexed in the field.

References: Anon 1996; Forsman 1980, 1984, 1993b; Cramp & Simmons 1980; Gensböl 1995; Kjellén 1992b, 1994, 1995; Noakes 1990; Sylvén 1977; Tucker & Heath 1995; Tyrberg 1994

Plate 45 *Juvenile showing creamy head and pale streaking to underbody as well as pale tips to greater underwing coverts. Note also marked colour contrast between lesser and median underwing coverts as well as dark iris. Oct 1996, Sweden (Jens B. Bruun).*

Plate 46 *Juvenile showing typical silhouette with narrower hand than arm and with long and narrow tail. Oct 1996, Sweden (Jens B. Bruun).*

Plate 47 *Juvenile showing pale underbody and dark subterminal tail band. Feb 1991, Spain (Markus Varesvuo).*

Plate 48 *Juvenile from above. The distinct dark centres of the upperwing coverts and the rufous tail are diagnostic against Black Kite. The pale rump and uppertail coverts and the pale tips to the greater coverts are juvenile characters. Oct 1996, Britain (David Cottridge).*

Plate 49 *Juvenile in 2nd cy spring with recently started primary moult. Juveniles are more compact in silhouette than adults. Note translucent wing-patches and tail, which differ from Black Kite. 19 Apr 1995, Spain (Dick Forsman).*

Plate 50 *Juvenile in 2nd cy spring showing diagnostic plumage features, including subterminal tail-band. Note moulted feathers on breast with adult-type broad black streaks. Mar 1997, Italy (Roberto Gildi).*

Plate 51 *Possibly a 2nd cy autumn bird with retained juvenile greater underwing coverts with pale tips but otherwise showing adult characters. The dark streaking on the breast and the broad dark trailing edge to the arm are both diagnostic of adult plumage. Oct 1996, Sweden (Jens B. Bruun).*

Plate 52 *Adult showing slimmer silhouette than juvenile, with longer wings and tail. Note deep rufous forewing and boldly streaked breast compared with juvenile, while the tail is more deeply cleft. Oct 1996, Sweden (Jens B. Bruun).*

Plate 53 *The upperparts of adults are less contrasting than in juveniles and the pale median coverts patch of the upperwing is smaller. Oct 1996, Britain (David Cottridge).*

Plate 54 *Adult showing largely yellow bill with darker tip only, yellowish iris and distinct dark streaking to breast. Apr, Germany (Alfred Limbrunner).*

BLACK KITE   *Milvus migrans*

Plates 55–70

Subspecies: Nominate *M. m. migrans* in Europe and NW Africa. Extralimital *M. m. lineatus* (Black-eared Kite) in E Palearctic to China and *M. m. aegyptius* (Yellow-billed Kite) in S Egypt, S Arabia and coastal E Africa. Another four subspecies recognized from Africa, Asia and Australia. Is known to have hybridized repeatedly with Red Kite in the wild.

Distribution: Widely distributed throughout the Old World. Absent as a breeding bird in maritime areas of W and NW Europe.

Habitats: Often breeds near wetlands, lakes and rivers. In winter less specialized and congregates around villages, at rubbish dumps, slaughter houses, fish farms, etc., wherever food is available.

Population: Palearctic population estimated at 77 000–105 000 pairs, with main populations in Russia (50 000–70 000 pairs), Spain (9000), France (6000–8000) and Germany (5000–7000). Locally increasing (in the west) while other populations stable or steadily but slowly decreasing (in the east).

Movements: Migratory; most winter in Africa south of Sahara, smaller numbers also in the Middle East, rarely in S Europe. Migrates in flocks using the main flyways over Strait of Gibraltar, Sicilian Channel and the Bosporus–Levant route. Bulk of C European breeding birds leave Europe as early as Aug over Gibraltar, with 39 099 counted there in 1972 (peak day 22 Aug with 13 356). Returns to C Europe from Feb to May, most during early Apr. Spring migration at Eilat, Israel peaks in late Mar–early Apr comprising mainly birds of more northeastern origin. Highest daily totals 20 450 on 29 Mar 1980 and 9956 on 29 Mar 1987.

According to ringing recoveries most C European birds do not return to breeding grounds in first summer (2nd cy), but summer further south, in N Africa and S Europe.

Hunting and prey: Omnivorous but European breeding birds prey mostly on fish, dead or alive. Swoops down to take prey from surface. Hunts mostly on the wing, quartering leisurely in rather low searching flight, following shorelines, roads and woodland edges. Also eats insects when abundant, as well as small mammals and birds, and uses carrion freely.

SPECIES IDENTIFICATION

Length 46–59 cm

wing-span 130–155 cm (*n*=51; Israeli migrants; W.S. Clark, unpubl.)

The identification of Black Kite is not always simple, especially when seen from a distance, owing to confusion risk with other rather similarly shaped darkish raptors. Important features to look for are silhouette and wing-formula, wing-action in active flight and wing-attitude when gliding. At closer range the plumage pattern on the upperwing and under-wing are important, as are the colour of the head, the streaking of the breast, and the colour and shape of the tail.

> **Identification summary:** In silhouette identified by long and parallel-edged wings with rather broad tip (usually six prominent fingers) and fairly long and shallowly forked tail, longer than the width of the wings. Flapping flight with loose, slow and shallow wing-beats; glides on smoothly arched wings. Plumage generally darkish, lacking striking patterns (except in some juveniles). Shows diffuse, paler diagonal bar across upperwing coverts and slightly paler and barred inner hand to otherwise dark underwings.

Fig 19 *Black Kite. When gliding long and smoothly arched wings make the shape reminiscent of an eagle, but wing-tips are narrow lacking obvious broom-shape.*

In flight, distant Active flight with wrists pressed forward, level with the head. Wing-beats shallow and elegant and the flight looks relaxed and effortless. When soaring, wings look parallel-edged with a broad tip. The tail is clearly, yet shallowly, forked when folded, but the fork is lost when the tail is maximally fanned; then looks like a triangle with sharp corners. Approaching Black Kites often appear very eagle-like, owing to slow wing-action and long wings in relation to small body. Glides on slightly and smoothly arched wings and soars on more or less level wings.

From above, distant Black Kites are mostly identified by their typical silhouette and their uniformly dark plumage, with a broad but rather diffuse paler diagonal patch across the median upperwing coverts. Head often appears clearly paler than the rest of the bird. From underneath, adults appear uniformly darkish, with a slightly paler area on the inner hand. Juveniles are more contrastingly patterned below and often show a distinct white patch on the outer hand and a pale underbody. The whitish wing-patch is smaller than in Red Kite, being most conspicuous near the leading edge and becoming gradually darker and more barred towards the rear.

In flight, closer Closer looks reveal the typical underwing pattern, with rather dense but coarse barring to generally darkish secondaries and primaries, but with variably paler inner hand. The paler window is usually grey and the barring is inconspicuous in adults, whereas most juveniles show a more distinct pattern. Underbody dark brown, often with a rufous tinge, and uniformly streaked, more heavily on the upper breast, with dark streaks in adults and pale in juveniles. Head paler than the body, greyish in adults and creamy in juveniles. Upperparts rather uniform and dull brown, a paler area across the upperwing coverts being the only notable plumage pattern. Tail usually concolorous with the upperparts; the dense and regular barring is rather indistinct in juvenile, more distinct in adult, showing more clearly when tail is fanned. Some birds show a faint rufous tinge to uppertail, but never anything like the luminant cinnamon tail of the Red Kite.

Perched Perched birds look very drawn-out with long wings and tail and very small feet; the legs look almost too short for the size of the bird. The wing-tips reach the tail-tip, or come very close to it. Adults are dull brown with dark streaks on the breast and a paler greyish head; juveniles are pale-spotted all over and the head is creamy with darker auriculars. The pale patch in the median upperwing coverts is less conspicuous than in the Red Kite, lacking its contrasting black shaft-streaks.

Bare parts Bill black; contrasts sharply with the yellow cere (cf. Red Kite); the feet are yellow. Iris dark brown in juveniles but becoming paler with age, turning pale brown at approximately 2–3 years of age and finally to pale yellowish brown in older adults (6–7 years of age), but little is known about individual variation in timing (cf. Ageing and sexing).

Variation: Plumage variation is normally rather slight in the Black Kite but extremely dark, almost uniformly blackish brown birds occur occasionally. These lack the normal upperwing pattern and appear all-dark from below, but the silhouette and flight-action are normal. Some juveniles may show a nearly white underbody, owing to extensive pale spotting, causing possible confusion with other species, e.g. pale juvenile Honey Buzzard or Booted Eagle, but the upperparts and flight-feathers are normal.

The Yellow-billed Kite *M. m. aegyptius* of Egypt and S Arabia (Plates 66–68) has a distinct plumage differing from nominate *migrans*. Adults show an all-yellow bill and a more sandy-brown overall colour with rather distinctly barred underwings and tail. Juveniles have a black bill and a yellow cere but the plumage is more uniformly sandy in colour than nominate juveniles. The pale streaking below is also less contrasting, with a fine dark shaft-streak and a pale apical spot to each feather.

The Black-eared Kite *M. m. lineatus* (Plates 69–70) is more similar to the nominate race and is not known to occur in the region, although birds resembling this form are reported seen on migration in the Middle East, possibly representing a population from the wide interbreeding zone between *lineatus* and *migrans*. Juveniles are rather similar in plumage to nominate, although they show on average a larger white underwing patch. Older immatures and adults show rather distinct rufous streaks to head and breast, unlike nominate *migrans*.

Confusion species:

Red Kite (page 55) Told by brighter coloured and much more contrasting upperparts, longer and narrower wings, and longer, more deeply forked tail, large white inner hand on underwing and five-fingered primaries. However, on migration in the Middle East some Black Kites have extremely rufous underparts, a wide and pale (but not translucent and white!) window on the inner hand, a pale head and a narrower wing-tip, with five-fingered primaries only.

Marsh Harrier (page 167) Female-type told by unbarred underwing and tail, pale forearm, crown and throat and often also by pale mottled upper breast and mantle. Wings are not parallel-edged as in Black Kite, but show a narrower hand than arm, with five fingers only, and they are held in a shallow V when soaring.

Booted Eagle (page 416) Dark form told by striking pattern of upperwings, pale uppertail coverts and more compact silhouette. When soaring, wings held prominently arched with splayed fingers, forming distinct broom in head-on views.

Buzzards (pages 30, 266) Told by shorter and more rounded wings and shorter tail, with diagnostic dark trailing edge to wing, although some juvenile Honey Buzzards may have a rather similar underwing pattern.

MOULT *(M. m. migrans)*

Complete moult annually. Starts to moult flight-feathers during breeding, but moult suspended for autumn migration to be resumed and completed in the winter quarters.

Juveniles (first moult) During first winter, juveniles replace some body feathers in a partial body moult, especially on head and forebody, but generally fewer than juvenile Red Kite. Complete moult as in adults, but beginning from mid Apr. By autumn migration 2nd cy birds still retain juvenile outer primaries, with distinct white bases in most individuals. In late Sep 2nd cy birds wintering in N Israel showed on average more advanced primary moult than adults, with moult proceeding at p7–8. Moult is completed in the winter quarters in Jan–Feb, but in some birds retained juvenile body feathers may allow exact ageing even after this (pers. obs.).

Adults (subsequent moults) Adults commence their complete moult while breeding, with females beginning earlier than males, usually at the time of egg-laying (Apr–May). Moult is suspended for the autumn migration and resumed on the wintering grounds. By late Sep–early Oct wintering adults studied in N Israel had replaced only about half of their primaries, with a distinct moult gap at p5–6. Moult is completed in Jan–early Feb prior to spring passage (pers. obs.).

AGEING AND SEXING *(M. m. migrans)*

In autumn three separable age-classes, in spring at least two, sometimes a third. Ageing is usually easy if the bird is seen close and in good light, typical individuals being possible to age even from a great distance. The main points to focus on when separating juveniles from adults are colour of head, details of upperwing and underwing, streaking of breast and colour of vent. Ageing second-winter birds is not always possible and requires careful scrutiny of remiges and body plumage.

> **Ageing summary:** Juveniles are extensively pale-spotted above and pale-streaked below. Head buffish with a dark mask through the eye; the primaries are distinctly barred in black and white underneath. First-adults may appear rather juvenile-like in plumage, but show signs of wing moult. Adults are much more uniform and most do not show any contrasting pattern to the underwings.

Juvenile (1st cy – 2nd cy spring)   Plates 55–58

Fresh juveniles are easily told by their extensively pale-spotted upperparts and pale-streaked underparts. Head creamy, with a darker auricular patch behind the eye. Iris darkish brown.

In flight, upperwings show a brighter diagonal patch than in adults, but the best character is the fine pale line formed by the pale tips to the greater primary and secondary coverts. Underparts show pale streaking, with vent and undertail coverts largely pale. Greater underwing coverts have pale tips, forming a narrow wing-band, and primaries are distinctly patterned, with bold dark bars on a whitish ground-colour and black fingers. The extent of white in the window of the underwing varies individually, with some showing extensively white bases to primaries, whereas others show only some white at the bases of the outermost.

By spring, upperparts are more uniform, because of wear, but the pale line along the greater covert tips is usually still visible. Underparts change less, although some birds have moulted their upper breast partially, showing darker feathers with black streaks.

Transitional or first-adult plumage (2nd cy autumn – 3rd cy spring)   Plates 59–60

By 2nd cy autumn, birds look like adults, but most are still possible to age accurately by their retained juvenile feathers. Retained juvenile outer primaries show distinctly white bases underneath (sometimes also distinct black-and-white barring) and contrast sharply with moulted, darker and more barred inner primaries. These birds usually also show partly retained juvenile body-feathers, with largely pale belly, vent and undertail coverts and (partly) retained juvenile greater underwing coverts with pale tips. Even the head may still be largely yellowish buff with a darker mask through the eye, and the breast may be partly pale-streaked as in juveniles.

In 3rd cy spring a small proportion of birds may still be aged by partly retained juvenile greater underwing coverts with pale tips and by largely pale feathers of underbody, similar to 2nd cy autumn. The head is creamy with a distinct dark patch behind the eye, and the eyes are dark.

Adult (3rd cy autumn and older)   Plates 61–65

Perched adults are very uniformly dark brown above, and the pale wing covert patch is mostly inconspicuous. Head slightly paler and greyer, with fine dark streaks and with a faint auricular patch behind the eye. Underparts dull brown with narrow black streaks. Iris varies from pale brown to pearl grey or yellowish, probably depending on the age of the bird.

In flight, adults appear rather uniformly dull brownish above. Only the paler greyish head and the broad diagonal area across the upperarm stand out. Tail mostly the same colour as the rest of the upperparts, but in some birds may show a slightly rufous brown tinge. It is, however, never as pale and brightly coloured as in the Red Kite. Also, from underneath, adults generally appear rather uniformly dark, and the typical streaking on the breast is visible only at close range. Vent and undertail coverts are dark brown, clearly darker than the undertail. Underwings appear dark, but the inner hand is paler grey and contrasts with darker fingers and secondaries. Remiges are densely barred, but often the barring is diffuse, making the underwing appear rather uniform.

From a distance, adults are usually picked out by their uniform appearance compared with more brightly patterned juveniles and first-adults. The plumage remains rather similar throughout the year.

Ortlieb (1996), studying the development of the plumage and iris colour on some captive nominate Black Kites, noticed that the colours of the head and iris change over a number of years after the transitional plumage. In the subsequent third and fourth plumages both head and iris are brown, in the fifth plumage the head becomes greyer but the eye is still brown and does not turn pale until the sixth plumage. Little is known about individual variation in the timing of these changes.

Sexing: The sexes are not known to be separable in the field.

References: Beaman 1994; Bernis 1975; Cramp & Simmons 1980; Forsman 1980, 1984, 1993b; Gensbøl 1995; Ortlieb 1996; Shirihai 1995; Shirihai & Christie 1992; Sylvén 1977; Tucker & Heath 1995

Plate 55   *Juvenile from below. Note uniform condition of plumage, pale vent, pale streaking to body and pale tips to greater underwing coverts. 8 Oct 1988, Israel (Dick Forsman).*

Plate 56   *Juvenile showing wider white primary-patches. Note also pale head with dark eye-mask, typical of juveniles. 8 Oct 1988, Israel (Dick Forsman).*

Plate 57   *Juvenile from above, showing diagnostic pale feather-tips above, with pale tips to greater coverts forming narrow wing-bands. 5 Oct 1995, Israel (Dick Forsman).*

Plate 58   *Fresh juvenile showing pale feather-tips above and pale streaking below. Sep, Finland (Mikko Pöllänen).*

Plate 59 *Transitional 2nd cy bird moulting to first-adult plumage and still retaining its juvenile outer primaries, with distinct pale bases, pale-tipped greater coverts, pale vent and pale streaking on breast. The head still appears rather juvenile-like. 8 Oct 1988, Israel (Dick Forsman).*

Plate 60 *Birds in first-adult plumage from below often still resemble juveniles, but lack the distinct pale streaking to underbody, while the new greater coverts lack pale tips. The head is still pale with dark eyes and a darker eye-mask. The pale patch on the inner hand of this bird is brighter and larger than usual. 14 Jan 1990, Israel (Dick Forsman).*

Plate 61 *Typical adult with dark greyish brown plumage and a paler grey head; breast and head finely streaked black. Note also inconspicuously marked, rather dark underwings with paler grey inner hand. Mar 1985, Israel (Dick Forsman).*

Plate 62 *Adult showing unusually rufous underbody, while the underwings are rather typical. Similar birds, but with paler inner primaries, can easily be mistaken for Red Kites. Mar 1985, Israel (Dick Forsman).*

Plate 63   *Typical adult from above showing grey head and diagnostic pale diagonal wing-patch with otherwise rather uniform upperparts. Mar 1985, Israel (Dick Forsman).*

Plate 64   *Younger adult. Like full adult, with breast showing rather fine dark streaks with pale margins, but head not yet pure grey and iris not as pale. Apr 1987, Israel (Paul Doherty).*

Plate 65   *Adult. Note grey and finely streaked head and yellow iris. Compared with Red Kite the wing-tips reach close to the tail-tip and the upperwing coverts are much less brightly patterned. The black bill contrasts sharply with the yellow cere even in old adults. Mar 1985, Israel (Dick Forsman).*

Plate 66   *A pale, fresh juvenile ssp. aegyptius. Note pale general impression and finer barring of flight-feathers and paler-mottled greater coverts compared with juvenile migrans. Bill and iris are dark in juveniles. Sep 1995, Egypt (Axel Halley).*

Plate 67 *A darker juvenile* aegyptius. *Note pale head and dark iris. Underwing coverts paler and more variably patterned than in nominate* migrans. *1 Nov 1989, Yemen (Magnus Ullman).*

Plate 68 *Adult ssp.* aegyptius. *Note diagnostic yellow bill of adult. The body plumage is rufous and finely streaked compared with nominate subspecies and the remiges appear paler. 10 Apr 1991, Egypt (Annika Forsten).*

Plate 69 *Juvenile (2nd cy) ssp.* lineatus. *In this subspecies the distinct tawny streaking of the body plumage is retained throughout life unlike the nominate subspecies. May 1985, Mongolia (Lasse J. Laine).*

Plate 70 *Juvenile ssp.* lineatus. *Note largely pale vent and prominently marked primaries. 5 Feb 1997, India (Tapani Numminen).*

WHITE-TAILED EAGLE   *Haliaeetus albicilla*
Plates 71–91

Subspecies: Monotypic. Slightly bigger birds from Greenland sometimes separated as *H. a. groenlandicus.*

Distribution: Widely scattered from Europe to N Asia, Japan, India and China.

Habitat: Found close to water, from sea shores to freshwater lakes and rivers, often far inland.

Population: Marked decrease in European population during twentieth century. Has recently increased locally because of protective measures and diminished persecution e.g. in N Europe, where bulk of European population breeds. Total breeding population of Europe estimated at 3500 pairs, with 1500 pairs in Norway.

Movements: Resident and dispersive or migratory depending on population. Birds of inland N Europe winter along the Baltic coasts and in S Scandinavia, even entering C Europe. Birds from coastal populations of NW Europe are resident, although young birds disperse during first years of life. Immatures abandon the northern breeding areas from late Aug and autumn migration peaks in Finland in late Sep–mid Oct, but continues well into Nov. At Falsterbo, S Sweden between 3 and 18 birds were counted in the autumns of 1986–1994, whereas 192 birds were counted on the Finnish south coast in autumn 1992, where days with more than 10 birds are not exceptional. Spring migration from Feb–Mar (breeding adults) to Apr and May (immatures), with most of the few hundred spring migrants of S Finland passing in Apr.

Hunting and prey: Feeds mainly on fish or waterfowl, with main prey depending on local supply. Also feeds on carrion and many birds wintering in the Baltic rely on feeding stations for food, with concentrations of up to 75 birds at one station at the same time!

Species identification

Length 78–102 cm (*n*=38; Gerdehag & Helander 1988)
wing-span 180–235 cm (*n*=5; Finnish birds, pers. obs.)
wing-span 205–244 cm (*n*=16; Gerdehag & Helander 1988)

Distant birds may be confused with similarly proportioned *Aquila*-eagles, such as Steppe and the spotted eagles. Adults and juveniles differ in plumage but also in silhouette and proportions. At closer range details of bill and feet exclude other eagles.

Identification summary: In powered flight long neck with protruding head and huge bill, broad wings and comparatively short tail. Adults are very pale-headed with huge yellow bill and the white tail is short and wedge-shaped. Wings are narrower than in juveniles, with straighter trailing edge, and appearing uniformly dark below. Immatures have a dark head and neck contrasting with streaked or blotched under-body. Tail longer than in adults, yet wedged, and the rectrices are variably dark with white centres or white mottling. Axillaries form a diagnostic pale triangle in the armpit and the remiges normally appear uniformly dark. Tarsi largely bare and yellow (cf. *Aquila*-eagles).

In flight, distant The powered flight looks surprisingly easy with long series of shallow wing-beats interspersed by short glides. Glides on flattish wings, often with hand slightly lowered and with strongly up-bent fingers. In active flight appears front-heavy, with long neck and protruding head and short stern. Soars on flattish or slightly arched wings kept level or lifted slightly above horizontal. Silhouette when soaring more like other eagles with neck appearing shorter.

Adult-type birds have rather rectangular wings and usually show a pale straw-coloured head, upper breast and mantle, becoming gradually darker towards the rear. Upperwings have paler coverts and dark flight-feathers, while the outer primaries often show a paler grey flash basally. Underwings appear uniformly darkish, sometimes with a diffuse paler crescent to the bases of the outer primaries. The white tail can be surprisingly difficult to note unless the bird is seen against a dark background or a blue sky, since in cloudy weather it merges with the sky leaving the dark brown undertail coverts as the only visible tail-stump.

Juveniles and immatures have broader and more rounded wings and are generally darker, with a dark head and neck contrasting with paler and mottled breast and mantle. Upperwing usually shows a large paler area on the coverts of the inner arm, while the remiges appear uniformly dark. Underwing appears dark, but often shows lines of pale spots in the underwing coverts, while the axillaries typically form a paler patch. Tail looks dark when folded,

Fig 20 *White-tailed Eagle. Glides on rather flattish wings or with slight angle between level arm and drooping hand.*

but shows white 'spikes' to feather-centres when fanned. Bill is dark initially, with a greyish cere and a pale bare loral area, but gradually becomes paler and yellower over the first 2–3 years.

In flight, closer Adults are unmistakable with a huge yellow bill and short, all-white tail. The rest of the plumage appears rather uniform, lacking any striking markings to e.g. wings or body. Immatures are more variable, but show a dark head and neck contrasting with paler and mottled breast and upperparts. The huge bill and the cere vary in colour depending on the bird's age, but the loral area is bare and pale, giving a typical facial expression different from other eagles. Axillaries typically paler than the surrounding tracts, a character that is retained until adult plumage is donned. The trailing edge of the wing of younger birds (first and second plumage) is distinctly serrated, whereas older birds show a more even contour-line. The remiges are never barred in White-tailed Eagles and, if seen well, the tail always shows some white, often as irregular mottling along the feather-shafts, or as predominantly white feathers with darker smudges to tips and fringes.

Perched On the ground appears short in the rear but with big forebody, which is further emphasized by less regal posture than in other eagles. Sits upright like other eagles when perching in a tree. Bill huge and often diagnostic in colour; crown appears either flat or shows distinct bump on forehead from raised feathers. Tail typically short and mostly hidden by the huge wings. Tarsi partly bare and yellow. Adults unmistakable by diagnostic bill and tail, juveniles identified by regular dark mesh-pattern of ochre upperwing coverts and by dark head with dark bill and cere, but large pale loral patch. Older immatures have similar head to juvenile but breast and mantle show increasingly white feather-bases and the bill and cere gradually turn more yellowish.

Bare parts Feet yellow at all ages. Colour of bill, cere and iris develop slowly and there is considerable individual variation in the timing of the maturing process. For further details see under Ageing and sexing.

Bill in 1st cy blackish, cere greyish and loral patch prominent and whitish; iris dull brown. By second winter bill becomes slightly paler at base and cere turns yellowish, but general impression still rather like juvenile; iris dark brown. By third winter bill colour varies from largely grey to largely yellow with a grey suffusion and the cere is yellow; iris paler brown than in juveniles, distinctly paler than black pupil. Fourth-winter birds are variable, but most show a predominantly yellowish bill and cere with some grey close to the tip; the iris colour varies from pale brown to yellowish. By fifth winter the bare parts are much as in adults, but there may still be some dark along the culmen and the iris colour is not yet as pale yellow as in adults. From sixth winter, birds are generally like adults, with a deep yellow bill and cere, and a yellow iris.

Variation: Scotland's last White-tailed Eagle was an albino and recently at least two very pale leucistic individuals have turned up in Sweden.

Some immatures show extensive white mottling to inner primaries and inner secondaries below, hence underwing-pattern may resemble immature Bald Eagle *H. leucocephalus*, Pallas' Fish Eagle *H. leucoryphus* and immature Golden Eagle.

Confusion species: Younger White-tailed Eagles can be mistaken for other large raptors with rectangular wings and short tails, like large vultures and several *Aquila*-eagles. Adults are unmistakable if white tail and yellow bill are seen.

Griffon Vulture (page 126) and Black Vulture (page 138) All-dark and proportionately shorter tails; not streaked or blotchy on the underbody, mantle and upperwing coverts.

Greater Spotted (page 332), Lesser Spotted (page 316) and Steppe Eagles (page 348) Dark tails and barred remiges in most plumages. They also mostly show at least some of the following characters: pale wing-bands, pale vent and undertail coverts, pale uppertail coverts and pale flashes above on the inner primaries; they also lack the immature White-tailed Eagle's pale axillaries and lores, notably indented trailing edge to the wing and the extensive mottling to breast and belly.

Golden Eagle (page 390) Much longer tail and the wings are narrower, with more rounded tips, narrower bases and distinctly bulging trailing edge. They also soar on slightly lifted wings. Immatures have diagnostic white tail with broad black terminal band and adults have greyish flight-feathers with a broad black terminal band.

MOULT

Complete moult annually, but does not comprise all flight-feathers. In the first moult only 30% of remiges moulted but amount increases to approximately 50% annually in older birds. Moults faster than e.g. Golden Eagle. (Account based on Fennoscandian birds; Forsman 1981. Also see Fig 11, page 5)

Juveniles (first moult) Primaries moulted from 2nd cy May–Jun to Sep–Oct, when moult is suspended. Usually only three or four inner primaries and some inner secondaries are moulted, whereas the tail is usually moulted completely. Also moults body plumage extensively, usually retaining juvenile rump, underwing coverts and some upperwing coverts.

Second moult (3rd cy summer) Commences earlier than first, from Mar to Apr and proceeds from where the moult waves stopped in previous moult. Another three or four primaries are moulted (mostly p4–6 or p5–8) and the secondary moult proceeds rapidly, leaving only a few juvenile secondaries unmoulted (usually s4 and s7–9) before the moult is suspended in Sep–Oct. The tail is moulted completely and most of the body-feathers have been moulted at least once by now, while very few juvenile body-feathers are retained, mainly among the upperwing coverts.

Third moult (4th cy summer) From Mar–Apr to Sep–Oct. In this moult the remaining juvenile primaries and secondaries are usually moulted, although some birds may retain the outermost (juvenile) primary even after this moult. New moult fronts start from the inner primaries and the inner secondaries gradually building up the serial moult found in adults.

Adults (subsequent moults) Between Mar and Oct, although odd remiges may be replaced during winter. In adults the primaries show two or three simultaneously active moult fronts whereas the secondaries are replaced simultaneously from three or four foci. Despite the serial moult adults need two moulting seasons to replace the entire set of remiges, while the tail is moulted nearly completely every year.

AGEING AND SEXING

Adults and juveniles/young immatures are usually easy to separate, since they differ significantly not only in plumage but also in flight silhouette and proportions. Since individuals vary as to how quickly they acquire certain age-related plumage characters, older immatures and subadults after the third plumage are best referred to as plumage-types.

> **Ageing summary:** Juveniles have dark heads, dark streaking to tawny underparts and the trailing edge of the wing is evenly indented. The second plumage differs in having extensive white mottling to breast and mantle and the pointed juvenile secondaries have been partly replaced by shorter feathers with more rounded tips. The third plumage still shows pale mottling to the underbody and the underwing coverts but the general impression of the upperwing is more uniformly greyish brown. Bill is mostly yellowish, often with extensive greyish shadowing.

The fourth plumage already resembles that of the adults but can be told by the pale axillaries and feather-bases to the underparts, the parti-coloured tail and by the not yet fully adult bill and eyes. Adults lack white markings on the underparts, the tail is pure white and the bill is bright or pale yellow. Head is often distinctly paler than the rest of the bird. Iris pale yellow.

Juvenile (1st cy – 2nd cy spring)   Plates 71–75

Perched juveniles are characterized by the regular pattern of the upperwing formed by the dark tips of the coverts. Head blackish brown, bill dark and cere greyish, bringing out the pale loral area. Breast tawny with dark streaks but normally lacks white except for the odd white feather-base. The 'trousers' are regularly patterned, like the upperwings, although they are mostly hidden in the belly feathering.

In flight from above, juveniles show tawny upperwing coverts, typically also including the inner greater coverts, with rows of darkish covert tips visible at close range. Remiges uniformly dark, often with paler mottling on the inner secondaries. Head dark and the pale lore is distinct. Rump tawny and variably streaked dark and mantle appears dark, both lacking the sometimes extensive white mottling of the two subsequent plumages. The relatively long tail appears dark when folded but when spread reveals the whitish feather-centres, although there is a great deal of variation in the amount of white in the tail.

From below, the body is tawny with dark streaking, sometimes contrasting sharply with

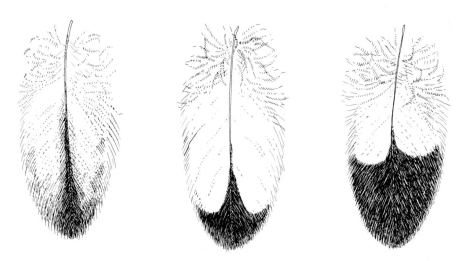

Fig 21 *White-tailed Eagle. Breast-feathers of immatures showing ochre and streaked feather of juvenile plumage (left) with distinctly marked white and dark feathers of second (centre) and third plumage (right). Note reduced amount of white in third generation feathers, with visible part of feather being largely brown (from Forsman 1981).*

the blackish head and neck. Axillaries pale tawny and form a conspicuous pale triangle in the armpit, a reliable feature when separating immature White-tailed Eagles from dark *Aquila*-eagles. Underwings variably patterned, but at least some rows of coverts usually show paler bases forming spotted wing-bars on the underwing. Remiges uniformly dark, rarely with irregular paler mottling on inner secondaries and inner primaries. Because of the pointed juvenile remiges, the trailing edge is deeply serrated, something that is lacking in other European eagles, but which is later lost in the moults.

Second plumage (2nd cy autumn – 3rd cy spring)   **Plates 76–80**
Birds in this plumage appear very blotchy. Head is still dark and contrasts sharply with the largely white-mottled underbody, while the trousers are contrastingly dark. Bill still predominantly dark but the cere is yellowish and the base is turning paler. Upperwing coverts are largely pale and mottled, showing a mixture of fresh and worn feathers, and they lack the neat pattern of the juveniles. Mantle and uppertail coverts are often distinctly mottled white, whereas the rump is still largely juvenile and tawny.

In flight rather similar to juvenile and best separated by the distinct white mottling to mantle and underbody. Tail often even darker than in juveniles, sometimes with nearly all-dark feathers, but normally at least the outer ones still show the diagnostic pattern with white centres and dark margins.

From below, the second plumage is characterized by the dark head contrasting with whitish mottled breast and belly and by contrasting dark trousers. Underwing still shows prominent wing-bars and white axillaries, much as in juvenile plumage. The shape of the bird is still rather similar to the juvenile, with serrated and bulging trailing edge to the wing.

Third plumage (3rd cy autumn – 4th cy spring)   **Plates 81–83**
This plumage is the link between the mottled immature plumages and more uniform adult-type plumages. Owing to individual variation in moulting speed some birds are more similar to second plumage, others are closer to fourth plumage. Head usually coloured as the rest of the plumage, not distinctly darker as in the previous plumages. Bill and cere predominantly yellowish, with a grey suffusion on the bill, while some still have a largely greyish outer bill with a yellowish base and cere; from a distance the bill appears yellowish and pale. Upperwing coverts mostly uniform in colour, either brown or grey, with only a few retained immature-type worn and pale coverts with a dark shaft-streak. Greater coverts form a darker band on the wing with some of the inner being pale and worn. Tail still mostly dark, often even darker than in the previous plumages, but the individual variation is considerable. Underparts still show some scattered white mottling on breast both as white feather-bases and as retained immature-type feathers with dark shaft-streaks.

Fourth plumage-type (*c.* 4th cy autumn – 5th cy spring)   **Plates 84–86**

The first adult-type plumage, but differs from full adult in having a darker head, a slight grey suffusion on the outer bill in most individuals and by showing a few white feather-bases among the upperwing and underwing coverts and breast feathers. Axillaries still largely pale and the rump and vent show extensive white feather-bases. Tail variable and can be either largely dark or largely white but mostly it consists of a mixture of largely white and darker mottled feathers.

In flight similar to adult from a distance and possible to age only by retained whitish markings to underbody and underwing coverts, usually also by largely dark feathers in mostly white tail.

Adult-type (from *c.* 5th – 7th cy autumn and older)   **Plates 87–91**

In the fifth and sixth plumages the last remaining pale feather-bases are lost, the bill turns pure yellow and the tail becomes white, while the rest of the plumage becomes greyer and the head paler. Some fifth-winter birds (5th cy autumn to 6th cy spring) already show an all-yellow bill, all dark underwings and a white tail and are thus indistinguishable from older birds in the field. Since individuals vary in how quickly the different characters mature, exact ageing is not possible, and e.g. some birds seem to retain dark tips to their tail-feathers through life. In flight, underparts appear dark brown with paler head, neck and upper breast and a translucent, white tail. Upperparts more greyish brown, with darker remiges and a distinct grey flash on the upper hand between the dark primary coverts and dark fingers.

Sexing: Sexing not possible by plumage characters, but males are smaller and lighter built than females in direct comparison and show a comparatively finer bill and more rounded head.

References: Ekman & Helander 1994; Forsman 1980, 1981, 1983, 1984, 1993a; Gerdehag & Helander 1988; v. Haartman et al. 1965; Helander et al. 1989; Kjellén 1995; Pöyhönen 1995; Rüger & Neuman 1982; Tucker & Heath 1995

Plate 71 *Juvenile (2nd cy spring) showing diagnostic tawny underbody with dark streaking, dark head and bill, and pale lores. Note also pale axillaries and wing-bands and serrated trailing edge of wing. Tail-pattern typical of juvenile. Mar, Sweden (Jens B. Bruun).*

Plate 72 *Juvenile (2nd cy spring) showing tawny-mottled underbody, pale axillary-patch and diagnostic tail-pattern. Apr 1985, Norway (Dick Forsman).*

Plate 73   *Juvenile (2nd cy spring) with typically serrated trailing edge of wing and showing diagnostic tail-pattern. Has dropped two innermost primaries. May 1986, Norway (Dick Forsman).*

Plate 74   *Juvenile (2nd cy spring) showing typically patterned upperwing coverts with feathers of uniform age. Note dark head and bill and brown iris. 11 Mar 1997, Finland (Dick Forsman).*

Plate 75   *Typical juvenile with uniform plumage and regularly patterned upperwings. 9 Dec 1993, Finland (Dick Forsman).*

Plate 76   *2nd cy bird moulting from juvenile to second plumage. Still retains most of its juvenile plumage but darker upperwing coverts and inner primaries are growing. Jul, Norway (Markku Huhta-Koivisto).*

Plate 77 *Second plumage bird. Rather like juvenile, but moulted secondaries shorter and with blunter tips than juvenile secondaries, which stick out from the trailing edge of the wing. Dark head and neck contrast sharply against largely pale belly. 22 Jan 1995, Israel (Dick Forsman).*

Plate 78 *Second plumage bird showing marked contrast between dark head and thighs and pale belly. May 1985, Norway (Dick Forsman).*

Plate 79 *Second plumage bird (left) with juvenile. Note mottled and varied appearance of upper-parts, with lots of white admixed and irregular pattern of upperwing coverts compared with juvenile. Bill still mostly dark. 9 Dec 1993, Finland (Dick Forsman).*

Plate 80 *Second plumage. Extensive white markings on mantle and upperwing coverts are diagnostic of this plumage. Most birds still show a dark iris and bill. 10 Dec 1993, Finland (Dick Forsman).*

Plate 81 *Third plumage shows on average less white mottling compared with previous plumage and the tail may show the juvenile pattern, as here, but it may also be largely dark. Best aged by the few retained juvenile remiges. 20 Sep 1995, Finland (Mikko Pöllänen).*

Plate 82 *Third plumage. White feather-bases still show through on the breast. The upperwing looks generally greyish brown, with only some juvenile-type pale mottled greater and median coverts left. The bill is yellowish with a duskier outer half and the iris has become paler brown. 9 Dec 1993, Finland (Dick Forsman).*

Plate 83   *Two third plumage birds. Note difference in tail pattern. 10 Dec 1993, Finland (Dick Forsman).*

Plate 84   *Fourth plumage. In flight appears largely adult but head not paler than body and pale axillary-patch still prominent. 11 Mar 1997, Finland (Dick Forsman).*

Plate 85   *Fourth plumage. Much like adult because of largely yellowish bill, but with rather darkish head. Some isolated immature-type pale feather-bases are still visible among the inner wing coverts and feathers of the underparts. 9 Dec 1993, Finland (Dick Forsman).*

Plate 86   *Two birds in fourth plumage. Individual differences in plumage may be quite noticeable, but the bill shows some darker shadowing distally. The tail is very variable and can be mostly dark, mostly white or show a mixture of darkish and whitish feathers. 9 Dec 1993, Finland (Dick Forsman).*

Plate 87 *Fifth plumage. Not possible to tell with certainty from older birds and best called adult in the field. Many birds of this age still have a dark speck at the tip of the culmen and the iris is not yet as pale as in many full adults. 11 Mar 1997, Finland (Dick Forsman).*

Plate 88 *Adult with adult Rough-legged Buzzard. Note uniform underwings, white tail and pale head and neck. 7 May 1991, Norway (Dick Forsman).*

Plate 89   *Adult in flight. Despite the very pale head, the smudged bill and the retained pale mottling to underwing suggests this is not yet a full adult. Jun 1988, Norway (Esa Sojamo).*

Plate 90   *Moulting breeding adult. 3 Jul 1997, Norway (Dick Forsman).*

Plate 91   *Adult. This bird, in its sixth plumage, already shows all the adult features with pale iris, pure yellow bill, pale head and forebody and greyish upperwing coverts. 10 Dec 1993, Finland (Dick Forsman).*

BEARDED VULTURE or LAMMERGEIER
Gypaetus barbatus
Plates 92–102

Subspecies: Two subspecies currently recognized, nominate *barbatus* in Eurasia and NW Africa and *meridionalis* in the rest of Africa. Birds from Europe, the Middle East and C Asia were once separated as ssp. *aureus*, birds from NW Africa as ssp. *barbatus*, birds from Arabia and NE to S Africa as ssp. *meridionalis* and birds from E Asia as *G. b. haemachalanus*.

Distribution: In Europe restricted to the Pyrenees, Crete and the Balkans. Recent re-introduction programme in the Alps.

Habitat: Confined to mountain massifs and rarely seen away from these, except when crossing valleys, often at high altitude.

Population: Dramatic decline during past century and now extinct over much of former European range, with fewer than 200 pairs remaining, and an additional 100–500 pairs in Turkey. The population in the Pyrenees is slowly and steadily recovering, thanks to conservation measures, increasing to more than 75 pairs. The populations of Corsica and Crete are fairly stable, with 8 and *c.* 15 pairs, respectively, whereas the few remaining in the Balkans are dwindling. More than 50 birds have been re-introduced into the Alps since the late 1980s.

Movements: Adults resident. Juveniles and immatures disperse but usually stay within natal mountain range.

Hunting and prey: Feeds mainly on bones, but is also capable of taking live prey. Takes large bones high up in the air and drops them on to flat rocks to crack them and make marrow accessible. A masterful flier; hovers occasionally while hunting. Unlike other European vultures carries food in talons.

SPECIES IDENTIFICATION

Length and wing-span of S African Bearded Vultures *Gypaetus barbatus meridionalis* (smaller than European birds) after Brown (1989).

	Length (cm) ± SD	**Wing-span** (cm) ± SD
juv	100 ± 1 (*n=5*)	254 ± 3 (*n=6*)
imm	99 ± 3 (*n=5*)	257 ± 4 (*n=5*)
subad	107 (*n=1*)	260 (*n=1*)
ad	104 ± 4 (*n=6*)	263 ± 7 (*n=5*)

Not likely to be mistaken for any other species. Adults and juveniles are very different in proportions and flight silhouette.

Identification summary: A bird of unique and impressive proportions, yet appearing light and agile in flight. Juveniles and young immatures have long but broad and rounded wings, with deeply serrated and bulging trailing edge, and broader, shorter and more rounded tail than adults. Underwings dark and the dark head contrasts with paler greyish brown underbody. The wings of adults and subadults appear long and rather narrow with an even trailing edge, and the tail is very long and distinctly wedged; when seen from below, the underwings appear dark in contrast to the pale body.

In flight, distant Unmistakable even at long range owing to distinct silhouette, with wings long and either rounded (younger birds) or rather narrow (older birds) and tail rounded (young birds) or long and wedged (older birds).

Mostly seen soaring above mountain slopes or gliding along cliffs on motionless wings. When gliding, wings kept flat, but diagnostically pressed down, with smoothly up-bent wing-tips. Flapping flight appears extraordinarily light for the size of the bird, with deep and flexible wing-beats, almost like a giant Montagu's Harrier in slow-motion. Extreme agility of flight becomes obvious when playing around with other large birds of prey, with quick manouvres, stoops and dives.

Adults are white-headed, with a pale underbody contrasting with dark underwings, and shiny, silvery greyish upperparts. Young birds are dark-headed with a grey body and dark underwings, often showing a prominent pale carpal-patch, and the upperparts are dark with pale patches on upperwing coverts and mantle. Subadults are intermediate in plumage with a pale head and black neck, pale underbody and mottled underwing and upperwing coverts but with the diagnostic silhouette of the adult.

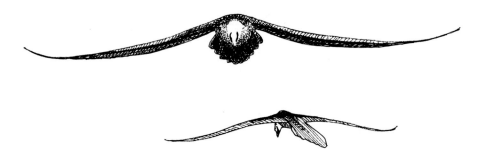

Fig 22 *Bearded Vulture. When hanging against the wind, Bearded Vultures show a diagnostic wing-attitude, with arms pressed down and hands bending smoothly upwards.*

In flight, closer Juveniles and young immatures have a grey underbody and a blackish head, neck and upper breast and the underwings appear fairly dark, with a distinct white carpal-patch varying in size between individuals. Upperparts are dark but frequently show irregular pale patches or wing-bars among the upperwing coverts, and the mantle shows a pale mottled triangle.

Older immatures and subadults may show a whitish head but they still retain the dark

Fig 23 *Bearded Vulture. Juvenile (upper) and adult showing different proportions to wings and tail. Note different wing-formulas and spiky trailing edge of juvenile.*

neck and breast-band, which contrasts with a pale, mottled underbody. Underwing coverts are mottled, with a mixture of pale and darker feathers, whereas flight-feathers are uniformly dark.

Adults are easily recognized alone by their typical falcon-like silhouette with long and rather narrow wings and a very long tail (clearly longer than the width of the wings). The head is whitish and the underbody and axillaries are pale, variably toned ochre. Underwings appear dark, but in good light the black forearm contrasts distinctly with paler grey greater coverts and remiges, with dark tips of latter forming black margin to wings. Upperparts appear uniformly silvery grey with a darker mantle.

Juveniles and adults differ significantly in wing-formula and roundness of tail. Juveniles have a more rounded wing-tip with p10<6 (counted descendantly), while adults show the opposite (p10>6), and the juvenile tail is more evenly rounded, with central feathers only 10 cm longer than the outer, whereas in adults the difference is 18 cm.

Perched Unmistakable, owing to short legs and very long and attenuated stern, with wing-tips reaching close to tail-tip. After first year, pale iris and diagnostic 'beard' add to unique appearance. Immatures and subadults show a mixture of irregularly spaced brown and pale feathers on upperwing coverts and the elongated neck-feathers are predominantly black. In adults the head is white, with a black eye-brow and lores, and a prominent 'beard'. Upperparts are black with silvery feather-centres and white shaft-streaks and tips.

Bare parts Feet greyish, feathered almost down to the toes; bill horn-coloured. Scleral-ring around eye brown-red in juvenile until about 8 months when turns dull red, becoming deep red at c. 24 months, and eventually bright blood-red by c. 40+ months. Iris yellow-brown to brown in juvenile until c. 12 months old, then turning yellow; by 36 months the iris is clear yellow, although still duller than in full adult.

The 'beard' lengthens with age (given here to the nearest mm): 4 mm long at age 3.5 months (in the nest); 7 mm at 4.5 months; 12 mm at 10–12 months; 32 mm at 22–24 months; 37 mm at 36 months; 43 mm at 42–44 months and 45–55mm at 60+ months (Brown 1989).

Confusion species: The huge size, diagnostic silhouette and slow-motion movements make the Bearded Vulture unmistakable and unlikely to be confused with any other bird of prey.

Egyptian Vultures (page 108) Immatures may appear rather similar to younger Bearded Vultures, but are much smaller, have more parallel-edged wings and the tail is comparatively shorter and distinctly wedged, not rounded, and the head is slim with a fine bill.

MOULT

Annually complete but comprising only some body plumage and some flight-feathers. Replacing the entire plumage takes *c.* 2.5–3 years, but individuals vary in speed and duration of moult. Thus some birds may show the first adult-type feathers from 3rd cy autumn while others do not acquire them until a year later, by 4th cy autumn (Adam & Llopis Dell 1995).

Juveniles (first moult) Commence moulting in 2nd cy late spring (Apr) at about 13 months. Only three to four innermost primaries are moulted; sometimes also the occasional secondary and rectrix.

Second moult Commences in spring of 3rd cy and is completed by Sep–Oct. Moults p4–6 and occasionally some secondaries. In one individual (BMNH) the distance between the tips of the moulted s1 and retained s2 was 3.5 cm, and between the moulted s14 and retained s13 8.5 cm, elucidating the difference in feather length (and wing width) between juveniles and older birds.

Third moult In 4th cy, the remaining juvenile outer primaries are moulted and replaced by feathers some 5 cm longer. After completing moult, some birds still retain an outermost juvenile primary or a few juvenile secondaries until the next moult in 5th cy.

Adults (subsequent moults) Moult primaries serially descendant, but it probably takes two or three moults to replace the remiges completely.

AGEING AND SEXING

Four distinct plumage-types recognizable from a distance in the field: juvenile type (carried until 21–24 months of age), immature plumage-type (from 21 to 43 months of age), subadult plumage-type (from 43 to 60 months of age) and adult plumage-type (from 60+ months of age). The first three or four plumages are possible to age reliably in the field, given close and prolonged views, but older birds not possible to age with certainty, as individuals vary considerably in speed of moult and development of plumage. Older immature and subadult plumages are hence better referred to as plumage-types.

Ageing summary: The first two plumages are generally dark and difficult to separate in the field, the main difference being the replaced inner primaries of the second plumage showing more rounded tips. The subsequent immature plumages show white mottling to the underwing coverts and underbody, the head becomes paler, and the secondaries are largely long and pointed juvenile feathers. The subadult plumages are similar to the adult plumage in silhouette (some may show the odd retained juvenile central secondary or outermost primary) but the underwing coverts and underbody are mottled. The adult plumage is distinct and attained in the 6th–7th cy. From above it is grey with contrasting white head and dark mantle and from below shows dark underwing coverts, greyish remiges and a pale ochre underbody.

Juvenile (1st cy – 2nd cy spring)   Plates 92–93

Whole plumage consists of fresh or evenly worn feathers. Face black, blackish collar of elongated and pointed feathers, some individuals showing whitish patch to throat. Underparts uniformly brownish grey, mixed with variable paler tips and darker feathers, vent slightly darker. Broad breast-band dark brown. When perched wing-tips fall about 10 cm short of tail-tip. Iris dark, turning paler from 2nd cy spring; scleral-ring dull reddish brown. Beard small and inconspicuous.

In flight, wings and tail broad and rounded. From below, remiges uniformly dark and very pointed (almost spiky), including the inner primaries. Greater underwing coverts are dark grey, but many birds show a distinct pale carpal comma, formed by pale tips to median primary coverts. Median and lesser secondary coverts are darker greyish brown contrasting with paler underbody, sometimes showing paler spots. Rectrices dark with variable, large pale spots at tips.

Upperparts are dark greyish brown with darker flight-feathers and large scapulars, with white mottling of mantle forming whitish triangle. Upperwing coverts appear generally dark, but some individuals show partly or largely pale median coverts forming pale wing-patch; lesser and greater coverts are dark, latter often with diffuse paler tips forming indistinct wing-band.

Second plumage (2nd cy autumn – 3rd cy spring)   Plates 94–95

Generally very similar to juvenile, but face turns greyer and black collar may show first pale feathers in some advanced birds. Dark breast-band prominent. Underbody somewhat mottled consisting of 50% faded juvenile feathers with pale tips and 50% freshly moulted and uniformly greyish brown feathers, with occasional pale tips. Upperwing coverts consisting of 50% worn brown and 50% freshly moulted brown feathers lacking pale tips. Greater upperwing coverts are largely worn and pointed juvenile feathers, with some inner being moulted and dark. Iris becomes yellow by 2nd cy autumn.

Silhouette in flight similar to juvenile, but innermost primaries are moulted, with more rounded tips. The whitish triangle on the mantle is less prominent than in juvenile plumage.

Third plumage (3rd cy autumn – 4th cy spring)   **Not depicted**
Still resembles juvenile, although plumage consists mainly of second generation feathers. Face consists of a mixture of pale and dark feathers. Iris is yellow and the scleral-ring red. The first white feathers start to emerge among the black neck feathers. Underparts are even more mottled than in previous plumages, consisting of three generations of feathers, with the most recently moulted being the darkest (*c.* 30% juvenile feathers and *c.* 70% moulted feathers of variable age). Upperwing coverts very chequered consisting of 20% juvenile feathers and 80% moulted feathers, both fresh and worn, with pale coverts still forming patches and bands; first adult-type coverts (black with whitish tips) start to appear. Central greater coverts of upperwing are extremely worn juvenile feathers.

In flight, best recognized by worn and faded juvenile outer primaries and by largely retained juvenile median secondaries projecting from the trailing edge of the wing, but silhouette otherwise resembles that of adult. Pale triangle of mantle even more diffuse than in previous plumage.

Fourth plumage (4th cy autumn – 5th cy spring)   **Plate 96**
Face largely white; collar and neck predominantly dark but with increasing proportion of whitish feathers. Underbody appears paler and more uniform in colour than previous plumages as proportion of white feathers increases. Upperwing coverts become gradually more uniform and the paler wing-patches and bands are lost as adult-type feathers appear. Pale triangle on mantle no longer discernible. Still retains a few pointed juvenile secondaries on inner arm. Underwing coverts mottled, generally paler than remiges, with largely pale outer vanes to greater coverts, brownish-ochre median coverts and brown lesser coverts.

Fifth plumage-type (*c.* 5th cy autumn – 6th cy spring)   **Plate 97**
Head and neck predominantly white with some retained dark feathers and with narrow dark breast-band. Underbody largely white, but still not uniform. Upperwing coverts still somewhat mottled, but gradually losing pale wing-bands and becoming more uniform, with increasing proportion of adult-type feathers. Silhouette similar to adult with long and rather narrow wings and a long tail.

Sixth plumage-type (*c.* 6th cy autumn – 7th cy spring)   **Not depicted**
Some individuals are known to have acquired a nearly fully adult plumage by this age, although another 1–2 years are usually required to replace the remaining subadult feathers. Face and neck predominantly pale, although the collar may still be partly dark. The breast-band has odd dark feathers. Underbody nearly uniform, but underwing coverts still mottled. Upperwing coverts may appear uniformly coloured, but they often still show odd paler feathers.

Adult plumage (from *c*. 7th cy autumn and older)   **Plates 98–102**

Head and neck white, with black lores and beard, body uniformly white but mostly stained deep ochre from contact with iron oxide from the breeding cliffs. Feathers of upperparts black with silvery centres and white shaft-streaks and tips. Flight-feathers are silvery grey with black margins, appearing silvery from a distance.

In flight from below, characterized by long and rather narrow wings with even trailing edge and by very long and wedged tail. From a distance, head and underbody appear white and tail and underwings dark, but when under-lit remiges and greater coverts appear grey contrasting with black lesser and median coverts, while the trailing edge of the wing shows a dark margin. Axillaries elongated and prominent, whitish with dark streaks. Seen from above, the wings and tail appear silvery, slightly varying in shade depending on the angle of the light, with white head and 'hump-back' of mantle and leading edge to arm distinctly darker.

Sexing: No significant difference in size or plumage between male and female. At least adults of African *meridionalis* differ in wing-shape in flight, with females having broader inner hand than males, which is best seen in direct comparison.

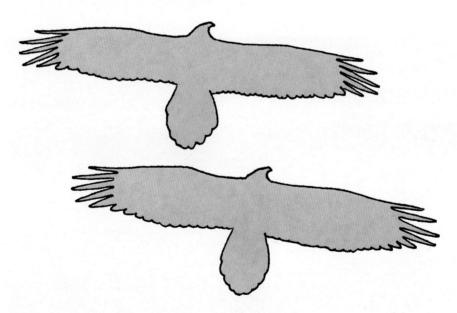

Fig 24 *Bearded Vulture. Note broader wings with bulging trailing edge of adult female (lower) compared with adult male (after Brown 1989).*

References: Adam & Llopis Dell 1995; Brown 1989; Mundy et al. 1992; Tucker & Heath 1995

Plate 92 *Juvenile showing more rounded wing-profile and shorter tail than adult. Note serrated wings and pale patch at carpal bend. Apr 1991, China (Jyrki Matikainen).*

Plate 93 *Juvenile from above. The whitish triangle on the mantle is diagnostic of juvenile, while the pale wing-bands vary individually. Note the uniform condition of the plumage and the serrated trailing edge to the wing owing to pointed remiges. Feb 1981, Nepal (Erik Mölgaard).*

Plate 94 *Second plumage* meridionalis. *Plumage still largely juvenile but the innermost few primaries are moulted as well as some of the median coverts. South Africa (Penny Meakin/Aquila).*

Plate 95 *Second plumage* meridionalis *(same as Plate 94). Note pointed juvenile greater coverts, rather worn by now, and fresh pale-mottled median upperwing coverts. South Africa (John F. Carlyon/Aquila).*

Plate 96 *Subadult (possibly 4th plumage). Silhouette much like adult while plumage still halfway between adult and juvenile. Sep 1988, Turkey (Markku Huhta-Koivisto).*

Plate 97 *Subadult* meridionalis *(possibly 4th (or 5th?) plumage). Face and nape white, but neck still largely dark. Remiges and greater coverts of adult type, with one retained and worn greater covert of younger immature-type. South Africa (John F. Carlyon/Aquila).*

Plate 98   *Adult. The long and rather narrow wings and long tail make the silhouette of adults unmistakable. 19 Nov 1996, Ethiopia (Dick Forsman).*

Plate 99   *Adult. In good light greyish remiges and greater coverts contrast with dark forewing and dark trailing edge. Note also elongated pale axillaries. 23 Apr 1996, Spain (Dick Forsman).*

Plate 100 *Adult in full soar showing diagnostic head-on silhouette with typically lowered hands and smoothly up-bent tips. 19 Nov 1996, Ethiopia (Dick Forsman).*

Plate 101 *Adult. The shiny upperparts reflect the light and often appear silvery with a darker mantle and a contrasting white head. 19 Nov 1996, Ethiopia (Dick Forsman).*

Plate 102 *Adult. Often the wings appear all-dark from below contrasting with the pale body. 19 Nov 1996, Ethiopia (Dick Forsman).*

EGYPTIAN VULTURE   *Neophron percnopterus*

Plates 103–126

Subspecies: Two subspecies, nominate *percnopterus* over most of species' range, ssp. *ginginianus* of India smaller with all-yellow bill in adult.

Distribution: Nominate subspecies in Europe, Africa and Asia to Pakistan and Tien-Shan mountains.

Habitat: Nests on steep cliffs and crags, but otherwise found in all kinds of open terrain. Usually confiding or indifferent towards people and commonly seen close to human settlements, on rubbish dumps and around villages.

Population: Population declining over most of its European range, owing to improved hygienic standards and decreased supply of suitable carrion. Now fewer than 2000 pairs in Europe (of which *c*. 1350 in Spain), with another 1000–7000 in Turkey.

Movements: Mainly migratory in W Palearctic parts of range with majority wintering in Africa south of Sahara. Some European birds winter around the Mediterranean and the island populations of Menorca, Canary and Cap Verde Islands are resident. Some of the juveniles and younger subadults oversummer in the winter quarters; adults migrate earlier than immatures.

On migration follows the main raptor routes at Straits of Gibraltar and Bosporus–Levant. Autumn migration from Jul to Oct, with numbers peaking in Sep; birds from Iberian peninsula leave somewhat earlier than E European birds. More numerous along western route, with 3768 passing Gibraltar between 21 Aug and 14 Nov 1972, with peaks of 435 on 22 Aug and 431 on 2 Nov. At Suez a total of 437 migrants between 4 Sep and 31 Oct 1981, with daily peak of 77 on 24 Sep.

Spring migration protracted with observations from late Feb to late May. At Eilat three migration peaks, around mid-Mar, mid-Apr and early May, with former two comprising mainly adults and latter non-breeders and immatures; adults formed *c*. 95% of all migrants in spring 1985. Iberian birds arrive in spring before the Balkan population. Migrates singly or in small parties, up to 10–15 birds together, occasionally in bigger flocks.

Hunting and prey: Does not feed exclusively on carrion but scavenges on all kinds of organic litter. Frequently seen around rubbish dumps, shores, roadsides and villages searching for food, often walking about or sitting on an exposed perch. Joins other vultures at carcasses, but does not descend to feed until larger species are about to finish.

SPECIES IDENTIFICATION

Length 56–65 cm

wing-span 164–168 cm (*n*=5; Israel, W.S. Clark, unpubl.)

Length 63–75 cm

wing-span 163–171 cm (*n*= 4 and 3, respectively; Dementev et al. 1966)

Adults and older immatures usually straightforward to identify, whereas juveniles and birds in second plumage may be mistaken for eagles, distant birds especially.

Identification summary: Diagnostic silhouette, with rather long and rectangular wings, a rather sharply wedged tail and a narrow and pointed head. Older birds show diagnostic plumage in black and white. Older immatures and subadults resemble adults but retain brownish feathers to underbody, and wing coverts. Juveniles and young immatures are predominantly brown, but tail is paler brown with a pale and translucent margin and with individually variable pale markings to rear body as well as to upper- and underwing coverts, often forming pale wing-bands.

In flight, distant Active flight relaxed and rowing with rather stiff wings and high wing-beats, somewhat reminiscent of Honey Buzzard or Booted Eagle. Soars on nearly horizontal and flattish yet smoothly arched wings.

Mostly rather easy to identify by characteristic plumage and silhouette. Largely brown juveniles and immatures can be superficially similar to *Aquila*-eagles, but show narrower hand than arm, pointed tail and different flapping flight.

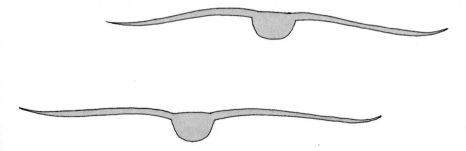

Fig 25 *Egyptian Vulture. Glides on rather flat but smoothly arched wings lacking prominent broom-shape.*

In flight, closer Adults are diagnostic: mostly white underneath with contrasting black remiges; more varied but predominantly white above, with black inner greater coverts and primary coverts, black mid-wing-band at base of secondaries, latter showing largely whitish outer vanes. The bare face is bright orange-yellow and the ruff around the neck often stained light brown by grit and dust.

Juveniles are mostly dark brown with a variable amount of pale feather-tips to body and wing coverts. Paler individuals have a pale rump and broad pale wing-bands on the upperwing, the belly and vent are largely paler and the underwing coverts may show distinct wing-bars, while dark birds may appear almost uniformly dark brown but mostly show paler rear body above and below. The darkish tail invariably shows diagnostic paler and translucent edges and the trailing edge of the wing appears serrated, because of pointed secondary-tips.

The second plumage is rather similar to the juvenile plumage and only with difficulty possible to separate from this (see under Ageing and sexing). The consecutive plumages show an increasing number of pale feathers in body and underwing coverts, the bird first looking mottled but gradually becoming paler, often retaining darker neck collar until later.

Perched Unmistakable if seen well, bare face and slender bill diagnostic. Rather long-winged and short-tailed with wing-tips reaching tail-tip. Adults easily recognized by their diagnostic plumage and yellow bare face. Older subadults are rather similar to adults but show some retained brownish or tawny feathers on upperwing and body. Juveniles and first-immatures are mostly dark brown with variable spotting to upperwing coverts, scapulars and body, while the bare face is pale bluish to nearly whitish. The feet are pinkish in all plumages.

Bare parts In adults face orange to orange-yellow, feet pink, bill black; in juveniles face pale bluish or whitish, feet and bill as in adult. Face changes colour with age, being pale with a pinkish base to the bill in 2nd cy, turning faint yellowish during 3rd cy and gradually becoming more brightly yellow by 4th cy.

Confusion species: *Adults* possible to mistake for other black-and-white raptors (or with White Stork *Ciconia ciconia*!).

Pale Booted Eagle (page 416) Very different proportions in flight to adult Egyptian Vulture, with shorter and more buzzard-like wings, a long and square-tipped tail and completely different upperparts.

Bonelli's Eagle (page 404) Adult has much broader and more rounded wings and longer tail than adult Egyptian Vulture and the upperparts are largely dark with pale mantle-patch.

Osprey (page 21), Short-toed Eagle (page 156), and pale Honey and Common Buzzards (page 30 and 266 respectively) All identified from below by pale or barred remiges.

Juveniles may be confused with other largish and uniformly dark birds of prey, especially Lesser Spotted Eagle, with which it may join on passage. Older immatures mostly identified by mottled plumage but otherwise resemble adult.

Lesser Spotted Eagle (page 316) More parallel-edged wings with broader tip and a blunter tail, and flies and glides on more arched wings. Most individuals also show pale upper-tail coverts and pale wing-flash on inner upperhand lacking in Egyptian Vulture.

MOULT

Complete moult annually, but does not replace whole set of remiges in first moults, at least not until serial moult is fully developed. Extent of wing moult in winter quarters still poorly known. Possibly a longer moulting period, and hence a more extensive annual moult, in non-migratory populations of N Africa and Arabia than in migratory birds from Europe (unpubl. data).

Juveniles (first moult) Moult of remiges commences in 2nd cy Apr, sometimes as early as Mar continuing until Nov, when moult is suspended. After the moult the outermost two to four primaries and usually up to seven median secondaries are retained juvenile feathers, being browner, narrower and more pointed than the replaced ones.

Second moult Starts in some as early as 3rd cy mid Feb (Eilat, Israel, Mar, with p9 half-grown and p10 a retained juvenile feather) from where it was suspended the previous autumn, while others do not show any signs of moult by May (Turkey) or even by 24 Jun (Greece). The remaining juvenile remiges are moulted during the summer when a new moult wave starts from p1. The moult is finished by Oct–Nov.

Subsequent moults The timing of moult in adults and near adults is poorly known. The numerous birds studied in Israel (Mar, Apr, Sep and Oct), Egypt (Apr), Greece (Jun), Turkey (Jun, Sep) and the United Arab Emirates (Dec) did not show active remex moult, while immatures at the same time were moulting actively (see above). Long-distance migrants may moult (at least partly) on the wintering grounds, as some of the spring migrants show growing secondaries.

AGEING AND SEXING

Easily divided into three plumage-types: a mostly dark plumage, a paler milk-coffee coloured plumage (often mottled) and the adult plumage, but exact ageing within each plumage-type is difficult and requires close views. The plumages of older immatures, which have replaced their last juvenile remiges, are best referred to as plumage-types.

Ageing summary: Exact ageing difficult because of slow plumage development and extensive individual variation. Mostly brown juvenile and second plumage possible to separate only at close range, if moulting details are seen. The third plumage shows increasing numbers of pale feathers in underwing coverts and underbody, often appearing biscuit-coloured from a distance but mottled from close up with a darker collar. The fourth plumage is predominantly white, but still shows lots of brown feathers among the underwing coverts whereas the collar is predominantly pale. The adult plumage is black and white from below with no dark feathers among the underwing coverts (a fifth plumage-type probably precedes the adult plumage, differing from full adult by a few retained dark feathers to the underwing coverts).

Juvenile (1st cy – 2nd cy spring)   Plates 103–108

Plumage fresh in autumn, evenly worn in spring and lacking signs of moult until Apr; largely dark brown with individually variable pale tips to wing-coverts, scapulars and rear underbody. Facial skin whitish or pale bluish with areas of darker bristles around the eyes, while the plumage of head and neck is uniformly dark.

In flight shows evenly serrated trailing edge to wing including pointed inner primaries. Upperparts variable but often show paler tips to greater upperwing coverts and a pale patch in the median upperwing coverts, paler mantle and scapulars and almost invariably pale rump and uppertail coverts. Tail brownish with a paler tip and edges. Remiges show the diagnostic pattern of the adults with paler outer vanes, although much fainter and browner, and the secondaries have more broadly dark bases with outer vanes only distally paler. The primaries and their coverts are darker than the rest of the upperwing.

Underparts appear rather uniformly dark apart from the pale face, the paler rear underbody and the regular pale lines to the forearm formed by pale covert bases. Remiges are uniformly dark whereas the diagnostically shaped tail shows distinctly paler edges.

During winter the pale markings are partly worn away and the upperwings especially become darker and more uniform.

Second plumage (2nd cy autumn – 3rd cy spring)   Plates 109–115

Similar to juvenile and told from this by the following characters. The moulted remiges show more extensively pale outer vanes above; body appears more uniform in colour, mottled greyish brown both above and below, with a distinctly darker blackish brown neck-collar; underwing coverts are more irregularly patterned, with dark lesser coverts and faded brown median and greater coverts, and often with some prominent whitish feathers among the axillaries and the coverts of the forearm. Face and tail still much as in the juvenile but the base of the bill is yellowish pink. Rump and vent merge in colour with the rest of the body (not distinctly paler as in juvenile), while the flanks and trousers tend to be dark brown, contrasting with paler brown belly and vent.

Individuals vary considerably: some birds may appear almost uniformly dark from below, while more advanced birds show quite a few whitish median underwing coverts and axillaries. Upperparts also vary and some birds show still largely brownish upperwing coverts while others show white and dark feathers in equal proportions.

When perched most individuals told from juveniles by whitish feathers appearing among wing coverts, darker and more uniformly brown individuals by partly moulted upperwing coverts, showing both fresh and worn feathers to upperwing, and by more extensively white outer vanes to moulted secondaries.

Third plumage-type (3rd cy autumn – 4th cy spring) Plates 116–118

Compared with previous plumage generally more pied in appearance with more white feathers appearing among the underwing coverts, including some of the greater coverts. Underbody shows a mixture of whitish and dark and faded brownish feathers and the ruff is paler because of an increasing proportion of long, white lanceolated feathers. Median and greater underwing coverts mostly white in some individuals, whereas the forearm still shows mostly darkish feathers. Face by now all-yellow but tail still greyish buff with paler edges.

Perched birds told from adults by buffish and tawny feathers to the upperparts and by not yet uniformly white collar.

Fourth plumage-type (4th cy autumn – 5th cy spring) Plates 119–120

From a distance similar to adult but differs by some retained grey greater underwing coverts and dark lesser underwing coverts, and by tail which still retains some greyish buff feathers among all-white ones.

Perched birds differ from adults by some retained coloured feathers among upperwing coverts and mantle, which may create an impression rather similar to soiled adults, although showing a more irregular pattern.

Adult (from *c.* 5th cy autumn) Plates 121–126

When perched looks generally white, more or less dirty, with dark inner greater coverts, secondary bases and primary projection. Bare orange-yellow face surrounded by a dense ruff of elongated white feathers; feet pinkish; bill black.

Unmistakable in flight with, from below, pure white body plumage and wedge-shaped tail contrasting sharply with black remiges. Upperparts are similarly black and white but more varied in pattern. Most of the body-feathers and the tail are white, but the inner greater coverts and primary coverts are black forming contrasting dark areas to the upperwing. Remiges generally dark, but show extensively silvery white outer vanes, with the exception of the fingers and the bases of the secondaries, the latter forming a distinct black wing-band.

Note that the collar, the underbody, the scapulars and the inner upperwing coverts are often dirty and soiled and may therefore appear coloured and darker than the rest of the white plumage tracts, and may hence resemble some of the subadult plumages, but adults always show clean, white underwing coverts. (Birds appearing in an otherwise full adult plumage but showing a few retained dark underwing coverts, usually confined to the carpal area, may represent a fifth plumage-type.)

Sexing: Not possible to sex in the field, as sexes similar in plumage and nearly so in size.

References: Bernis 1975; Bijlsma 1983; Mundy et al. 1992; Shirihai & Christie 1992; Tucker & Heath 1995

Plate 103 *Fresh juvenile. Note uniform condition of plumage with well preserved pale feather-tips and lack of ruff on head. 10 Sep 1997, Spain (Dick Forsman).*

Plate 104 *Fresh juvenile from above. Note extensive white areas to upperparts of this individual. 9 Sep 1997, Spain (Dick Forsman).*

Plate 105 *Juvenile in more worn plumage. Uniform condition of plumage and pointed remiges reveal the age. Note diagnostic pale rump, greyish brown tail with paler edges while the secondaries are diffusely paler distally. 24 Nov 1996, Oman (Hanne & Jens Eriksen).*

Plate 106 *Fresh juvenile. Note uniform condition of plumage with well preserved pale feather-tips and lack of ruff on head. 3 Sep 1992, Oman (Hanne & Jens Eriksen).*

Plate 107 *Juvenile growing new inner primaries. 4 Mar 1993, Oman (Hanne & Jens Eriksen).*

Plate 108 *Worn juvenile at beginning of first moult (note missing upperwing coverts). Told from second plumage by just faintly paler outer vanes to secondaries. 10 Apr 1991, Egypt (Annika Forsten).*

Plate 109 *Moulting to second plumage. Second plumage still very similar to juvenile but differs by partly moulted remiges and partial body moult. 2 Oct 1987, Israel (Dick Forsman).*

Plate 110 *Second plumage showing retained four outermost primaries. Note dark neck-collar and dark forearm. This rather typical individual shows some pale median underwing coverts. Dec 1996, UAE (Markku Huhta-Koivisto).*

Plate 111 *Advanced second plumage showing partly whitish underwing coverts. Note, however, retained juvenile outer two primaries and one inner secondary, dark neck-collar and brownish breast. 17 Dec 1992, UAE (Markku Saarinen).*

Plate 112 *Second plumage moulting to third (3rd cy spring). The overall impression becomes more buffish as the proportion of pale feathers increases. 10 Apr 1991, Egypt (Heikki Assinen).*

Plate 113 *Second plumage from above. Note brighter secondary bands compared with juvenile and new tawny and whitish feathers on forewing and mantle. Black neck-collar still prominent in most. This bird has retained its juvenile s4 and s11–13. 8 Apr 1991, Egypt (Tapani Numminen).*

Plate 114 *A rather juvenile-like second plumage bird. Aged by irregularly mottled upperwing coverts, brighter secondaries and growing outer primaries. Spring, Israel (Urban Olsson).*

Plate 115 *Second plumage moulting to third. This rather advanced individual already shows lots of white on forewing and scapulars but the head and neck are still mostly dark. Note the growing outermost primary. 10 Apr 1991, Egypt (Tapani Numminen).*

Plate 116 *A rather dark third plumage-type bird. Best told from second plumage by different moult-pattern, partly white greater underwing coverts and emerging white neck-collar. Dec 1996, UAE (Markku Huhta-Koivisto).*

Plate 117 *Third plumage-type. This rather typical individual shows partly white greater underwing coverts, a whitish neck-collar and a uniformly mottled plumage. Dec 1996, UAE (Tom Lindroos).*

Plate 118 *Third plumage-type. Overall appearance mottled including partly white underwing coverts. Note long white feathers of neck-collar. 24 Aug 1995, Oman (Hanne & Jens Eriksen).*

Plate 119 *Fourth plumage-type. Differs from adult by greyish tail, by retained greyish greater underwing coverts and body feathers (here also partly grey neck-collar). Dec 1991, UAE (Matti Rekilä).*

Plate 120 *Fourth plumage-type. Apr, Israel (Göran Ekström).*

Plate 121 *Near adult (fifth plumage-type) with some retained greyish underwing coverts. 10 Apr 1991, Egypt (Heikki Assinen).*

Plate 122 *Adult from below. The smudged collar, breast and carpals is a common feature in adults. 10 Apr 1991, Egypt (Heikki Assinen).*

Plate 123   *Adult. Unmistakable plumage and silhouette. Note wedged tail, yellow face and long, fine bill. 15 Mar 1995, Israel (Dick Forsman).*

Plate 124   *Adult from above. Upperwing pattern diagnostic with largely white outer vanes to remiges, black wing-band and black primary coverts. 28 Mar 1996, Israel (Dick Forsman).*

Plate 125 *Two adults (right) with second plumage bird. 29 Nov 1994, Oman (Hanne & Jens Eriksen).*

Plate 126 *Adult. 10 Apr 1991, Egypt (Tapani Numminen).*

GRIFFON VULTURE *Gyps fulvus*
Plates 127–142

Subspecies: Two subspecies. Nominate *fulvus* in W Palearctic, extending from Iberian Peninsula in the west to NW Pakistan and Altai Mts. Extralimital *G. f. fulvescens*, from Kashmir, N and C India to Assam and S Himalayas.

Distribution: From Spain and Morocco scattered and sparsely distributed around the Mediterranean, Near East and C Asia to India and Assam. Formerly over much of S Europe. Now common only in Spain and locally in Greece (Crete).

Habitat: Breeds on steep cliffs in mountainous areas. When foraging, patrols all kinds of landscapes, from high mountains to lowland deserts and plains.

Population: As in other vultures populations dramatically diminished during the last few centuries because of changes in livestock rearing, locally (Balkans and the Iberian peninsula) also as a result of poisoning large carnivores. Recently, captive bred birds have been released in several places (S France, Alps) in attempts to reintroduce the species to former breeding grounds. The Spanish population shows a steady increase and, in 1989, totalled *c.* 7487 breeding pairs, with another 544 possible pairs, comprising in all 22 945–24 535 individuals. Total European population (including Turkey) *c.* 9000–11 000 pairs.

Movements: Adults mainly sedentary, staying close to the breeding colony. Juveniles and non-breeding immatures straggle outside breeding areas. Some younger birds migrate, singly or in small groups, following the major flyways for large raptors (Gibraltar, Bosporus–Levant). Main migration periods Sep–Oct (Levant) and Oct–Nov (Spain), return passage from Feb to May. Iberian migrants winter in NW Africa from Morocco to Mauretania and Senegal, Asian birds in Arabian peninsula and NE Africa.

Hunting and prey: Feeds on all kinds of carrion. Patrols high in the air for much of the day covering large areas in search of food. Gathers rapidly around carcass, where tens of birds may flock. Dependent on thermals or wind for flying, leaving roosts later than e.g. Black Vulture.

SPECIES IDENTIFICATION

Length 95–105 cm

wing-span 240–280 cm (Cramp & Simmons 1980); wing-span 240–256 cm (*n*=2; Dementev et al. 1966)

Mostly easily identified by distinct upperwing contrast, comparatively small and pale head and, in flight, by long wings with slightly narrower hand than bulging arm.

> **Identification summary:** One of the largest raptors of the region. Usually not difficult to identify by clearly bi-coloured upperparts (shadowed underparts often less distinctive), long wings with bulging trailing edge to arm and slightly tapering hand, small whitish head and short, ample tail. When soaring, wings kept typically slightly lifted in shallow V, with bulky, barrel-shaped body hanging well below wing-plane.

In flight, distant Best told from other large raptors by clearly two-toned upperparts in combination with characteristic silhouette. Long and fairly broad wings, slightly tapering towards tips, tail short and square, head small and whitish. When soaring, wings kept in shallow V, glides on flat or slightly arched wings, often with moderately drooping hand, thus at times resembling Black Vulture, and with fingered primaries strongly bent upwards forming a wide 'broom' at the wing-tip in head-on views. Active flight laboured, with

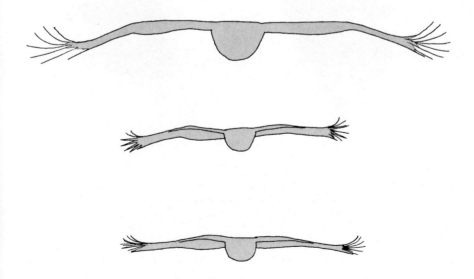

Fig 26 *Griffon Vulture. Different wing attitudes when gliding. Note bulging arm and narrower hand than arm and compare with Black Vulture (Fig 28).*

wing-beats even heavier and deeper than in Black Vulture. Mostly seen in flight, soaring for hours on motionless wings or gliding along ridges and slopes in search of food.

In flight, closer Unmistakable, with huge body and small pale head, short tail and long wings, fingers deeply splayed at tip. Flight-feathers dark and unbarred, rest of upperparts sandy brown with dark-centred greater coverts and large scapulars, former creating prominent upperwing band. Underwing coverts vary from largely pale to darker, often showing paler and darker bands, but generally paler than uniformly dark remiges. Head small and downy, either whitish or slightly rufous, bill pale or slate grey; feet grey.

Perched Unmistakable. Large and sandy brown with a small, downy head, and huge wings covering most of body including tail. Long and downy neck visible during interactions between birds e.g. around a carcass, but, when resting, keeps head tucked between the shoulders. Feet and cere greyish, bill slate or pale horn.

Fig 27 *Griffon Vulture. Greater covert of right wing of juvenile (left) and adult. Note pointed and narrowly marked tip of juvenile and compare with shape and pattern of adult.*

Bare parts Legs and cere grey at all ages. Iris dark brown in juvenile turning paler with age and becoming finally pale yellowish brown in adult. Bill dark grey in juvenile, taking several years to become pale horn in adult (see Subadults under Ageing and sexing).

Confusion species: Possible to confuse with faded adult Black Vulture, but told from other large raptors by combination of typically shaped wings, comparatively small whitish head, very short tail and marked contrast of upperwings.

Black Vulture (page 138) In adult plumage also shows brownish upperparts and whitish head but lacks the distinct contrast of upper- and underwing of Griffon. The Black Vulture is also more eagle-like in silhouette, with slightly longer and more parallel-edged wings (wider hand), longer and wedge-shaped tail and a comparatively larger, more protruding head.

MOULT

Annually complete during breeding season, but comprising only part of plumage. Whole plumage takes more than a year to replace.

Juveniles (first moult) First primary moult commences in 2nd cy Apr–Jun (17 Apr p1–2 missing, Spain; Jun innermost primary missing, Greece). By the time the moult is suspended in Oct–Nov, only two or three innermost primaries are replaced (e.g. Israel, 13 Oct, p1 new and p2 missing; Spain, 21 Feb, p1–3 moulted). Some birds also replace a few secondaries and the central tail-feathers.

Second moult Commences in 3rd cy Feb (Spain) starting where previous moult stopped. When moult is suspended in Oct–Nov birds still retain some juvenile outer primaries (usually p8–10) and some median secondaries, which are replaced in the 3rd moult the following (4th cy) summer.

Adults (subsequent moults) The remiges are moulted serially, the whole set taking approximately 2 years to replace. The moult is more extended than in juveniles, commencing Jan–Feb and continuing into Nov. Occasional remiges can be moulted during mid-winter.

AGEING AND SEXING

Ageing usually difficult, although juveniles and adults are rather straightforward to tell apart, whereas the ageing of older immatures requires good conditions, as many of the ageing characters are visible only at close range and even so may be difficult to assess on flying birds. Important points to look for are moult pattern of primaries and details of trailing edge to arm, colour of bill and eye, structure and colour of ruff, colour of upperparts and pattern of greater coverts on upperwing.

Ageing summary: In flight, juveniles are more slender-winged than adults, with markedly narrower inner hand and with clearly indented trailing edge to arm; the remiges are black underneath, the underbody is rufous brown with pale shaft-streaks, and the bill is dark. Adults are paler and more greyish above, the trailing edge of the wing is even, the remiges from below are grey with black margins, and the bill is pale. The adult plumage takes several years to acquire, but already by 3rd cy summer (2 years old) distant birds appear largely like adults. After this it still takes several years before the ruff becomes white and the bill turns pale horn. Immatures are possible to age accurately only by moult pattern of the remiges.

The pattern of the underwing coverts, which used to be given as one of the main ageing characters, is not reliable, as juveniles with dark and patterned 'adult-type' coverts frequently occur.

Juvenile (1st cy – 2nd cy spring) Plates 127–134

During favourable conditions not difficult to identify. General plumage colour rufous brown, clearly darker than in adults, with less pronounced contrast between coverts and flight-feathers above. Upper greater coverts pointed and dark brown with narrow paler tips only, lacking the broad margins and distinct black centres of the adult (Fig 27). All body-feathers (including wing coverts) are narrow and pointed and the underparts especially show more or less prominent whitish shaft-streaks.

Compared with adult, head looks longer and slimmer, with less woolly down, and dirtier in colour, pale brownish, greyish or yellowish, and the face is greyer. Iris dark brown; bill and cere dark grey. Ruff around base of neck is rufous and consists of narrow, lanceolated feathers, not of fluffy and white hair-like down as in adult.

Underwing coverts are, on average, paler and plainer in juveniles, but individual variation is great and adult-type darker and mottled underwing coverts are not rare. Remiges uniformly black below, darker than in adults, with the pointed tips of the secondaries giving a diagnostic dentation to the trailing edge of the wing.

From a distance, juveniles are best told from adults by their slimmer silhouette (especially narrower hand), browner, less contrasting colour of the upperparts, less distinctly marked upper greater coverts, and by their dark bill and brown ruff.

Second plumage (2nd cy autumn – 3rd cy spring) Plates 135–136

Still very similar to juvenile, from which best told by signs of moult to upperparts and wings. Remex moult commences in Apr–May. By autumn only a few innermost primaries and tertials have been replaced, the wing thus still consisting largely of juvenile remiges. After moulting the innermost primaries, the typical slender-winged appearance of the juvenile is lost. Most birds still retain the serrated trailing edge to the arm, although some

individuals may have replaced a few secondaries as well. By the end of the year a varying number of lesser and median upperwing coverts have moulted, but only single or no
greater coverts. The new greater coverts are more rounded in shape with dark centres and
pale margins, being widest at the tip, thus differing markedly from the retained narrow,
pointed and very faded brown juvenile greater coverts. Bill, head, collar and iris colour
as in juvenile, though some individuals show a paler outermost tip to bill. Plumage of
underparts mainly juvenile, brownish with paler streaks.

Third plumage (3rd cy autumn – 4th cy early spring)   Plates 137–138

Still rather juvenile-like, with brownish plumage and ruff, and with largely dark bill (some
pale at tip). Most of the remaining juvenile lesser and median upperwing coverts are
moulted during the summer and adult-type greater coverts appear. The first replaced greater
coverts are intermediate in pattern between juvenile and adult, whereas feathers replaced
later in the summer are identical to the greater coverts of adults. Primary moult proceeds
to the median fingered primaries and blunt adult-type secondaries start to appear, dis-
turbing the regular dentation of the trailing edge of younger birds. After moult is suspended in autumn birds appear largely adult in body plumage, save for extremely worn
juvenile greater coverts on the inner arm of some individuals. Bill, eye and ruff are still
much as in juvenile.

From a distance best identified by retained, very pointed and faded brown juvenile outer
primaries and median secondaries and by juvenile-type head.

Fourth plumage (4th cy autumn – 5th cy spring)   Not depicted

During 4th cy summer identified by outer moult-wave progressing among very faded brown
outermost primaries (p8–10). Some birds (not all) can still be identified after the moult
by their retained outermost primary and a few retained median secondaries, now extremely
worn and pale brown. (See also Subadult-type below).

Subadult-type (from c. 4th cy autumn/5th cy spring – 6th/7th cy spring) Not depicted

Slowly moulting individuals are best aged by their retained juvenile remiges, which are
moulted early in 5th cy (see previous age-class). Although the plumage is largely adult,
the birds still show some immature characters. Characters such as bill colour, eye colour
and colour of head down and ruff 'mature' independently, explaining varying individual
combinations of partly immature, partly adult characters. The fluffy white ruff and downy
white head seem to take longest to acquire, whereas bill colour and iris colour change earlier. The bill turns paler starting from the tip and following the culmen inwards. Breeding
birds may thus still show e.g. a partly dark bill, a brownish ruff and a greyish face. (See
also Fourth plumage above.)

Adult (from *c*. 7th cy autumn and older) **Plates 139–142**

Adults are more compact in silhouette than juveniles, with broader wings and broader-based tail. Secondaries have blunt tips making the trailing edge to the wing more even. The upperwing contrast is striking, and the coverts vary from pale sandy brown to almost pearl grey in some individuals. All feathers (including wing coverts) on the upperparts are rounded and the pattern of the greater coverts is diagnostic: the centres are black with a wide sandy margin (Fig 27). The distinctly coloured greater coverts band is often apparent from afar. The pale horn-coloured bill with grey cere, the fluffy white ruff and the whitish, down-covered head are also diagnostic, but be aware of soiled birds with darker, juvenile-like heads. Iris is pale, yellowish-brown, but this is discernible only at close range. Breast and belly are either uniformly pale sandy or greyish, or faintly streaked paler. Underwing coverts are variably mottled dark and remiges are paler grey than in juveniles, with narrow dark margins.

Sexing: Sexes similar in plumage; slight size difference not noticeable in the field.

References: Arroyo 1989; Cramp & Simmons 1980; Dementev et al. 1966; Tucker & Heath 1995

Plate 127 *Juvenile showing contrasting black flight-feathers with pointed tips creating regularly serrated trailing edge to wing. Note also dark bill and rufous ruff. Sep 1990, Israel (Klaus Bjerre).*

Plate 128 *Juvenile with typically dark and pointed remiges. 1 Oct 1995, Israel (Dick Forsman).*

Plate 129 *Juvenile. Note dark bill and iris, uniform plumage and pointed dark flight-feathers. This individual lacks the pale area in the underwing coverts found in many juveniles. 20 Nov 1988, Spain (Dick Forsman).*

Plate 130 *Typical juvenile from above showing uniformly black flight-feathers, narrow pale tips to greater coverts and rufous brown body plumage. 28 Jan 1988, Spain (Dick Forsman).*

Plate 131 *Juvenile from above. Note uniform condition of plumage and poorly marked greater coverts as well as dark iris and bill. 24 Jan 1995, Israel (Dick Forsman).*

Plate 132 *Fresh juvenile showing uniform plumage condition with pointed and poorly marked greater coverts. The bill and iris are dark. Autumn, Israel (Hadoram Shirihai).*

Plate 133 *Juvenile (2nd cy) moulting to second plumage. Apart from shed inner two primaries plumage still juvenile. 17 Apr 1995, Spain (Dick Forsman).*

Plate 134 *Worn juvenile moulting to second plumage. Note retained and pointed juvenile greater upperwing coverts. Bill is paler at the tip but the iris is dark. Jun, Greece (Alfred Limbrunner).*

Plate 135   *Second plumage (3rd cy) from above. Told from juvenile only by moulted, darker three inner primaries and central tail-feathers. 28 Jan 1990, Spain (Dick Forsman).*

Plate 136   *Second plumage, starting moult to third (3rd cy). Overall impression like juvenile, but moults median primaries, while most of the secondaries are still juvenile and pointed; bill and iris still dark. 27 Mar 1996, Israel (Dick Forsman).*

Plate 137   *Third plumage (3rd cy). Note faded juvenile outer primaries and median secondaries, dark bill and iris, brownish ruff and distinctly streaked underbody. 1 Oct 1995, Israel (Dick Forsman).*

Plate 138   *Third plumage moulting to fourth (4th cy). Outermost primary still juvenile while all the secondaries have been moulted. Bill and iris still dark and ruff brownish. 25 Jan 1995, Israel (Dick Forsman).*

Plate 139 *Adult. Aged by pale bill, iris and ruff and by greyish remiges with darker margins. Note variable age and wear of flight-feathers. 20 Feb 1997, Israel (Dick Forsman).*

Plate 140 *Adult. Typical bird with pale bill and iris, white woolly ruff and greyish remiges with darker margins. Note also the dark neck-pouch. 1 Oct 1995, Israel (Dick Forsman).*

Plate 141 *Adult from above. Note pale bill, distinctly marked greater coverts and pale edges to secondaries. 24 Jan 1995, Israel (Dick Forsman).*

Plate 142 *Adult from above showing pale bill and ruff and milk-coffee coloured upperwing coverts. Note also greyish edges to flight-feathers and rounded greater coverts with broad pale margins. 20 Nov 1988, Spain (Dick Forsman).*

BLACK VULTURE *Aegypius monachus*
Plates 143–154

Subspecies: Monotypic.

Distribution: In Europe found only in Spain and Greece (the Balkans) with occasional stragglers north of these areas. From Turkey and Crimea eastwards in a wide zone across C Asia to China.

Habitat: Breeds in Europe in wooded mountains and foothills at moderate altitudes (less than 1000 m). Hunts over all kinds of terrain from barren mountains to vast plains, often at considerable distance from nest-sites. Non-breeders straggle more widely outside breeding range.

Population: European population decreased markedly during the past century. Largest subpopulation found in C Spain (1027 pairs in 1994; steadily increasing), with small isolated populations on the verge of extinction on Mallorca (10 pairs) and in continental Greece (20 pairs). Recent recolonization of Bulgaria, two pairs in 1994.

Movements: European birds are resident or stragglers, Asian birds being more dispersive. Usually seen singly on migration and only single birds recorded at e.g. Bosporus and eastern Turkey. Winters mainly within breeding range but some individuals reach Israel, Egypt and even Sudan. Rare on passage in Eilat, Israel in Feb–Mar and Oct–Nov.

Hunting and prey: Feeds mainly on carrion, but will take small live prey. Searches for food by soaring for hours on motionless wings, covering large areas. Often seen together with Griffon Vultures, joining them at carcasses. On the ground, dominant over other scavenging raptors. Usually seen singly or a few birds together, but may congregate in groups of 20–30 birds at favourable sites.

SPECIES IDENTIFICATION

Length 100–110 cm

wing-span 250–295 cm (Cramp & Simmons 1980)

Usually easily identified by colour of head and bill and general uniformity of plumage. Silhouette in flight bearing some resemblance to large *Aquila*-eagle, for which browner adults especially may be mistaken.

> **Identification summary:** The largest of all European raptors with impressive proportions. Plumage uniformly blackish (juveniles) or dark brown (adults). Wings long and broad with parallel edges, prominently indented trailing edge and with seven deeply splayed fingers at tip. Tail short and wedge-shaped, in length about half of width of wings. Head and beak powerful.

In flight, distant At a distance appears uniformly blackish or dark brown with impressive proportions. Head appears comparatively smaller and wedge-shaped tail shorter than in any eagle; wings look longer and more rectangular. Arm long, primaries long and deeply

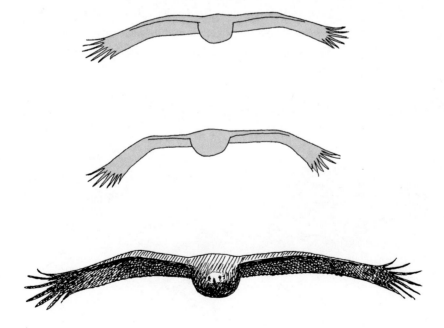

Fig 28 *Black Vulture. Different wing attitudes when gliding. Note rather parallel-edged wings and compare with Griffon (Fig 26).*

fingered. Soars on slightly arched wings; when gliding, arms are held flat and hands drooped, often with a notable kink at carpal joint (cf. Greater Spotted Eagle) and with heavy body and head hanging well below wing-plane. In flight, mostly easy to identify by huge size and overall dark colour, but when size not apparent, may, from some angles, greatly resemble *Aquila*-eagle or other vulture species. In active flight, wing-beats appear lighter than in smaller Griffon, more similar to the slow and buoyant flight of the White-tailed Eagle.

In flight, closer Wings are long with parallel edges and the tail is clearly wedge-shaped (most obvious on approaching birds) measuring in length about half of width of the wings. The trailing edge of the wing is deeply indented at all ages. Old birds can be very faded brown on back and upperwing, and coloration of upperparts may approach young Griffon, but Black Vulture lacks the clear-cut upperwing contrast of latter. The pale, woolly head of adults may, at a distance, resemble the whitish head of Griffon, but the head is proportionately bigger with the huge beak being prominent from afar. The underwings of older birds frequently show a diffuse paler wing-bar formed by the greater coverts.

Perched Sits mostly upright, with large wings almost concealing body and with head tucked between the shoulders. When alert erects head revealing dense ruff formed by elongated feathers to sides of neck reaching almost to the nape. Head typically black in younger birds with contrasting paler cere and base to bill. Adults paler-headed but most show at least some traces of blackish face-mask around the eyes. On the ground the Black Vulture is clearly bigger than a Griffon.

Fig 29 *Black Vulture. Head-pattern of juvenile (left) and two adults. Note very pale head and paler bill of old adult (far right).*

Bare parts Cere, base of bill and orbital ring pink or violet pink in juvenile, pale cobalt blue in adult. Feet violet pink in juvenile, purer pink in adult. Bill partly horn-coloured in adult, black in juvenile becoming gradually paler with age starting from base of bill. All changes in colours of bare parts take years to develop (see also Ageing and sexing). Iris dark brown at all ages.

Confusion species: Possible to confuse with several other dark and large raptors, most likely with *Aquila*-eagles and other vultures.

Griffon Vulture (page 126) The most likely confusion species as the two often occur together. In flight, Griffons show a narrower hand than arm (latter with bulging trailing edge), a shorter and more squarish tail, a smaller and paler head, and a marked contrast on both upper- and underwing. Griffons also soar on wings lifted in shallow V. On the ground, Griffons have a proportionately smaller head, the neck is long and slender and lacks the dense feathering of Black Vultures, and the contrast between wing coverts and remiges is distinct.

Aquila-*eagles* Can be very similar in silhouette (especially adult Greater Spotted and Steppe Eagle; pages 332 and 348, respectively), but always show comparatively shorter wings, lacking the serrated trailing edge, and showing some paler areas to upperwings and patterned underwings. They also have yellow cere, gape and feet.

Egyptian Vulture (page 108) Juvenile has distinctly narrower wings with six fingers and a longer, more pointed tail with paler edges. The head is small with a slim bill. Frequently shows paler markings on the wing coverts both above and below.

Bearded Vulture (page 94) Juvenile has a much longer tail, narrower wing-tips and a distinctly greyer underbody than head.

Moult

Annually complete, but comprising only part of plumage. Juvenile plumage takes 3–4 years to replace, adult plumage probably 2 years. Moults between Jan and Oct/Nov.

Juveniles (first moult) Innermost primary is shed in 2nd cy May–Jun (Greece) and by the end of 2nd cy only three innermost primaries and one or a few tertial(s) are moulted, together with some smaller upperwing coverts. After the moult is suspended the plumage still consists mostly of juvenile feathers.

Second moult Commences earlier, by Jan–Feb of 3rd cy. After this moult the four outermost primaries (p7–10) and about half of the secondaries (irregularly spaced, but larger group around s7–11) are still retained juvenile feathers. The last juvenile feathers are not replaced until the next moult in 4th cy summer/autumn. Even after this some individuals may retain their outermost juvenile primary and one or two of the median secondaries, which by then are extremely worn and faded brown.

Adults (subsequent moults) Moult their flight feathers serially between Jan–Feb and Oct–Nov, showing several simultaneously active moult fronts in each wing. Adults, however, cannot replace the complete plumage in one moult cycle, but need at least two moults for this. Odd flight-feathers may also be replaced during the winter.

AGEING AND SEXING

The changes in the plumage are rather small from year to year, making ageing in the field quite difficult, unless the moult pattern of the remiges can be reliably noted. Ageing mainly based on moult pattern of especially the primaries used in combination with changes of coloration of head and bill.

> **Ageing summary:** Juveniles and 2nd-year birds are almost identical and are as a group rather easily told from adults, whereas older immatures and subadults are more difficult to age as they show characters of both younger and older birds. Juveniles are predominantly black, whereas adults are clearly brown. With age the black feathering of the head gradually recedes and is eventually replaced by pale woolly down in old adults. The birds retain their juvenile characters with blackish plumage and dark head for about 2 years after which the plumage turns browner and the head becomes paler. Adult plumage acquired in approximately 6–7 years.

Juvenile (1st cy – 2nd cy summer)   **Plates 143–145**

Juvenile Black Vultures are predominantly black, even glossy in fresh plumage. From a distance they look all-black. In good light, upperwing coverts are slightly browner than the black flight-feathers. Sometimes the greater coverts appear a degree darker than the rest of the coverts, with faintly paler tips. Underwings show a more marked contrast between coverts and remiges. The narrow area consisting of lesser and median coverts is absolutely black, while the remiges are more shiny looking, distinctly paler and greyer from most angles. The greater underwing coverts form a wide and pale grey wing-band, which, however, varies according to the changing light conditions e.g. during soaring. The trailing edge of the wing shows pointed 'spikes', sharper than in adult, although the difference in shape is difficult to see in the field. The evenness and uniformity of the dentation is obvious, something that is lacking in older birds.

Up to early 2nd cy summer, juveniles are best told from older birds by the combination of fresh plumage lacking signs of moult and by the head-pattern. The head is covered with solid black down leaving only a pale area behind the gape naked. Bill all-black. Bare parts of the head, such as cere, gape, base of lower mandible, eye-brow and orbital ring pink or violet, with the intensity of the colour varying individually. Feet bluish pink or violet pink, clearly visible under the tail in flight.

Second plumage (2nd cy autumn – 3rd cy spring)   Plate 146

Birds in their second winter are still confusingly juvenile-like, with a neat and very dark, blackish plumage and a juvenile-like head-pattern. The innermost primary is moulted in 2nd cy May–Jun and by the end of the year only the three innermost primaries are replaced together with one or a few of the tertials. With very few moulted feathers in the arm, the juvenile-like regular dentation to the trailing edge is retained even after the moult and the plumage looks tidy without any notable signs of moult. The first paler, brownish wool appears on top of the head and nape during the summer. Most reliably separated from juvenile by difference between black inner three and slightly browner outer primaries, slightly paler and browner upperparts, with slight mottling from new smaller coverts, and a paler nape. Cere varies from pink to pale violet, gape sometimes bluish. Bill mostly blackish.

Third plumage (3rd cy autumn – 4th cy spring)   Plates 146–147

During and after moult told from second plumage by more advanced moult of upperwing coverts, turning upperparts brown as in adult, and by more advanced remex moult. By Oct–Nov moult has reached p6/7 and about one third to half of the secondaries are moulted (seemingly irregularly) leaving only one larger group of retained juvenile secondaries in mid-arm. Sides of head still quite dark, but 'supercilium' and crown paler. Colour of cere much as in previous plumage. Bill still very dark from a distance, but turning paler at base in some individuals.

Fourth plumage (4th cy autumn – 5th cy spring)   Plate 148

Birds in this age-class can be aged only under very favourable conditions before completion of moult during summer and early autumn by their extremely worn and faded, almost pale brown, juvenile outermost primaries and median secondaries. After these feathers are moulted by late autumn, birds can no longer be separated from 'subadult-type'. Some individuals, however, retain the outermost primary and one or two juvenile secondaries until the following moult in 5th cy summer. The crown is usually pale and the pale nape reaches the throat, leaving an isolated, dark and solid face-mask. The bill turns increasingly paler from the base.

Subadult-type (from 4th cy autumn/5th cy spring – *c.* 6th/7th cy spring) Not depicted
After having lost their last juvenile remiges birds can no longer be aged exactly. Subadults differ from adults in having a darker head and bill and by their more uniform underparts. The dark areas of the head and bill gradually decrease, the cere and gape turn from violet to pale blue and the feet change from pale violet pink to pure pink, while the underbody and underwing coverts become browner and more streaked.

Adults (from *c.* 6th/7th cy autumn and older)   **Plates 149–154**
Head distinctly paler than in juveniles and younger subadults, but the head-pattern varies with age. All adults have at least a woolly and pale crown and nape, the latter reaching around the neck. With age the dark areas gradually shrink and are finally confined to the lores, the area below the eye and around the ear openings. The oldest birds have a uniformly pale head, with a dark peering eye as the only prominent feature. The pale head may, from a distance, resemble a Griffon Vulture's. The dense ruff of long plumes is best visible when the birds are on the ground stretching their necks. It reaches from the armpits up along the sides of the neck almost to the nape, creating a totally different appearance to the slender-necked Griffon. Above the ruff is a collar of paler skin, whereas the bare throat and foreneck are dark.

From a distance adults in flight may be difficult to separate from younger birds, but in favourable light they are brown above with a paler head and a slightly darker hand. Underparts are normally rather uniformly dark, with hardly discernible contrast between darker coverts and paler flight feathers (cf. juvenile). Coverts often look untidy and mottled, owing to ongoing moult and missing feathers. Like juveniles, adults also show a paler, light-reflecting wing-band along the greater coverts of the underwing. In old birds the underparts are faded brown with paler streaking on breast, somewhat resembling Lappet-faced Vulture.

Feet pink and show well in flight under the tail. Cere and gape pale cobalt blue. The bill turns paler with age starting from the base of the upper mandible and proceeding along the cutting edges and up towards the culmen (cf. adult Lappet-faced Vulture), with dark culmen retained longest. Oldest birds show entirely pale, horn-coloured bill (cf. adult Griffon).

Sexing: Black Vultures are not possible to sex in the field.

References: Anon 1995b; Cramp & Simmons 1980; Shirihai & Christie 1992; Tucker & Heath 1995

Plate 143   *Juvenile. Note fresh and uniform plumage with all feathers of same age while the head is mostly black. Nov 1986, Israel (Hadoram Shirihai).*

Plate 144   *Juvenile. Nov 1986, Israel (Hadoram Shirihai).*

Plate 145   *Juvenile in 2nd cy summer. Aged by uniformly worn plumage and pointed feathers. Note faded crown compared with fresh juvenile plumage. Jun, Greece (Alfred Limbrunner).*

Plate 146   *Second (left) and third plumage birds. Ageing based on the primary moult pattern. Left bird has moulted inner four primaries while the outer are juvenile feathers and the older bird has moulted up to p6. 28 Jan 1990, Spain (Dick Forsman).*

Plate 147 *Third plumage from above with Griffon. Aged by moult-pattern showing recently moulted p4–6, while the outer four are still juvenile feathers. 20 Nov 1988, Spain (Dick Forsman).*

Plate 148 *Subadult (probably fourth plumage). Still retains its juvenile p10 and a juvenile median secondary (c. s10) in both wings, while the body shows paler streaking commonly found in adults. 20 Nov 1988, Spain (Dick Forsman).*

Plate 149 *Adult in full soar. Note rectangular wings with deeply serrated trailing edge also in adult. The feet are pinkish and the head is largely pale. Underwing contrast less pronounced than in juvenile. May 1992, Spain (Markku Saarinen).*

Plate 150 *Adult. The head is largely pale with dark around the eyes and a dark chin. The bill is proximally paler. 17 Apr 1995, Spain (Dick Forsman).*

Plate 151 *Adult showing contrast on upperwing between browner coverts and darker remiges and a pale head with dark eye-mask. Note also serrated trailing edge and huge bill. 17 Apr 1995, Spain (Dick Forsman).*

Plate 152 *Adult showing typical gliding posture with arched wings. 17 Apr 1995, Spain (Dick Forsman).*

Plate 153 *Two adult-type Black Vultures together with Griffons. The birds' ages cannot be assessed accurately from the photograph. Jun, Greece (Alfred Limbrunner).*

Plate 154 *This breeding adult shows a typically dull brown plumage and a pale, downy head with a dark eye-shadow. Note also rather pale ruff and partly pale bill. Jun, Turkey (Alfred Limbrunner).*

LAPPET-FACED VULTURE *Torgos tracheliotus*
Plates 155–162

Subspecies: Three subspecies: *T. t. negevensis* in Arabia and S Israel, *nubicus* in S Egypt, Sudan and Sahara and nominate *tracheliotus* in most of sub-Saharan Africa. Individual variation extensive within each subspecies and individuals of one subspecies may show characters of another; frequency of gene flow between populations not studied. Sometimes also considered monotypic.

Distribution: Widespread in sub-Saharan Africa south to Cape Province. Rarer and more local in Sahara and north of it reaching S Egypt, S Israel (now extinct) and the Arabian peninsula.

Habitat: In W Palearctic confined to deserts, breeding in areas with scattered acacias, upon which nest is built. Does not depend on mountains like e.g. Griffon Vulture.

Population: Breeding population of ssp *negevensis* in S Israel now extinct after dramatic decline from 25–30 pairs in 1945 to extinction by late 1980s, although a few individuals may still survive. A rather healthy population breeding in the interior of Saudi Arabia shares phenotypic characters with *negevensis*; up to 100 birds seen in area of 300 km^2 during survey in 1991.

Movements: Resident, but non-breeders may disperse widely before settling to breed.

Hunting and prey: Feeds on carrion, joining other vultures at carcass, where dominant.

SPECIES IDENTIFICATION (*T. t. negevensis*)

Length 95–105 cm

wing-span 255–290 cm (Cramp & Simmons 1980)

Most likely to be confused with Black Vulture, with rather similar uniformly darkish plumage, but silhouette and plumage details diagnostic.

> **Identification summary:** The largest vulture of the region. Head big and pale, wings broad and long with S-shaped and serrated trailing edge, tail short and wedged or rounded. Upperparts uniformly brownish with diffuse contrast between paler coverts and darker remiges. Underparts darkish with paler trousers and paler band through underwing coverts.

In flight, distant Active flight on slow yet surprisingly light wing-beats. Soars on flattish but slightly arched wings, with prominently up-bent primaries forming wide 'broom' at wing-tip. Glides on arched wings with rather level arm but drooping hand. Prominent kink between arm and hand further out on wing than on Griffon or Black Vulture, indicating a proportionately longer arm in Lappet-faced.

Upperparts uniformly dull brownish with slight and diffuse contrast between paler coverts and darker rest of upperwing. Head big and appears white from a distance, which may cause confusion with both Griffon and adult Black. Underparts appear dark from a distance with paler rear underbody, and sometimes with diagnostic pale underwing band to lesser/median coverts. The underwing coverts often appear darker than the shinier and more greyish remiges. Pale feet are not as conspicuous as in Black Vulture because of paler body plumage.

In flight, closer Head big and pale with pinkish flush to nape in close views, bill massive with paler cutting edges, prominent especially in adults. Body variegated below with streaked sides to breast and with pale wool shining through on belly and trousers. Owing to pale rear underbody, pale greyish feet not prominent as on Black Vulture in similar situations. Remiges and rectrices pointed and narrow, creating distinct serration to trailing edge of both wings and tail. Irregular pale underwing band between lesser and median coverts and one at the tip of the greater coverts less obvious or lacking in young birds.

Perched A huge vulture with a big head and a massive beak appearing rather uniformly dull brown to faded medium brown. Head appears bare and pale with a pinkish nape (uniformly pale in juvenile) with prominent ruff of lanceolated feathers to sides of neck reaching almost to the nape, as in Black Vulture. The dark eye is conspicuous and the huge beak is darkish, broadly pale along the upper cutting edge in adult. The breast is sparsely covered with long, lanceolated feathers with pale edges and with whitish down showing through.

Bare parts Feet greyish; beak dark horn-coloured with prominent pale lower edge of upper mandible in adult; cere appears greyish from a distance but may be bluish or violet when seen from close-up; iris dark.

Variation: Adult *nubicus* are darker above than *negevensis*, with more pinkish head and slightly more prominent face-lappets and the trousers are brownish or cream-coloured. Nominate *tracheliotus* is darkest above, almost blackish brown, with deeper red head, prominent face-lappets, distinct white band across underwing coverts and whitish thighs. However, some *negevensis* show white underwing band and rather pale trousers like African birds, while African juveniles and subadults can appear rather uniformly brownish resembling *negevensis*.

Confusion species: Possible to confuse with other large vultures of the region.

Griffon Vulture (page 126) Always shows marked contrast on upperwing between pale coverts and darker remiges and a similar contrast also to the underwing. Wing-shape rather similar to Lappet-faced, but Griffon shows even more marked difference between broader arm and narrower inner hand and lacks deeply serrated trailing edge to wing.

Black Vulture (page 138) More rectangular wings and uniformly dark rear underbody, with distinctly contrasting pale feet. Upperparts more uniformly coloured than in Lappet-faced; tail longer and more clearly wedge-shaped.

Moult

Moults probably like other large vultures, but *negevensis* not studied in detail.

Juveniles (first moult) Replace only a few innermost primaries during first moult, as in other large vultures. Last juvenile feathers probably not moulted until in 4th or 5th cy.

Adults (subsequent moults) Moult probably like e.g. Black Vulture. Breeding adults in Israel were moulting actively in Jan. Even adults probably take 2–3 years to replace the entire set of flight-feathers, as in other large vultures.

AGEING AND SEXING

Moult and plumage sequences for *negevensis* not studied, but plumage development prob-ably similar to e.g. Black and Griffon Vultures. Distant birds are difficult to age, since plumage stays rather similar.

> **Ageing summary:** The juvenile plumage is browner and appears darker above show-ing feathers of uniform age and wear. Older birds always show feathers of different age and wear next to each other, the upperparts are more faded brown, while the underparts show more prominent pale trousers and a paler underwing band.

Juvenile (1st cy – 2nd cy summer)   Plates 155–156
Upperparts brown with rather distinct contrast between coverts and somewhat darker remiges. Head is pale, whitish grey, with 'hairy' nape and less pink than in adults and bill is all-dark. Underparts darker than in adult, with darkish underwing coverts and brown-ish trousers and the remiges appear dark from below.

Second and third plumage (2nd cy autumn – 4th cy spring)   Plates 157–160
Second plumage aged by largely juvenile plumage with uniformly worn remiges, except for moulted inner primaries.

Third plumage birds told by retained and extremely worn juvenile outer primaries and median secondaries.

Adult (probably from *c.* 5th cy autumn and older)   Plates 161–162
Upperparts more faded brown with very diffuse contrast between upperwing coverts and remiges. Head shows distinct pinkish tone especially to nape and neck and bill has broadly pale cutting edge to upper mandible. Underparts more varied than juvenile's, showing dis-tinctly paler trousers and often also a pale underwing band. Remiges are more greyish below than in juveniles.

Immatures and subadults can possibly be aged by recording the moult of the juvenile remiges following the principles given for Griffon and Black Vulture (which see).

Sexing: Not possible to sex in the field, although females are somewhat bigger than males in direct comparison.

References: Bruun 1981; Bruun et al. 1981; Cramp & Simmons 1980; Goodman & Meininger 1989; Leshem 1984; Mundy et al. 1992; Shirihai 1987, 1995; Weigeldt & Schulz 1992

Plate 155 *Juvenile. Aged by uniform and sharply pointed upperwing coverts. Note naked head with peering dark eye. 13 Mar 1993, Oman (Hanne & Jens Eriksen).*

Plate 156 *Juvenile (2nd cy summer) ssp.* negevensis *moulting to second plumage. Jul, 1987, Israel (Hadoram Shirihai).*

Plate 157 *Second plumage (2nd cy). Aged by its freshly moulted four inner primaries while the rest of the remiges are juvenile. Note sharply pointed secondaries creating a deeply serrated trailing edge to wing. 24 Nov 1996, Oman (Hanne & Jens Eriksen).*

Plate 158 *Second plumage ssp.* nubicus *(3rd cy) starting to moult to third plumage, chased by Yellow-billed Kite. The primary moult has resumed where it stopped the previous autumn, at p4 and p5, respectively. 10 Apr 1991, Egypt (Annika Forsten).*

Plate 159 *Second plumage (3rd cy; ssp.* nubicus*) moulting to third plumage. This bird still retains its sharply pointed juvenile secondaries and four outermost primaries. 10 Apr 1991, Egypt (Annika Forsten).*

Plate 160 *Most probably a third plumage bird (3rd cy), with a Brown-necked Raven* Corvus ruficollis*. Still retains groups of juvenile median secondaries in both wings, while the juvenile primaries have mostly been replaced (p9 is still retained in far wing). 28 Oct 1994, Oman (Hanne & Jens Eriksen).*

Plate 161 *Adult ssp.* negevensis. *Underbody appears pale and streaked and head is deeper in colour than in younger birds. Note also variably aged (coloured) remiges. 18 Mar 1993, Israel (Dick Forsman).*

Plate 162 *Adult ssp.* negevensis. *Although the trailing edge of the wing is serrated in adults, too, the tips are not as pointed as in juveniles. Note almost completely feathered forearm (patagium) in this subspecies. 14 Mar 1985, Israel (Dick Forsman).*

SHORT-TOED EAGLE   *Circaetus gallicus*

Plates 163–177

Subspecies: Monotypic. Forms superspecies with *C. beaudouini* and *C. pectoralis* of sub-Saharan Africa, which are sometimes considered conspecific.

Distribution: From W Europe to Lake Balchas in C Asia.

Habitat: Prefers broken country with partly wooded and partly open habitats. Nests in woods but hunts mostly over open country. Most often seen hunting above sunny hillsides with low vegetation.

Population: Decreased over much of its northern range during the past 100 years. European population scattered over large area from the Mediterranean to the Baltic states, with strongholds in Spain, France, Italy and Greece. Total European population estimated to be between 5900 and 14 000 pairs and W Palearctic population 8700–18 400 pairs, with largest concentrations in Spain, S France, Russia and Turkey.

Movements: Mainly migratory in Europe, sometimes wintering in Spain. Winters across Africa in the savanna-zones south of Sahara, but rarely reaching the Equator. Autumn migration in Europe starts late Aug–early Sep, and peaks late Sep–early Oct. Passage concentrated along traditional routes for soaring birds with bulk of population leaving Europe over Strait of Gibraltar and via Bosporus, with peak day at Gibraltar 1 Oct 1972 with 1328 birds compared to 850 on 26 Sep 1971 at Bosporus. Autumn totals from different migration surveys include 8000 counted at Kfar Kasem, Israel in 1986, 12 000 at Suez, Egypt in 1984 and 9000 at Gibraltar, Spain.

Returns to Europe from late Feb, with majority arriving between early Mar and mid-Apr, adults before yearlings. In Israel fairly scarce at Eilat, with 345 passing during spring survey in 1985, more common closer to the Mediterranean coast with 3000 in spring 1982. Appears at northern breeding sites late Apr–early May.

Usually migrates singly or a few birds together, rarely in smaller flocks, but mixes freely with other soaring raptors en route.

Hunting and prey: Hunts from elevated posts such as tree-tops or poles or walks around on ground. Most often, however, seen hunting on wing patrolling hills and fields at moderate heights, stopping every now and then to scan the ground while hovering. Specialized on catching snakes but also takes lizards. Amphibians, birds and mammals are also taken occasionally.

SPECIES IDENTIFICATION

Length 59–62 cm

wing-span 175–195 cm (*n*=5; Israeli birds, W.S. Clark, unpubl.)

One of the easier large raptors to identify because of diagnostic plumage. Pattern of under-wings, upperwings and tail important.

> **Identification summary:** Underparts appear uniform and bleached from a distance, lacking prominent pattern except for more or less well developed darker hood in most. Upperwings characterized by greyish coverts (lesser and median) contrasting with darker rest of upperwing. Plumage variation relatively limited, occurring mainly as variation in amount of markings to underparts.

In flight, distant Usually not difficult to identify by bleached and pale overall impression of underparts in combination with large and broad wings and slow and heavy wing-beats. Upperparts typically bi-coloured with darker greyish-brown remiges and paler greyish coverts.

A large and sluggish eagle, appearing in powered flight even bigger and heavier than it actually is, with slow and laboured wing-action, almost as in slow-motion. The empha-sis is on the upstroke, at times creating a wing-action recalling huge owl with large wings and comparatively small body mass (low wing-loading). In head-on views body smaller in comparison to wing-span than in any other large raptor. Wings mostly held practically flat and level when soaring, and just slightly arched, with gently drooping hand, when gliding. When hunting, stops every now and then to hover, moving its wings in a more relaxed, twisting manner than e.g. Osprey.

Shape often characteristic, especially when gliding, as wrists pressed well forward form-ing a notably sharp angle to the leading edge of the wing. Tail rather short and narrow at base with sharp corners. Head does not appear particularly big in flight, whereas perched birds always seem to have a large and owl-like head because of fluffed-out feathers of crown and nape.

In flight, closer Plumage diagnostic, usually appearing bleached and featureless. Never shows all-black fingers, like most other raptors, but rather pale fingers with darker mar-gins and tips. In closer view, sparse barring of rectrices and secondaries becomes appar-ent, as well as heavy and sparse barring of body-feathers, latter varying individually and with age. Upperparts less variable and wing-coverts always show a diagnostic greyish or brownish-grey tone, with lesser and median upperwing coverts contrasting with darker

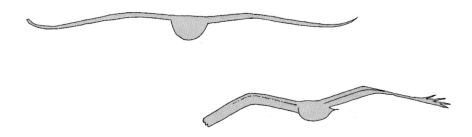

Fig 30   *Short-toed Eagle. Glides on rather flat but slightly kinked or smoothly arched wings, with bend of wing increasing with steepness of glide.*

remiges and greater coverts. Tail appears dark when folded, with a paler base, but when fanned shows extensively pale sides with typically three or four broad and sparse dark bars.

Perched When perched always looks top-heavy and big-headed with an owl-like face. Perches prominently on tree-tops, telegraph-poles and pylons or on boulders or mounds. Big head with yellow eyes in combination with pale bluish feet and sparsely barred or spotted underparts make the bird unmistakable. Upperparts appear rather pale, greyish brown, with darker wing-tip only. Darker birds are clearly hooded when perched, whereas many just appear streaked on upper breast, until they take to the wing when the hood becomes more obvious. Tarsi are long and bare and wing-tips reach close to tail-tip.

Bare parts Legs bluish grey at all ages. Cere grey, bill horn grey with darker tip. Iris yellow, paler in juvenile and more orange yellow in adults.

Variation: Some birds, mainly juveniles and immatures, can appear extremely pale and featureless, nearly white underneath with no visible pattern in the field. The upperparts are, however, normal, except for the head which may appear entirely whitish.

Confusion species: Possible to confuse with other largely pale raptors, but the only one to have pale remiges from below.

Osprey (page 21) Heavily patterned underwings with darker remiges, a striking head-pattern and rather uniformly dark brown upperwings, lacking the upperwing contrast of Short-toed.

Booted Eagle (page 416) Pale phase much smaller, has dark remiges below contrasting sharply with whitish coverts and a diagnostic pattern on upperwings and mantle.

Common Buzzard (page 266) and Honey Buzzard (page 30) Always have distinctly marked remiges below with notably dark wing-tips and a dark trailing edge to the underwing. Secondaries appear rather dark in pale birds.

Bonelli's Eagle (page 404) Adult has uniformly dark upperparts with white patch on mantle, bi-coloured tail and darkish underwings with pale forearm and mostly black underwing coverts.

MOULT

Complete annually, but not comprising all remiges in one season. Moult-pattern thus useful for ageing birds in 2nd cy autumn – 3rd cy spring.

Juveniles (first moult) Commences Mar–Apr (May) of 2nd cy: 28 Feb, Etawah, no traces of moult; 24 Mar, Sudan, and 5 May, Siwa, both replacing p1–2, latter more advanced (BMNH). Others starting seemingly late: Greece 1 Jun missing p1–3. Moult suspended in Sep–Oct (–Nov), leaving some juvenile outer primaries and central secondaries unmoulted.

Adults (subsequent moults) Probably starting slightly later than in 2nd cy birds, from Apr–May continuing until Oct–Nov. Probably not capable of replacing all remiges during one season despite time-saving serial moult, since adults always show a mixture of fresh and worn feathers in wing.

AGEING AND SEXING

Adults and juveniles are usually separable in the field, although good views are required. Plumage differences between juveniles and adults are generally rather subtle, especially in the more patterned birds. Details of moult and trailing edge of wing are essential when ageing more difficult individuals, but note also amount, distinctiveness and colour of spotting below, as well as type of barring to secondaries. Separating second-plumage birds from adults requires excellent conditions and close views.

Ageing summary: Juveniles show a uniform pale tail-tip and trailing edge to wing, paler and more contrasting median upperwing coverts and pale tips to greater upperwing coverts, while the underwing is poorly and/or faintly marked and lacks a distinct grey subterminal band. Adults show an irregular white trailing edge to wings and tail, darker and less contrasting median coverts above and the remiges are more distinctly barred below with a broad, grey subterminal band.

Juveniles (1st cy – 2nd cy spring)   **Plates 163–169**

Appears narrower-winged than adult and difference in structure obvious when adults and juveniles are seen together, e.g. on migration. Trailing edge smoothly S-curved with a whitish even margin and the tail has a similarly white tip. The most typical birds appear very pale and uniform below, lacking practically any pattern. A plain underwing with practically unbarred secondaries, often in combination with a uniformly whitish body plumage, strongly suggests a juvenile. More richly patterned juveniles are possible to tell from older birds by differences in secondary barring and spotting of underparts. Juveniles lack the distinct grey subterminal band of the wing, which is typical of adults, and the secondaries have finer and less distinct bars. Underbody in juveniles is spotted or streaked rufous brown and the pattern is less contrasting than the greyer barring of adults. Hood rufous brown, often leaving a largely pale chin and throat, the rufous colour being most striking on the sides of the bib.

Upperparts less variable, typically bi-coloured, with dark remiges, slightly paler greater coverts and pale sandy greyish median and lesser coverts. In fresh plumage the pale tips to the greater coverts form a pale band on the upperwing visible from afar. Tail appears dark brown above with a whitish tip, but when fanned, e.g. when hovering, the paler base and sides show well. Tail sparsely barred, usually with three or four darker bars, but this varies individually. More importantly, all bars are of equal width including the subterminal band.

Second plumage (2nd cy autumn – 3rd cy summer)   **Plates 170–171**

Second-plumage birds are still rather juvenile-like in appearance, being generally paler with less contrasting underparts than adults. The best way to age them is by the pattern of the remex moult: they still retain two to four juvenile outer primaries (p7/9–10) and several juvenile secondaries (normally s3–4 and s7–10). These are shorter, narrower, paler and much more abraded than the moulted neighbouring feathers. The retained juvenile secondaries also differ in pattern from the fresh ones, being translucent and more or less uniformly pale, whereas the replaced feathers are more distinctly barred, often with a wider subterminal band close to the white tip. After the last juvenile feathers have been replaced, usually in 3rd cy summer, birds are not possible to age with certainty.

Adults (3rd cy autumn and older)   **Plates 172–177**

Adults are usually possible to tell from juveniles by signs of moult in remiges and rectrices. Wings and tail consist at all times of feathers of different age, i.e. fresh and worn feathers side by side. Adults thus never show the even and neat pale trailing edge of the juveniles, but a broken and uneven white margin with broadly white-tipped and worn feathers side by side. But care is needed when ageing distant birds, since distant adults also appear to have a regular white margin. Adults also have broader and more rectangular wings with fuller hand and they lack the S-curved trailing edge of the juveniles. Underparts variable but markings generally darker and more contrasting than in juveniles, with broad and dark grey bars. The barring of the secondaries is broader and more distinct as well, with a broader grey subterminal band to wings and tail. Hood variably well developed, but is grey rather than rufous. Paler birds may have a large paler and streaked area on central upper breast, recalling juveniles, but the throat itself is darker than in juveniles.

Upperparts rather similar to juvenile, but adults lack the pale band along the tips of the greater upperwing coverts and the upperwing coverts are darker and the contrast is less distinct. The irregular white trailing edge to wings and tail can also be seen from above.

At least some 3rd cy autumn birds are possible to separate from 2nd cy and adults by the following characters: the inner 2–3 primaries and the outermost are fresh, while some birds still retain a faded and bleached juvenile outermost primary (less than 50% of the birds); paler birds appear strikingly pale, with a whitish head and rather unmarked underwing coverts, while more patterned birds are more difficult to tell from full adults, although they seem to retain the brownish colour to their underbody markings. By 4th cy spring it may not be possible to distinguish from older birds.

Sexing: Sexing in the field normally not possible, unless a pair is seen together, because of similar plumage and negligible size difference.

References: Bernis 1975; Bijlsma 1983; Cramp & Simmons 1980; Gensbøl 1995; Shirihai & Christie 1992; Svensson 1976; Tucker & Heath 1995

Plate 163   *Juvenile showing poorly marked remiges and brownish hood diagnostic of juvenile. 10 Sep 1997, Spain (Annika Forsten).*

Plate 164   *Juvenile showing diagnostic plumage including uniform white tips to remiges and rectrices. 10 Sep 1997, Spain (Dick Forsman).*

Plate 165   *Fresh juvenile from above aged by pale greyish upperwing coverts with uniform pale tips to greater coverts and showing typically sparsely barred tail for the species. 10 Sep 1977, Spain (Dick Forsman).*

Plate 166   *Fresh juvenile. Note the uniform plumage, the broad and pale fringes to the median coverts and the brownish hood all typical of juveniles. 15 Oct 1988, Israel (Dick Forsman).*

Plate 167 *Juvenile showing typically rufous hood and markings to underparts. 29 Dec 1991, Israel (Tomi Muukkonen).*

Plate 168 *Juvenile (2nd cy spring). Despite loss of pale trailing edge from wear, the plumage condition is uniform, the wing-barring faint, and the hood and underparts markings are rufous indicating juvenile. Apr 1992, Israel (Markus Varesvuo).*

Plate 169 *A very worn juvenile in spring. Possible to age just by uniform condition of plumage lacking feathers of different age. Apr 1992, Israel (Tom Lindroos).*

Plate 170 *A typically pale bird, with p1–5 in both wings, and s1 and s5 in the other wing replaced, the other remiges being juvenile. Note faded pattern of retained juvenile fingers. 10 Sep 1997, Spain (Dick Forsman).*

Plate 171 *Second plumage (3rd cy). A slightly more patterned but still light individual. Note the frayed and bleached outer three juvenile primaries. 31 Mar 1996, Israel (Dick Forsman).*

Plate 172 *Adult. This individual has a rather poorly marked greyish hood, but shows the broad subterminal wing-band and the more prominent wing-barring typical of adult birds. Apr 1990, Israel (Göran Ekström).*

Plate 173 *Approaching adult showing the typical silhouette of the species and the diagnostic underwing pattern. Mar 1996, Israel (Markus Varesvuo).*

Plate 174 *A rather heavily marked adult showing size and proportions compared with Black Kite. 27 Mar 1996 (Dick Forsman).*

Plate 175 *Heavily marked adult. Note complete greyish hood, distinctly barred remiges with broad dusky trailing edge and growing p7 in both wings. 30 Sep 1997, Israel (Dick Forsman).*

Plate 176 *Adult from above. Less contrasting upperwing coverts than in juvenile. Note the diagnostic tail-barring for the species. 28 Mar 1996, Israel (Dick Forsman).*

Plate 177 *Adult from above. Note slight upperwing contrast and ragged trailing edge to wings and tail. Mar 1996, Israel (Axel Halley).*

MARSH HARRIER   *Circus aeruginosus*
Plates 178–197

Subspecies: Nominate *aeruginosus* in Europe, the Middle East and C Asia and *C. a. harterti* in N Africa from Morocco to Tunisia.

Distribution: Occurs all over Europe but rare or local over much of western and central parts, although locally increasing, more common in the east.

Habitat: Always confined to open country, where especially attracted to wetlands, wet meadows, reed-beds, etc. Breeds almost exclusively in tall reeds, where nest built either on ground or floating on water. On migration seen hunting in different types of open terrain from cultivated fields to steppes and semi-deserts, often together with other harrier species.

Population: A notable decline in breeding numbers in western and central parts during the twentieth century because of persecution and habitat destruction (draining of wetlands). During last few decades continued decline in southern part of range. Recent increase locally in W and N Europe. Total population for W Palearctic estimated to be approximately 55 000–75 000 pairs, with majority in Russia and neighbouring parts of E Europe.

Movements: Northern and eastern populations migratory, southern populations partly migratory or resident. Nordic populations winter mainly in S Europe or in sub-Saharan Africa. Migrates on broad front but certain attraction to major flyways can be seen e.g. at Strait of Gibraltar. On migration usually seen singly or in small groups of up to five birds. In N Europe non-breeding immatures usually start the autumn migration in late Jul–early Aug, followed later by adults and juveniles. Northern populations leave their breeding grounds mainly before the end of Sep, with peak in late Aug–first days of Sep. At Falsterbo, S Sweden between 261 and 915 were counted in autumn migration surveys in 1986–1994, with peak days of 169 and 181 on 19 and 20 Aug 1992, respectively, and with 106 on 26 Aug 1993. Migration across the Gibraltar Strait peaks in late Sep, but small-scale movements observed into Nov. Small numbers winter further north in W Europe.

Returns to Europe from early Mar, with passage continuing until late May. Peak in S Europe in second half of Mar–early Apr. In Eilat, Israel 371 were counted during the spring migration survey in 1983, with peak day of 22 passing on 3 May 1985. First birds arrive at northernmost breeding grounds during first half of Apr, with majority arriving by early May.

Hunting and prey: Hunts mainly on the wing, quartering low over fields and meadows. Prey taken by surprise. Feeds mainly on small mammals, such as water voles, and various wetland birds up to the size of ducks and Coot, including high proportion of nestlings, fledglings and injured birds.

SPECIES IDENTIFICATION

Length 42–53 cm

wing-span, males 115–128 cm, females 123–139 cm (*n*= 96; Israeli migrants; W.S. Clark, unpubl.)

Adult males rather straightforward to identify, subadult males, females and juveniles more often confused with other darkish raptors, most frequently with Black Kite, Booted Eagle and Common and Honey Buzzards. A typical harrier in shape and behaviour, although adult females are heavier and may appear buzzard-like. Considerable individual variation in plumage at all ages. A black form exists (probably more common in eastern populations) being most conspicuous in adult males. Flight-feathers generally unbarred, but may show coarse barring to inner primaries in certain plumages. Pattern of head and wings diagnostic in all plumages. Wing-formula important for separation from Booted Eagle and Black Kite.

> **Identification summary:** A long-winged and long-tailed raptor with slim proportions typical of a harrier. Hand narrower than arm with five-fingered primaries. Soars and glides on lifted wings. Juveniles and adult females largely dark brown with pale crown and throat, often also pale forearm, and with remiges and rectrices dark and unbarred, often with distinct pale crescent at base of outer primaries on underwing. Adult males usually unmistakable from above with black outer hand, largely brown upperwing coverts and silvery mid-wing and tail; from below, extensively black wing-tip but otherwise with largely pale remiges and brown rear underbody.

In flight, distant A medium-sized raptor with fairly long wings and a long, rather narrow tail, juveniles slimmer than adults. Mostly seen hunting low over wetlands, reed-beds and meadows, following ditches and edges. Searching flight slow and ponderous for a harrier, the bird stopping every now and then against the wind to check the ground below. Wing-beats during hunting quite heavy but smaller and lighter male can at times appear very fast and agile. In the sky, at altitudes, e.g. when on migration, birds look slimmer and narrower-winged and adult males especially can easily be mistaken for smaller harrier species. Stockier females more buzzard-like with broader wings and comparatively shorter tail than in adult males, and may easily be confused with Black Kite and dark Booted Eagle, but identified by narrower wing-tip, lighter and faster wing-beats and by habit of keeping wings in shallow V when gliding and soaring. Juveniles clearly narrower-winged than adults, with S-shaped trailing edge because of tapering inner hand, compared with more rectangular wing-shape in adults. Females and juveniles uniformly dark brown with paler head (and forearm). Adult males are tri-coloured above, with black wing-tips, largely brown mantle and wing coverts and silvery grey tail, secondaries and inner primaries. Head pale as is often also the forearm. Transitional males (2nd cy summer to 3rd cy summer) may be extremely female-like, but by 3rd cy late autumn acquire the distinct plumage of the adult male.

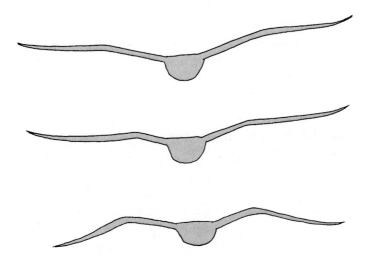

Fig 31 *Marsh Harrier. Various wing-attitudes of gliding birds. Upper two are rather typical with wings raised in V and showing kink between inner and outer wing. Lowest shows bird in steep glide or heading into a strong head-wind.*

In flight, closer Shows narrower hand than main confusion species, with only five fingers at wing-tip instead of six in Black Kite and Booted Eagle.

Juveniles are uniformly dark brown with variable head-pattern: most have an orange crown and throat divided by a dark mask through the eyes, others just the paler crown or even only a nape-patch, while some have all-dark heads. Wing coverts above and below vary from uniformly dark in most to variably pale-spotted, and the most patterned individuals have pale forewings like adults. Flight-feathers are uniformly blackish brown above but the primaries show paler bases below, with a whitish crescent around the carpal in most birds and with slightly paler inner hand than rest of underwing. Spring juveniles are more faded brown with pale areas on head bleached off-white.

Adult females resemble juveniles but are browner with variable amounts of pale blotching on wing coverts, breast and mantle. Underwings are, on average, paler, with widely paler brown inner hand and more contrasting dark wing-tip.

Adult males vary individually and with age but are identified by distinctly black outer hand and largely grey upperwing with partly or completely brown upperwing coverts. Tail grey above, either uniform or with faint barring on outer rectrices. Head and forebody variably deep or pale ochre with darker streaking and belly and rear underbody uniformly rufous brown. Underwings show distinct black outer hand and pale secondaries and inner primaries, while the underwing coverts vary from whitish to deep ochre with or without darker streaking.

Perched Marsh Harriers perch mostly on the ground on mounds or low posts, not more than a few metres high, rarely on top of small trees or bushes. When perched usually adopts a horizontal stance, with long wings and tail protruding well behind forward set long legs. Wing-tips almost reach tail-tip. When perched on a pole or tree-stump also sits more upright, like a buzzard, but is recognized by long stern, slim build with long and thin tarsi and a smallish head. Adult males easily recognized by dark primaries, largely grey secondaries and brownish wing coverts and by pale head and neck with darker streaking. Lower breast and belly deep rufous brown. Juveniles and females are largely dark brown, with variable amount of pale feathers on crown and throat, but also on mantle, upper breast and forearm.

Bare parts Bill dark, cere and legs yellow at all ages. The brown iris of the juveniles turns yellow in some males in first winter, while it remains brown in females for at least another year, to become amber and then yellow over a number of years.

Variation: The Marsh Harrier occurs in a rare dark form, which originates from more eastern populations migrating through the Middle East and is only exceptionally seen further west.

Adult males are especially conspicuous, whereas females and juveniles can be identical to all-dark juveniles lacking ochre markings, which do occur in western populations. Adult males differ from normal males in having all-dark head, body and both upper- and underwing coverts. The grey area of the upper wing is darker bluish grey and smaller than in normal males and can be hard to discern in the field, while the dark trailing edge of the wing is correspondingly broader. Tail seems more or less normal, being the palest area of the upperparts. Underwing looks very dark, with a conspicuous and wide dark trailing edge, leaving only a comparatively small whitish area at the remex-bases.

Confusion species: Adult males usually unmistakable, except for exceptionally pale individuals that may be mistaken for male Hen or Montagu's Harrier.

Hen Harrier (page 183) Male always told by white belly and rear body and grey forebody and upperwing coverts.

Montagu's Harrier (page 215) Male identified by much slimmer outline, barred secondaries below, grey forebody and lack of brown on upper forewing.

Females and juveniles often mistaken for Black Kites and Booted Eagles, sometimes also for dark Montagu's Harrier or buzzard.

Black Kite (page 65) Barred remiges below and a diagonal paler patch across coverts of upper arm. Hand broader with six fingers and tail shallowly forked. Black Kites soar and glide on flattish, slightly arched wings.

Booted Eagle (page 416) Broader hand with six fingers. Dark form has upperparts distinctly patterned with pale areas across upperwing coverts, scapulars and uppertail coverts. Booted Eagles soar and glide on distinctly arched wings with clearly splayed fingers.

Montagu's Harrier, dark form (page 215) Much slimmer with narrower and more pointed wings with only three to four-fingered primaries; body uniformly dark. Powered flight light and elegant.

MOULT

Complete annually, but some remiges are occasionally left unmoulted.

Juveniles (first moult) Juveniles undergo a partial body moult in winter, varying individually in extent. During this moult most birds replace their uppertail coverts, some of their upperwing coverts (especially lesser) and mantle feathers, as well as some feathers on upper breast and crown. Many birds also replace some tail-feathers, usually starting with the central pair. Advanced birds may moult most of their body-feathers, even including some greater upperwing coverts. Remiges are always retained, as are mostly also the underwing coverts and feathers of rear body. The first complete moult starts in 2nd cy May or early Jun, earlier than in older birds. During the summer approximately half of the remiges are moulted before the autumn migration. The remex moult is completed in late Sep–early Oct, earlier than in adults (in N Israel on 5 Oct 1995 2nd cy birds had completed or were about to complete their primary moult, while adults still had one or two outer primaries unmoulted; pers.obs.)

Adults (subsequent moults) Adults undergo a complete annual moult starting in females, during incubation in May–early Jun and, in males, up to 6 weeks later. During the nestling period adults may suspend the moult to ensure maximal flight abilities for the period when both sexes take part in hunting (pers.obs.). After young are fledged remex moult resumes in Aug. The moult takes about 5 months, and is usually finished by late Oct–early Nov.

Some median secondaries (usually s4 and s7–8) are occasionally retained until next summer.

AGEING AND SEXING

Non-juvenile males can often be divided into three different age-classes, while females and juveniles are very similar and in many situations not possible to separate, unless seen close and well.

From above, ageing is based on coloration of upperwing and tail and from below, on plumage details of body and underwing. Adult males are easy to tell from female-type birds, whereas separating adult females and juveniles is more difficult, especially in spring, as is separating females from 2nd cy males later in the summer. Note that the heavy abrasion of the plumage, which is·typical of this species, changes plumage characters considerably from autumn to spring. Eye colour is important when ageing female-type birds.

> **Ageing and sexing summary:** Fresh juveniles are blackish brown above with a deep ochre crown-patch and very dark below, usually with a distinct paler crescent at the carpal. Juveniles have narrower hands than adults. Adult females are duller brown, usually with variable pale mottling to underwing coverts, upper forearm, mantle and upper breast. Transitional and first-adult males show adult male wing-pattern, but are dull in colour. Adult males are brightly coloured and distinctly patterned above. From Jul to Oct non-juveniles are in wing moult, whereas juveniles show a mint plumage (see Moult).

Juvenile (1st cy – 2nd cy spring) Plates 178–183

The fresh juvenile plumage is the darkest of all Marsh Harrier plumages. In late summer and early autumn juveniles appear almost blackish brown in strong light and a shade browner in overcast conditions. Remiges are only a shade darker than the rest of the upperparts and the whole plumage is fresh and neat. Cap and throat deep rusty yellow. In good conditions the rusty tips to the greater and primary coverts are visible as a narrow band on the upperwing.

From below, the bird looks as uniformly dark as from above. Remiges appear slightly paler (with a greyish sheen) than the blackish brown coverts. Inner hand often slightly paler than the secondaries with a distinct whitish crescent at the bases of the outer primaries; fingers black.

Some juveniles show adult female plumage characters. They may show a large ochre patch on the upper forearm, which, however, is of the same rich colour as the crown, not whitish. Others have their ochre head-markings reduced to just a band across the nape, or, rarely, the head might be all-dark. Some birds show small ochre spots to their innermost underwing coverts or axillaries and some even show some pale streaking on upper breast. All these characters can occur freely combined in different individuals. Despite these 'adult-type' characters all juveniles can be aged by the uniform condition of the plumage.

As the autumn progresses the ochre tracts soon bleach and by Oct are much paler, yellowish buff. By this time the rest of the juvenile plumage can, because of wear, appear paler than in adult females, which in turn are finishing their moult and have just acquired a fresh and dark plumage. Juveniles have a dark brown iris.

In 1st winter juveniles undergo a partial body moult that varies individually. Usually some feathers on mantle, head and upper breast are moulted, as well as some median and lesser upperwing coverts and the uppertail coverts. It is not rare for some inner greater coverts and tail-feathers to be replaced. Depending on the extent of the body moult the juveniles can look very different in spring. Those birds with just a few feathers replaced are still generally quite like autumn juveniles, though extensive wear, typical of Marsh Harrier, has bleached the plumage considerably. The birds are dull dark brown with a clear demarcation between faded and much paler upperwing coverts and darker brown remiges. The deep ochre markings of the autumn juvenile have faded into nearly buffish white. Birds with extensive partial moult can have replaced a great deal of their body-feathering, superficially resembling adult females (also the juvenile males), with streaked crown, pale forewing and pale breast-patch. Juveniles that have replaced some of their rectrices can be reliably sexed. The new tail-feathers in females are dark brown, whereas young males grow brownish grey or greyish feathers with a darker subterminal spot. The grey colour is dull and difficult to note from a distance. The iris can be yellow in some males, whereas other males and all females have a dark brown iris.

Transitional male plumage (2nd cy summer and autumn)　　　　　　Fig 32

During summer the progressing moult changes the appearance of the juvenile males. By Jul males have usually replaced some inner primaries, which are whitish below with broad black tips. From above, these feathers show a dark bluish grey cast, which varies individually and can be difficult to note in less brightly coloured individuals. The corresponding upper primary coverts are dull bluish grey, whereas most of the secondaries and their coverts appear dark brown (also the moulted ones), although they may show some dull grey at the base. Unmoulted remiges are faded brown above and clearly paler than the moulted feathers. The new tail is dull grey, often with some rusty brown admixed, and with a darker subterminal band. The body plumage resembles that of an adult female, with similar head-pattern and pale-mottled areas on upper breast, mantle and upper forewing. In all, the upperparts look rather uniformly dull brown; only the greyish cast of the inner primaries and tail reveal the sex of the bird. From below, these birds appear uniformly dark brown, except for the pale innermost replaced primaries with distinct black tips. Iris is yellow.

Fig 32 *Marsh Harrier, transitional male with suspended moult. Typical plumage of 2nd cy males in Aug–Sep. Note female-like head, some retained, brown juvenile flight-feathers and greyish tail with dark subterminal band.*

First-adult male (2nd cy late autumn – 3rd cy summer)   Plates 184–186

Even after completing the moult, by Oct, the 2nd cy males are still very dark and female-like above and lack the sharp contrasts of older males. The grey areas of upperwing and tail are, in some individuals, so dull that they hardly stand out from the generally dark brown upperparts. Many individuals have a pale upper forearm, similar to adult females. The dullest individuals may be very difficult to separate from adult females if the under-parts are not seen. The body still appears dark brown, often with a paler breast-band and the head-pattern is rather similar to the adult female, with a pale crown and throat and a dark eye-mask. Only the remiges, with, from below, whitish or pale cinnamon bases and distinct black tips, differ from the female. There is more black in the wing-tip than in older males and the inner arm appears dark. Brighter individuals also have pale bases to their secondaries with a broad dark trailing edge to the wing. The underwing coverts are deep rusty brown with darker streaks, appearing dark against the paler bases of the remiges. This plumage is retained until the following moult in 3rd cy summer.

Transitional and first-adult female (2nd cy spring – 3rd cy spring)   Plate 194

2nd cy females in spring are usually possible to identify by narrower hands and dark underwings with a distinct pale crescent around the carpal until these characters are gradually lost in the moult during the 2nd cy summer. On the upperwings the worn coverts contrast with darker remiges and there may be a hint left of the pale tips to the greater coverts. Towards the end of the moult 2nd cy females may be identified by extremely faded brown outer primaries and median secondaries, the former with distinct pale bases below. After completed moult (for timing in relation to older adults see 'Moult') often possible to separate from older females, as the plumage is still rather juvenile-like, but showing clear signs of moult, such as remiges of different age and shade. From below, the remiges appear rather dark with a paler crescent at the carpal and the tail is darker than in older females. Iris still dark brown. In fresh plumage (late autumn) adult females are darker and more brightly coloured than juveniles, which by then are bleached from extensive plumage wear.

Adult male (from 3rd cy autumn and older)   Plates 187–193

The adult plumage is attained in the second complete moult during 3rd cy summer–late autumn and differs from the previous plumage in having more contrasting upperparts. Adult males may further be divided into, 'younger adults' (probably from 3rd cy autumn to 4th/5th cy summer) and 'old adults' (at least in their 6th cy), but since the individual variation is not yet fully understood these types are better referred to as plumage-types, rather than exact ages.

Younger adult-type male Upperwing distinctly patterned with black outer hand, silvery grey mid-wing and brownish inner wing and coverts, often with paler coverts on forearm. Tail silvery grey, but, like the wings, usually not as pale as in older males and frequently with a darker but faint subterminal band. Uppertail coverts rufous brown. Head and upper breast ochre with darker brown streaking, but there may still be a hint of a darker auricular spot. Lower breast, belly and vent uniformly rusty brown. Underwing coverts vary from rusty ochre to paler straw with sparse or more intense dark streaking and the wing has a prominent dark trailing edge.

Old adult-type male As males get older they become paler and brighter. Full adults show extensively pale silvery upperparts. Upper greater coverts silvery grey, only the innermost are brown (more brown coverts in younger adults). Tail pale silvery grey and lacks any darkening to the tip; many old males show pale grey or even whitish uppertail coverts. Head off-white to pale straw with fine dark streaks and lacks the darker ear coverts. Underbody largely pale with rather fine darker streaking and only lower belly, vent and undertail coverts are more intensely streaked rusty-brown; the border between pale forebody and rufous belly runs lower down than in younger adults. Underwing coverts white or very pale ochre and often practically unmarked; the black in the wing-tip is mostly restricted to the fingers. Old males lack the dark trailing edge to the wing, although there may be a hint of a diffuse band in some.

Adult female (3rd cy summer and older)   Plates 195–197

Adult females are generally distinguished by their chocolate-brown plumage, with rusty-yellowish crown, throat and upper forearm. Lesser and median upperwing coverts extremely variable and range from dark brown to largely buffish with darker mottling and

Fig 33 *Marsh Harrier, dark morph adult male. Note all-dark body plumage and broad black margin to underwing leaving small pale area in the remiges.*

some females show extensively pale-mottled mantle. Some females are just uniformly dark brown, with no pale markings whatsoever. In late summer the pale crown and forewing are paler, more distinctly streaked and not so deep in colour as in fresh juveniles, and the rest of the upperparts are browner and tattier. Compared with juveniles the tail-feathers are paler rufous brown, being most apparent when the tail is fanned. From below, adult females are paler and less uniform than juveniles, often with extensive pale mottling to upper breast and underwing coverts. From underneath, remiges paler brown than in juveniles and younger adult females, with pale, often slightly rufous or sandy inner hand, while the fingers and the secondaries contrast as darker brown. This may vaguely resemble the wing-tip-pattern of adult males, but females lack the distinctly black outer hand and the darker trailing edge of adult males. Iris colour takes several years to change from brown to amber and finally to yellow in old females.

Some (very old?) adult females show a greyish tinge to their flight-feathers above, being thus very similar to transitional/first-adult males. Others may show darker bars to their innermost primaries and outer tail-feathers, features that are normally connected with subadult males. These females, however, lack the conspicuous dark trailing edge and the distinct division between black tip and pale inner hand typical of subadult males and show a diffuse and gradual change between pale sandy inner hand and darker brown fingers on the underwing.

Sexing: Males are slightly smaller and slimmer than females, with narrower wings, longer tail and slimmer belly and vent but experience is required to note this difference unless both sexes seen together. Adults also differ in plumage, while juveniles are similar.

References: Bavoux et al. 1991; Clark 1987b; Clark & Forsman 1990; Forsman 1980, 1984, 1993b; Gensbøl 1995; Kjellén 1992b, 1994, 1995; Shirihai & Christie 1992; Zuppke 1987

Plate 178 *Recently fledged juvenile. Note dark underwings with small pale patch at base of outer primaries only and dark brown tail. Sep, Finland (Mikko Pöllänen).*

Plate 179 *Juvenile showing typical restricted pale carpal crescent below and pale tips to remiges and greater coverts above. 23 Nov 1996, Ethiopia (Dick Forsman).*

Plate 180 *Juvenile (or first adult female?). Winter juveniles are often very difficult to tell from adult females, but uniform plumage suggests juvenile. 11 Jan 1990, Israel (Dick Forsman).*

Plate 181 *Juvenile from above. Note uniform plumage and dark brown tail. 30 Nov 1996, Ethiopia (Dick Forsman).*

Plate 182 *Recently fledged juveniles. The plumage is very dark and uniform with rufous feather-tips and uniformly ochre crown and throat. Aug, Finland (Mikko Pöllänen).*

Plate 183 *Dark juvenile with ochre of head reduced to nape (may lack ochre altogether). Aug, Germany (Alfred Limbrunner).*

Plate 184 *First-adult male. Body plumage like adult female, but identified by broad dark trailing edge to wing and distinctly dark wing-tip. Sep, Turkey (Göran Ekström).*

Plate 185 *First-adult male. Note extensively black wing-tips, broad dark subterminal wing-band and largely dark underbody. Dec 1996, UAE (Tom Lindroos).*

Plate 186 *First-adult male (2nd cy; same as Plate 185). Body plumage much like adult female but secondaries at least partly grey above. The iris of this bird is not yet bright yellow. Dec 1996, UAE (Markku Huhta-Koivisto).*

Plate 187 *Younger adult-type male (possibly moulting from first-adult to adult plumage) showing extensively brown underbody, heavily mottled underwing coverts and dark trailing edge to wing. 31 Aug 1996, Finland (Markku Huhta-Koivisto).*

Plate 188 *Younger adult-type male (same as Plate 187). Note largely brown upperwing coverts, broad dark trailing edge to arm and dark subterminal spots in tail. 31 Aug 1996, Finland (Markku Huhta-Koivisto).*

Plate 189 *Adult male. This bird is overall rather dark and brown, but the grey in the wings is silvery, compared with previous plumages. May 1987, Israel (Hadoram Shirihai).*

Plate 190   *Old adult-type male. Note very pale underwings with black of wing-tip restricted to the fingers and faint trailing edge. Rear underbody still rufous brown. Jul 1996, Finland (Esa Sojamo).*

Plate 191   *Old adult-type male. Probably a very old bird with reduced amount of black in wing-tip and very pale underwing, body and head. Aug 1992, Finland (Esa Sojamo).*

Plate 192   *Adult male from above. The upperparts become even more contrasting with age, with grey areas turning more uniform and silvery. May 1992, Finland (Mikko Pöllänen).*

Plate 193   *Adult male (same as Plate 189). May 1987, Israel (Hadoram Shirihai).*

Plate 194 *First-adult female (2nd cy). Extremely juvenile-like plumage best separated by signs of moult. Note advanced stage of primary moult in relation to date compared with older females. 19 Oct 1988, Israel (Dick Forsman).*

Plate 195 *Adult female. Older females typically show dark fingers contrasting with paler, sandy-coloured inner hand, but the fingers are not black and the contrast is not clear-cut as in males. Note also pale mottling of underwing coverts and breast. 23 Nov 1996, Ethiopia (Dick Forsman).*

Plate 196 *Adult female from above. Distant birds are very difficult to tell from juveniles, but close views reveal signs of moult, such as variably aged remiges and coverts. Note also more rufous tail of adult females. 23 Nov 1996, Ethiopia (Dick Forsman).*

Plate 197 *Adult female. Note streaked crown and pale iris compared with juvenile female. Apr, Germany (Alfred Limbrunner).*

HEN HARRIER   *Circus cyaneus*
Plates 198–213

Subspecies: Two subspecies. Nominate *cyaneus* in Eurasia, *C. c. hudsonius* in N and C America; adult males of latter less uniform above and patterned on breast, juveniles unstreaked on lower breast and belly, adult females rather similar to nominate.

Distribution: From W Europe in a wide belt through Asia to the Pacific.

Habitat: Prefers open ground, such as moors, heaths, bogs and fields, both during breeding and on migration and in winter. In N Europe also nests in open woods on swampy ground and, in the British Isles, in reforestation plantations.

Population: European population 22 000–32 000 pairs, with an estimated two thirds in Russia and additional important populations in Sweden, Finland and France.

Movements: Northern and eastern populations migratory, birds from W and C Europe dispersive. Nordic birds start to appear at migration localities in late Jul–early Aug (adults) and late Aug–early Sep (juveniles) with peak-days between late Aug and early Oct. Both timing of migration and autumn numbers vary from year to year depending on breeding success. Numbers are generally fairly low, e.g. 149–356 Hen Harriers passed Falsterbo, S Sweden in 1986–1993, with highest daily total of 38 on 24 Sep 1986. The migration levels off during Nov. Migrants winter from W and C Europe to N Africa and the Middle East.

In spring rare on migration in Eilat, Israel, mainly from late Feb to mid-Mar. Birds return to Finland from late Mar, with peak in second half of Apr, when 10–20 birds can pass a station in a day; all-time peak 58 migrants on S coast on 27 Apr 1975. Regularly seen on passage until early Jun, with yearling predominance among late-comers.

Hunting and prey: Specialized in catching small rodents, such as voles and mice, but also takes small passerines. Boreal populations depend on cyclic vole populations for breeding, with considerable annual variation in breeding populations and breeding success. Hunts from low quartering searching flight following ditches and hedges. When prey is spotted makes a split-second loop and pounces on it from above. Hunts small birds, like a Sparrowhawk, taking them by surprise, approaching low over ground at good speed using any available cover to get as close as possible, eventually catching the birds as they flush.

SPECIES IDENTIFICATION

Length 44–53 cm (v Haartman et al. 1965)

wing-span 114–121 cm (*n*=3; D. Forsman & W.S. Clark, unpubl.), 102–121 cm (Noakes 1990)

Adult males rather straightforward to identify, if diagnostic plumage features, such as amount of black to wing-tip, are seen reliably. Females and juveniles are more difficult to tell from 'ring-tails' (female-type birds of Pallid, Hen and Montagu's Harrier) of other species, but broader wings with fuller wing-tip and barring of remiges on underwing diagnostic. Flight slower and less elegant than in the smaller harriers.

> **Identification summary:** Adult males are identified by combination of black outer hand and trailing edge to arm but otherwise unbarred secondaries and by white lower breast and belly. Females and juveniles (ring-tails) resemble ring-tails of Montagu's and Pallid Harrier and are best identified by broader wings, with five-fingered primaries at wing-tip, heavier flight and different underwing pattern, with bold barring of secondaries continuing onto primaries. Juveniles differ further by distinctly streaked underbody. Heavier flight and build, and broader wings, exclude small, light and narrow-winged Montagu's, but some adult female Pallid Harriers can appear as big and heavy and are separated from Hen only by their more pointed wing-tip and different plumage characters.

In flight, distant Easy to recognize as harriers by fairly long wings and longish tail and by the habit of quartering low over the ground when hunting. The wings are typically kept slightly lifted in a shallow V when soaring or gliding. Ring-tail Hen Harriers are difficult to tell from other harriers in similar plumage and differences in structure and flight are important when separating the species. Wings are comparatively broader with a broad and rounded tip, while the hand is not clearly narrower than the arm. The wing-shape can be rather *Accipiter*-like rather than falcon-like, as in the smaller species, the shape being easiest to assess when the bird is soaring. The powered flight is also heavier and slower than in the two smaller species and the body is heavier with a fuller belly and vent.

In flight, closer Broad and rounded wing-tips with five clearly fingered primaries. Adult males are grey above, with a 'cut-off' black outer hand, prominent white uppertail coverts, no distinct barring in the wings apart from a dark trailing edge, and a clear-cut division between grey forebody and pure white underparts.

'Ring-tails' show distinctly barred underwings, with three broad dark bars in the sec-

Fig 34 *Hen Harrier. Glides in typical harrier fashion with slightly lifted wings, but with varying angle as in Marsh Harrier.*

ondaries (including the trailing edge) seemingly continuing on to the primaries. Primaries distinctly and regularly barred, although some juveniles (males only?) may show irregularities and may approach the primary pattern of a 'ring-tail' Pallid Harrier.

In late 2nd cy summer males appear in a plumage rather similar to that of a male Pallid Harrier. When the primary moult has reached the wing-tip, which usually happens in Aug–Sep, a Pallid Harrier-like black wedge is formed. The retained outermost juvenile primaries are extremely worn and pale and appear plain from a distance, while the missing/growing primary helps create a pointed wing-tip. These males can always be told from male Pallid by their heavier flight, considerably broader wings and by the broad dark tip to the moulted secondaries, and from 2nd cy summer Montagu's males by broad wings and heavier body, pale and unbarred inner primaries and axillaries, and by the absence of the latter's rufous streaking on the lower breast and belly.

Perched Rather short-winged compared with other harriers, with wing-tips reaching about three quarters down the tail. The spacing of the primary tips on the folded wing differs between the three species. Adult males appear pale bluish grey with largely black primaries and a distinct border between the white and grey on the breast.

Ring-tails can be extremely difficult to identify. The structural details in the wing are reliable features, but these are mostly difficult to see in the field. Head-pattern diagnostic in most: the Hen shows 'loosely' streaked ear coverts, while they are darker and more uniform in most adult Pallids. This also makes the pale, dark-spotted collar more contrasting in adult Pallid, although it may be identical in the two species.

Bare parts Legs and cere yellow. Iris dark in older nestlings, turning grey in males before fledging and becoming yellow in the autumn. Adult males have a yellow iris. Females have dark brown irides by fledging, remaining brown until 2nd–3rd cy. Iris colour gradually changes in females from pale chocolate brown (2nd cy) to amber (4th–5th cy) to bright yellow in old adults (7th+ cy). There is considerable individual variation in the speed of the process and iris colour can therefore be used only as a rough guide for ageing.

Variation: From time to time juveniles showing characters similar to the N American ssp.

hudsonius occur in the Eurasian population: the streaking of the underparts is confined to the upper breast and neck-sides, forming a distinct darker neck-band. These birds also resemble juvenile Pallid Harriers in that the lower breast is practically unstreaked. A juvenile male in this plumage may appear as narrow-winged and light as a Pallid, and great care is needed to separate them from juvenile Pallids. The wing-formula and the underwing pattern remain the best separating characters.

Confusion species: Can be confused with other harriers. Told from other medium-sized raptors by silhouette and typical hunting flight and wing-carriage when soaring, and always by diagnostic underwing pattern.

Pallid Harrier (page 196) The most similar species. Adult females especially can be very similar to ring-tail Hens, being as big and heavy, but in flight they always show a narrower hand than arm and a more pointed wing-tip. Most ring-tail Pallids also show partly reduced barring on primaries below, but some juvenile (male?) Hens may show a similar pattern. Pallid usually has darker and more uniform ear coverts than Hen, making the pale collar more distinct. Some juvenile Hens, however, have rather contrasting heads, while some old female Pallids may show extremely featureless heads. Most reliably identified by different wing-shape and underwing pattern. Pallid males are considerably smaller and lighter than Hen Harriers with a faster and more agile flight and with slimmer and more pointed wings, with a black wedge at the tip (cf. 2nd cy male Hen Harrier in summer).

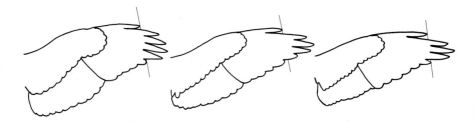

Fig 35 *Wings, from left, of Hen, Pallid and Montagu's Harrier showing differences in wing-formula, with five fingers in Hen, but four in Pallid and Montagu's. On average Pallids, the tip of p10 falls between p5 and p6, while on average Montagu's it roughly equals the tip of p6, with age-related variation. Note also different wing-shape between the species with length of hand in relation to arm increasing from left to right.*

Montagu's Harrier (page 215) Notably slimmer and lighter, with long and narrow, pointed wings (cf. wing-formula) and a long and narrow tail. Females are told from Hen by their distinctive underwing and axillary pattern, adult males by their barred secondaries and tricoloured upperparts, with slightly darker innerwing and mantle, silvery mid-wing and largely black hand.

Marsh Harrier (page 167) Old males may be extremely pale and thus resemble adult male Hen Harrier. Although the underwings may be as pale as in Hen even the palest Marsh males show some rufous streaking to rear underbody and head, with most showing uniformly rufous belly and vent. The palest (very old?) Marsh males also seem to lack the darker trailing edge of the wing, which is distinct in male Hen Harriers.

Goshawk (page 256) Juveniles may resemble ring-tail Hens when suddenly gliding by. They are told by paler underwings, with finer and lighter barring, and they lack the white uppertail coverts of the ring-tails. Any prolonged views of a Goshawk in flight will reveal its broader arm than hand and its different way of flying compared with any harrier.

MOULT

Annually complete during breeding.

Juveniles (first moult) Single body-feathers and tail-feathers may be replaced from late winter, but to a lesser extent than in Montagu's and Marsh Harrier. The complete moult, including the flight-feathers, takes place between May and Sep–Oct, starting, on average, earlier in the season than in breeding birds. Occasionally single secondaries and body-feathers may be left unmoulted.

Adults (subsequent moults) The plumage is moulted completely between May–Jun and Sep–Oct, with breeding females starting up to several weeks ahead of their males. As in the first moult some secondaries are occasionally retained.

AGEING AND SEXING

Adult-type males are easy to identify, while juveniles and females appear very similar, especially in worn plumage in spring. When ageing ring-tails ground-colour of breast and upperparts, as well as pattern of underwings, upperwings, breast and head are important.

> **Ageing summary:** Adult-type males can be aged by the colour of the upperparts and head. Definite adults are pure bluish grey while first-adults (2nd cy autumn – 3rd cy spring) are mottled brownish grey above and show smudgy ear coverts, crown and nape. Fresh juveniles are dark brown above, with uniformly dark secondaries and a pale line along the tips of the greater upperwing coverts. The body is ochre below and the secondaries appear darker than the primaries. Adult females are broader-winged than juveniles and the remiges and greater coverts are greyish above with visible darker barring. The breast is whiter and the secondaries are paler below with distinct black bands.

Juvenile (1st cy – 2nd cy spring)   **Plates 198–203**

In fresh plumage, perched juveniles are characterized by dark brown upperparts with rufous feather-tips and fringes, while the underparts are ochre with dark streaking. Secondaries blackish brown without apparent bars and there are no grey colours on the upperparts. Head-pattern tends to be rather contrasting with a dark crown and cheek-patch surrounded by a pale but dark-spotted collar.

In flight, autumn juveniles are identified by dark brown upperparts and rich ochre underparts. The rufous tips to the upper greater primary and secondary coverts form a distinctive fine line across the wing. Secondaries greyish below, being often clearly darker than the primaries, with broad dark bars, and the barring is not as distinct as in adult females. Juveniles have narrower wings than adults, with a slightly tapering inner hand and bulging secondaries and they do not show traces of wing moult until late in 2nd cy spring.

Males are smaller than females and have a paler iris that turns from greyish to bright yellow in the autumn. The pale iris is, however, surprisingly difficult to see in the field, unless the bird is seen perched or very close in flight, when the black pupil is apparent. Females have dark brown irides and the eye appears all-dark in the field.

Spring juveniles are very similar to adult females. In winter, upperparts bleach to faded grey and juveniles can often be identified by their extremely bleached and faded upperparts, which are distinctly paler than in adult females. Mantle and upperwing coverts are dull greyish, contrasting sharply with the uniformly dark secondaries. Underparts have bleached to off-white, as in the adult female. The banding of the underwing secondaries is still diffuse but the whole underwing appears distinctly paler than in autumn because of wear.

First-adult male (2nd cy autumn – 3rd cy spring)   **Fig 36**

Generally like adult male, but possible to identify if seen well. In late summer–early autumn recognized by unmoulted juvenile remiges, which are brown above and pale with barring below (outermost primaries and median secondaries are retained longest). After completing moult, differs from adult male by blotchier and dusky brownish mantle, scapulars and inner arm, and by retained faint juvenile-like head-pattern, with brownish nape-patch and slightly darker auriculars. Diffusely darker tips of inner greater and median upperwing coverts often form dusky wing-bands on inner wing, while the tail frequently shows a diffuse dark subterminal band. From below, more similar to adult male but axillaries and greater underwing coverts often show fine dark barring; the upper breast may show diffuse streaks until late autumn. The barring and streaks, however, are visible only at close range.

In worn plumage in 3rd cy spring told from adult male by blotchy and brownish grey instead of uniformly silvery upperparts and faintly patterned head, sometimes also by retained juvenile flight-feathers, but ageing generally more difficult than in autumn.

Fig 36 *Hen Harrier, 2nd cy male in Aug–Sep. Note Pallid Harrier-like black wedge to wing-tip caused by moulting primaries. Identified by broad dark trailing edge to wing, broader wings and steadier flight.*

Definite adult male (3rd cy autumn and older) Plates 204–208

Adult males are beautifully coloured silver-grey, white and black. Head and upperparts silvery bluish grey, with black wing-tips. The blue-grey upper breast contrasts sharply with the white lower breast and belly.

In flight, adult males are easily recognized even from afar by their uniformly bluish-grey upperparts with largely black outer hand and by conspicuously white uppertail coverts. From below, underwings are white with a black outer hand and a broad dark trailing edge, most conspicuous along the tips of the secondaries. The grey forebody contrasts sharply with the white belly and the fine grey tail barring is usually hidden, becoming visible when the tail is fanned.

Distant adult-type males that cannot be exactly aged can be referred to as adult-type males, which includes all grey males from 2nd cy autumn and older.

Adult female (2nd cy autumn and older) Plates 209–213

Adult females resemble juveniles but have greyish upperwings with clearly visible darker barring to remiges and greater coverts and with secondaries and primaries similarly coloured, without the contrast between dark secondaries and paler primaries of the juveniles. Underwing distinctly banded underneath with similarly pale ground-colour to both primaries and secondaries. Underbody whiter with broad brown streaks to vent, under-tail coverts and upper breast, where they may form a collar and conceal the ground-colour completely. Head often appears rather featureless, but shows in close views slightly darker but streaked crown and cheeks, a narrow pale collar with dark spots and a rather extensive white area around the eye. Adults have broader wings than juveniles, with broader inner hand. Iris colour may give further hint of bird's age (see Bare parts).

Sexing: Adults are easy to sex by plumage but juveniles are more similar. The size difference is rarely of use in the field unless male and female are seen together. With experience, extremes can be sexed even in the field, as small, narrow-winged and lightly flapping males differ markedly from the heavy and broad-winged females. Iris colour is a good character but surprisingly difficult to note reliably in the field, since the pale irides of males are far less obvious than might be expected and usually appear fairly dark even from close up.

References: Balfour 1970; Forsman 1980, 1984, 1993b, 1995b; v. Haartman et al. 1965; Kjellén 1994, 1995; Lontkowski 1995; Noakes 1990; Picozzi 1981; Pöyhönen 1995; Shirihai & Christie 1992; Tucker & Heath 1995

Plate 198 *Juvenile showing typically ochre underbody. Note five fingers compared with Pallid and Montagu's. This young female (by iris colour) has rather well marked secondaries, with barring continuing typically to primaries. Aug, Finland (Mikko Pöllänen).*

Plate 199 *Juvenile showing the typical curved lines of the wing-profile. The primaries are unusually poorly marked in this bird, indicating a young male. Oct, Sweden (Jens B. Bruun).*

Plate 200 *Juvenile showing deeply coloured underparts and rather uniformly broad wings with a rounded wing-tip. Autumn, Finland (Harri Muukkonen).*

Plate 201 *Juvenile male moulting to first-adult. The moulted inner primaries are of adult male type while the rest of the plumage is still juvenile. Note bleached (hence pale) body and forewing. 8 Jul 1985, Finland (Pekka Helo).*

Plate 202 *Juvenile female moulting to adult plumage. The pale breast with the narrow streaks, the rather solidly dark cheek, the brownish iris and the darkish secondaries are retained juvenile characters, soon to be moulted. 8 Jul 1985, Finland (Pekka Helo).*

Plate 203 *Juvenile female moulting to adult plumage (same as Plate 202). Differs from adult by retained juvenile and worn upperparts, uniformly brown juvenile secondaries, distinctly marked head and thinly streaked breast and belly. 8 Jul 1985, Finland (Pekka Helo).*

Plate 204 *Adult male. Note broad wings and black outer hand with five black fingers. Note also broad dark trailing edge to wing and distinct grey hood. 1 Jul 1993, Finland (Dick Forsman).*

Plate 205 *Adult male (same as Plates 204 and 206). 1 Jul 1993, Finland (Dick Forsman).*

Plate 206 *Adult male from above showing uniformly grey upperparts apart from cut-off black wing-tip, white uppertail coverts and faint darker trailing edge to wing. 1 Jul 1993, Finland (Dick Forsman).*

Plate 207 *Adult male. 5 Jul 1979, Finland (Pekka Helo).*

Plate 208 *Adult male (same as Plate 207) showing relatively short wings in relation to tail-length. 5 Jul 1979, Finland (Pekka Helo).*

Plate 209 *Adult female. Note rounded wing-shape with five prominent fingers and with barring continuing from the secondaries to the primaries. 1 Jul 1993, Finland (Dick Forsman).*

Plate 210 *Adult female (same as Plates 209 and 212). Differs from female Pallid by distinctly barred primaries and dark trailing edge to hand, from juvenile Hen by broad streaks of upper breast, spotted undertail coverts and distinctly barred secondaries. 1 Jul 1993, Finland (Dick Forsman).*

Plate 211 *Moulting adult female showing 'wrong' wing-formula causing confusion risk with female Pallid Harrier. Despite the pointed wing-tip the wings are broad and the distinct barring of the secondaries continues to the primaries. Sep 1985, Finland (Dick Forsman).*

Plate 212 *Adult female from above. Shows greyish secondaries with dark banding and more distinctly barred primaries than juvenile. 1 Jul 1993, Finland (Dick Forsman).*

Plate 213 *Breeding adult female. The banded greater upperwing coverts, secondaries and primaries and the loosely streaked head and cheeks show this to be an adult, further confirmed by the paler iris. 5 Jul 1979, Finland (Pekka Helo).*

PALLID HARRIER   *Circus macrourus*

Plates 214–239

Subspecies: Monotypic.

Distribution: Breeds in Russia from Black Sea to Yenisei River and Lake Baikal in the east.

Habitat: A bird of open mainly dry grassy habitats. Hunts over fields and farmland as well as over wetlands and semi-deserts.

Population: An estimated 1000–2000 pairs in European part of Russia, declining in numbers and showing considerable contraction of range. Regular breeding outside Russia confined to the Dobrogea in Romania, to Moldova and Ukraine, with some tens to a few scattered pairs each. Changing of virgin steppe into agricultural farmland has probably had a negative effect on the population.

Movements: Migratory, winters from SE Europe and the Middle East to India and in most of Africa. Main wintering area probably in central E Africa. Autumn migration from Aug to Oct–Nov, on average later than Montagu's, with peak around late Sep through to end of Oct. Migrates on broad front usually singly or in small groups of two and three. Crosses Mediterranean freely and does not concentrate into certain flyways as do many larger raptors, hence numbers usually small. Spring migration in Mar–May, with main peak in the Middle East in early Apr. Also spring migration earlier than Montagu's. On spring passage frequently takes more westerly route crossing the Mediterranean as far west as Cap Bon in Tunisia, or even at Gibraltar. This may suggest a westward movement in Africa during winter.

Hunting and prey: Feeds on small to medium-sized mammals and birds, which it hunts in normal harrier manner flying low over ground and pouncing on prey from flight, probably partly relying on its hearing. Birds are also taken when flushed or after short pursuit.

SPECIES IDENTIFICATION

Length 40–49 cm

wing-span males 102–109 cm, females 109–119 cm (*n*=25; Birds from Israel and Kazakhstan; W.S. Clark & D. Forsman et al., unpubl.)

Adult males unmistakable. Females and juveniles easily confused with other ring-tail harriers, but underwing pattern in combination with head pattern diagnostic. Birds in transitional plumage best identified by underwing pattern of primaries.

Identification summary: Males small and slim with narrow wings and light flight, females considerably bigger and heavier, but still with pointed hand, and only four visible fingers. Adult males generally pale with contrasting black wedge to wing-tip. Adult females show mostly a contrast in the underwing between dark secondaries and pale primaries. Secondaries usually show one or two pale bands gradually tapering and dissolving towards the body, while hand shows a pale trailing edge and most of the barring confined to the median portion of each primary, leaving largely pale fingers and a pale crescent around the carpal area. Head-pattern variable, but usually shows complete but narrow pale collar bordering face from behind. Juveniles show similar underwing pattern to females, although secondaries are, on average, darker and the primaries are more boldly barred. Fingers pale with dark barring, and the pale bases to the primaries often form a 'boomerang' around the carpal. Head-pattern is contrasting, with extensively dark cheeks, small white spots above and below the eye, and a distinct and complete collar running from nape to throat.

In flight, distant Males are considerably smaller and lighter than females and the two may appear like two different species. Adult males can readily be identified over long distances by their very pale plumage, with dark wedge at wing-tip, in combination with shape and light flight.

Ring-tails most difficult to tell from Montagu's Harrier (adult females also from ring-tail Hen), but Pallid appears to have a slightly fuller body and slightly broader wings, with comparatively shorter and more triangular hand, and the flight is less buoyant and graceful than Montagu's. Juveniles of the two are more similar in flight silhouette and are usually not possible to identify by shape (except perhaps for heavy Pallid females). Males are very fast and agile in flight with rather fast but stiff wing-action and may recall a falcon at times. Females are much heavier and approach juvenile male Hen Harrier in both shape and wing-action; some broad-winged adult females differ in shape from Hen Harrier only by narrower and more pointed hand. Soars and glides on lifted wings; on soaring birds wing broadest at carpal with hand tapering towards tip. Moulting adult female Hen

Fig 37 *Pallid Harrier. Typical head-pattern of juvenile showing extensively dark cheeks, extending on to lower mandible, distinct collar running from nape to throat, small white eye-patches and dark lores.*

Harriers should be carefully considered when identifying adult female ring-tails in late summer, as they may show a pointed wing-tip because of moult, although showing typically broad wings.

Adult females and juveniles especially are difficult to tell from Montagu's in corresponding plumage, unless details of e.g. underwings are seen. Adult females typically show a dark inner third and a pale outer two thirds of underwing, corresponding to dark secondaries and pale primaries. Underwing coverts (and the axillaries) appear largely dark, adding to the impression of a dark arm, while the forearm is paler, and the pale hand shows a distinct dark carpal crescent. Head and forebody often darker than the rear underbody, the margin following roughly the line between darker and paler underwing coverts. Secondaries appear genearally rather dark above, being the darkest area of the entire upperparts.

Juveniles are very similar to juvenile Montagu's Harriers from a distance, but appear to have a paler and a more 'open' hand, because of less black in wing-tip. Many individuals (but far from all!) also show the pale 'boomerang' around the carpal, which is obvious from afar when present. Head and sides of neck appear dark with a distinct pale collar often surrounding the whole head from nape to throat.

In flight, closer Hand narrower than arm, with four fingers and longest three forming wing-tip.

Adult males easily identified by slim proportions and characteristic plumage: generally very pale with distinct black wedge in wing-tip but lacking other distinct features. When fanned, tail shows fine greyish barring to outer rectrices, which is finer and denser than e.g. on adult male Montagu's. Uppertail coverts white with grey barring but appear pale grey in the field.

Adult females resemble female Montagu's Harrier and even more adult female Hen Harrier, but are identified by the underwing pattern. Secondaries are variable, but generally appear dark with, usually, just one pale band near the trailing edge of the wing. Some birds have another pale band closer to the coverts, but, regardless of number of bands, they are broader and clearer further out and tend to taper and dissolve before reaching the body, resulting in the whole wing gradually darkening inwards. Primaries appear generally pale, often with restricted dark tips, and the barring is mostly confined to the median section of each primary leaving prominently paler bases, which contrast with the dark carpal crescent. The trailing edge of the hand is typically faint and inconspicuous giving the whole hand an 'open' expression (cf. ring-tail Montagu's). Underwing coverts vary in ground-colour and amount of markings, but appear mostly rather dark with paler forearm. This adds to the impression of a pale hand and a dark arm. If any pattern can be discerned in the underwing coverts it is usually pale spots to rather dark greater coverts, whereas median and lesser coverts appear darkish with pale fringes.

The head-pattern is extremely variable. Some adult females have an almost juvenile-like and contrasting head while others are almost identical to adult female Hen Harriers. Head tends to show a more extensively dark ear coverts patch, being more uniformly dark than in other adult ring-tail females, with the dark reaching the lower mandible, but some females have very washed-out head-markings. The pale collar is usually distinct, narrow and regular in width and runs from nape to throat, but unlike juvenile shows dark spots. The white spots above and below the eye are usually small.

Upperparts appear rather uniform and dark in fresh plumage and more greyish in spring with somewhat darker secondaries and a paler wing covert patch. The barring of the secondaries is sometimes visible from above, usually with trailing edge looking darkest, but Pallid does not show the distinct dark band across otherwise greyish secondaries as in typical adult female Montagu's. The streaking of the underbody varies as well, often with bolder streaking on upper breast and finer streaking lower down. In contrast to Montagu's the streaking of belly and thighs often shows narrower shaft-streaks with drop-shaped tips.

Juveniles can be very similar to juvenile Montagu's, but differ in pattern of underwings and head. Primaries are rather similar to adult female Pallid, but juveniles tend to show bolder barring covering the entire hand and the fingers. Still, many individuals show paler primary-bases and the trailing edge is diffuse and inconspicuous, creating a pattern rather similar to adult female. Secondaries vary a lot, from almost uniformly dark to regularly barred, the most common type being dark with one pale band, as on adult female. Underwing coverts also variable, with plain ochre lesser and median, and faintly streaked greater, being the most common type.

Head diagnostic, with black cheek-patch extending to lower mandible and with a complete pale collar from nape to throat. In addition the lores appear dark, the white spots below and above the eye are small, and the side of the neck is uniformly brown.

Underbody does not show any streaking in autumn birds, although the flanks may appear somewhat smudged.

Perched Frequently perches on the ground where normally adopts horizontal posture like other harriers. Not possible to separate from Hen or Montagu's on shape alone, although Pallid, like Hen, frequently appears bigger-headed than Montagu's. Adult Montagu's have the longest wings, reaching almost to the tip of the tail, while Pallid has slightly shorter wings and Hen the shortest, with wing-tips falling *c.* 5 cm short of the tail-tip.

Adult male is identified by pale plumage with unstreaked underparts and unbarred secondaries and by complete collar to head (although not differing in colour and hence difficult to see).

Adult female Pallid and Montagu's best separated by different head-pattern and breast-pattern. Pallid females have more heavily streaked upper breast with finer streaking towards the belly, whereas Montagu's have a uniformly patterned breast with lanceolated streaks. Pallid told from very similar female Hen by more uniformly dark ear coverts and greater upperwing coverts, darker lores and by comparatively longer wings.

Juveniles identified by typical head-pattern from both Montagu's and Hen.

Bare parts Iris pale greyish in juvenile male after fledging, turning lemon yellow in autumn–early winter. Iris dark brown in juvenile female, remaining dark until at least 2nd cy summer, probably even later, becoming yellow with age as in Hen Harrier, although exact timing unknown. Cere and legs yellow at all ages, bill and claws dark.

Confusion species: Most likely to be confused with other harrier species, juveniles especially with Montagu's, adult females also with Hen.

Montagu's Harrier (page 215) Narrower wings with longer and narrower hand (does not necessarily apply to juveniles) and a more swaying flight. Adult males are tri-coloured above with darker grey mantle and head than Pallid and with extensively dark hand and dark bands on secondaries above and below. Adult females have pale underwings with distinct dark barring and boldly patterned coverts and axillaries and the head is rather pale and streaked with pale lores, lots of white around the eye, and with a dark ear coverts spot. Juveniles have dark fingers, a dark trailing edge to hand and dark secondaries and the head shows more white around the eye, paler lores, smaller ear coverts patch and a less complete pale collar than juvenile Pallid.

Hen Harrier (page 183) Broader wings with more rounded tip (five fingers) and a heavier and more laboured flight. Adult males show more black to hand, a broad dark trailing edge to wing and a clearly demarcated grey hood. Adult females can be very similar to adult female Pallid, but show distinctly barred secondaries with barring continuing onto primaries, which show a distinct dark trailing edge. Juveniles may be very similar to adult female Pallid, but show different flight silhouette and wing-formula and also distinct dark trailing edge to hand.

MOULT

Complete annual, but some median secondaries may be left unmoulted. Moult begins and is finished earlier than in Montagu's Harrier.

Juveniles (first moult) Undergo a partial body moult in winter in which normally only a few feathers around neck and upper breast are moulted. Moults thus, on average, clearly less than first winter Montagu's. Complete moult commences May–early Jun and in 2nd cy birds is finished earlier than in adults. Birds in fresh plumage are found from the end of Aug (e.g. 14 Aug 2nd cy female with p10 and s8–9 growing, rest of remiges moulted (ZMK) and 2nd cy males, from 9 and 24 Sep in fresh plumage; BMNH).

Adults (subsequent moults) Complete moult starting earlier in females (May) than in males (Jun). Moult is finished during Sep–Oct, later than in 2nd cy birds but earlier than in Montagu's: 3rd cy male with completed moult on 13 Sep (Kazakhstan); adult male missing p10 and with p8–9 growing on 9 Sep (ZMK); adult female 8 Sep with completed moult (Kazakhstan); adult female from 18 Oct still growing s4, rest of plumage moulted (BMNH). Single remiges, especially median secondaries, may be left unmoulted. Some feathers, mainly body-feathers or rectrices may occasionally be shed in the winter quarters prior to spring migration.

AGEING AND SEXING

Adults and juveniles fairly easy to separate as well as a first-adult plumage in males. However, separation between first-adult and definite adult females requires good views and experience of the plumage variation.

> **Ageing and sexing summary:** Juveniles have unstreaked underbody and contrasting head-pattern; males and females differ only in size and iris colour. Advanced 2nd cy spring males identified by mixture of juvenile and adult male characters in plumage, later in summer like adult males but with dull brownish grey upperparts and streaked or deep rufous breast and pale collar. In 3rd cy spring males still possible to age by dull, often mottled upperparts, dark trailing edge to wing, faintly banded uppertail and traces of juvenile head-pattern. After completed moult in 3rd cy summer like adult, but still shows more extensively dark wing-tip, duller upperparts and subterminal tail-band. Adult male is pale silvery grey above lacking streaking to underbody and lacking darker markings to head or wings apart from contrasting black wedge to wing-tip.
>
> 2nd cy females in spring may be impossible to separate from sparsely moulted 2nd cy males, unless iris colour is seen. In early 2nd cy summer told from older females

by unstreaked juvenile belly and forearm, very worn upperparts and juvenile-like head-pattern. After completed moult, in late 2nd cy summer, from older females by darker iris and darker overall appearance and strikingly contrasting head-pattern. Adult females are more greyish brown above and paler, less rufous below, with finer streaking and less contrasting head-markings, finer and reduced markings to primaries on underwing, and a yellow iris.

Juvenile (1st cy – 2nd cy spring)   Plates 214–219

Juveniles principally coloured like juvenile Montagu's and told from adults by very dark upperparts and brightly coloured, unstreaked yellowish ochre underparts. Underwing and head-pattern best for separation from other ring-tailed harriers.

Juvenile Pallid shows the most contrasting head-pattern of all harriers. Crown and cheek-patch blackish brown, latter large and dominant, normally reaching the lower mandible. In some individuals the crown may appear rather pale ochre because of extensive pale tips to crown feathers. Behind the dark cheek and ear coverts runs a strikingly distinct, pale collar of even width, separating dark sides of head from almost equally dark and uniform sides of neck. The pale collar appears to continue around the throat and is apparent from afar and from all angles. The size of the white patches above and below the eye are, on average, smaller than in juvenile Montagu's and the lores are typically dark. Both species show a prominent whitish double-spot on the nape differing from the streaked and less conspicuous nape-patch of Hen.

The primary-pattern is usually diagnostic and rather similar to adult female (see In flight, closer). The secondaries appear dark below, but at closer range some birds show rather diffuse, paler greyish bands.

Upperparts blackish brown with rusty tips, including greater coverts, while median and some lesser coverts have more extensive rusty fringes forming an individually variable rusty patch to mid-arm. Secondaries uniformly dark, nearly black, whereas primaries are somewhat paler and brownish, with dark tips and barely visible darker barring, especially on upper inner hand. Uppertail coverts white or tawny. Central tail-feathers brown with four darker bands, outer feathers paler, rufous to pale straw with dark bands.

Underparts resemble juvenile Montagu's but upper breast and flanks lack streaking. Underwing coverts are coloured like the body with darker streaking to the greater coverts but with less patterned or uniformly ochre median and lesser coverts. The dark greater primary coverts form a crescent at the base of the primaries, as in Montagu's.

During winter the plumage wears and fades considerably. Virtually all rusty feather edges of the upperparts are worn off, save for some fragments left on the inner vanes of the greater coverts (still visible under favourable conditions in flight as a band on the upperwing). All upperparts wear into a faded, dull greyish-brown colour, with only secondaries remaining dark. Underparts fade into pale straw or almost off-white and the head-markings can be even more distinct than in autumn juveniles.

Transitional plumage (2nd cy spring – 2nd cy summer)   **Plates 220–221**

By spring sexes differ in eye-colour, males having bright yellow and females dark brown irides.

In winter some advanced juveniles start to moult the head, neck and upper breast, but on average juvenile Pallids moult less than Montagu's and most juveniles appear in spring in a bleached juvenile plumage. The first replaced feathers on the upper breast show brown streaks in both sexes, recalling feathers of the adult female, but males soon start to acquire pale greyish feathers with diffuse streaks.

Males A small percentage of advanced males have replaced most of the body plumage. Upperparts are grey-brown and the underbody is off-white with some fine streaks on the breast. The juvenile head-pattern is replaced by a less conspicuous one, with paler grey-brown cheeks and crown but with distinct pale collar and white spots below and above the eye. They may appear rather similar to 2nd cy males in autumn, apart from the juvenile remiges.

During the summer males gradually attain a plumage resembling the adult male. In early summer they differ from Montagu's Harrier in corresponding plumage by plain inner primaries, axillaries and belly (see First-adult male).

Females 2nd cy spring females are mostly still in complete juvenile plumage. They are much paler than fresh juveniles owing to extensive plumage wear. Many birds have not moulted anything upon their return to the breeding grounds and are thus easy to age. Others have, at the most, moulted their head and neck, rarely also the upper breast, and have acquired a collar of streaked feathers around the neck. 2nd cy spring females can be reliably separated from older females by their unstreaked, uniformly pale straw-coloured breast, belly and lesser underwing coverts. They are told from retarded 2nd cy males only by their dark brown irides (yellow in males). The secondaries form the darkest area above and a variable paler area can be seen on the upperwing coverts.

In summer, females moult their plumage more or less completely, and by autumn migration they have nearly completed their moult. Head-pattern is still very juvenile-like, with dark crown and cheeks and a striking pale collar, although dotted with dark spots. The sides of the neck are dark, although some paler fringes can be seen. Females in this plumage differ from older females further by their darker brown upperparts and their darker underparts, often with deep rusty-ochre breast with blackish brown streaks. Also, the secondaries appear very dark from below. Iris still predominantly dark (brownish).

Adult plumages (2nd cy autumn and older) After the moult in 2nd cy autumn Pallid Harriers wear a first-adult plumage, which is diagnostic and separable in the field. Males older than this may still be divided into two groups, here called 'Second-adult plumage' and 'Definite adult plumage', which are separable in the field under optimal conditions. Second-adult plumage is better referred to as a plumage-type, as it is not known whether it actually relates to birds of a certain age-class or merely just reflects individual variation between males after their second moult.

The plumage development in females is even less well known and is further confused by extensive individual variation.

First-adult male (2nd cy autumn – 3rd cy summer) Plates 222–227

By Sep the moult is completed and the birds can be separated from older males by their dull brownish grey upperparts with diffuse but widely dark wing-tips. The dark area of the wing-tip is on average larger than in older males, including p9. Uppertail brownish grey and shows a darker suffused subterminal bar and additional finer barring to the central tail-feathers. Head brownish grey, darker than in adult males, and frequently shows a pale collar, whitish areas above and below the eye and mostly also a darker cheek-patch. Brown and streaked feathers are often visible on the crown or around the retained white nape-patch.

Underwing pattern is rather similar to adult males, but the black in the wing-tip is, on average, more extensive, reaching closer to the leading edge (p6–9 largely black). The trailing edge shows a darker band, similar to, but narrower than, male Hen Harrier. Greater underwing coverts variably barred greyish, forming a slightly darker crescent around the carpal area and/or a darker band along the base of the secondaries, which may also show faint bars. From below, the tail-feathers are principally patterned as in adult males but a diffuse dark subterminal bar, lacking in adult males, can be seen when the tail is fanned.

Upper breast extremely variable in autumn, being more or less diffusely streaked or mottled in grey and/or deep rufous. Lower breast and belly are white, with sparse, fine greyish streaks extending in some birds to the undertail coverts, but these cannot normally be seen in the field. The line between the greyish upper breast and the white lower breast and belly is rather sharp (as in Hen) as opposed to the very gradual margin in older males. Montagu's Harrier males in corresponding plumage show well defined and rather broad rusty red streaks to the whitish belly, visible also in the field.

By 3rd cy spring breast colours are largely lost (probably moulted in 2nd cy late autumn–winter?) and birds thus resemble adult males. They can still be aged by the brownish tinge to the upperparts with less distinct dark wing-tip above, faintly barred central tail-feathers, darker trailing edge to wing and greyish markings to the greater underwing coverts. The white areas around the eye and the greyish barring of the greater underwing coverts are retained.

Second-adult male (3rd cy autumn – 4th cy summer)   **Plates 228–230**

Like definite adult male but somewhat duller grey above, appearing unevenly coloured and slightly blotchy on scapulars and upperwing coverts and with less contrasting and wider black area to wing-tip above. Underwing shows a faint and diffuse darker trailing edge to the arm and there is more black in the wing-tip than in older males. Many individuals also show some darker feathers to crown and nape plus a small darker smudge on the ear coverts and the tail-tip, and the grey upper breast is rather clearly demarcated from otherwise white underparts, giving a distinctly hooded appearance.

Definite adult male (4th cy autumn and older)   **Plates 231–232**

Adult male Pallid Harriers are among the palest of all raptors. From a distance they can appear all-white save for the black wedge in the wingtip (distal parts of p6–8). Upperparts very pale silvery grey with only uppertail coverts appearing paler (barred grey at close range). The black wing-tip is distinct on the upperwing in contrast to younger males. Tail silvery grey lacking any bands to the central pair, but showing rather dense and fine barring in the outermost feathers (approximately six to seven grey bars), as opposed to the three or four wide, rusty red bars of the male Montagu's. Head appears very pale, whitish grey. Upper breast whitish grey blending smoothly with the white lower breast and belly. Underwings white except for the black wing-tips, extending from p6 to p8 and the tip of p9.

Adult females (after 2nd cy autumn and older)   **Plates 233–239**

Adult females are variable, and it is difficult to distinguish between age-dependant and individual variation. The most reliable indication of age in females is the iris colour, which changes from dark brown (in 1st cy up to probably second winter/3rd cy summer) to light brown or amber (probably by 3rd cy summer–4th cy summer) and to bright yellow (probably not before 4th cy summer), but the exact timing is unknown and probably individually variable. The plumage tends to get paler below and greyer above with increasing age, while at the same time the streaking of underbody gets finer and the dark areas of the head become less distinct. Underwing pattern seems to vary individually, rather than changing with age, although the barring of the primaries seems to get finer and the hand hence paler with age.

Easily identified from autumn juveniles by streaked underparts but may be difficult to separate from advanced 2nd cy female in spring. Even advanced juveniles mostly carry their faintly streaked juvenile underwing coverts in 2nd cy spring, while the underwing coverts of adult females are darker and distinctly patterned.

The head varies in darkness considerably and the pattern is variable. Some (younger) females resemble juveniles, while older females may be very similar to juvenile Hen Harriers especially, but most females are easy to recognize as Pallid Harriers by the dark face with dark lores and solid and extensive dark cheek-patch connecting with the lower mandible, by small white spots above and below the eye, and by a narrow but distinct and complete collar. The sides of the neck vary from uniformly brown to paler brown with dark streaking.

Underbody shows broader streaks to upper breast and finer streaks to lower breast and belly. The streaks vary from blackish brown to chestnut and the ground-colour of the underparts, including the underwing coverts, varies from buffish white to pale ochre or deep rufous brown. Greater underwing coverts and axillaries often darkish with pale spotting.

Upperparts vary from largely dark to faded greyish brown, being darker in younger adults and greyer in older birds but also darker in fresh plumage (autumn) and more faded in spring. The majority of adults appear rather dark above, lacking the juvenile's distinct pale tips to the greater coverts, with barring visible only on inner primaries. Greyer (older) females may even show faint barring to secondaries above and may hence approach adult female Montagu's in this respect. Uppertail varies from dark brown (younger) to more greyish brown (older) with sparse dark bars. Outer rectrices paler ochre with distinct dark bands.

Sexing: Juveniles are similar in plumage. Size difference is obvious in direct comparison and experienced observers may be able to note the lighter and more agile flight of the males. By the late nestling period the iris of males turns greyish (later yellow) whereas females have dark brown irides. The iris colour of males, however, is surprisingly difficult to see in the field.

After 2nd cy summer males predominantly greyish with black wing-tip pattern, females predominantly brown and streaked below.

References: Christensen 1977; Delin 1989; Forsman 1980, 1984, 1993b, 1995b; Lontkowski 1995; Piechocki 1955a; Svensson 1971, 1991

Plate 214 *Juvenile female (sex by iris colour) with dark cheek-patch typically reaching out to lower mandible and with distinct pale collar surrounding the head. Also notice typically irregular barring in the primaries. 16 Sep 1993, Kazakhstan (Antti Mikala).*

Plate 215 *Juvenile with boldly barred primaries but showing pale bases forming a 'boomerang' around the carpal area. Apr 1982, Israel (Bertil Breife).*

Plate 216 *Juvenile. Note fairly broad arm and clearly narrower hand (cf. Hen Harrier) and diagnostic primary-pattern. 2 Sep 1996, Finland (Tom Lindroos).*

Plate 217 *Juvenile showing diagnostic head- and primary-pattern. 14 Sep 1993, Kazakhstan (Dick Forsman).*

Plate 218 *Typical juvenile with conspicuous pale collar between dark face and dark sides of the neck. Note pale bases to primaries below. 25 Jan 1995, Israel (Dick Forsman).*

Plate 220 *Juvenile male in transitional plumage (2nd cy). This individual shows a diagnostic juvenile underwing, while most of head and underbody are moulted. Note white axillaries and breast-feathers, which in male Montagu's in corresponding plumage would show distinct rufous markings. May, Israel 1987 (Hadoram Shirihai).*

Plate 219 *Juvenile male (yellow iris) showing diagnostic head-pattern. The pale collar acquires dark spots during winter. Note the broken tail of this individual. 7 Feb 1996, Israel (Dick Forsman).*

Plate 221 *Juvenile male in transitional plumage (same as Plate 220) with moulted central tail-feathers, some median coverts and mantle. May, Israel 1987 (Hadoram Shirihai).*

Plate 222 *First-adult male showing rufous breast-markings, dark ear coverts and prominent white eye-patches. Dec 1996, Israel (Hadoram Shirihai).*

Plate 223 *First-adult male from above (same as Plates 222 and 224). Upperparts are dusky brownish grey and the tail shows faint barring. Dec 1996, Israel (Hadoram Shirihai).*

Plate 224 *First-adult male. Note dusky, brownish upperparts with lots of brown in head as well as brownish markings on breast and thighs. Dec 1996, Israel (Hadoram Shirihai).*

Plate 225 *First-adult male. Note darkish hood with prominent white eye-patches, streaking on breast, dark subterminal wing-band and barred primary coverts. 4 Oct 1995, Israel (Dick Forsman).*

Plate 226 *First-adult male in 3rd cy spring. Note dark trailing edge to wing and darker crown and auricular crescent, but lack of markings to underbody compared with plumage of 2nd cy autumn. Apr 1993, Germany (Axel Halley).*

Plate 227 *First-adult male in 3rd cy spring (same as Plate 226). Like adult, but faint streaking on crown, collar and breast are indications of immaturity. Apr 1993, Germany (Axel Halley).*

Plate 228 *Second-adult male. Not always possible to tell from definite adult plumage in the field, but tends to show a rather contrasting grey upper breast and dark smudges to crown and ear coverts. 13 Sep 1993, Kazakhstan (Markku Huhta-Koivisto).*

Plate 229 *Second-adult plumage male (same as Plate 228). The grey upper breast contrasts with the white underbody. 13 Sep 1993, Kazakhstan (Dick Forsman).*

Plate 230 *Second-adult plumage male. Differs from adult male by duskier upperparts, rufous markings on crown and cheeks and by dusky subterminal tail-band. Dec 1996, Israel (Hadoram Shirihai).*

Plate 231 *Adult male showing very pale underbody and head and uniformly grey uppertail. Winter, Israel (Hadoram Shirihai).*

Plate 232 *Adult males are practically white below with a small black wedge in the wing-tip. Jun 1987, Kazakhstan (Markku Huhta-Koivisto).*

Plate 233 *Adult female showing typical underwing-pattern with irregularly barred primaries and pale trailing edge to hand. Note also extensively dark cheeks and small white eye-patches. Mar 1988, Israel (Klaus Bjerre).*

Plate 234 *Adult female. Note two-coloured impression of underwing, with dark arm and pale hand resulting from dark greater coverts and secondaries and largely pale and unbarred distal portions of primaries. Many females also show marked contrast between more heavily streaked upper breast and paler lower breast. Apr 1982, Israel (Bertil Breife).*

Plate 235 *Adult female showing diagnostic underwings and head-pattern. 5 Feb 1996, Israel (Dick Forsman).*

Plate 236 *Rather pale adult female showing typically dark secondaries and translucent tips to inner primaries. 14 Sep 1993, Kazakhstan (Markku Huhta-Koivisto).*

Plate 237 *Adult female from above. Note darkish secondaries with trailing edge darkest and compare with female Montagu's. Mar 1993, Israel (Lars Jonsson).*

Plate 238 *Adult female. Note uniformly dark secondaries and greater coverts differing from female Hen Harrier while the wings are shorter and legs longer than Montagu's. The darkish iris shows this to be a younger adult female. Dec 1996, Israel (Hadoram Shirihai).*

Plate 239 *Younger adult female. Note narrow but distinct pale collar and dark cheeks. The uniform greater coverts and secondaries and the denser and finer tail-barring differ from Hen Harrier. Mar 1993, Israel (Lars Jonsson).*

MONTAGU'S HARRIER   *Circus pygargus*

Plates 240–267

Subspecies: Monotypic.

Distribution: In a wide zone from W Europe (Iberia, France) to Yenisei River, roughly between 40° and 60° N.

Habitat: A bird of open landscapes. Prefers open plains with special liking for river valleys or lakes; more closely associated with wetlands than Pallid Harrier. Nests in tall vegetation among reeds or cereals or in wetland meadows. Hunts over all kinds of open terrestrial habitats from open farmland and heathlands to meadows, steppe and semi-desert.

Population: W Palearctic population estimated to be 25 000–40 000 pairs, with strongest population in Russia. The Iberian peninsula and France both hold 3000–4000 pairs, compared with some tens to some hundred pairs in other European countries. Marked decline documented in many European subpopulations during the last 50 years, probably from habitat destruction. Numbers increasing locally in northern part of range (Sweden, Denmark), with apparent recent northward expansion in Finland. Colonial nesting and polygamy observed in the best habitats, where birds are numerous.

Movements: Migratory, European population winters in Africa south of Sahara. The wintering area stretches from the Atlantic to the Indian Ocean and to the Cape Province in the south. Autumn migration earlier than in other harriers with first movements recorded late Jul. Peak migration in S Europe in late Aug to early Sep with numbers dropping sharply in Oct. Migrates on broad front and crosses the Mediterranean freely, still concentrating at Strait of Gibraltar, with 1727 there between 11 Aug and 9 Oct 1972. Smaller numbers recorded along the Levant route. Occasional winter records from W Europe.

Spring migrants return to Europe from Mar with peak during first half of Apr but continuing until late May. Ringing recoveries and museum specimens show that unknown percentage of 2nd cy birds oversummer in their winter quarters.

Hunting and prey: Hunts like other harriers in a slow searching flight, low over the ground, following ditches and hedges and relying partly on hearing for finding prey. Stoops or drops on prey direct from flight or flushes birds which are then taken in the air. Feeds mainly on various small vertebrates such as rodents, passerines, reptiles and amphibians, but larger insects are also taken. Prey composition varies locally depending on supply.

SPECIES IDENTIFICATION

Length 38–44 cm

wing-span 102–116 cm (*n*=13; Israeli migrants; W.S. Clark, unpubl.)

Adult males are fairly easily identified and focus should be on extent of black in wing-tip and three-coloured upperparts as well as on pattern of secondaries, underwing coverts, rectrices and belly. Ring-tails are very similar to Pallid Harrier in corresponding plumages and are best identified by pattern of remiges from below and by pattern of axillaries, but, with prolonged views, attention should also be paid to head-pattern, pattern of underwing coverts and pattern of secondaries above. Transitional males show diagnostic moulted inner primaries and typical streaking on underbody.

Identification summary: Graceful in flight, with slender, long wings, a slim body and a narrow and long tail. Juveniles have considerably shorter wings and tail than adults, creating silhouette and flight rather similar to juvenile Pallid Harrier. Juveniles are dark above with rich ochre patch on upperwing coverts, white uppertail coverts and white nape-patch. Underbody uniformly rich ochre or copper-red with dark secondaries and paler primaries with dark fingers. Dark wing-tip more extensive and dark trailing edge to hand more prominent than in juvenile Pallid. Adult males easily identified by tri-coloured upperparts with largely black hand, silvery mid-wing and tail and darker grey wing coverts and mantle/scapulars. Underwings show two dark bars in the secondaries (one on upperwing) and a dusky trailing edge; the belly is white with rufous streaks. Adult females are greyer above than juveniles with streaked underparts and the secondaries show distinct dark barring below on pale ground-colour, much as in adult male. Axillaries distinctly barred. Head shows extensive white patches around the eye and a dark cheek-patch with no bordering pale collar.

A rare dark morph of the Montagu's Harrier occurs in all age-classes. It seems to reach its highest frequencies in the western populations, especially in Iberia. These birds can be mistaken for all-dark juvenile/female Marsh Harriers, but their lighter build, slender silhouette and their buoyant and graceful flight are diagnostic.

In flight, distant A medium-sized raptor of extremely slender proportions, females and males practically equal in size. Wings long and narrow. Hand long and tapering with a pointed tip in active flight and clearly narrower than arm when soaring. When hunting glides on wings in shallow V. Body slim, broadest around upper breast and tapering markedly to the vent; tail long and narrow. Long tail together with smallish body create a 'lollipop'-impression, differing from more full-bodied appearance of both Pallid and

Fig 38 *Montagu's Harrier. Note slim body in relation to wing-span and long, kinked wings held in V when gliding and soaring.*

especially Hen. Flight very light and elegant with buoyant and almost flowing wing-beats differing from stiffer flight of Pallid. Adults appear small-headed and slim-bodied with very long and narrow tail and long wings with especially long, narrow and pointed hand. Juveniles are shorter-winged and shorter-tailed than adults and are virtually identical to juvenile Pallid Harriers in shape.

Adult males are usually straightforward to identify by diagnostic plumage of upperparts, with extensively black hand and rest of upperparts in two distinct shades of grey. Distant ring-tails are very similar to Pallid Harriers and plumage details are needed for a positive identification. Adult females appear to have rather pale underwings generally, with distinctly barred secondaries and axillaries, and rather pale head with a dark cheek-patch. Old adult females show a distinct dark bar across the secondaries on upperwing. Juveniles are uniformly ochre underneath with dark secondaries, like juvenile Pallids, but they show more dark in the wing-tips (all-dark fingers) and a dark trailing edge to the hand. Upperparts dark with an ochre covert-patch and whitish or tawny uppertail coverts and nape-patch.

In flight, closer Wings long and rather narrow, with short arm and long hand with four fingers, the longest three forming the tip.

Adult males are easily identified by characteristic plumage. Primaries black except for the innermost, which in some are silvery grey with two distinct black bars, but dark in others. On the upperparts the secondaries, the primary coverts and the folded tail are silvery grey and contrast with the rest of the upperparts which are darker grey. Fanned tail shows four rich chestnut red bars on the outer rectrices, sparser and broader than on male Pallid or Hen. Uppertail coverts white with grey barring but usually blend with the upperparts. Head grey, but may show white areas around the eye and on the nape. Breast grey and belly white with rufous streaking. Underwings diagnostic with a dusky trailing edge and two distinct black bars on the secondaries, continuing on to the inner primaries in many birds. The rest of the primaries are black. Underwing coverts and axillaries white with a diagnostic bold chestnut red pattern formed by bars or transverse spots.

Adult females can be difficult to tell from adult female Pallid Harriers, but the underwings are diagnostic. The whole underwing appears rather pale with distinct dark bars and uniformly chequered underwing coverts. Secondaries show the diagnostic pattern of adult males and the primaries are regularly barred from base to tip, with a dark trailing edge to inner hand. Axillaries pale with bold chestnut barring and the same general pattern is repeated in the underwing coverts. Upperparts rather similar to those of other ring-tail females, but old females (not necessarily in first-adult plumage) show a diagnostic black transverse band across the secondaries. Head-pattern varies, but typical individuals show large white spots above and below the eye, a contrasting dark ear coverts patch (the darkest part of the head) and no sign of a prominent pale collar behind the ear coverts. Underbody pale buffish with rufous brown streaking, which appears uniform and regularly spaced from upper breast to belly.

Juveniles are very similar to juvenile Pallids and differ mainly in pattern of underwing and head. Fingers all-dark in most individuals and inner primaries have dark tips. The rest of the hand is pale with barring mostly confined to the inner primaries. Some birds have completely barred primaries, more resembling Pallid Harrier, but the trailing edge is dark and the barring is finer and regularly spaced from base to tip. Secondaries dark and rarely reveal any barring at all. Head-pattern is contrasting and may appear Pallid-like, but usually shows more white around the eye, paler lores and face, smaller dark cheek-patch

Fig 39 *Montagu's Harrier. Variation in head-pattern of juveniles. Note size of dark cheek-patch and details of pale collar bordering it as well as the amount of white around the eye and compare with juvenile Pallid (Fig 37).*

barely reaching the gape and an incomplete pale collar which often has the shape of a moon-crescent. The sides of the upper breast are often faintly streaked in juvenile Montagu's and some juveniles also show the diagnostic barring in the axillaries, as in adults.

Perched Longer-winged than other harriers when perched, with wing-tips reaching tip of tail, although wings appear shorter in 2nd cy spring birds with longer moulted rectrices. Adult males identified by white belly with rufous streaking and by dark bar on upperwing, usually barely visible outside the greater coverts on the outermost secondaries. Projecting primaries largely black. Adult females identified by restricted dark cheek-patch, extensive white around eye, no pale collar on head and by uniform streaking of underbody. Old adults show clearly greyish remiges above, including inner half of primary projection, with dark bar across secondaries also visible on perched birds. Juveniles identified by head-pattern, with more white around the eye and smaller dark cheek-patch than in Pallid, and with incomplete and less distinct pale collar. Upper breast and flanks are often faintly streaked.

Bare parts Cere and legs yellow at all ages, sometimes nearly orange yellow in adult males. Juveniles are possible to sex by iris colour at the time of fledging: males show paler, greyish irides, whereas females have dark brown irides, but the grey colour of the males is usually discernible only on perched birds. In males iris colour changes permanently to yellow in their first autumn. The females acquire a yellow iris in the course of several years, as the iris changes gradually from brown to amber and finally to yellow. The process is slow and, as shown for other species, the timing probably varies between individuals (for details see Hen Harrier).

Variation: The Montagu's Harrier occurs in a rare dark morph in all plumages (Fig 40 and Plates 266–267). In good views the normal pattern of the remiges and rectrices can be seen, allowing ageing and sexing of the birds. At greater distances the birds appear more or less dark with paler underwing remiges. Females and juveniles are dark coffee brown to blackish brown with barring of underwing and tail discernible at close range. The paler bases to the primaries often form the palest area below. Ring-tails are best aged by the secondary pattern, which is visible in good conditions. Adult males are dark ashy grey with blackish primaries. Shape differences between adults and juveniles are also helpful for ageing.

Juveniles The whole plumage blackish brown with head darkest, but with white nape-patch shining through. Tail-feathers equally dark with barely discernible darker banding. In certain light the secondaries appear almost black, being darker than rest of upperparts,

Fig 40 *Montagu's Harrier. Dark morph birds, from left to right: juvenile, adult male and adult female. Note rather normal pattern of remiges of juvenile and adult female, while males have dark underwings but show grey on upperwing.*

especially noticeable on spring birds. From below, the primaries appear almost normal whereas the secondaries are black and the body plumage is blackish brown. The rectrices are paler below, appearing greyish and glossy.

Adult males Upperparts dark ashy grey with blackish remiges and dark grey rectrices and uppertail coverts. Primary coverts dark silvery grey. Greater coverts and median coverts dark grey whereas lesser coverts, mantle and scapulars appear blackish. The division of the upperparts into differently shaded areas is visible under good conditions and follows that of normal males. Head blackish grey with slightly paler grey crown and nape. Underparts darkish grey, being palest on upper breast and darkening towards lower breast and belly. The underside of the tail is the palest part of the whole bird. Primaries and underwing coverts blackish, secondaries dark silvery grey.

Adult females General colour blackish brown. Resembles juveniles but are, on average, slightly paler with more of the normal pattern showing through. Crown and cheek-patch form the darkest parts of the head. On the upperparts the primaries and their coverts are paler greyish with visible darker barring and the typical dark bar across the secondaries can be seen. Tail dark brownish grey, paler than in juveniles and with more distinct darker barring. Underparts mainly blackish brown but the remiges appear nearly normal with clearly banded primaries on a yellowish-buff ground-colour. The diagnostic barring of the secondaries is also clearly visible.

Confusion species: Most likely to be confused with Hen and especially Pallid Harrier. Species identification easier if age (juvenile or adult) first determined. For identification of ring-tails pattern of underwing and head most useful. Experienced observers also find differences in flight and silhouette useful.

Pallid Harrier (page 196) Males are paler and more uniformly coloured and show a black wedge at the wing-tip.

Adult females show mostly dark secondaries to underwing contrasting with pale primaries, latter lacking dark trailing edge and with barring irregularly spaced and confined to median portion of feathers, leaving pale boomerang at base of primaries in many birds. Face darker with less white around the eye and larger dark cheek-patch extending on to lower mandible; narrow pale collar extending from nape to throat.

Juveniles show paler and barred fingers, ill-defined dark trailing edge to hand and often irregularly spaced barring of primaries, as in adult female. If primaries completely barred then barring bolder than in Montagu's. Secondaries often more distinctly barred than in juvenile Montagu's, with one pale bar close to trailing edge of wing being the commonest type. Head-pattern similar to adult female, but even more contrasting, with distinct pale collar from nape to throat between dark sides of neck and dark face, latter with small white spots above and below the eye and dark 'cheeks' reaching to the lores and the lower mandible.

Hen Harrier (page 183) Identified in all plumages by heavier flight, stiffer wing-beats and broader wings with more rounded tip (five fingers), but be aware of moulting birds in late summer–early autumn. Adult males lack the tri-coloured appearance above, as well as the barring to the secondaries. Ring-tails are always streaked on underbody, and the underwing coverts and remiges are more like Pallid Harrier, lacking adult female Montagu's chequered coverts and axillaries and pale underwing.

Marsh Harrier (page 167) Usually not possible to confuse with Montagu's, except for the dark morph, which may appear similar to dark morph Montagu's. Always identified by broader wing-tip (five fingers), heavier flight and more uniform remiges below, whereas dark Montagu's show a normal, although less conspicuous underwing pattern.

MOULT

Annually complete starting in the breeding areas but suspended for the autumn migration and completed in the winter quarters. Juveniles undergo a partial body moult in winter.

Juveniles (first moult) Start to moult their body plumage during winter, but the extent varies individually. By spring advanced birds may have replaced the whole plumage except for the remiges! The least moulted individuals only replace some feathers on upper breast, mantle and scapulars. The average bird returns in 2nd cy spring with upper breast, neck and head largely moulted, and often also mantle and scapulars as well as lesser and median upperwing coverts are partly moulted. Many birds also replace one or a few tail-feathers, normally starting with the central pair. On average, juvenile Montagu's Harriers moult more in winter than juvenile Pallid Harriers and appear in spring in a more advanced plumage. In extreme cases even the primary moult can start on the wintering grounds (2nd cy male, Israel, May, had replaced all of its body-feathers, all tail and even the innermost primary and its covert, retaining only the rest of its juvenile remiges).

The first complete moult starts with p1 earlier than in adults, in mid May–early Jun, and it also advances further before it is suspended for the autumn migration, showing six to nine moulted primaries by late Aug. The appearance of the body plumage depends mainly on the extent of the partial body moult in previous winter, varying accordingly. There is some evidence suggesting that 2nd cy birds summering in Africa replace their remiges faster than birds returning to the breeding grounds, although individual differences seem to be great.

Adults (subsequent moults) Adults commence their complete moult during breeding. Females start earlier than males, in late Jun–early Jul, but individual variation is considerable (one adult female had replaced p1–2 by 6 Jul, while another adult female had p1 fresh and p2–3 recently shed on 22 Jul, both ZMK). By late Aug four to six inner primaries are replaced, before moult is suspended.

Males start to moult their primaries in late Jun–early Aug, on average later than females (adult male with innermost primary replaced on 2 Jul; another with all remiges old on 2 Aug, both ZMK). By late Aug up to five (0–5) primaries are replaced before moult is suspended. Males thus replace, on average, fewer primaries than females before migrating.

For both males and females moult is resumed in the winter quarters, where it is finished during Nov–Feb (adult male growing p9–10 on 21 Oct, BMNH).

AGEING AND SEXING

Given good views juveniles and older birds are not difficult to separate. In autumn three age-classes can be separated for both sexes: juveniles, transitional and adult. Sometimes a fourth age-class, a first-adult plumage, can be separated from definite adult plumage. Pattern of primaries and secondaries on underwing as well as coloration of upperwing and body plumage are essential when ageing ring-tails. Grey males are best aged by retained immature characters in the remiges and head; type of streaking of underparts, pattern of underwing coverts and tail as well as general colour of upperparts serve as additional characters.

> **Ageing and sexing summary:** Juveniles appear unstreaked below with dark secondaries and the upperparts are dark, while adult females are streaked on underbody and the secondaries are distinctly barred below. Autumn juveniles can be sexed only by iris colour, but subsequent plumages differ between the sexes. In spring and early

summer, 2nd cy birds can, nevertheless, be difficult to age and sex because individuals vary in extent of body moult (see under Moult). Advanced 2nd cy females in spring can closely resemble females in first-adult plumage (3rd cy spring), while retarded birds still carrying their juvenile plumage can be impossible to sex. With age females become paler below and greyer above, whereas males become lighter, more silvery grey above and the streaking of the underbody becomes finer.

Juveniles have shorter wing- and tail-feathers than adults, and thus lack their extreme proportions, resembling more Pallid Harrier in silhouette. Also the flight of the juveniles appears steadier, hence resembling Pallid Harrier.

Juveniles (1st cy autumn – first winter/2nd cy spring)   Plates 240–247

Autumn juveniles are best told from older females by practically unstreaked, rich rusty or ochre underparts and, in most individuals, very dark secondaries below. Upperparts dark brown, with blackish secondaries darkest, and with rich ochre tips and fringes to upperwing coverts. Some variation occurs in the colour of the underparts and in the extent of the rusty markings on upperwing coverts.

The head-pattern of juvenile Montagu's Harriers is the same as in juveniles of other ring-tail harriers, with two main-types. Darker birds (deep copper brown underbody) have a quite uniformly coloured dark brown head, with small whitish markings above and below the eye and a cheek-patch slightly darker than the rest of the head. Paler juveniles (yellowish ochre underbody) have larger white areas around the eye and a prominent blackish cheek-patch contrasting strongly with the paler sides of the neck. The cheek-patch typically reaches only to the gape and leaves much of the face pale, which is evident in frontal views, although dark juveniles also tend to have a darker face. The paler collar crescent, which can often be seen between the dark cheeks and the streaked sides of the neck, typically has the shape of a half-moon tapering at both ends. The crown varies from dark to more ochre with darker streaking, and the sides of the neck are mostly ochre with diffuse darker streaking, although birds with darker necks occur.

Two types of primary-pattern of underwing occur. In the more common type the outer primaries have all-dark fingers and uniformly grey inner parts, while most of the barring is confined to the inner primaries. The barring is regular and rather fine. The rarer type shows completely and regularly but finely barred primaries, which may appear rather similar to the pattern of Pallid Harrier, but juvenile Montagu's show finer bars and a dark trailing edge to the hand lacking in Pallid.

The secondaries of most juveniles appear just 'dark' from below. Some birds show diffusely barred secondaries, but the barring is inconspicuous and can be seen only in good light and at close range. The barring varies considerably with no reliable difference from Pallid Harrier.

In fresh plumage many juvenile Montagu's appear almost copper brown on underbody, while others are paler and more yellowish ochre. The faint dark streaking along the sides of the breast and flanks seems to be a regular feature among juvenile Montagu's. The streaking, which varies individually, is difficult to see in most field situations, but is rather obvious in good light at close range. Some juveniles, but not all, also show axillaries with the typical 'chess-board'-pattern of the adult females.

Transitional plumage (2nd cy winter/spring – 2nd cy autumn)   **Plates 248–254, 266**
In winter the juveniles undergo a partial moult which varies immensely between individuals. The most retarded individuals may still be in nearly complete juvenile plumage in May, although extremely worn and faded, whereas advanced birds have moulted their body-feathers extensively and may hence recall adults, especially the females. Birds with retarded moult and lacking obvious plumage characters for sexing can be sexed only by iris colour: males bright yellow, females dark brown. Most birds, however, show newly moulted feathers especially around head and upper breast. The males acquire bluish grey feathers to upper breast and neck and the new feathers of the lower breast and belly are white with distinct rusty streaks. In females the uniformly straw-coloured feathers on the upper breast are replaced by pale ochre feathers with rufous brown streaks. The new feathers of the lower breast are similar in colour, but with finer streaking. If only a few feathers have been replaced on the upper breast the sex can be difficult to determine, as the first few feathers in many males still lack grey and are streaked as in females. At this stage most birds, regardless of sex, have moulted their axillaries, which are boldly barred and serve as a good character against Pallid Harrier. Many 2nd cy spring Montagu's have also replaced the central tail-feathers, which are about 2–3 cm longer than the juvenile feathers, and protrude from the tail-tip.

Normally 2nd cy birds retain most of their juvenile plumage with only head, upper breast, parts of mantle and scapulars partly or completely moulted. If the central tail-feather(s) are replaced they can be used for sexing: dark brown and barred in females and uniformly grey in males. The remaining juvenile upperparts are normally bleached and faded with the wing covert area palest and the secondaries darkest. The ochre patch of the upperwing of fresh autumn juveniles is often completely worn away. In most females the upper breast is moulted and streaked, whereas the vent is still juvenile and uniformly pale. Males are variably mottled bluish grey on the upper breast and sides of head and neck but juvenile-type head-markings normally show through. Many birds also show some fresh feathers on the lower breast and vent, which are then pure white with distinct rusty-red streaks.

Males The most advanced males may have moulted the body plumage completely. At first glance they recall adult males, but are always easy to age by the wing-pattern. The secondaries are dark from both above and below and contrast with paler primaries on underwing. First-summer males often show a surprisingly distinct and complete pale collar.

Females The most advanced females are difficult to separate from females in first-adult plumage as the plumage can be completely moulted except for the remiges! The juvenile secondaries are very dark from below (although they appear paler and more clearly barred than in fresh plumage) and are usually also much darker above than the rest of the wing. In females with replaced upperwing coverts the wing looks much as in adult, but the secondaries are uniformly dark above and contrast strongly with browner and more faded primaries. The shape of the bird is also different from adult female, with shorter and blunter wings and a shorter tail.

First-adult plumage (2nd cy late autumn – 3rd cy summer)   Plates 255, 260, 265
Probably not all birds of this age-group are possible to tell from older adults, but indviduals showing the following characters are separable.

Males Similar to adult males and have to be seen close up to note the differences. Upperparts, such as mantle and wing coverts, are unevenly coloured, often with a brownish tinge and mottled darker, while the general colour is a dusky grey, darker and less silvery than in adult males. Head shows traces of a pale collar and rather contrasting whitish patches around the eyes. Some brown and streaked feathers are left on the crown and around the whitish nape-patch. Tail-bars broad, distinct and chestnut red in colour. The rusty red streaks of the lower breast are broad and lanceolated, compared with the finer and more irregular streaking of older males, and the border between grey breast and white belly is sharp and runs across the upper breast, higher up than in older adults. Underwing coverts richly patterned with chestnut red bars, the individual marks being bigger and covering more of the white ground-colour than in old males.

Females Iris colour medium brown to amber. Head still rather dark and the pattern contrasting and resembling the juvenile's. Upperparts appear dark in flight, with dark secondaries, showing a faintly darker central band visible from certain angles. Primaries and central rectrices appear dark, brownish rather than grey above, with inconspicuous barring. From below, the secondaries are similar to adult female, although they often appear slightly darker than the primaries and the barring is less distinct than in older females. Underbody pale ochre with even rusty brown streaks over the whole breast.

Adult (3rd cy late autumn and older)   **Plates 256–259, 261–264, 267**
Males Tri-coloured above with bluish ashy-grey head, mantle, scapulars and lesser upperwing coverts, silvery grey tail, primary coverts and outer secondaries and their coverts,

and a largely black hand. The amount of black in the wing-tip varies individually and some males may have all the primaries dark, whereas others have the four innermost primaries grey with black bars. A black band across the secondaries can be seen on the upperwing in flight. The folded tail appears silvery grey from above, but when spread the barring of the outer rectrices is finer and shows more grey admixed compared with younger adults. Although some adult males show white patches around the eye most birds appear uniformly grey-headed.

Underparts strongly patterned. Head and breast bluish ashy-grey blending smoothly into the white belly on the lower breast, with faint and irregular rufous streaking on the rear underbody. Primaries black apart from the inner few, which are paler with or without dark bars. Secondaries pale grey with a diffuse darker trailing edge and two black bars further in, the innermost often partly hidden under the coverts. Underwing coverts white with bold rusty-red markings to the greater and median coverts and the axillaries. The pattern of the underwing coverts and axillaries is finer and more reduced than in first-adult plumage. Tail appears pale from below with only faint barring visible when folded.

Females Very bleached and greyish brown above and pale below, almost completely lacking any rich, warm tones. The head-pattern is diagnostic: the whole head and neck look rather pale and uniformly streaked with a distinctly darker and isolated cheek-patch and large white patches below and above the eye, while there is usually no paler collar to speak of. On the bleached upperparts the dark barring of the remiges and the greater coverts is distinct and the primaries are extensively greyish. Compared with younger females, the whole upperwing looks pale greyish brown, lacking the contrast between paler coverts and darker secondaries. Also, the central tail-feathers are greyer with distinct barring. The size and shape of the pale patch formed by partly paler median coverts varies both individually and as a result of wear and state of moult.

In flight from below, the bird appears uniformly coloured and patterned and the underwing-pattern especially is a good character in separation from Pallid females. The ground-colour of the wing is very pale, often clearly buffish in tone, with distinct blackish barring to primaries and secondaries. The ground-colour of the secondaries does not appear darker than that of the primaries, as it does in most female Pallids. The distinct black bars of the secondaries stand out well against the pale interspaces, which in turn continue unchanged in paleness and width to the body. The dark tips of the inner primaries in female Montagu's form a dark trailing edge to the hand and the primaries are regularly barred from base to tip. Underwing coverts evenly patterned with chestnut markings and blend in general paleness with the rest of the underwing. At close range the greater coverts and axillaries show the typical loose and bold 'chess-board' pattern, typical of adult Montagu's.

Sexing: Plumage differs significantly after partial body moult in first-winter, although birds with retarded moult may appear similar into 2nd cy summer. Sexing autumn juveniles possible only if colour of iris is seen: greyish in males at fledging but turning yellow in autumn, while females have a dark brown iris throughout first year.

References: Arroyo & King (in press); Christensen 1977; Cramp & Simmons 1980; Delin 1989; Forsman 1980, 1984, 1993d, 1995b, 1995c, 1995d; Lontkowski 1995; Svensson 1971

Plate 240 *Juvenile. The dark fingers and dark trailing edge to hand are typical of juvenile Montagu's. Note that primary barring is concentrated on inner hand, which is common among juveniles. Very dark secondaries and poorly marked head are further features of juvenile Montagu's. 4 Sep 1993, Kazakhstan (Markku Huhta-Koivisto).*

Plate 241 *Juvenile with more regularly barred primaries, but the barring is finer than in Pallid. Isolated ear-coverts patch typical. 14 Aug 1994, Finland (Dick Forsman)*

Plate 242 *Juvenile. Note typical primary- and head-pattern. Upper breast shows faint narrow streaking. Aug 1991, Portugal (Tom Lindroos).*

Plate 243 *Juvenile, with typically dark fingers and trailing edge to hand and faintly streaked breast-sides. 9 Sep 1992, UAE (Tapani Numminen).*

Plate 244 *Juvenile from above. Note lack of pale collar and scaly upperwing coverts. 17 Aug 1995, Finland (Dick Forsman).*

Plate 245 *Juvenile with prominent pale collar, but still showing typically extensive white area around the eye, pale lores and face and broadly pale throat. Dark auricular patch appears isolated and reaches only to gape. Note also faint streaks to breast-sides and flanks. 14 Sep 1996, Finland (Henry Lehto).*

Plate 246 *Juvenile. Birds with darker face normally lack pale collar altogether. Aug 1987, Germany (Axel Halley).*

Plate 247 *Juvenile female (by iris colour) in somewhat bleached juvenile plumage. Note extensive white around eye and small ear-coverts patch. 18 Feb 1987, Kenya (Veikko Salo).*

Plate 248 *Transitional male (2nd cy). Note the diagnostic pattern on the retained juvenile primaries as well as the typically patterned fresh belly and axillaries. Apr, Israel (Hadoram Shirihai).*

Plate 249 *Transitional male (2nd cy). Note the juvenile remiges with dark fingers and almost unbarred primaries often found in juvenile males. Body largely moulted including some wing coverts. Summer, Sweden (Jan Rittfeldt).*

Plate 250 *Transitional male (2nd cy) moulting to first-adult plumage. Note retained outermost four juvenile primaries while most of the secondaries are still juvenile. Aug 1992, Hungary (Tom Lindroos).*

Plate 251 *Transitional male (2nd cy) in nearly complete first-adult plumage. Like adult, but still retains juvenile p10 and several dark, juvenile secondaries. 7 Sep 1993, Kazakhstan (Dick Forsman).*

Plate 252 *Transitional (2nd cy) female showing retained juvenile wings but moulted body, axillaries and part of tail. These birds are easily misidentified as female Pallid Harriers but can be told by diagnostic pattern of axillaries and largely dark fingers. 17 Apr 1995, Spain (Dick Forsman).*

Plate 253 *Transitional (2nd cy) female with retained juvenile remiges while most of body-plumage moulted and hence resembling adult female. 24 Apr 1995, Spain (Dick Forsman).*

Plate 254 *Transitional female (2nd cy spring). At first glance similar to adult female, but brown iris and extremely worn and pointed primaries show it is a juvenile with an almost completely replaced body plumage. 5 May 1994, Oman (Hanne & Jens Eriksen).*

Plate 255 *Adult male. The rather extensive streaking on belly and underwing coverts and the sharply marked grey hood indicate a younger bird (possibly 3rd cy). Jun 1995, Germany (Axel Halley).*

Plate 256 *Adult male showing diagnostic underwing pattern. The sparsely marked belly and underwing coverts and extensively grey chest indicate an older bird. 17 Jul 1992, Sweden (Dick Forsman).*

Plate 257 *Adult male from above showing diagnostic tri-coloured upperwings with distinct black secondary-band. 24 Apr 1995, Spain (Dick Forsman).*

Plate 258 *Adult male. The dark wing coverts are worn adult-type feathers not yet moulted. The secondary-band is partly hidden behind the fluffed belly feathers. 23 Jan 1995, Oman (Hanne & Jens Eriksen).*

Plate 259 *A ringed adult male, known to be in its 8th cy, showing largely unmarked underwing coverts and underbody and pale silvery upperwings, diagnostic of old birds. May 1989, Sweden (Lars Jonsson).*

Plate 260 *Adult female. The dusky secondaries may indicate a younger bird, possibly in first-adult plumage. May, Sweden (Jens B. Bruun).*

Plate 261 *Adult female showing diagnostic coarsely marked axillaries as well as typically patterned remiges and head. May 1990, Sweden (Jan Rittfeldt).*

Plate 262 *Adult female. Note coarsely marked axillaries and underwing coverts and regularly barred primaries with dark trailing edge to hand and compare with adult female Pallid Harrier. May, Sweden (Jens B. Bruun).*

Plate 263 *Old adult female (yellow iris!) showing greyish upperwing with diagnostic black band across secondaries, not shown by females in first-adult plumage. May, Sweden (Jens B. Bruun).*

Plate 264 *Adult female. The brownish iris and the fairly dark secondaries indicate a younger bird. Note typical head-pattern as well as long wings in relation to tail and compare with female Pallid Harrier. May, Sweden (Jens B. Bruun).*

Plate 265 *Adult female. Probably in first-adult plumage moulting to definite adult plumage (3rd cy summer) owing to all-brown secondaries above and lack of grey tones to primaries and tail. 10 Aug 1991, Sweden (Dick Forsman).*

Plate 266 *Dark morph 2nd cy male moulting to first-adult plumage. Underwing shows moulted inner primaries of adult male-type, whereas the outer four and the secondaries are retained juvenile feathers. 18 Jul 1982, France (Arnoud van den Berg).*

Plate 267 *Dark morph adult female. Note that remiges are normally patterned from below. 10 Jul 1992, Poland (Jan Lontkowski).*

LEVANT SPARROWHAWK   *Accipiter brevipes*

Plates 268–283

Subspecies: Monotypic.

Distribution: Breeding range confined to W Palearctic. Breeds from the Balkans (north to former central Yugoslavia and Romania) eastwards, with majority in areas north of the Black Sea. Assumed to be rare in Turkey and areas between Black and Caspian Seas, but numbers probably underestimated (cf. Movements).

Habitat: Prefers fragmented broad-leaved forests at low altitudes, with a liking for river valleys. Occurs also in lowland areas with no forest, making use of isolated woods, riparian woodlands, hedgerows, etc.

Population: European population estimated to be between 3600 and 5800 pairs (Tucker & Heath 1995) with most breeding in Russia, Ukraine and Greece and generally regarded as stable. According to spring migration counts in Eilat, Israel (see Movements) the total population passing through would be no smaller than 20 000–25 000 pairs!

Movements: Migratory. Highly gregarious during migration, occurring in dense flocks of up to hundreds of birds. Migration highly synchronous, with narrow peaks both in autumn and spring. Highest numbers recorded along eastern flyway at Bosporus and Levant, concentrated in central Israel in autumn and at Gulf of Aqaba, Eilat in spring. Autumn movement starts mid-Aug, with marked peak during latter half of Sep and ceasing during first half of Oct; highest total 44 600 at Kfar Kasem, Israel in 1986. At Eilat usually in small numbers in autumn, but 25 522 counted there on 25 Sep 1994. Spring migration even more synchronous, with majority of birds passing Eilat in second half of Apr. Highest spring total 49 836 (1987) with 22 747 passing on 25 Apr. Wintering area presumed to be in central E Africa north of the Equator.

Hunting and prey: Hunts from low search-flight but also by using sit-and-wait technique; prey taken mostly by surprise. A skulking species, not much seen when hunting. Wide spectrum of prey includes smaller songbirds, small mammals, lizards and large insects; diet thus more varied than in Sparrowhawk.

SPECIES IDENTIFICATION

Length 29–37 cm

wing-span 63–76 cm (n =60; Israeli migrants; W.S. Clark, unpubl.)

Similar to Sparrowhawk but wing-formula diagnostic (beware of moulting Sparrowhawks in early autumn) as well as colour of wing-tip, colour of head, eyes, bill and cere.

> **Identification summary:** Resembles Sparrowhawk, but has contrasting dark wing-tip below (also above in adults), uniformly coloured sides of head, blackish bill with distinct yellow cere, and dark eyes. Wing-tip more pointed and wings proportionately slightly longer and tail shorter than Sparrowhawk's. Breast and flanks boldly patterned in juvenile.

In flight, distant Occurs on migration in massive flocks, swarming like insects when gaining height. After reaching migration altitude birds shoot out from the swarm, dashing off to form a loose raft. In favourable conditions long distances are covered like this by circling and gliding, whereas Sparrowhawks, which frequently mix with these flocks, always stick to their diagnostic flap-and-glide flight. Levant Sparrowhawks may also migrate by flapping and gliding, but the flight-path is straighter and the wing-beats are faster and shallower, more falcon-like. Normal powered flight, e.g. when searching for prey, very similar to Sparrowhawk.

Wings comparatively longer and tail shorter than sparrowhawk, shape thus more resembling juvenile Goshawk. Told from below, apart from shape in flight, even from a distance in all plumages by darker wing-tips than rest of underwing. Adults have pale underwings with black tips, paler males at times even confused with male Lesser Kestrel, especially when soaring. Juveniles show more patterned underwings with slightly darker fingers only, with dark tip obvious only from certain angles.

In flight, closer Only four distinct fingers (two less than in Sparrowhawk and Goshawk), which gives a more pointed and 'closed' wing-tip and showing a more linear leading edge to the hand and a more prominent angle at the carpal than Sparrowhawk. Eyes dark and the sides of the head uniformly dark contrasting with paler throat only. The black bill is heavier than in Sparrowhawk, and contrasts markedly with the swollen yellow cere, a useful field character. Adult males show barring only on the outermost primaries, whereas females show more barring and juveniles have completely barred remiges below.

Perched Generally like Sparrowhawk in shape, long-tailed and short-winged, with wings falling well short of tail-tip (reaching about half way), but head is comparatively bigger, with dark eyes and bill, latter contrasting markedly with swollen yellow cere. Cheeks uniformly darkish. Juveniles show a dark gular stripe and bold streaking on breast changing to broad bars on flanks. Adults have a pale throat (gular stripe on female) and fine rufous barring on breast.

Bare parts Bill black, cere and feet yellow at all ages. Iris appears dark from a distance, being dark brown in juveniles and in 2nd cy spring birds and dark red in older birds. Toes considerably shorter and stouter and tarsus much thicker than Sparrowhawk's.

Confusion species: Mostly confused with slightly smaller Sparrowhawk, gliding/soaring birds also with Goshawk when size difference not apparent. From a distance, underparts of adult males may appear confusingly similar to adult male Lesser Kestrel.

Sparrowhawk (page 245) Uniformly dark upperparts. The wing-tip is broader and rounder (six fingers) and appears uniformly pale from below. Lower cheeks always paler than ear coverts. Perched Sparrowhawks have mostly yellowish eyes (pupil discernible) and the bill is dark only at tip, hence lacks marked contrast between bill and cere.

Goshawk (page 256) Considerably bigger with more powerful flight and shows more rounded wing-tip (like Sparrowhawk). Eyes, bill and wing-tip as in Sparrowhawk (see above). Juveniles have generally paler heads, adults show prominent supercilium.

Lesser Kestrel (page 429) From below adult male distinguished by broad black subterminal tail-band. Upperparts largely rufous.

MOULT

The complete moult, including the flight-feathers, starts during breeding. Unlike Sparrowhawk, juveniles largely moult their body-feathers in winter.

Juveniles (first moult) Body plumage moult begins with upperparts (mantle, scapulars, etc) and head. The proportion of moulted feathers varies individually, but most birds appear nearly adult by spring migration. In advanced birds only remiges, the underwing coverts and most of the rectrices remain juvenile. The complete moult, involving remiges and rectrices, commences in early May and lasts until Sep. Some individuals retain a few juvenile feathers after the first moult (mostly median secondaries, sometimes even body-feathers of breast and underwing). In a 3rd cy male from 16 Jan the retained juvenile p9–10 and s4 and s7–9 were worn almost to the shaft (BMNH)!

Adults (subsequent moults) Adults undergo annually a complete moult during breeding, starting during first half of May. An adult female from 13 May had p1 missing; another adult female from 17 May had p1 growing and p2 missing, while an adult male from 21 May had dropped p1 (BMNH). Moult presumably completed by most before autumn migration in Sep, but material scanty. Some moult still while on passage: adult male 3 Oct growing last secondaries (Turkey, pers. obs.); adult female 10 Oct still growing outermost primary and last secondary (Riyadh/BMNH), while an adult male from 19 Oct had completed its moult and appeared in a fresh plumage (no loc./BMNH).

AGEING AND SEXING

Usually two separable age-classes, in autumn sometimes a third. Amount of barring on underwing remiges, pattern of breast and flanks and colour of upperparts are diagnostic.

> **Ageing and sexing summary:** With good views, juveniles and adults are easily separated. Juveniles are uniformly dark above and heavily streaked/spotted on breast and show distinctly barred underwings. The wing-tip is dark below only along the fingers of the leading edge. By 2nd cy spring immatures moult into a partly adult plumage and are more difficult to tell from adults in the field.
>
> Adults are grey above with darker outer hand, with more prominent contrast in males. Breast and underwing coverts are finely barred and the wing-tip is distinctly black. Distant birds are difficult to sex but males show whiter underwings with less barring.

Juvenile (1st cy autumn) Plates 268–269

Upperparts uniformly dark brown; when perched often showing white bases to scapulars. Underparts whitish with bold spotting/streaking on breast and also with rather coarsely patterned underwing coverts and completely barred remiges. Throat white with a dark gular stripe, which, in combination with the bold flank bars, are usually the first plumage characters to become apparent on an approaching bird. Head and bill dark with contrasting yellow cere. Iris dark brown. Sexing not possible by plumage, although males tend to show uniformly greyish fingers below, whereas females have barred fingers.

Transitional plumage (2nd cy spring – summer) Plates 270–274

By 2nd cy spring juveniles have moulted partially into adult plumage. Many birds appear adult-like on the underbody showing fine rufous barring on breast. On advanced individuals the few remaining streaked juvenile feathers can be difficult to note, whereas the majority show a mixture of streaked and barred feathers. The juvenile underwing, with narrowly dark leading edge of tip, distinctly barred remiges and boldly patterned underwing coverts, is a reliable ageing character. The upperwing remains in most rather dark and uniform, often contrasting with freshly moulted greyer mantle and scapulars. The birds can be sexed, like adults, by colour of new feathers of upperparts and underparts.

First-adult (2nd cy summer – 3rd cy spring)   Not depicted

Like adult but until first moult is completed birds can be aged by their coarsely spotted, juvenile underwing coverts, which are among the last feathers to be replaced. A small number of birds can be aged even after the moult by single retained juvenile feathers on e.g. breast. These feathers are retained until the following moult, in 3rd cy summer.

Adult male (2nd cy autumn and older; also see above)   Plates 275–279

Both in flight and when perched the dark wing-tips contrast sharply with the bluish grey upperparts and head. Gular stripe usually inconspicuous and grey. From a distance breast appears pinkish turning gradually white towards belly. At closer range fine gingery barring can be discerned, sometimes turning more uniform on upper breast. At a distance the underwing appears almost white with a black fringe around tip, but at close range fine rufous barring can be seen on the coverts as well as some reduced barring on the outer primaries.

Adult female (2nd cy autumn and older; also see above)   Plates 280–283

Duller and darker grey above than adult male, showing little or no contrast between upperparts and primary projection when perched. Dark gular stripe usually prominent. In flight outer hand slightly but clearly darker than rest of upperwing. Barring on breast and underwing coverts is a more distinct rufous brown, and the border between barred breast and paler belly is more sharply defined than in males. Females also have distinctly barred remiges, like juveniles, but show contrasting black wing-tips like adult males. From a distance the underwing looks duskier than adult male.

Sexing: Males are distinctly smaller than females, but size is of little use in the field without direct comparison. Juveniles cannot be sexed with certainty by plumage (although pattern of fingers below on average different) whereas adults can.

References: Anon. 1995a; Gensbøl 1995; Shirihai & Christie 1992; Tucker & Heath 1995

Plate 268 *Juvenile. Boldly streaked upper breast and prominent barring to flanks are diagnostic characters of autumn juveniles, as well as completely barred remiges. Note also darker cheeks and wing-tips compared with Sparrowhawk. Sep 1996, Israel (Klaus Bjerre).*

Plate 269 *Juvenile. Note diagnostic pattern of underbody and narrow wing-tip with only four fingered primaries. 27 Sep 1987, Israel (Dick Forsman).*

Plate 270 *Transitional male in 2nd cy spring. Underbody largely moulted, but retained breast-streaks, juvenile coarsely patterned underwing coverts and barred remiges differ from full adult. Reliably sexed by fine rufous barring on breast. The uniformly dark fingers are also strongly indicative of male. May 1995, Israel (Hadoram Shirihai).*

Plate 271 *Transitional female. Aged by juvenile underwing and retained streaks on breast. Sexed by darker and more distinct barring of breast than in male, while the barred fingers act as an additional indication, although some juvenile males also have barred fingers. May 1995, Israel (Hadoram Shirihai).*

Plate 272   *Transitional male showing diagnostic wing-formula with four clearly fingered primaries. Note also proportionately longer wings and shorter tail than in Sparrowhawk. Spring, Turkey (Lasse J. Laine).*

Plate 273   *Transitional male showing brownish upperwings and tail while the underbody is largely moulted. May 1990, Israel (Paul Doherty).*

Plate 274   *Transitional male. Note juvenile, brown wings contrasting with largely moulted grey mantle. Spring, Israel (Hadoram Shirihai).*

Plate 275   *Adult male. Fine rufous barring of breast and underwing coverts and largely unbarred remiges with black fingers are diagnostic. Spring, Israel (Hadoram Shirihai).*

Plate 276 *Adult male. More distant birds appear pale pinkish on breast while the underwings look pale with contrasting black wing-tips. 28 Sep 1992, Israel (Dick Forsman).*

Plate 277 *Adult male from above. Note pale grey upperwing with sharply contrasting black wing-tip. Apr 1987, Israel (Esa Sojamo).*

Plate 278 *Adult males have a bluish grey head and a finely barred rufous breast. Also note dark iris and bill and conspicuous cere and compare with Sparrowhawk. Spring, Israel (Hadoram Shirihai).*

Plate 279 *Adult male showing bluish grey upperparts with contrasting dark primaries. Spring, Israel (Hadoram Shirihai).*

Plate 280 *Adult female. The breast and underwings are more distinctly barred than in adult males and the remiges are barred. Spring, Israel (Hadoram Shirihai).*

Plate 281 *Adult females lack the pinkish blush below of adult males. Note pointed hand with dark fingers and compare with Sparrowhawk. May 1995, Israel (Hadoram Shirihai).*

Plate 282 *Adult female. May 1988, Israel (Hadoram Shirihai).*

Plate 283 *Adult female. Note dense and distinct barring of breast and darker upperparts and head compared with adult male. Dark cheeks, dark iris, dark bill and swollen yellow cere differ from Sparrowhawk. Apr 1995, Israel (Hadoram Shirihai).*

SPARROWHAWK *Accipiter nisus*

Plates 284–299

Subspecies: Polytypic, with nominate *A. n. nisus* in W Palearctic to W Siberia and *A. n. wolterstorffi* on Corsica and Sardinia. Extralimital *A. n. punicus* in NW Africa north of Sahara, *A. n. granti* on Canary Is. and Madeira, *A. n. nisosimilis* from C and E Siberia to Manchuria and Japan and isolated *A. n. melaschistos* in the mountains of C Asia and the Himalayas.

Distribution: Widely distributed over most of W Palearctic.

Habitat: Habitat preferences during breeding adapted to local conditions. Always nests in woods, primarily in dense and not too old stands. May choose either broad-leaved, mixed or coniferous woods and anything from dense thickets to old parks. Hunts mainly along woodland edges but also inside woods and in open country. Migrants found in all kinds of habitats.

Population: Suffered earlier from persecution. During 1950s and 1960s declined markedly over much of Europe owing to pesticide contamination. Has widely reached pre-crash population levels since and recent increase noted in many areas, e.g. in N Europe. Now one of the most common raptors in Europe (with Common Buzzard and Kestrel) with an estimated 300 000–400 000 pairs for W Palearctic.

Movements: Northern populations are migratory, southern are resident or dispersive. Northernmost populations start to leave breeding grounds in late Jul–early Aug and numbers build up during late Aug and early Sep, when a first peak is noted. After this, continued good passage through Sep and Oct, after which numbers start to decline. Migration ceases in Fennoscandia by mid-Nov. Juveniles migrate earlier than adults and juvenile females before juvenile males. In Aug and Sep most birds are juveniles, with adults appearing in late Sep and especially during Oct. Daily totals of around 1000 birds occur at Falsterbo, S Sweden from late Aug to early Oct. An autumn total of 19 881 was counted there in 1994, and in 1988 peak counts of 1895 and 1362 were registered on 1 and 2 Oct 1988, respectively. Migration peaks in S Europe in late Sep–Oct.

Winters mainly within Europe, from Fennoscandia and south, with northernmost winterers confined to towns and villages. Some enter Africa, both via Middle East and crossing the Strait of Gibraltar and the Sicilian Channel (500 at Bosporus and 1000 at Gibraltar, mainly juveniles in Sep–Oct). Winter visitors noted as far south as Equatorial E Africa.

Return movement starts from late Feb. Migrates through Eilat, S Israel from late Feb to mid May with peak between mid Apr and early May; 456 seen in spring 1983 with peak of 30 birds on 6 May. First migrants reach Nordic breeding grounds from late Mar, with majority arriving around mid-Apr.

Hunting and prey: Specialized on small songbirds, with finch-sized passerines forming bulk of prey. Females also hunt bigger prey, like thrushes and starlings, and are even capable of killing Jays, Woodcocks, Woodpigeons and Hazel Hens. During rodent peaks also takes e.g. bank voles (*Clethrionomys*).

Hunts mainly by sit-and-wait strategy, perching well hidden for a short while before moving to new perch. Also takes prey by surprise from low flight and stoops on ground-dwelling prey from considerable height.

SPECIES IDENTIFICATION

Length 28–37 cm

wing-span in males 58–65 cm, females 68–77 cm (*n*=46; Israeli migrants; W.S. Clark, unpubl.).

Often mistaken for other *Accipiters*, although typical wing-formula and flight as well as underwing pattern diagnostic.

> **Identification summary:** A small and short- but broad-winged and long-tailed raptor. Wing-tips rounded, especially when soaring, with hand and arm equally broad. Wing-beats are rather fast and flappy with flight path ascending when flapping and falling when gliding. Underparts uniformly and finely barred lacking any contrasting pattern, while upperparts appear uniformly dark. When perched appears small-headed with long tail, short wings and long, very thin legs and toes. Eyes mostly yellowish, bill bluish grey at base with black tip.

In flight, distant Small raptor with shortish, rounded wings and long square-cut tail and small head (cf. Goshawk). Active flight typical with series of flaps interspersed by short glides, the bird slightly rising when flapping and descending when gliding. Upperparts appear uniformly dark, underparts uniformly pale, only a slight darkening can be seen towards the wing-tips. When soaring, wings pressed slightly forward with hand appearing as broad as arm; tail always appears narrow at base, even when fanned. Glides on short, half-folded wings, with pointed tips but retaining diagnostic curved leading and trailing edge. Wings held distinctly arched in head-on view when gliding.

In flight, closer At closer range the barred underparts are diagnostic and the sparse and fine, yet distinct barring of the remiges retained through life (cf. Goshawk). The wing-tip is formed by six barred fingers, making it look broad and rounded when spread and with two outermost shorter primaries creating typically curved leading edge when wing folded. Tail shows three complete dark bands outside the undertail coverts. Head-pattern rather conspicuous with a pale supercilium in juveniles and adult females and the dark ear coverts form a dark eye-mask, more prominent and solid in adults. Eye is yellow. Upperparts appear uniformly coloured, dark brown in juveniles, more greyish in adults.

Perched A small raptor with comparatively small head, long tail and short wings, wing-tips reaching only half way down the tail. Legs and toes extremely long and slender, but tarsi often hidden in the belly-feathering. Upperparts of juveniles dark brown with rusty brown feather-tips and with some white bases showing on scapulars and tertials when plumage fluffed. Underparts whitish with dark rufous brown barring, which on upper breast especially is coarse and irregular. Adults are greyish above, males purer bluish grey, females duller brownish grey, and white below with fine and regular barring. Lower cheeks always paler than dark ear coverts mask (cf. Levant Sparrowhawk), streaked in juveniles, more uniform in adults. Juveniles and adult females have a prominent whitish supercilium, which some adult males may lack. Iris yellow (cf. Levant Sparrowhawk).

Bare parts Bill bluish grey with dark tip, cere greenish yellow and indistinct compared with large and swollen cere and all-black bill in Levant, a good field-mark even from a distance. Feet yellow, paler and greenish tinged in juveniles, deeper lemon to chrome yellow in adult. Iris yellow to orange, with small percentage of very old birds acquiring red eyes. Iris colour changes with age from pale lemon yellow in 1st cy autumn to a deeper yellow in both sexes at 1 year of age. At the age of 2 years some birds have already developed an orange iris. Most adult females remain yellow-eyed, although some acquire orange irides, whereas adult males mostly develop an orange iris, some even a reddish, while some remain yellow-eyed. The colour change is faster in males than in females. The great individual variation lessens the importance of the iris colour as an ageing character.

Confusion species: Most likely to be confused with other *Accipiters*, sometimes also with small falcons.

Goshawk (page 256) Heavier and steadier flight. Wings comparatively longer, tail shorter with a rounded tip and body stronger with a fuller belly and a longer neck. Adult Goshawks have a prominent head-pattern and paler underparts than Sparrowhawks, juveniles are streaked below and usually show more mottled upperwing coverts. Birds giving brief views and especially if only gliding pass on motionless wings remain difficult to identify.

Levant Sparrowhawk (page 235) The most similar confusion species. When soaring, Levant differs in having slightly longer wings and shorter tail, while the wing-tip is more pointed (four separable fingers only) and darker than rest of underwing. On migration, flapping flight of Levant shows typically shallow and more falcon-like wing-beats and the flight path is straight. Juvenile Levants are boldly streaked on breast with heavy barring on flanks/axillaries; adults are pale underneath with distinct black wing-tips. At close range the swollen cere, the prominent black bill and the dark eye of Levant are additional diagnostic characters.

Fig 41 *Sparrowhawk and Levant Sparrowhawk. Soaring Sparrowhawk (left) shows more rounded wings, with more curved lines, whereas Levant Sparrowhawk has more uniformly broad and straighter-lined wings with pointed tip. Note also longer tail of Sparrowhawk.*

Kestrel (page 443) and Merlin (page 495) May appear broad-winged like Sparrowhawks when soaring. Small falcons are always identified by narrower and straighter wings than Sparrowhawk, with a more pointed wing-tip (different wing-formula).

MOULT

Annually complete during breeding.

Juveniles (first moult) Juveniles may show single moulted feathers on mantle or scapulars by winter, probably lost by accident. The complete annual moult starts, as in adults, during laying or early incubation in females (start between 2 May and 12 Jun for all females), in males during hatching some 5–6 weeks later (start between 24 May and 13 Jul). The rapid change in appearance from juvenile to adult takes place during late Jun–Jul, when the body plumage is rapidly moulted. Some juvenile feathers, especially on rump, back and uppertail coverts are regularly (always?) retained. Single median secondaries may also be left unmoulted.

Adults (subsequent moults) As in juveniles, although adult females seem to commence moult slightly later than 2nd cy birds. Both parents may suspend their remex moult for the late nestling period, usually sometime between mid-Jun and mid-Aug, for up to 37 days and even longer, having replaced before this four to six inner primaries in females and two to four in males (Newton 1986). Moult is resumed after young fledge. Single body-feathers, sometimes also the odd rectrix or secondary, may be left unmoulted, whereas primaries tend to be replaced completely. The primary moult takes 110–130 days in females and 100–120 days in males and is usually completed by Sep–Oct: in British females between 23 Aug and 10 Oct and in males between 6 Sep and 2 Nov.

AGEING AND SEXING

Usually only two separable age-classes. Ageing Sparrowhawks in the field require good conditions so that the breast- and head-patterns can be reliably recorded. The colour of the upperparts is diagnostic in fresh plumage in autumn, but by spring juveniles appear more greyish. Sometimes a first-adult plumage is separable, but rarely in the field.

> **Ageing summary:** Juveniles, up to 2nd cy summer, are dark brown above and rather coarsely barred on upper breast, some, predominantly males, appearing almost spotted on upper breast. Adults are greyish above with finer and more regular barring below, rufous in males and greyish or rufous in females. Eye colour changes with age.

Juvenile (1st cy autumn – 2nd cy spring) **Plates 284–290**

Juveniles are readily aged by their dark brown upperparts, with rusty margins. The amount of rufous tinge above and below varies individually, but, on average, males tend to be more rufous than females. The neck shows at least some ochre streaking. The barring of the breast varies considerably, from rather narrow and regular dark bars, similar to adult female, to more irregular barring, changing to spots on the upper breast. Males tend to have a more irregular breast-pattern than females. The barring is broader in juveniles than in adults, and, at close range, the distal bars show rufous shaft-spots. Ageing birds in flight is more difficult, but at close range the irregular pattern of the upper breast is quite obvious. Also, the underwing coverts are more boldly barred in juveniles and cover more of the whitish ground-colour than the finer and more regular bars of the adults.

By spring juveniles appear greyish above, as most of the rusty fringes are worn, and are more difficult to tell from adult females in particular.

First-adult (2nd cy autumn – 3rd cy spring)   **Not depicted**
Like definite adult plumage but some may be aged after complete moult by brown unmoulted juvenile upperwing coverts contrasting with fresh grey feathers. Birds of this age normally retain some juvenile rump feathers and uppertail coverts, but these are rarely seen in the field. Many also have almost juvenile-like deep rusty edges and tips to their new lesser upperwing coverts, something that is replaced by narrow whitish tips in later plumages. This character may, however, be inconsistent, and it is not known whether all birds of this age shows this character.

Definite adult (2nd cy autumn and older)   **Plates 291–299**
Adults are greyer above than juveniles, but birds may be difficult to separate by this char-acter, especially in spring. Hindneck uniformly dark in adults, but streaked in juveniles. As a rule, adults have slightly darker primaries above than the rest of the upperwing, whereas the opposite is the case in juveniles. Underparts of adults are finer and more reg-ularly barred, with a marked difference especially in the pattern of upper breast and under-wing coverts. Juveniles and adults are often separable even from a distance: adults appear nearly white below, the barring of the underparts is discernible only at close range, and the contrast between upperparts and underparts is distinct, whereas juveniles appear more dusky below with coarser barring and therefore the contrast between upperparts and under-parts is less pronounced.

Adult males Usually easy to tell from juveniles by their colourful plumage. Upperparts bluish grey and underparts whitish with individually variable rufous barring. Some birds are evenly barred, whereas others are more or less uniformly rufous on throat, cheeks and flanks. The white supercilium, normally prominent in juveniles and adult females, is incon-spicuous or absent.

Adult females Duller brownish grey above, but may appear pure grey in the field. The barring on the breast is normally greyer than in males, with rufous confined to throat, cheeks and ear coverts. Some females, however, show rufous barring to the entire breast thus appearing rather similar to males, but usually differing by more prominent white supercilium and nape-patch and bigger size.

Sexing: Although the size difference between the sexes is considerable, it is often not pos-sible to sex single birds in flight without direct comparison with the other sex. Experience helps in assessing the slight differences there are in proportions and flight between the sexes. For plumage differences see above.

References: Forsman 1980, 1984; Gensbøl 1995; Kjellén 1995; Newton 1986; Newton & Marquiss 1982a,b; Newton et al. 1981; Opdam & Müskens 1976

Plate 284 *Juvenile (female?) showing typical silhouette with rather broad and blunt wings, with smoothly curved wing-profile and long and narrow tail. Irregular upper breast-pattern separates from adult female. Autumn, Sweden (Jens B. Bruun).*

Plate 285 *Juvenile (male?). Note small, rounded head and slim body compared with Goshawk. The upper breast is typically irregularly barred in juveniles and the underwing coverts are more coarsely barred. Aug, Sweden (John Larsen).*

Plate 286 *Juvenile (female?). A finely barred individual resembling an adult female, but identifiable by prominent supercilium, irregularly barred upper breast and streaked cheeks and crown. Note that the fingers are no darker than the rest of the underwing (cf. Levant Sparrowhawk). Aug, Sweden (John Larsen).*

Plate 287 *Juvenile (female?) showing diagnostic rufous hindneck and brown upperparts with rufous feather-tips. Aug, Sweden (John Larsen).*

Plate 288   *Juvenile from above showing brown upperparts and pale-streaked neck. Oct 1988, Sweden (Jens B. Bruun).*

Plate 289   *Juvenile female showing rufous spots to upperbreast and rufous fringes above. Note short wings, thin legs and yellow eyes. 4 Sep 1997, Finland (Dick Forsman).*

Plate 290   *Juvenile male with even more rufous and spotted underparts. Apr, Denmark (John Larsen).*

Plate 291   *Adult male (left) and adult female showing size difference between sexes, but also how close in plumage the two can get. Note the duller upperparts of the female, her distinct supercilium and her less rufous cheeks compared with the male. Apr, Denmark (John Larsen).*

Plate 292   *Adult male. Uniformly dark crown and ear coverts contrast with bright orange lower cheeks. This bird shows less orange below than average. Oct 1988, Sweden (Jens B. Bruun).*

Plate 293   *Adult male. Note vividly rufous lower cheeks and sides of breast. Oct, Finland (Markus Varesvuo).*

Plate 294   *Adult male. Uniformly deep rufous lower cheeks and sides of breast are typical of adult males. Feb 1992, Sweden (Lars Jonsson).*

Plate 295   *Adult female. Note the regularly barred breast of this moulting bird. Autumn, Sweden (Jens B. Bruun).*

Plate 296 *Adult female. Fine and regular barring to body and underwing coverts and a rufous wash to the lower cheeks characterize adult females. Sep, Finland (Markus Varesvuo).*

Plate 297 *Adult female. Note uniformly dark ear coverts and finely streaked rufous lower cheeks as well as fine barring to underbody. The deep orange iris indicates an older bird. Nov 1995, Sweden (Jens B. Bruun).*

Plate 298 *Adult female. Females are normally duller grey above than males while the rufous is restricted to the lower cheeks. Mar, Sweden (Lars Jonsson).*

Plate 299 *Adult female on the nest showing typical head-pattern and barring on breast. 21 Jun 1981, Finland (Dick Forsman).*

GOSHAWK *Accipiter gentilis*

Plates 300–315

Subspecies: Three subspecies in Europe. Nominate *gentilis* over most of region, larger and paler *buteoides* in far NE, and smaller and darker *arrigonii* in Corsica and Sardinia. N American *atricapillus* occurring as a rare vagrant to W Europe.

Distribution: Holarctic, from W Europe in a wide zone across Asia and N America. Occurs all over Europe, but population unevenly distributed.

Habitat: Originally confined to mature forests, but also nests in smaller woods and younger stands. Usually found close to woodlands but also hunts in the open, especially outside the breeding season.

Population: Population of W Palearctic estimated at 140 000–170 000 pairs, with bulk nesting in Russia, Fennoscandia, Germany and E Europe. Locally populations mirror degree of century-long persecution and availability of suitable habitat. Generally scarce in W Europe and more common in E and N, but with recent increase locally in W Europe. Reintroduced to Britain, where still rare.

Movements: Sedentary over large parts of Europe. In northern populations juveniles are partly migratory, whereas adults remain close to their territories if the food supply permits. In northern populations autumn dispersal of juveniles starts in Aug and peaks in S Finland during late Sep–first half of Oct, in adults somewhat later. At Falsterbo, S Sweden numbers low (only some tens per autumn, mainly juveniles), with peak in late Oct–early Nov. The spring migration is hardly noticeable and takes place in Mar–Apr.

Hunting and prey: Hunts mostly using sit-and-wait technique perched well hidden in a tree. Prey taken by surprise after short attack, as in Sparrowhawk, often from ambush. Also soars at moderate heights and capable of impressive stoops. Most prey taken on ground, birds also when flushed. Preys mostly on medium-sized birds such as corvids, pigeons, ducks and grouse, but during breeding also feeds on fledglings of smaller birds. Mammal prey includes rabbits, hares, squirrels, etc.

SPECIES IDENTIFICATION

Length 54–67 cm (v. Haartman et al. 1965)

wing-span 98–120 cm (*n*=40; D. Forsman et al., unpubl.)

Despite different silhouette and more powerful flight often confused with Sparrowhawk, especially in brief views. In closer views differs by pattern of head and breast as well as by barring of tail and wings.

Identification summary: Told from other medium-sized raptors by characteristic silhouette, with comparatively short, broad and rounded wings, and a long and rounded tail, and by typical *Accipiter*-flight, with series of powerful wing-beats interrupted by short glides. Wings generally appear pale and unpatterned underneath. From a distance told from other Accipiters by comparatively longer neck and wings, with clearly narrower hand than arm, shorter tail with rounded tip and more powerful wing-action. In closer views identified by evenly streaked underparts in juvenile and by diagnostic head-pattern and faintly barred underwings in adults.

In flight, distant When soaring, the silhouette resembles a cross with longer neck (*c.* one third to a quarter of width of wings), longer wings and shorter tail than T-shaped Sparrowhawk. Juveniles and adults differ in silhouette: juveniles slimmer with narrower wings and longer tail (tail length approximately same as wing width in adult, distinctly longer in juvenile). Powered flight steadier than Sparrowhawk's, with series of powerful, slower and stiff-looking wing-beats interspersed by short glides, and flight-path straighter. Goshawks soar on almost flattish, slightly arched wings. Corvids react very differently towards Sparrowhawks and Goshawks: Sparrowhawks are often chased and mobbed in flight, whereas at the appearance of a Goshawk the birds flee in panic and climb as high as possible.

In flight, closer At closer range told by typical silhouette: fairly short and broad wings, with broader arm than hand, more marked in juveniles, and broad and rounded wing-tip with six fingers. Underwing lacks striking patterns and appears rather pale and uniform.

Fig 42 *Goshawk. Glides on gently arched wings. Body appears large in relation to shortish wings.*

Tail fairly long with three or four broad dark bands and a rounded tip. In profile shows powerful head, with heavier bill and a longer neck, and the body appears stronger with a fuller chest and vent, latter continuing well under the tail.

Adults appear almost whitish below with finely barred body and underwing coverts and washed-out barring on remiges (more prominent on fingered primaries). Head-markings prominent with broad white supercilium sandwiched between dark crown and eye-mask. Upperparts appear uniformly dark grey or brownish grey. More distinctly barred on chest and underwings in first-adult plumage.

Juveniles show uniform dark streaking to pale, often ochre-tinged breast. Underwing coverts streaked or spotted and remiges finely barred, making the whole underwing appear rather pale and featureless. Upperparts less uniform and also somewhat paler brown than in either Sparrowhawk or Levant Sparrowhawk, often with distinct buffish markings to coverts and scapulars.

Perched Goshawks usually sit upright and mostly well hidden in a tree. The long tail shows three or four broad dark bands and the short wings reach only halfway down the tail, excluding most other raptors of similar size (cf. Gyrfalcon). Eyes yellow or orange with a fierce look. Juveniles are uniformly streaked on the underparts and the facial pattern is rather bland but a darker cap and a pale supercilium stand out. Neck ochre with dark streaking. Upperparts brownish with buffish tips and margins, often also with paler pattern on inner upperwing coverts, tertials and scapulars. Adults have a prominent head-pattern, with dark cap and ear coverts and a prominent white supercilium. Underparts finely barred; upperparts uniformly greyish.

Bare parts Bill bluish grey at base with dark tip. Feet and cere yellow, deeper in adults. Eyes greenish yellow on recently fledged juveniles, turning bright yellow during first autumn. Adults have either yellow, orange or orange-red irides, with colour deepening with age and being, on average, darker in males than in females of same age.

Variation: Variation clinal with size increasing from south to north and plumage becoming paler and more finely patterned underneath from west to east. Nominate *A. g. gentilis* over most of Europe with smaller and darker *A. g. arrigonii* in Corsica and Sardinia. In NE Europe *A. g. buteoides* is larger and, on average, paler above and more finely patterned below than *gentilis*. Juveniles show variably pale barring on lower scapulars, upperwing coverts, remiges and rectrices, but similar individuals also found occasionally among *gentilis* further south. Adult *buteoides* are paler above than *gentilis*, with diagnostic barring on hindneck and mantle in some, and more finely barred underparts, sometimes with reduced barring. Only the most typical individuals can be subspecifically identified, since intermediates are not rare in the Fennoscandian population. Extralimital *A. g. atricapillus* of N America recorded in Ireland and Britain as a vagrant. Juveniles are similar to *gentilis* but adults show a contrasting black-and-white head-pattern and the barring of the underparts is finer, forming a greyish vermiculation with distinct black shaft-streaks.

Confusion species: Mostly confused with other *Accipiters* because of generally similar silhouette and flight (see also above), sometimes also with Gyrfalcon or female Hen Harrier. Given good views always told from other medium-sized raptors by combination of silhouette, underwing pattern, flight and behaviour.

Sparrowhawk (page 245) Considerably smaller and slimmer (broadest around upper breast) with a faster and more erratic flight. Wings comparatively broader and shorter, tail comparatively longer with sharp corners. Head and bill comparatively smaller. Sparrowhawks are barred below in all plumages, thus excluding juvenile Goshawk. Told from adult Goshawk by less striking head-pattern, distinctly barred remiges below (note, however, more prominent barring in first-adult plumage of Goshawk) and rufous tinge to throat and upper breast in most.

Levant Sparrowhawk (page 235) Always identified by dark face, dark eyes and dark bill, and in flight by dark wing-tips below. Adults are barred rufous or rufous-brown on breast; juveniles show bold dark streaks or spots on white breast changing to broad barring on flanks/axillaries.

Gyrfalcon (page 542) Very different flight, covering long distances on shallow and flexible wing-beats with occasional short glides. Wings more angular, with a straight trailing edge and a pointed tip. Wings and tail more densely barred. Head with more or less pronounced dark eye-line and moustache, and pale supercilium. Iris dark.

Hen Harrier (page 183) Female can at first glance appear to have similar underbody and tail to juvenile Goshawk, but is always identified by very prominent underwing pattern, with boldly barred primaries and secondaries and distinctly paler sides of tail with striking dark bands. The low searching flight and the habit of soaring on lifted wings are also diagnostic.

MOULT

Annually complete, but some median secondaries are frequently retained until next moult.

Juveniles (first moult) Some body feathers may be moulted occasionally (accidentally?) during the first autumn, but primary moult starts in early May of 2nd cy, in breeding females earlier, corresponding to laying dates. The moult is completed during Aug–Sep, but occasionally some median secondaries are left unmoulted.

Adults (subsequent moults) Females begin to replace their primaries during laying or early incubation, and the innermost four or five primaries are shed in a rapid sequence. Males begin their primary moult 2–3 weeks later. Nesting birds seem to suspend the moult of the flight-feathers for the late nestling period, as shown for Sparrowhawk, until after the young are fledged. The moult is finished during Sep, but some median secondaries are sometimes left unmoulted (reflecting food shortage?) and replaced the following year.

AGEING AND SEXING

Ageing juveniles and adults is usually straightforward and based on plumage characters of, especially, the head, breast, underwing and upperparts. Separating first and definite adult is more difficult and focus should be on head-pattern and type of barring of upper breast and underwings, but also on details of hindneck.

Ageing summary: Juveniles are easily told by their streaked underparts and brown upperparts. Adults have a distinct head-pattern, a fine and regularly barred breast and a rather diffuse wing-barring. First-adult plumage told from definite adult by coarse and irregular barring on the upper breast, less distinct head-pattern and more distinctly barred remiges below. From a distance juveniles mostly appear yellowish buff underneath, whereas adults always appear whitish or greyish white. Juveniles also show different silhouette in flight from adults, with narrower hand, more bulging trailing edge to wing and comparatively longer tail.

Juveniles (1st cy – 2nd cy spring)   **Plates 300–307**

Juveniles show regular and even brown streaking on breast, often on a slightly yellowish-buff ground-colour. Lacks prominent head-pattern, but shows a paler supercilium between darker crown and streaked ear coverts. Upperparts brown with buffish tips and variably pale buffish markings on inner median and greater coverts and tertials. Remiges rather distinctly but narrowly barred underneath and the bold tail barring is best seen when the tail is fanned.

Iris of newly fledged Goshawks is pale greenish yellow but changes to bright yellow by early autumn.

Some variation occurs in darkness and amount of mottling of upperparts (pale mottling increasing from south to north), as well as in coloration of underparts: some birds are whiter underneath, others are deeper tawny, while the streaking varies from narrow lanceolated streaks to more drop-shaped spots.

First-adult (2nd cy autumn – 3rd cy spring)   **Plates 308–309**

Similar to adult but upperparts brownish grey, often with fine whitish tips to upperwing coverts and scapulars. Dark bars of uppertail still complete and conspicuous. Head-pattern less striking than definite adult, with some retained juvenile characters: streaked ear coverts and crown and partly streaked nape and hindneck make pale supercilium less conspicuous. Underparts rather coarsely barred with barring on upper breast more irregular and pointed (V-shaped) than on full adults. Remiges still show prominent barring below differing from older adults. Often retains some brown and worn juvenile secondaries or upperwing coverts until next moult.

Definite adult (3rd cy autumn and older)   **Plates 310–315**

Upperparts appear uniformly grey with uniformly dark crown and ear coverts and a distinct white supercilium. Dark bands on central tail-feathers often restricted to washed-out spots around the feather shaft. Underparts show fine barring with a regular and uniform pattern and, from a distance, the whole underparts appear pale and uniform. Barring of the underwing often diffuse and inconspicuous, even partly washed-out, with more prominent barring retained on outer hand only.

Adults have deep yellow to yellowish orange irides, which may turn orange or reddish with age.

Sexing: Sexes are similar in juvenile plumage. Adult males are more bluish grey above compared with the more brownish grey females and they also show a more distinct head-pattern. The barring of the underparts is finer in males than in females of the same age.

The size difference between males and females is obvious when the sexes are seen together, but sexing single birds on size in the field often proves difficult.

References: Bond & Stabler 1941; Bährmann 1941; Fischer 1983; Forsman 1980, 1984, 1993b; Gensbøl 1995; v. Haartman et al. 1965; Voipio 1946

Plate 300 *Juvenile (male?). Breast and underwing coverts show distinct spotting while the remiges and tail are distinctly barred. Autumn, Sweden (Jens B. Bruun).*

Plate 301 *Juvenile (female) with more ochre-toned and streaked underparts. Note broad wing-tip and uniform barring of remiges. 11 Oct 1990, Finland (Dick Forsman).*

Plate 302 *Juvenile of the white-breasted and more spotted type. Dec, Finland (Markku Huhta-Koivisto).*

Plate 303 *Juvenile (2nd cy) moulting to first-adult. Plumage still mostly juvenile, but inner five primaries are replaced. 27 Jun 1991, Finland (Dick Forsman).*

Plate 304   *Juvenile in fresh plumage. The short wings in relation to the long tail are typical of the species. Birds from C and S Europe are browner and less variegated above. Sep, Finland (Mikko Pöllänen).*

Plate 305   *Juvenile. Note short wings and typical head- and breast-pattern. Dec, Finland (Tapani Räsänen).*

Plate 306   *Juvenile (2nd cy) of ssp. buteoides. Note very pale head and pale overall impression. Apr 1995, Finland (Mikko Pöllänen).*

Plate 307   *Juvenile of ssp. buteoides (same as Plate 306). Note extensive pale markings to all upperparts. Apr 1995, Finland (Mikko Pöllänen).*

Plate 308 *First-adult plumage (3rd cy). Note rather indistinct head-pattern, much as in juvenile, and rather coarse barring of upper breast, with bars shaped like arrowheads. Apr, Finland (Tapani Räsänen).*

Plate 309 *First-adult plumage showing some retained juvenile lesser upperwing coverts and two juvenile secondaries. Head-pattern diagnostic. Apr, Finland (Tapani Räsänen).*

Plate 310 *Adult in moult. Note broader tail and longer wings than Sparrowhawk and distinctly narrower hand than arm. 10 Jun 1991, Finland (Dick Forsman).*

Plate 311 *Adult. Note finely barred underbody, distinct head-pattern and diffusely barred remiges. 7 Jul 1991, Finland (Dick Forsman).*

Plate 312   *Adult male. Finely barred underbody and wing and poorly marked remiges are diagnostic. The distinct head-pattern is typical of male. Dec, Finland (Tapani Räsänen).*

Plate 313   *Adult male with typically distinct head-markings. The barring below is finer and denser than in first-adults. Mar 1996, Finland (Pekka Helo).*

Plate 314   *Adult female. Females are usually browner above than males and the head-markings are less distinct. Feb, Finland (Tapani Räsänen).*

Plate 315   *Adult female. The fine barring below, the reduced dark head-markings and the red iris indicate a greater age (or perhaps buteoides influence). Mar 1990, Finland (Pekka Kokko).*

COMMON BUZZARD *Buteo buteo buteo*

Plates 316–329

Subspecies: Four subspecies in Europe, nominate *buteo* in W and C Europe and slightly smaller *vulpinus* in the east, from N Sweden and Finland, down to E Greece and eastwards (see page 277 for full treatment); *B. b. arrigonii* in Corsica and Sardinia and *menetriesii* in Crimea and the Caucasus. Birds in the zone of overlap between *buteo* and *vulpinus* (e.g. in Finland) and showing intermediate characters were formerly recognized as ssp. *intermedius,* no longer considered valid.

Distribution: Occurs over most of Europe and is the continent's most numerous bird of prey.

Habitat: Prefers a mosaic of woods and open areas such as pastures and meadows.

Population: Now considered fairly stable in Europe, with populations largely recovered since the 1950s thanks to pesticide bans and local protection measures. Total European breeding population estimated at *c.* 500 000 pairs.

Movements: Mainly resident and dispersive, but northern populations are migratory. Birds from N Europe winter in C and W Europe and Swedish birds enter NW Africa. Autumn migration begins at Falsterbo S Sweden in late Aug and peaks in late Sep–early Oct to level off during early Nov; 36 000 counted here in autumn 1950 and 17 200 in 1974 with 31 300 at Stigsnaes on the Danish side of the Strait, with passage numbers showing a declining long-term trend. Proportion of juveniles has varied between 31 and 51%. In 1972 and 1974 2700 and 2800, respectively, crossed the Strait of Gibraltar to Africa. In spring, returns to northern part of range from early Mar to mid-May, with breeding birds peaking in late Mar–early Apr; immatures return later.

Hunting and prey: Hunts either from perch or from the air, where it hangs against the wind and scans the ground. Also walks around looking for smaller ground prey. Feeds mainly on small or medium-sized mammals, depending on local supply. Rabbits form the staple food where common, otherwise voles and mice form the basic diet. Also takes all sorts of birds, often injured individuals and fledglings, and preys on snakes, lizards, frogs and larger insects. Feeds on carrion, especially in winter.

SPECIES IDENTIFICATION

Length 51–57 cm

wing-span 113–128 cm (Cramp & Simmons 1980), wing-span *c*. 112–130 cm (Haftorn 1971)

Extensive plumage variation complicates identification. Pattern of remiges and rectrices as well as wing-action during powered flight and wing-posture when gliding and soaring are the most reliable characters when separating from confusion species such as Honey Buzzard.

Identification summary: A fairly compact, long- and broad-winged and rather short-tailed raptor which is often seen soaring on slightly lifted wings. Upperparts generally dark brown, but largely pale and partly white individuals are locally rather common in W and NW Europe. Remiges below rather finely and evenly barred with prominent dark tips forming dark lining to wing-tip and trailing edge. Regardless of plumage type and age most individuals show a dark shield on the upper breast, bordered by a pale breast-band, dark flanks and a pale belly; darkish lesser underwing coverts, forming dark triangle to patagium; and pale median underwing coverts. For pale individuals see Variation.

In flight, distant Powered flight on rather shallow, stiff and fast wing-beats which are regularly interspersed with glides on flattish but kinked wings. Wing-action shallower, faster and stiffer than e.g. in Honey and Rough-legged Buzzards. Soars on slightly lifted wings often with clear kink at elbow in head-on profile (cf. Honey Buzzard) and with more clearly splayed 'fingers' than in Honey Buzzard; body comparatively larger in relation to wing-span than in latter. Display flight with stoops and loops in descending and undulating flight-path; intruders greeted with owl-like flight on high and slow wing-beats.

Upperparts generally brown, often with slightly paler patch on primary-bases and inner tail but lacking distinct white markings. Adults and juveniles differ (see Ageing and sexing). From below, identified by dark upper breast, pale breast-band, pale belly and darker flanks/thighs. Underwing shows rather pale remiges with dark tips and typically patterned underwing coverts with darkish lesser and pale median coverts.

In flight, closer Most reliably told from similar species by barring of flight-feathers: remiges are rather finely and evenly barred underneath, with darker tips. Tail also shows rather fine and dense barring above, sometimes becoming paler with suffused markings towards the base. Underwing coverts show a typical pattern with darkish

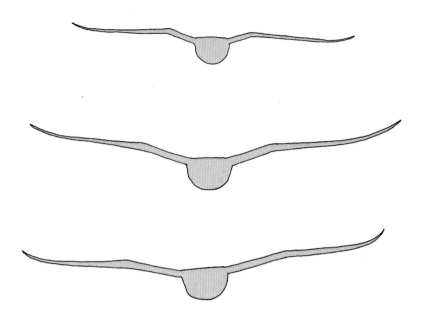

Fig 43 *Common or Steppe Buzzard (upper) and two Long-legged Buzzards gliding, showing different proportions. Note comparatively longer wings and smaller body of Long-legged, with wings held in higher V with more marked kink between inner and outer wing.*

lesser, paler median and again more patterned greater coverts, leaving a broad pale wing-bar across the central covert area. The dark carpal-patch is often irregular or consists of two dark crescents, rarely being all-dark and solid. Vent and undertail coverts are pale.

Perched A broad and compact bird of prey with wing-tips reaching close to tail-tip. Mostly identified by typical 'segmentation' of underbody, with darker upper breast, pale breast-band, paler belly and darker flanks, and with pale tracts either streaked, spotted or barred. Tail is dark above, often slightly paler towards base, with dense and fine barring.

Bare parts Feet and cere yellow at all ages, deeper in adults than in juveniles; bill dark. Iris pale grey, brownish grey or light brown in juvenile, with black pupil clearly visible. Adults show a very dark brown iris and the pupil is not discernible in the field. First-adults (2nd cy autumn – 3rd cy spring) show, like other *Buteo*s, an intermediate, often bi-coloured iris, with a darker base and lighter top.

Variation: Although the Common Buzzard is a highly variable species the plumage variation is mainly confined to the body, whereas the remiges remain rather constant. The darkest birds (practically always adults) are nearly uniformly dark brown on breast and belly, with just a hint of a paler breast-band. The palest birds are nearly all white with just a darker carpal comma (greater primary coverts) and some dark spots to flanks and sides of breast. Less extreme pale individuals usually show hints of darker bib of upper breast, darker thighs and flanks and a dark malar stripe. Upperparts vary less but the amount of white in the upperwing coverts varies from none to nearly all white, except for the greater coverts which tend to remain dark. The tail of pale birds also varies from normal to largely white, but most show a whitish base and a normal outer half with the white entering as spikes into the brown. From below, many pale Common Buzzards appear to show rather darkish secondaries, which may cause confusion with both pale Booted Eagle and pale juvenile Honey Buzzard. For identification of Steppe Buzzard see page 278.

Confusion species: Mostly confused with other largely dark and medium-sized raptors, sometimes even with eagles.

Honey Buzzard (page 30) The most likely confusion risk but flies with slower and higher wing-beats (more like Booted Eagle or Egyptian Vulture); glides and soars on flat wings lacking angled kink at elbow in head-on views. Adults further identified by diagnostic barring of underwings and tail; juveniles by darkish secondaries and broadly black-tipped and coarsely barred remiges below, pale greater underwing coverts and relatively uniformly coloured body below.

Rough-legged Buzzard (page 303) Told by white inner tail with distinct and broad dark subterminal band, best seen from above. Flight is slower and more powerful than in Common Buzzard and the wings show a more pronounced kink at the elbow in head-on views.

MOULT

Complete annually, but some remiges are frequently left unmoulted, more regularly so in the first moult.

Juveniles (first moult) Primaries moulted from 2nd cy Apr–May to Sep apart from the outermost few, which are left unmoulted. Duration of primary moult 158 days in captive male. Some of the juvenile secondaries are often retained. These are often replaced first during the next moult.

Adults (subsequent moults) Remiges moulted between Apr/May–Sep/Nov. Females begin to moult during incubation, males usually weeks later. Primaries moulted serially descendant, with active moult taking place simultaneously at two centres and hence primaries are mostly replaced in one season.

AGEING AND SEXING

Normally two age-classes, juveniles and adults, easily separated, whereas recognition of first-adults requires favourable conditions and close views. Separating adults and juveniles usually straightforward, but some juveniles may show a rather adult-like distinct black trailing edge to the underwing. In some juveniles the pattern of the underbody may resemble that of the adults.

> **Ageing summary:** Juveniles have a slimmer silhouette with longer tail and narrower wings, paler wing coverts above than secondaries, streaked underparts, a rather diffuse trailing edge to the underwing, rather pale iris and a narrow subterminal tailband. Adults are more uniformly brown above with a dark trailing edge to the wing, the underparts are barred, the trailing edge to the underwing is broad and distinct, the iris is dark and the subterminal tail-band is broad. Pale birds sometimes almost completely lack darker markings below; the iris colour and the tail-barring, as well as the trailing edge of the underwing, remain reliable ageing characters.

Juvenile (1st cy – 2nd cy spring) Plates 316–322

Perched juveniles show a pale iris with a distinctly darker pupil, the underparts are regularly streaked and the upperwing coverts are neatly fringed buffish, rufous or whitish.

 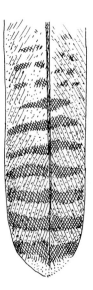

Fig 44 *Common Buzzard. Central tail-feathers from above showing differences in barring between adult (left) and juvenile. Note broad and dark subterminal band of adult while all bands are narrow in juvenile.*

Flying juveniles usually show rather dark secondaries above, whereas the upperwing coverts stand out as a distinctly paler tract. Uppertail shows narrow bars and lacks the broad subterminal band of the adult. From below, juveniles show a greyer and more diffuse trailing edge to the wing (although some may approach adults in this character) and the body and underwing coverts are streaked rather than barred. Distant birds show the typical two-coloured upperwing with paler brown coverts and darker secondaries. Silhouette differs slightly from the adults: the wings show an S-shaped trailing edge, with a narrower inner hand than in adults and the tail is longer and narrower.

During the winter the pale fringes of the upperparts wear off making them dull and greyish brown, but the contrast with the darker secondaries remains.

First-adult plumage (2nd cy autumn – 3rd cy spring)   Plates 323–326

Like adult but often possible to separate in favourable conditions. Iris colour intermediate between paler brown of juvenile and dark brown of adult and pupil still discernible (see Bare parts). Pattern of underbody and underwing coverts also intermediate between juvenile and adult and the dark trailing edge of the underwing shows a rather diffuse inner margin. The subterminal band in the tail is on average narrower than in full adults. Until the second moult starts in 3rd cy spring they can also be aged by the retained juvenile outermost primaries, which are comparatively shorter, faded brown and pointed.

Adult plumage (3rd cy autumn and older)   Plates 327–329

Perched adults are best identified by their uniformly dark eye, the irregularly worn upperwing coverts and by the pattern of the lower breast and belly, with a tendency towards transverse spots or barring.

In flight at close range the upperparts look rather uniformly dull brown but the trailing edge shows a broad dark lining to the wing and the tail shows a dark subterminal band which is broader than the other tail-bars. From underneath, adults typically show a broad, black and contrasting trailing edge to the wing, while the underwing coverts and lower body show a transverse barring. Distant birds may be more difficult to age but the uniform upperparts are usually discernible from afar. Adults are also slightly shorter-tailed and broader-winged than juveniles, being more bat-like in silhouette, although the difference is not as clear as in the Steppe Buzzard.

Plumage wear does not affect the appearance of the adults, as it does juveniles, and the plumage remains largely the same throughout the year.

Sexing: Normally not possible unless male and female are seen together. In direct comparison males are slightly smaller than females and show shorter tail, bigger head and narrower wings.

References: Bährmann 1969; Dittrich 1985; Forsman 1980, 1984; Gensbøl 1995; Ginn & Melville 1983; Hafton 1971; Kjellén 1995; Svensson 1976, 1981; Ulfstrand 1970, 1977

Plate 316 *Juvenile. This dark bird is unusually adult-like in showing a broad dark trailing edge to wings and a broad subterminal tail-band while the underbody and underwing coverts appear almost barred. The barring of the secondaries is mostly broader and duskier than in* vulpinus. *Oct 1996, Sweden (Jens B. Bruun).*

Plate 317 *Juvenile. Individuals with reduced dark markings below usually still show darker bib and trousers and darker lesser than median underwing coverts. 3 Nov 1987, Sweden (Dick Forsman).*

Plate 318 *Juvenile. Pale birds are told from Rough-legged Buzzard by tail-pattern, generally darker secondaries and by different head- and breast-pattern. 18 Sep 1995, Germany (Axel Halley).*

Plate 319 *Juvenile. Extremely pale bird with retained dark carpal-crescent, vestigial malar-stripe and dark markings on upper breast. Note white face with isolated dark eye (cf. pale juvenile Honey Buzzard). Oct 1996, Sweden (Jens B. Bruun).*

Plate 320 *Juvenile. Note pale iris, uniform condition of plumage, narrow subterminal tail-band and longitudinally marked breast. Apr, Finland (Tapani Räsänen).*

Plate 321 *Juvenile. A darker bird showing pale iris, uniform plumage and streaking to pale breast-band. Nov 1994, Germany (Axel Halley).*

Plate 322 *Pale morph juvenile. Extremely pale birds often show a largely white head and extensive white markings to the upperwing coverts. Note pale iris and uniform plumage. Aug 1994, Germany (Axel Halley).*

Plate 323 *Juvenile moulting to first-adult (2nd cy autumn). Note short retained juvenile outer primaries and median secondaries, latter showing less distinct dark tips than the moulted ones. Iris still pale. Sep, Sweden (John Larsen).*

Plate 324 *Juvenile moulting to first-adult (2nd cy). Only inner primaries moulted, all other remiges juvenile. Also body plumage largely juvenile. Note pale iris. Sweden (John Larsen).*

Plate 325 *First-adult? Plumage as in adult, with barred breast-band and underwing coverts, but pale iris and frayed and bleached longest primaries indicate a first-adult. Dec 1995, Germany (Axel Halley).*

Plate 326 *First-adult. Plumage characters intermediate between juvenile and adult. Note e.g. pale iris and a retained juvenile secondary. Apr, Finland (Tapani Räsänen).*

Plate 327 *Adult plumage. Dark iris, finely barred underbody and wing-coverts as well as broad dark trailing edge to wings and tail are adult characters. Oct 1996, Sweden (Jens B. Bruun).*

Plate 328 *Pale morph adult. This probably 2nd cy bird (with retained juvenile outer primaries) shows typically patterned remiges for the species. 3 Nov 1987, Sweden (Dick Forsman).*

Plate 329 *Adult. Variably worn remiges and coverts and broad subterminal tail-band distinguish from juvenile, dark iris also from first-adult. The barring of the lower breast is coarse, differing from typical adult* vulpinus. *Apr, Finland (Tapani Räsänen).*

STEPPE BUZZARD *Buteo buteo vulpinus*

Plates 330–352

Subspecies: Subspecies of Common Buzzard (page 266) given here full treatment, since often recognizable in the field and the most common form migrating along the eastern flyway.

Distribution: From N and E Europe (N Sweden and Finland through the Baltic states, E Poland and E Greece) to W Siberia (Yenisei River, N Kazakhstan and the Altai Mts.). Majority of population breeds in the forested parts of Russia.

Habitat: A forest buzzard breeding close to edges and open areas in woodland, often near bogs, rivers and meadows.

Population: European population poorly known because of difficulties in identification. Finnish population *c.* 10 000 pairs and total W Palearctic population, based on migration counts, probably in the order of 200 000–300 000 pairs.

Movements: A long-distance migrant wintering in Africa down to the Cape. Ringing recoveries show that Finnish breeding birds migrate mostly east of the Black Sea. Birds from the intergradation zone between *vulpinus* and *buteo* (*'intermedius'*) winter in the Balkans, Turkey and in the Middle East.

Massive spring migration at Eilat, Israel, where appears from mid-Feb, with period of heavy passage from mid-Mar to mid-Apr. In spring 1986 a total of 465 827 birds were counted, with all-time peak day of 130 000 on 2 Apr. Two main migration waves noted, first in late Mar–early Apr comprising adults and second wave after mid-Apr comprising mainly juveniles. Grey-brown morph migrates on average earlier than fox-red and dark morphs. Finnish birds arrive at northernmost breeding sites (70° N) during Apr.

Autumn migration fairly early, coinciding in Finland with the migration of the Honey Buzzard, starting during Aug and peaking in first half of Sep. Important migration routes follow W and E shores of Black Sea (32 000 at Bosporus in 1971) crossing into NE Turkey (205 000 in autumn 1976), where migration peaks late Sep–early Oct. Rare in Eilat in autumn, taking more easterly route over Arabian peninsula and Djibouti, where 98 000 crossed the Red Sea in 1987.

Hunting and prey: Hunting similar to Common Buzzard, but more confined to woodlands. During breeding, specialized in hunting small rodents, with field, bank and water voles forming the staple food. When small mammals scarce switches partly to reptiles, amphibians and birds, especially nestlings and fledglings. Also eats larger insects. Hunts from perch like Common Buzzard but also hovers regularly and for long periods.

Subspecies identification

Length 39–47 cm

wing-span 100–125 cm (*n*=60; Israeli migrants; W.S. Clark, unpubl.)

Extensive plumage variation complicates identification and adults especially appear in several distinct colour morphs. Pattern of remiges and rectrices as well as the wing-action during powered flight and wing-posture when gliding and soaring are the most reliable characters when separating from confusion species like Long-legged Buzzard. Not always possible to tell from nominate Common Buzzard.

> **Identification summary:** Generally very similar to Common Buzzard, but smaller and lighter and more agile in flight with faster wing-beats. The remiges are whiter below than in Common and the barring of the remiges and rectrices is finer and more distinct. Compared with Common Buzzard the underbody shows generally warmer colours and the barring of the breast is finer and more regular in adults, whereas juveniles tend to be more regularly streaked than Common. According to plumage adults especially can be divided into grey-brown, fox-red, dark rufous and black morph birds. A white phase, as known from the Common Buzzard, does not occur in the Steppe Buzzard. Juveniles and adults have different flight silhouettes.

In flight, distant Very similar to Common Buzzard and more agile flight, narrower wings and smaller size are normally impossible to assess reliably. Shows on average greyer upperparts than Common, probably because of heavy plumage wear in the winter quarters. Upper hand often shows a rather extensive grey or whitish panel and the tail becomes paler towards the base. Told from Honey and Long-legged Buzzard by different powered flight and wing-position when gliding/soaring (see Common Buzzard, Fig 43, p 268). Adults and juveniles differ in silhouette more than in Common, with juveniles being distinctly longer-tailed and slimmer-winged than the adults.

In flight, closer Like the Common Buzzard most reliably told from similar species by barring of flight-feathers: remiges are rather finely and evenly barred underneath, with darker tips. Tail shows similarly rather fine and dense barring above, sometimes becoming paler with suffused bars towards the base. Underwing coverts show a typical pattern with darker lesser, paler median and again more patterned greater coverts, leaving a broad pale wing-bar across the central covert-area. Carpal-patch can be rather dark and solid in some individuals adding to confusion risk with Long-legged. Vent and undertail coverts regularly pale. Upper hand often shows a paler patch outside the darkish primary coverts;

it is small and usually restricted to the bases of the fingered primaries in adults, but may be large and distinct in some juveniles recalling Long-legged Buzzard.

Perched A typical buzzard with wing-tips reaching close to tail-tip. The majority of individuals identified by typical pale breast-band between darker upper breast and belly. Tail either rufous, greyish or brown above, often slightly paler towards the base, with dense and fine barring. Many adults, especially in the fox-red and dark morphs, are more or less uniformly coloured below, lacking a breast-band.

Bare parts Feet and cere yellow at all ages, deeper in adults than in juveniles; bill dark. Iris pale grey, brownish grey or light brown in juvenile, with black pupil clearly visible. Adults have a very dark brown iris and the pupil is not discernible in the field. First-adults (2nd cy autumn – 3rd cy spring) show an intermediate, often bi-coloured iris, with darker lower and paler upper half and the black pupil is discernible in favourable conditions.

Variation: Occurs in three to four different plumage-types, often also referred to as colour morphs: the grey-brown, fox-red, dark rufous and black morph (latter two often combined under dark morph). The Steppe Buzzard lacks the whitish form found in the Common Buzzard, although some individuals (always juveniles) are very pale and sparsely patterned below, but even the palest birds show normally coloured head and upperparts, whereas they tend to be partly white in white morph Common Buzzard.

Grey-brown morph The most common form in the western part of the range and predominates in the early stages of the spring migration through Eilat, Israel. Adults are greyish brown above and the ground-colour of the tail is mostly greyish brown or grey, with or without some rufous distally. Underparts off whitish with greyish brown pattern on breast and the underwing coverts. Juveniles are more variable and often not possible to assign to a certain colour morph, although the ground-colour of the underbody is more whitish buff and the underwing coverts show less rufous brown markings than typical juvenile fox-red birds. Many juveniles appear to show intermediate characters between the two morphs.

Fox-red morph Slightly more easterly origin than the grey-brown, but still occurs e.g. in the Finnish breeding population, albeit rarer than the grey-brown. It is by far the most numerous morph migrating through Eilat in spring, starting its migration on average slightly later than the grey-brown birds. From above, the adults are much like the grey-brown birds, but the tail is more or less rufous and many birds also show extensive rufous fringes to mantle and upperwing coverts. Underbody and underwing coverts vary from uniformly rufous to normally patterned but rufous. Juveniles often difficult to assign to colour morph but typical birds have a deep yellowish buff ground-colour to the plumage of the underbody with rufous brown rather than dark greyish brown markings.

Dark rufous morph Southeasterly origin. Distant birds are often difficult to tell from the black morph and are therefore best lumped together as a dark morph. Dark birds are much rarer than the two aforementioned forms and comprise only about 2–5% of the spring population migrating through Eilat. Upperparts much as in grey-brown birds, although on average somewhat darker. Tail often clearly grey, or rufous and grey, with normal but distinct barring. Body plumage below is uniformly deep rufous brown, both in adults and juveniles, often showing slightly darker carpal-patches and somewhat paler forebody, thus greatly resembling Long-legged Buzzards of the same colour morph.

Black morph Same distribution as the dark rufous morph and the two morphs may in fact just represent the pale and the dark end of the same morph. Upperparts blackish brown, distinctly darker than in the previous morphs and the body plumage below is uniformly dark tar brown, blackish brown or nearly black. In adults the dark trailing edge to the wing and the dark subterminal tail-band are usually very broad and distinctive.

Subspecific identification Not always possible to tell from nominate Common Buzzards and birds of the grey-brown morph especially may appear very similar. Many birds from the intergraduation zone (e.g. from Finland) between *vulpinus* and *buteo* often show intermediate or mixed characters. In the past these birds were regarded as a separate subspecies *intermedius*, no longer considered valid.

Confusion species: Possible to confuse with several medium-sized raptors, but especially with Long-legged Buzzard since plumage is practically identical in many individuals.

Long-legged Buzzard (page 291) Distinctly bigger, with a more powerful and almost eagle-like active-flight and with wings held in a diagnostic dihedral when soaring and gliding. Most adults told from Steppe Buzzard by white tail with translucent gingery outer half, evenly patterned underwing coverts with contrasting dark carpal-patch; pale forebody contrasting with dark flanks and belly and by distinctly greyish and barred remiges above. Juveniles can be almost identical in plumage, but tail usually paler greyish with a whitish base and shows fine bars to distal half only; pale head and forebody contrast with dark belly; underwing lacks the dark triangle in the lesser coverts of the Steppe and upperwing shows more contrasting pale coverts and a wide and prominent pale panel on the inner hand.

Honey Buzzard (page 30) Another confusion risk but active flight on slower and higher wing-beats (more like Booted Eagle or Egyptian Vulture); glides and soars on flat wings lacking angled kink at elbow. Adults further identified by diagnostic barring of underwings and tail, juveniles by darkish secondaries and broadly black-tipped and coarsely barred primaries below, pale greater underwing coverts and relatively uniformly coloured underbody.

Rough-legged Buzzard (page 303) Sympatric with the Steppe Buzzard in the north and told from this by white inner tail with distinct and broad dark subterminal band, best seen from above. Flight is slower and more powerful than in Steppe and the wings show a more pronounced kink at the elbow in head-on views, as in Long-legged.

MOULT

Complete annually, starting during breeding but suspended for the autumn migration and finished in the winter quarters. The odd flight-feather is frequently left unmoulted.

Juveniles (first moult) Primary moult started in 2nd cy spring, normally in Apr–May, but sometimes prior to spring migration as early as Feb–Mar (Feb, Transvaal, S. Africa moulting p1 in both wings (Schmitt et al. 1980); p1–2 replaced in both wings, Eilat 5 Apr 1996, pers. obs.). Body plumage moulted from Jan onwards. By 2nd cy Sep, when moult suspended, three to five outermost primaries are still retained juvenile feathers, recognized as being shorter and faded brown (personal observation). Median juvenile secondaries often retained. In Transvaal, S Africa birds arrive with five to eight replaced primaries. Moult resumed in the winter quarters and completed there by majority of birds. Some birds still recognizeable in 3rd cy spring by a few retained juvenile remiges.

Adults (subsequent moults) Start to moult remiges during the breeding season, females during incubation in May, males considerably later. Moult is suspended before autumn migration but resumed and completed in the winter quarters, with body moult peaking in Nov and primary moult in Dec–Jan. Primaries moulted serially descendant, with two simultaneously active moult waves.

AGEING AND SEXING

Normally at least two recognizable age-classes, juveniles and adults, but in favourable conditions adults can be further split into first-adults and older, especially in autumn. Ageing usually straightforward: the pattern of the underbody is a more reliable ageing character in Steppe than in Common and also the upperwings and uppertails differ between juveniles and adults. First-adults are best told from adults by the moult pattern of the remiges and by the iris colour.

Ageing summary: Juveniles are streaked (or uniformly dark) on underbody and underwing coverts, the dark trailing edge of the underwing is dusky grey, the upperwing shows paler coverts than secondaries and the subterminal bar of the tail is narrow. Juveniles have narrower wings and clearly longer tail than adults.

Adults have finely barred (or uniformly dark) underbody and underwing coverts, the trailing edge of the underwing is distinct and black, the upperwing appears rather uniformly brown with a darker trailing edge and the tail shows a broad subterminal band.

First-adults resemble full adults but frequently show retained juvenile outer primaries, a paler iris and several of the underbody and underwing coverts are intermediate in pattern between juvenile and full adult.

Juvenile (1st cy – 2nd cy spring)   **Plates 330–338**

Perched juveniles show a rather pale iris with a distinctly darker pupil, the underparts are regularly streaked and the upperwing coverts are neatly fringed ochre, rufous or whitish forming a regular pattern.

Flying juveniles usually show rather dark secondaries above, whereas the fringed upperwing coverts stand out as somewhat paler. Upperwing greater coverts show distinct pale tips forming a diagnostic narrow band, whereas the primaries are variable above and may show extensively pale bases in some individuals (cf. Long-legged Buzzard). Uppertail shows narrow bars and lacks the broad subterminal band of the adult, while the tail-tip is broadly buff. From below, juveniles show a greyer and more diffuse trailing edge to the wing (although some may approach adults in this character) and the breast and especially the median underwing coverts are streaked rather than barred. Distant birds show the typical two-coloured upperwing with paler brown coverts and darker secondaries. The silhouette clearly differs from the adults: the wings are narrower with an S-shaped trailing edge, with a narrower inner hand, and the tail is longer and narrower.

By spring the pale fringes and feather tips of the upperparts wear off and the plumage is as a rule extremely worn and dull greyish brown above, with an even more clear-cut contrast between the darker secondaries and the faded greyish upperwing coverts.

Colour morphs Assigning juveniles to a certain colour morph is often difficult, except for dark morph birds. Fox-red and grey brown birds form a continuous intergrading series and only the most typical birds can be typed. Underparts in fox-red birds have a clearly yellowish buff ground-colour and the body and underwing coverts show rufous brown markings. Uppertail can be either brown or rufous with dark barring. Grey-brown juveniles are more whitish buff underneath with duller grey-brown markings. Tail similar to fox-red birds. Juvenile Steppe Buzzards, especially those of the grey-brown morph, can be extremely similar to juvenile Common Buzzards. Dark morph juveniles are very similar to dark morph adults, with uniformly deep rufous, tar-brown or blackish body plumage. They can be aged by the pale iris, the less distinct dark trailing edge of the underwing and by the tail-pattern, which lacks the broad subterminal band of the adults.

First-adult (2nd cy autumn (– 3rd cy spring))   Plates 339–340

Autumn birds with retained juvenile outer primaries (usually 3–5) can be reliably aged. Juvenile primaries can be recognized both from above and below by their faded brown colour, their pointed tips and they appear 'too short' to fit into the wing-formula. From above, they often also show distinctly paler bases which contrast sharply with the darker moulted inner primaries. These birds often also show a few retained median secondaries, which are diagnostically shorter than the moulted ones and appear more translucent because they lack the broad and distinct black tip.

Iris colour also paler than in full adults and the black pupil is still discernible, a character that, however, is seen only on perched birds in favourable lighting conditions.

Plumage pattern of the breast and underwing coverts often appears intermediate between juvenile and adult, showing a rather coarse barring or transverse spotting instead of the fine barring typical of older birds; the dark subterminal band in the tail is, on average, narrower and less regular in shape than in full adults and the dark trailing edge on the underwing shows a rather diffuse inner margin.

By 3rd cy spring the outer primaries may all have been replaced, making ageing of such birds extremely difficult, if not impossible.

Colour morphs as for adults.

Adult plumage (from 3rd cy (spring) autumn and older)   Plates 341–352

Perched adults are best identified by their uniformly dark eye, the irregularly worn upperwing coverts and by barring to lower breast and belly.

In flight at close range the upperparts look rather uniformly dull greyish brown but the trailing edge shows a broad dark lining to the wing and the tail a dark subterminal band, which is broader than the other tail-bars. From below, the adults typically show a broad, black and contrasting trailing edge to the whitish and distinctly barred remiges. Underwing coverts and lower breast are barred. Distant birds may be more difficult to age but the rather uniform upperparts are usually discernible from afar. Adults are also clearly shorter-tailed and broader-winged than juveniles, being more bat-like in silhouette.

Plumage wear does not affect the appearance of the adults, unlike the juveniles, and the plumage remains largely the same throughout the year.

Colour morphs Adults of the grey-brown morph are patterned in grey-brown underneath with a prominent pale breast-band. Their tail can be either rufous, brown or grey with fine black bars and a broad subterminal band. Fox-red birds are rufous or rusty-red below, either uniformly coloured or showing a pale breast-band. The tail is similar to the grey-brown morph, but some fox-red adults show a deep rufous tail with just the broad black subterminal band. Dark morph adults differ from dark juveniles by their dark eye, their distinct and broad black trailing edge to the wing and by the broad and black subterminal band in the barred, greyish tail.

Sexing: Normally not possible to sex in the field unless male and female are seen together. In direct comparison males are slightly smaller than females and show a comparatively bigger head, shorter tail and narrower wings and on average more finely barred underparts.

References: Broekhuysen & Siegfried 1970, 1971; Doherty 1992; Forsman 1980, 1984, 1993b; Saurola 1977; Schmitt et al. 1980; Shirihai & Doherty 1990; Shirihai & Forsman 1991; Shirihai & Christie 1992; Svensson 1976; Welch & Welch 1988

Plate 330 *Juvenile showing streaked underbody and underwing coverts and fine barring to secondaries, both typical of juvenile* vulpinus. *12 Sep 1993, Kazakhstan (Dick Forsman).*

Plate 331 *Juvenile. Tail-barring of juvenile typically narrow, as here, whereas trailing edge of wing is often fainter than in this individual. 14 Sep 1993, Kazakhstan (Dick Forsman).*

Plate 332 *Juvenile (2nd cy spring). Note uniform plumage and tail-barring and streaked median underwing coverts and breast. Remiges and tail show broader barring than usual. 6 Apr 1996, Israel (Dick Forsman).*

Plate 333 *Juvenile (2nd cy spring) showing moulted inner primaries with black tips, whereas tail is still juvenile. Apr 1992, Israel (Paul Doherty).*

Plate 334 *Juvenile dark morph (2nd cy). Aged by indistinct dark trailing edge to wings. Spring, Israel (Hadoram Shirihai).*

Plate 335 *Fresh juvenile from above. The upperwing coverts are neatly fringed rufous, the greater coverts tips form a pale band and the secondaries appear uniformly dark above. 12 Sep 1993, Kazakhstan (Dick Forsman).*

Plate 336 *Worn (2nd cy) juvenile from above. Note uniformly worn and faded upperwing coverts, which contrast with dark secondaries. Spring, Israel (Hadoram Shirihai).*

Plate 337 *Fresh juvenile showing pale iris, streaked underbody, rufous fringes to upperparts and narrow tail-bands. Sep, Finland (Mikko Pöllänen).*

Plate 338 *Worn (2nd cy) juvenile showing uniformly worn plumage with darker secondaries and pale iris. Apr 1994, Israel (Tom Lindroos).*

Plate 339 *First-adult (2nd cy autumn) showing suspended moult. Three outer primaries and some median secondaries are shorter juvenile feathers with less dark tips. 14 Sep 1993, Kazakhstan (Dick Forsman).*

Plate 340 *First-adult plumage (3rd cy spring) possible to age by retained juvenile p9–10 and s8–9. Note also rather pale iris and that the pattern of underbody and underwing coverts is rather juvenile-like. Apr 1992, Israel (Markus Varesvuo).*

Plate 341 *Adult fox-red morph. Note rufous brown lesser coverts and ochre tinge to entire body plumage. Distinct trailing edge and broad subterminal tail-band typical of adult. Mar, Israel (Paul Doherty).*

Plate 342 *Adult fox-red morph. Mar 1993, Israel (Markus Varesvuo).*

Plate 343 *Adult grey-brown morph. Note barred belly and underwing coverts typical of adults while the whitish remiges with fine barring are typical of this subspecies. Spring, Israel (Hadoram Shirihai).*

Plate 344 *Adult grey-brown morph. Apr 1987, Israel (Paul Doherty).*

Plate 345 *Adult fox-red morph. Birds like this can be confusingly similar to Long-legged Buzzard, but this individual told by its distinct dark subterminal tail-band. Mar 1989, Israel (Paul Doherty).*

Plate 346 *Adult dark rufous morph. Best told from very similar Long-legged Buzzard by different proportions and flight and by on average paler secondaries below. 6 Apr 1996, Israel (Dick Forsman).*

Plate 347 *Adult of dark rufous morph. Apr, Israel (Klaus Bjerre).*

Plate 348 *Adult dark morph. Best told from very similar dark Long-legged Buzzard in the field by different proportions and flight. Mar 1989, Israel, (Paul Doherty).*

Plate 349 *Adult dark morph. 12 Sep 1993, Kazakhstan (Dick Forsman).*

Plate 350 *Adult from above showing rufous tail with broad subterminal band. Note dark trailing edge to uniformly brownish upperwing typical of adult. 12 Sep 1993, Kazakhstan (Dick Forsman).*

Plate 351 *Adult from above showing typical broad subterminal tail-band. Note also dark trailing edge of wing, variably worn upperwing coverts and dark iris. May 1988, Israel (Hadoram Shirihai).*

Plate 352 *Adult. Note dark iris, broadly dark-tipped secondaries and broad subterminal tail-band. The head is typical of adult* vulpinus, *being pale greyish with a paler supercilium and a dark eye-line. Apr, Israel (Göran Ekström).*

LONG-LEGGED BUZZARD *Buteo rufinus*

Plates 353–370

Subspecies: Two subspecies. Nominate *rufinus* from E Europe to C Asia and smaller ssp. *cirtensis* in N Africa from Morocco to Egypt, possibly reaching deserts of S Israel. Streaked juveniles especially of latter subspecies may appear practically identical to juvenile Steppe Buzzards *(B. buteo vulpinus)*.

Distribution: In Europe breeds in Bulgaria, former Yugoslavia, Greece and Turkey outside Russia. Stragglers, especially juveniles and subadults, disperse north and west of breeding range prior to autumn migration. Smaller N African ssp. *cirtensis* occasionally reaches Iberian peninsula.

Habitat: Frequents open and arid areas, preferring steppes and semi-deserts and barren hills or rocks, but wintering birds also found around more fertile farmland. Usually nests on precipitous cliff or rock overlooking open areas or in narrower gorges. In the Balkans also inhabits more wooded mountains. In summer reaches mountain areas at higher altitudes.

Population: Population of W Palearctic estimated at 5000–15 000 pairs, with 1000–10 000 pairs in Turkey and 800–1500 in Russia. Remaining European population *c.* 230–370 pairs in Bulgaria, Greece and Ukraine. Recent increase, e.g. in Bulgaria, and increasing post-breeding dispersal to Hungarian steppes (puszta) has led to northward range expansion.

Movements: European birds mainly migratory but some winter in southern Greece and Turkey, most in Middle East and N Africa. Migration follows the Levant-route crossing into Africa at Suez. Migrates later in the autumn than other buzzards, peaking in late Oct and continuing well into Nov. In 1981, between 4 Sep and 5 Nov, 1816 migrants were counted at Suez, with marked peak during last 10 days of Oct. Returns in spring from late Feb to May, with peak during second half of Mar; at Eilat 105 counted in spring 1985, with 12 on 23 Mar.

Hunting and prey: Hunts from elevated posts, such as dead trees, pylons, telegraph poles or rocks. Often perches on ground, where long-legged stance becomes obvious. When searching for prey hovers frequently and persistently like Rough-legged Buzzard. Also hangs motionless against the wind, coming down step by step before final stoop. Prey consists of various smaller to middle-sized vertebrates including birds, mammals and reptiles in various proportions according to local food supply.

SPECIES IDENTIFICATION

Length 50–57 cm

wing-span 136–163 cm (*n*=37; W.S. Clark & D. Forsman, unpubl.)

Heavily streaked birds as well as uniformly rufous and dark birds are very difficult to separate from Steppe Buzzards in corresponding plumage. Silhouette, wing-action and wing-posture remain important characters when separating from similar Steppe.

> **Identification summary:** A large and long-winged buzzard with slow and deep wing-action, making active flight heavy for a buzzard, almost eagle-like. When soaring keeps wings diagnostically lifted in shallow V with distinct kink between hand and arm. Soars more slowly and in wider circles than Steppe Buzzard.
>
> Typical birds easily identified by pale plumage below with dark belly and dark, round carpal-patches. Tail typically whitish at base with orange outer half, but tail colour and pattern are variable.
>
> Can be very difficult to separate from certain Steppe Buzzards, especially in the black and dark rufous morphs. The shape of the bird, the proportions and wing-action in flight, as well as the wing-posture when soaring/gliding, are always important when separating the two species, not to mention the notable size difference in direct comparison.

In flight, distant Long-legged Buzzards of the more easily identified pale and intermediate forms are usually picked out by their sandy coloured upperwing coverts, the rather pale tail and head, and the typically pale underparts with distinctly darker carpal-patch and dark flanks and belly. More difficult birds, such as heavily marked or dark individuals, are best told from similar looking Steppe Buzzards by different proportions and flight.

The powered flight of the Long-legged Buzzard is slower and more majestic compared with Steppe, with deeper, slower and more powerful wing-beats on longer and more flexible wings. The silhouette is characterized not only by longer wings but also by a more protruding head and a heavier bill, making the bird look almost like an eagle. One of the most characteristic features in flight is the habit of keeping its wings lifted. When gliding, arms are clearly lifted with a sharp kink before the more level hand and, when soaring, the wings are held in a shallow V, as in Rough-legged Buzzard or Golden Eagle. When Long-legged and Steppe Buzzards are seen soaring together the circles of Long-legged are wider, slower and more stable and it also stands out as much bigger and longer-winged. Compared with Steppe the wing-tips of soaring and gliding Long-leggeds bend more strongly upwards because of their greater wing-loading, this also adding to the more eagle-like impression (see Fig 43, p 268).

In flight, closer Typical Long-legged Buzzards are not difficult to identify. From below, the combination of rather uniformly pale straw-coloured head, neck and upper breast contrasting with darker, often rufous, flanks and belly and rather pale underwing coverts, with a round dark carpal-patch strongly indicate Long-legged. From above, the combination of rather pale and sandy coloured lesser and median upperwing coverts, a large pale flash on the upper hand and a basally whitish tail turning cinnamon towards the tip is similarly a strong indication of Long-legged. However, be aware of heavily streaked, brownish juveniles greatly resembling juvenile Steppe Buzzards and also of uniformly coloured rufous and black birds that are almost identical in plumage to the corresponding colour morphs of Steppe Buzzard. Consider also Rough-legged Buzzard in areas where and at times when both might occur together.

Perched Long-legged Buzzards can be extremely difficult to separate from Steppe Buzzards. They appear on average heavier and comparatively smaller-headed, but without direct comparison or with inadequate experience these characters are difficult to assess. Typical birds are separated by their rather uniform, pale head, with a dark line through eye and dark triangle on nape, by the pale breast contrasting with darker flanks and belly, and by their typically coloured tail, with paler base and cinnamon distal half. More heavily streaked birds and dark birds are practically inseparable from Steppe by plumage characters. The bill of the Long-legged is, however, bigger than in Steppe, and the prominent hook gives it a more rapacious appearance; the tarsi are larger.

Bare parts Cere and feet yellow at all ages. Iris colour changes from pale pearl grey or greyish brown in juvenile to very dark brown in adults; subadults show an intermediate iris. Iris colour can be assessed even in the field, especially on perched birds. In practice, the black pupil stands out clearly in juveniles, whereas the eye looks all-dark in adults. Subadults show rather pale and juvenile-like irides in 2nd cy autumn. Even a year later in 3rd cy autumn many (most?) birds show paler brown eyes than adults, with the pupil still discernible.

Variation: Long-legged Buzzards can, at all ages, be divided into four main plumage-types: pale, intermediate, rufous and dark birds. The different types are not distinct morphs, except for the dark morph, and a wide variety of intermediates occur.

Pale type Pale birds are the most characteristic and easy to identify. From below they appear largely pale, with darker belly and carpal-patches and dark-tipped remiges. Typically head, upper breast and underwing coverts appear largely unstreaked. In juveniles the tail is normally whitish basally getting gradually more greyish brown towards the tip with faint and narrow barring distally. Adults show a practically unmarked tail, with a white base and orange outer half.

Intermediate type Intermediate birds are more richly coloured and more extensively marked on upper breast and underwing coverts. Upperparts are on average darker brown than in pale birds, showing narrower rufous fringes to upperwing coverts, mantle and scapulars. Tail more distinctly barred, with juveniles often showing a brownish grey, all-barred tail (a pattern very similar to juvenile Steppe Buzzards) and even adults retaining some bars or traces of bars on distal part of tail (although never a broad and conspicuous subterminal bar as in Steppe Buzzard).

Rufous type Rufous birds have uniformly rufous body and underwing coverts except for darker carpal-patches. The rufous colour varies from pale yellowish ochre to a deep rufous brown, with all possible intergrades. The dark rufous birds may appear almost black from a distance. Upperparts are much as in the previous plumage-types, although dark rufous birds often show a pale grey tail with fine black bars and a slightly broader subterminal band.

Fig 45 *Long-legged Buzzard. Tail-pattern of dark morph birds. Juvenile tails (left) are browner with broad dark bands while adult tails are pure grey with a broad subterminal band and individually variable barring proximally.*

Dark type The true colour, which varies from tar brown to black, is usually only seen at close range; distant birds look just dark. All birds, regardless of age, have a uniformly dark body and under- and upperwing coverts. Black birds also have blackish upperwing coverts. Paler individuals may show suggestions of darker carpal-patches and of a border between dark belly and slightly paler forebody. Tail-pattern variable, but frequently shows distinct black barring on greyish ground-colour. The dark subterminal band may be broad and contrasting as in adult Steppe Buzzard and the finer bars may be either fine and distinct (as in Steppe) or broad and sparse, or they may be absent altogether. Difficult to separate from similar forms of Steppe Buzzard, except on size, shape, wing-attitude and wing-action. However, dark Long-legged Buzzards tend to show from below greyish secondaries and a whiter flash only to the bases of the outer primaries, whereas dark Steppe Buzzards seem to show typically uniformly pale and finely barred remiges with distinct black tips.

The smaller ssp. *cirtensis* of N Africa is closer to Steppe Buzzard in size and proportions and would be very difficult to separate from this if the two occurred together. Possibly reaches the deserts of S Israel, where some birds in the resident population are distinctly smaller than the migrants passing through the area (pers. obs., see also Shirihai 1995).

Confusion species: Most likely to be confused with Steppe Buzzard, as certain plumage-types are almost identical and as both species occur together on migration. Theoretically also possible to mistake for Rough-legged Buzzard, although the two rarely occur together.

Steppe Buzzard (page 277) In all plumages told by faster and stiffer wing-beats and proportionately shorter wings, which are nearly flat and only marginally kinked at elbow in head-on views. Soars in smaller and faster circles than Long-legged. In most plumages told by darker and completely barred tail above, distinctly three-coloured underwing coverts with darkish lesser, pale median and darker greater coverts and less distinct carpal-patch and by mostly darker head and upper breast, which contrast with pale breast-band. Dark birds very similar to dark Long-leggeds.

Rough-legged Buzzard (page 303) Always separated by wide dark tail-band and feathered tarsi and the juveniles lack the dark line along the greater coverts of the underwing, which is commonly found in juvenile Long-legged. As size, proportions and flight behaviour are rather similar it is fortunate that the two as a rule do not occur together.

MOULT

Annually complete, but some remiges may be left unmoulted; outermost primaries regularly retained in first moult.

Juveniles (first moult) Starts earlier than in adults, often prior to spring migration, as migrants frequently show a fresh or growing inner primary in Mar–Apr (1 Apr p1 missing; another 4 Apr no moult yet). In Jun, Kazakhstan, innermost four primaries replaced and p5–6 missing. Moult arrested Sep–Oct, leaving outermost one to four primaries and frequently also some median secondaries unmoulted.

Adults (subsequent moults) Primaries moulted usually from two simultaneous foci. Thus may replace all remiges, although some may be left unmoulted. Starts to moult remiges during laying period, completing moult by (Sep–) Oct.

AGEING AND SEXING

Separating juveniles and adults in pale and intermediate morphs is rather straightforward but more difficult in dark birds. First-adults usually separable from adults only if seen close and well.

Ageing summary: Pale and intermediate birds are aged by trailing edge of wing, tail-pattern and basal flash on upper hand. From below juveniles show a greyish and narrower, less distinct trailing edge to wing and the tail is faintly but rather regularly barred, at least distally. From above, the primaries mostly show a large whitish panel and the secondaries are dark brown. Adults show a distinct black trailing edge to the underwing and the tail is either unbarred or shows distinct fine black bars (distally) with a marginally broader subterminal bar. Remiges grey above with dark tips, primaries often with pale bases on outer hand. Dark birds are difficult to age from below, but from above adults show greyish remiges and distinct barring to tail and the secondaries are distinctly barred from below, whereas juveniles show uniformly dark remiges above, and broad, rather diffuse and often irregular barring to underwings and uppertail. Possible to age in all colour morphs by iris colour.

Juvenile (1st cy autumn – 2nd cy spring)   Plates 353–360

Perched juveniles can be aged by their regularly patterned upperparts, with pale tips to the greater coverts and neatly fringed median and lesser coverts, and by distinctly pale iris colour.

In flight, juveniles appear slimmer than adults. Wings narrower, with an S-shaped trailing edge and tail is longer and narrower. The dark trailing edge of the wing is narrower and duskier than in adults (sometimes with a fine black central bar).

Seen from above, the tail is mostly whitish basally becoming pale greyish brown towards the tip with regular and fine barring distally. Secondaries appear uniformly dark brown and contrast sharply with the pale inner hand. Most individuals show a whitish primary flash above, with partly white bases to at least the fingered primaries, but some individuals show white bases to all primaries. The innermost four primaries are usually distinctly barred, whether whitish or brownish.

Dark juveniles are mostly very difficult to separate from dark adults in the field. Pale iris distinctive. Tail either all-dark or heavily barred, with few but very broad dark bands, often being wider than the pale interspace. From below, the dark trailing edge can be very wide, which, together with the generally dusky greyish ground-colour to the secondaries and the broad but diffuse barring, creates a much darker arm than hand (in dark Steppe Buzzards the dark trailing edge is narrower and it is sharply defined). Some birds show a paler patch on mid-breast, often with dark streaking. Juveniles tend to be more brownish than adults, especially in worn plumage in spring.

First-adult (2nd cy autumn – 3rd cy spring)   Plate 361

Possible to tell from full adults in the field when seen close. Iris still predominantly pale and the pupil is clearly visible. Most (all?) second winter birds can be aged by retained and faded juvenile outer primaries being shorter (creating an irregular 'step' in the wing-tip) and more pointed than the replaced ones (be aware of moulting autumn adults!). Others (not all) also carry some retained juvenile median secondaries, which are shorter and lack the distinct black tip. From above, retained juvenile outer primaries (mostly) show white bases contrasting sharply with moulted greyer inner primaries.

Plumage generally intermediate between juvenile and full adult and intermediate birds still show quite extensive longitudinal streaking on underparts. Tail of intermediate birds still shows hints of distal tail-bars with subterminal bar slightly broader.

Adult (3rd cy autumn and older)   Plates 362–370

Distant birds especially not always possible to tell from second winter birds, but the all-dark eye is a reliable character when seen properly.

From below, pale and intermediate birds are aged by their distinct and sharply defined, black trailing edge of the underwing. From above, remiges greyish with clearly darker tips forming a darker trailing edge to the upperwing. Upper hand greyish but often shows a diffuse whitish flash outermost. Tail typically predominantly white, with distal half orange or cinnamon, often with some grey admixed. Intermediate birds may show hints of bar-ring close to tail-tip, with slightly better defined subterminal bar.

In dark morph pattern of tail and remiges most important when separating adults from juveniles. From above, secondaries show a greyish cast and a blackish trailing edge and the tail is either pearly grey with just one wide black subterminal band or with additional finer black bars across the tail (as in adult Steppe Buzzard; see Fig. 45). From below, the trailing edge of the wing is broad, black and sharply defined. Dark barring of remiges below is often wider than in paler forms, leaving only bases to outermost primaries uni-formly pale.

Sexing: Sexing normally not possible in the field. When pair is seen together shows slight size dimorphism in favour of female.

References: Bijlsma 1983; Forsman 1992a; Shirihai 1995; Shirihai & Forsman 1991; Shirihai & Christie 1992; Tucker & Heath 1995

Plate 353 *Juvenile. Note pale body with dark trousers only. Aged by poorly marked trailing edge of wing and finely barred tail. 25 Nov 1988, Israel (Sampsa Cairenius).*

Plate 354 *Juvenile showing typically pale body and uniformly coloured underwing coverts with prominent dark carpal-patch. Note diffuse trailing edge to wing and uniformly barred tail typical of juvenile. 9 Oct 1996, Israel (Annika Forsten).*

Plate 355 *Juvenile. A rather heavily marked juvenile in plumage very similar to many juvenile Steppe Buzzards. Note pale tips to remiges and rectrices typical of fresh juvenile. 2 Oct 1990, Turkey (Dick Forsman).*

Plate 356 *Juvenile (2nd cy spring). Note the rather prominent dark trailing edge to wing of this bird with two fresh inner primaries. Mar 1993, Israel (Antti Below).*

Plate 357   *Juvenile dark morph. The broad bars on remiges and rectrices separate dark juvenile Long-legs from similar Steppe Buzzards, apart from differences in proportions and flight. Feb 1988, Israel (Hadoram Shirihai).*

Plate 358   *Juvenile showing typically pale head and upper breast and darker lower breast and flanks. Note pale iris and pale tips to greater coverts and secondaries typical of juvenile. Nov 1983, Israel (Lasse J. Laine).*

Plate 359   *Juvenile in rather worn plumage. Ageing of this slightly more patterned bird by pale iris and uniformly coloured secondaries and greater coverts. Feb 1988, Israel (Hadoram Shirihai).*

Plate 360   *Juvenile dark morph. Aged by pale iris and uniformly dark upperwing. Feb 1988, Israel (Hadoram Shirihai).*

Plate 361 *First-adult (3rd cy) aged by retained juvenile p9–10. First-adults are on average more marked below on body and underwing coverts than older birds. 5 Feb 1996, Israel (Dick Forsman).*

Plate 362 *Adult. A rather classic individual showing translucent gingery tail and unmarked underwing coverts with dark carpal. Apr 1985, Israel (Pekka Komi).*

Plate 363 *Adult. A pale bird with dark of body restricted to the thighs. Distinct dark trailing edge of wing and uniform tail indicate adult. Mar 1996, Israel (Axel Halley).*

Plate 364 *Adult. Note typical tail and underwings and dark belly contrasting with pale forebody. 29 Mar 1995, Israel (Dick Forsman).*

Plate 365 *Adult dark rufous morph. Can be confusingly similar to adult Steppe Buzzards of same colour morph and best identified by different proportions and flight. 5 Feb 1996, Israel (Dick Forsman).*

Plate 366 *Adult dark morph. Long wings diagnostic of the species. Note that most dark adults have a broad dark subterminal band in the tail. 18 Mar 1992, Israel (Dick Forsman).*

Plate 367 *Adult dark morph. Not always possible to tell from dark morph Steppe Buzzard by plumage, but Long-legs tend to have more heavily marked secondaries contrasting with pale inner hand. Oct 1995, Israel (Tom Lindroos).*

Plate 368 *Adult pale morph showing diagnostic tail, pale head and sandy upperwing coverts. Adults have greyish and barred remiges with distinct dark tips. 12 Dec 1986, Israel (Pekka J. Nikander).*

Plate 369   *Possible first-adult showing intermediate iris-colour and tail-pattern between juvenile and full adult. 23 Nov 1990, Oman (Hanne & Jens Eriksen).*

Plate 370   *Adult pale morph showing dark iris and uniformly gingery tail. The pattern and coloration of mantle and upperwing coverts are also diagnostic. 5 Sep 1995, Oman (Hanne & Jens Eriksen).*

ROUGH-LEGGED BUZZARD   *Buteo lagopus*

Plates 371–389

Subspecies: Nominate *B. l. lagopus* in W Palearctic, *menzbieri* east of Yenisei River, *kamtschatkensis* in Kamtschatka and Kuril Islands and *sanctijohannis* in N America.

Distribution: Holarctic, from the mountains of Fennoscandia east through northern Russia and N America. Absent from Greenland and Iceland. Breeding numbers and distribution vary from year to year depending on cyclic food resources. Migratory.

Habitat: A raptor of open tundra penetrating south into the coniferous taiga-zone. Relies on open areas for hunting and frequents bogs and clear-fellings in forested areas. On migration and in winter found in various types of open areas from steppes to moors, shores and cultivated fields.

Population: Fennoscandian population estimated roughly at 10 000–25 000 pairs with a total of 80 000–120 000 for the whole W Palearctic. Owing to specialization on cyclic prey, numbers of breeding pairs vary considerably between years and areas. In peak vole years most of the pairs of a given area breed, while no pairs nest in years with low vole populations.

Movements: Migratory, Fennoscandian birds wintering in C and E Europe from the North Sea coasts to the Black Sea. Leaves breeding grounds from late Aug and autumn passage peaks at Nordic migration sites between late Sep and late Oct. Onset of migration is probably affected by food situation in the breeding area: if the food supply is good migration starts later. At Falsterbo, S Sweden autumn numbers varied between 601 and 1480 in 1986–1994, with daily maxima of 247 on 24 Sep 1986 and 261 on 30 Sep 1987. On Bornholm, Denmark, in 1978 a total of 1151 birds were counted between 17 and 19 Oct. In Finland 3222 Rough-legged Buzzards were counted on passage at Virolahti in SE Finland between 9 and 12 Oct 1982, and 1100 were counted there on 23–24 Sep 1992. Spring passage peaks in S Finland between mid-Apr and mid-May, with adults arriving before yearlings. In Apr 1984 3910 were counted crossing the Bothnian Gulf at Quarken Straits, from Finland to Sweden, with 1200 on peak day 23 Apr.

Hunting and prey: Specialized in hunting small rodents, mainly voles, but also takes a great variety of birds especially when rodent prey is scarce. Hunts either from a perch, on migration usually from a post or an isolated tree and on the breeding grounds from a prominent rock, or hovers for prolonged periods when wind conditions are favourable.

Species identification

Length 50–60 cm

wing-span 127–148 cm (*n*=16; D. Forsman et al., unpubl.)

Identification mostly straightforward. Pattern of uppertail important in all plumages, also wing-action in powered flight and wing-carriage when gliding/soaring. General plumage colour as well as pattern of underbody and underwings give additional clues for identification.

> **Identification summary:** Although variable in plumage the Rough-legged Buzzard is rather easy to identify by its typical tail-pattern, with a white inner tail and a broad dark tail-band. Wings held at a dihedral when soaring and gliding with lifted arm and an obvious kink between inner and outer wing. Frequently hovers when hunting. Juveniles and most adult females have a very pale underwing with a prominent dark carpal-patch and the generally rather pale body has a solid dark belly. Adult males have more patterned underwing coverts and show a dark throat and upper breast and a more loosely barred belly, some even resembling Common Buzzard in plumage pattern.

In flight, distant The flapping flight is looser than in Common Buzzard, with more powerful, slower and higher wing-beats. When soaring or gliding the wings are typically held at a dihedral, with an obvious kink between lifted inner arm and more level outer wing. In frontal views the carpal bend is distinctly pale, extending over entire leading edge of arm in some. Hovers frequently and for long periods if wind conditions are suitable.

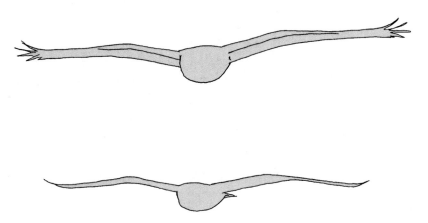

Fig 46 *Rough-legged Buzzards showing different wing-carriage when gliding. Note kink between lifted arm and level/lowered hand.*

Can be picked out even at great distance by the shining white inner tail, best visible from above. The rest of the upperparts appear rather uniformly dark, save for whitish primary-bases and paler upperwing coverts of juveniles. Underparts vary considerably depending on age and sex. Some are pale and the diagnostic underwing pattern with largely pale coverts and a distinct rounded dark carpal-patch are visible from afar. Others are more variegated and much darker and do not differ markedly from paler Common Buzzards. The tail-pattern is often difficult to discern from below.

In flight, closer The most reliable character, the tail-pattern, varies a lot depending on age and sex. The width of the dark tip varies from just one distinct black subterminal band to almost half of the outer tail being dark brown, but the base is always white. The white area on the inner tail may be either unpatterned or it may show distinct but sparse dark bars all the way to the white uppertail coverts, which show dark spots/bars. The rest of the upperparts are either predominantly brown, with pale ochre edges and tips (juveniles) or more mottled in grey, brown and black with clearly barred remiges (adults). Underwings very sparsely patterned in most juveniles and adult females, with sparsely barred remiges and almost unpatterned coverts, except for the prominent dark carpal-patch. Adult males show more patterned coverts, often appearing clearly darker than the remiges, and the carpal-patch is less prominent.

Perched Perched birds appear pale-headed, but the general appearance varies depending on age and sex. Usually the lateral crown and upper cheeks are pale and there is a prominent dark line through the eye in all plumages. Upperparts vary from greyish brown with pale ochre feather margins (juveniles) to grey with black streaking (adult males) or more dark brown with grey and ochre markings (adult females). Underparts either show a paler upper breast and a dark belly (juveniles and adult females) or a dark throat and upper breast and more loosely patterned flanks and belly (adult males). At close quarters the feathered tarsi distinguish it from other buzzards. Wing-tips reach close to tail-tip.

Bare parts Toes and cere yellow at all ages, bill black. Iris pale grey or brownish grey in juveniles, with black pupil showing clearly. Adults have a dark brown iris and the eye looks all-dark. First-adults (second winter) have an intermediate iris colour with the pupil discernible in close views (see Common Buzzard (page 268) for details).

Variation: A black morph of the Rough-legged Buzzard occurs in N America and Siberia, but it is not known from the European breeding population. A single specimen is known from Sweden, where a black morph bird was collected on Öland, 26 Oct 1950 (specimen no. 26 in NRM, Stockholm) and two birds are known from Britain (D'Urban & Mathew 1892 and Mather 1986). These individuals are possible vagrants from N America or N Asia.

A small proportion of juveniles show a largely dark uppertail with white restricted to base of tail only, whereas the rest of the plumage is normal.

Confusion species: Rough-legged Buzzards, especially juveniles, can be rather similar to other pale buzzards, particularly to some Long-legged Buzzards. Told from other medium-sized raptors by typical pattern of uppertail, by dark carpal-patch and by dark lining to underwing and diagnostic pattern of underbody.

Long-legged Buzzard (page 291) Shows strong rufous or yellowish colours in the most similar plumages and the tail lacks a prominent dark tail-band, showing either finer barring distally or a basally white tail turning gingery towards the tip. The long tarsi are bare and yellow.

Common Buzzard (page 266) Some individuals may appear rather similar, but they never show the distinct tail-pattern of Rough-legged Buzzard. Pale individuals can have a white inner tail but the outer part is brown or gingery with finer barring and the division between white inner half and dark outer half shows irregular border with pale and dark spikes. In addition, pale Common Buzzards often show partially white upperwing covert area and reduced dark pattern to underbody and underwing coverts, which are rare in Rough-legged Buzzard.

Honey Buzzards (page 30) Identified by their flat wings when gliding/soaring and from below by their typically barred remiges. Even the palest Honey Buzzards do not show an extensively whitish inner tail, as the white is restricted to the uppertail coverts only.

MOULT

Complete moult annually. First moult regularly incomplete, but some remiges may be left unmoulted in later moults too.

Juveniles (first moult) Starts to moult remiges in Apr–May of 2nd cy, earlier than in adults, sometimes starting even before spring migration. Actively moulting birds show only one moult gap in the primaries. As a rule moult arrested in Sep, when wings still show some retained outer juvenile primaries. Some juvenile secondaries and rectrices are also frequently retained.

Adults (subsequent moults) Complete moult from May–Jun to Sep–Oct. Actively moulting birds usually show two moult gaps in the primaries. Females start to moult remiges at the time of egg-laying, males later. Birds on autumn migration often show growing remiges and rectrices.

AGEING AND SEXING

Adults and juveniles distinctive and easy to separate given good views, with differences in trailing edge of wing and tail, from both above and below. For sexing of adults note plumage pattern of body and underwing coverts and type of barring of upper tail. A first-adult plumage is separable in good conditions.

Ageing and sexing summary: From below juveniles show a dusky trailing edge to wings and tail, and from above uniformly dark secondaries, often also largely whitish bases to primaries. From below adults show a distinct black trailing edge to wing and tail and from above barred remiges and darkish upperwing coverts. Adult males have finely barred belly, heavily patterned underwing coverts, more bars on uppertail and greyer upperparts than females, which are more solidly dark on belly, show less well-marked underwing coverts and fewer bars on uppertail and are more brownish above.

Fig 47 *Rough-legged Buzzards. Adults (upper two) have a distinct trailing edge to wings and tail compared with juvenile (lower). Adult males (left) mostly show a darker hood than belly, more patterned underwings and a poorly defined carpal-patch while females mostly show a paler hood than belly, less marked underwings and a prominent dark carpal-patch. Juveniles resemble the adult female, but usually show even less marked forebody and underwing coverts.*

Juvenile (1st cy – 2nd cy spring)   Plates 371–379

Perched juveniles are recognized by their uniformly brownish greater coverts and secondaries, the brownish and pale-fringed median covert patch and the pale iris. Head and forebody creamy buff with variable dark streaking and belly uniformly dark brown. Iris either greyish brown or pearl grey and the pupil shows clearly.

In flight from above, juveniles are identified by uniformly brownish secondaries and greater coverts, latter with distinctive pale tips, and by a variable pale (often white) flash basally on the primaries and a paler area in the median upperwing coverts. In good light the dark tail-band is brownish from above and blends gradually with the white inner tail. From below, the trailing edge to the wing as well as the tail-band are diffuse, the trailing edge to the wing often also narrow, never broad and distinctly black. Underwing coverts and remiges very pale and almost unmarked, while the belly is uniformly dark brown. Juveniles never show any trace of wing moult until in late 2nd cy spring. Sexes are not known to differ in juvenile plumage.

First-adult (2nd cy autumn – 3rd cy spring)   Plates 380–381

Birds in their first-adult plumage can mostly, but perhaps not always, be separated from older birds. Individuals showing the following criteria should be safe to age as first-adults. All(?) individuals seem to retain the one to four outermost juvenile primaries. The fingers of these are clearly browner, more pointed and comparatively shorter than on the replaced neighbouring feathers and from above show often extensively white bases contrasting sharply with grey and barred moulted primaries. Some individuals also retain some juvenile secondaries, which are shorter and lack the prominent black tip of the replaced feathers, resulting in a broken black trailing edge; seen from above they are shorter and faded brown compared with their neighbours. Upperwing often shows a variable number of worn juvenile median coverts, which form a paler irregular patch. Eye still paler than in older birds with the black pupil discernible in optimal conditions.

Sexing first-adults is more difficult than sexing older birds, as many males have not yet

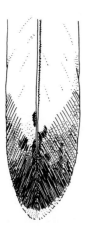

Fig 48 *Rough-legged Buzzard. Central tail-feathers from above showing diffuse and brown subterminal band of juvenile (left) compared with black bands of adults. Adult males (centre) typically show additional bars proximally, whereas most adult females (right) just show a subterminal band (see text for variation).*

acquired all the adult male characters, but show fewer tail-bars, paler forebody and solidly dark belly. However, most birds can be sexed using a combination of several criteria.

Males More heavily patterned underwing coverts (darker than bases of remiges) with less distinct carpal-patch and the uppertail has at least one black bar (usually one or two) inside the subterminal band.

Females Like adult females with pale underwings, sparsely patterned remiges and coverts but prominent and solid dark carpal-patch. Uppertail normally shows only the black subterminal band (only rarely an additional inner bar).

Adult (from 3rd cy autumn and older)   Plates 382–389

Perched adults show barred remiges and the eye looks black. In flight from above, adults show greyish flight-feathers with prominent dark bars and dark trailing edge to wing and lack the large white flash of many juveniles (although bases of outermost primaries may show some white in full soar). From a distance the upperwing appears uniformly dark with a diffuse grey flash on the upper hand in some, but lacking the pale coverts and the prominent pale primary flash of juveniles. The tail-barring is distinctive and black. From below, both remiges and rectrices show broad and distinctive black tips. Sexes distinct and possible to separate in the field.

Males Darker underwings, with more heavily patterned underwing coverts often appearing darker than bases of remiges. Secondaries and inner primaries distally more heavily barred than in females. Lower cheeks, throat and upper breast dark, whereas the belly is often paler and distinctly barred, as are the 'trousers'. Upperparts grey and black with distinctly barred remiges above. Uppertail shows one to four, normally two or more, additional black bands inside the broad subterminal band (not all narrow bands necessarily visible from below).

Females Normally show sparsely patterned and pale underwing coverts with a prominent dark carpal-patch. As the remiges are more sparsely barred, the whole underwing appears rather similar to the juvenile's, save for the distinct black trailing edge. Underbody rather juvenile-like, with a paler forebody and a rather solidly dark belly, but adult females tend to show a more heavily streaked and darker throat and upper breast, while the belly is blackish, not brown as in juvenile. Compared with adult males the dark belly is more solid, or, if reduced, it tends to be broken up in spots rather than bars. Upperparts browner than in adult males, and the secondaries especially are less prominently barred. Uppertail usually shows only a broad subterminal band, but some females show one additional dark bar (very rarely two) inside it.

Sexing: Adult males and females differ in plumage, but juveniles and most first-adults cannot be reliably sexed by plumage characters. Males are slightly smaller than females, but difference not notable in the field without direct comparison.

References: Danko 1988; D'Urban & Mathew 1892; Forsman 1980, 1984, 1992b, 1993b; Gensbøl 1995; Kjellén 1995; Mather 1986; Mebs 1989; Pöyhönen 1995; Svensson 1982

Plate 371 *Juvenile showing diagnostic pale iris, greyish trailing edge to wing, diffuse subterminal tail-band and brown belly. Sep 1985, Finland (Dick Forsman).*

Plate 372 *Juvenile. Poorly barred remiges and diffuse dark tail-band are typical juvenile characters. Oct, Finland (Mikko Pöllänen).*

Plate 373 *Juvenile with more marked underwing coverts but showing typical pattern of flightfeathers and pale iris. Oct, Finland (Mikko Pöllänen).*

Plate 374 *Juvenile with typically poorly marked underwing, uniformly brown belly and faint tailband. Autumn, Sweden (Jens B. Bruun).*

Plate 375 *Juvenile. Sep 1988, Sweden (Lars Jonsson).*

Plate 376 *Juvenile. The secondaries are distinctly darker than the primaries in most juveniles and the tail-band is brown, not black. Autumn, Sweden (Jens B. Bruun).*

Plate 377 *Juveniles normally show pale-mottled upperwing coverts, darkish secondaries and a pale flash on the primaries. 3 Nov 1987, Sweden (Dick Forsman).*

Plate 378 *Juvenile. Pale iris and pale fringes to upperwing coverts are juvenile characters. 5 Nov 1987, Sweden (Dick Forsman).*

Plate 379 *Juvenile. Note same characters as for Plate 378. 3 Nov 1987, Sweden (Dick Forsman).*

Plate 380 *First-adult male. The retained juvenile secondaries, shorter and lacking dark tips, stand out clearly on this bird. Note also retained and faded juvenile p9–10. Sex by patterned underwing coverts, variegated carpal-patch and dark upper breast. Autumn, Sweden (Jens B. Bruun).*

Plate 381 *First-adult female with retained juvenile p8–10 and s4 and s8–9 in each wing. Sex by pale underwing coverts, prominent carpal-patch and pale forebody. Autumn, Sweden (Jens B. Bruun).*

Plate 382 *Adult male. Note dark bib, barred flanks and thighs and heavily marked underwing coverts of this rather average male. 8 May 1991, Norway (Dick Forsman).*

Plate 383 *Adult male. Note same characters as for Plate 382. May, Finland (Tapani Räsänen).*

Plate 384 *Adult male. Paler males typically show darker bib than belly, as opposed to females. 8 Jul 1982, Finland (Dick Forsman).*

Plate 385 *Adult male from above. Note darkish upperwing coverts, greyish and distinctly barred remiges and multiple tail-bands. Sweden (Jens B. Bruun).*

Plate 386 *Adult male. Note multiple tail-bands, distinctly barred secondaries and pied mantle. 13 May 1989, Norway (Dick Forsman).*

Plate 387 *Adult female. Often resemble juveniles, but the tail-band and the trailing edge of the wing are distinct and black and the bib is better developed. Most females also show uniformly dark belly, darker than bib. 2 Aug 1997, Finland (Dick Forsman).*

Plate 388 *Adult female. Note single tail-band, less marked underwing coverts and paler bib of this pale individual compared with adult male in Plate 384. 13 May 1989, Norway (Dick Forsman).*

Plate 389 *Adult female. Uniformly dark belly and brown secondaries and greater coverts are typical of adult females. 10 Jul 1987, Finland (Jukka Rysä).*

LESSER SPOTTED EAGLE *Aquila pomarina*
Plates 390–409

Subspecies: Two subspecies, nominate *pomarina* in European part of range and resident ssp. *hastata* in India.

Distribution: A species of E European origin reaching the Baltic countries in the north, Germany in the west and Greece in the south.

Habitat: A bird of mature forests often near meadows and river valleys. Nests in trees, often close to woodland edges. Also hunts above forest, but depends mainly on open areas for foraging. On migration found in variable habitats. Winters mainly in savannas of E and S Africa.

Population: The total European population is estimated to be 6700–9500 pairs, with important populations in Belarus, Poland, the Baltic states and Slovakia. Population (of Russia?) probably still gravely underestimated, since counts from autumn migration in Israel suggest even 140 000 birds passing in a single season, indicating that the total breeding population numbers tens of thousands of pairs, perhaps 30 000–40 000 in total.

Movements: Migratory, wintering in E, south C to S Africa. Leaves breeding grounds from late Aug, with marked peak during last week of Sep–first week of Oct along the Levant flyway. Great concentrations noted Bosporus, SE Turkey, Israel and Suez in Egypt. Largest autumn totals counted at Kafr Qasim, near Tel-Aviv, Israel where 141 868 birds were seen in autumn 1983, with 46 579 birds on 29 Sep. Last birds leave the Middle East during Oct–Nov. In winter found over a large area, mainly in savanna, from Chad and Sudan to S Africa. Main wintering areas probably south C Africa: Zimbabwe, Zambia, Botswana and Angola. Returns to Europe from early Mar, with peak passage around end of month and early Apr in Israel. Spring passage of mainly non-breeding younger birds continues until mid-May, when breeders have already settled.

Hunting and prey: Hunts largely by sit-and-wait technique, much like buzzard, often hidden in a tree. Walks freely on ground when hunting small vertebrates. Soars above hunting grounds for long periods searching for prey. During circling stops frequently against the wind to scan the ground below with drooping head. Food consists mainly of amphibians and small mammals, particularly rodents.

SPECIES IDENTIFICATION

Length 61–66 cm

wing-span 145–168 cm (Mebs 1989; D. Forsman, unpubl.)

The smallest of the true *Aquila*-eagles, although size difference only average and useless for field identification. Wings fairly long and broad, tail rather short and wide, adults bulkier in silhouette than juveniles. When soaring wing-tips more rounded (corners cut-off) and compact, with less splayed fingers than in larger species. Can be very difficult (some adults actually impossible) to tell from Greater Spotted Eagle, but also resembles subadult Steppe Eagle. Plumage variation extensive in juveniles, which often have irregular ochre areas on underbody and underwing coverts.

Identification summary: A darkish *Aquila* similar in proportions to Greater Spotted, but also to Steppe. Juveniles mainly confused with certain juvenile Greater Spotted, or even juvenile Steppe, adults and subadults with adult Greater Spotted and subadult Steppe. The most reliable characters for identification of Lesser Spotted Eagles are: the double carpal comma, with the inner being usually more prominent (double-comma also frequent in juvenile Greater Spotted); the seventh primary (counted ascendantly) not fingered in juvenile and rather short and moderately emarginated in adult; the fingered primaries of the two spotted eagles are uniformly blackish grey, lacking barring (though bases often appear paler) as opposed to Steppe and Imperial, which show barred primary bases; shows distinctly two-coloured upperwing (similar in subadult Steppe Eagle), also in juvenile plumage (cf. Greater Spotted); the wings are rather short, with particularly short arm, and the tip is rounded with short and 'closed' fingers; in head-on views shows flatter wing-profile and smaller broom at wing-tip than other *Aquila* spp.; the head appears comparatively large and rounded in relation to smallish body (cf. Steppe).

In flight, distant Wing-beats lighter and faster than in larger *Aquila* spp, not much different from a buzzard. When soaring, arms held level with softly drooping hands; when gliding, wings slightly more arched. In head-on silhouette fingered primaries and drooping 'hind-corner' of hand less conspicuous, not forming prominent 'broom' of splayed fingers found in larger species. Also looks as if wings attached to mid-body, when seen approaching, unlike in larger species where wings seem to be attached higher on the body on a level with back.

Very difficult to identify in older subadult and adult plumages as many plumage characters very similar to old Greater Spotted Eagles and subadult Steppe Eagles. Differences in wing-shape and wing-formula important but only to be used by the experienced. Normally told from Greater Spotted Eagle by more contrasting, clearly two-toned upper-wing together with whitish double carpal comma on underwing. From Steppe by propor-tions and silhouette and by differently patterned flight-feathers below, whereas upperparts may be almost identical. These three species should always be identified using as many characters as possible, since every single character varies and overlaps extensively between the species.

In flight, closer The barring of the remiges of underwing is diagnostic in non-adults, but this character is difficult to discern. The diagnostic double carpal crescent of the under-wing, one at the bases of the outer primaries and a second and often clearer at the bases of the primary coverts, is mostly a diagnostic character, when present, especially when separating adult Greater and Lesser Spotted. The colour contrast of the underwing, between somewhat paler and warmer brown coverts and darker and more greyish remiges, is *not* a reliable character, since similar underwings are common among adult Greater Spotted Eagles. Upperparts normally show a marked contrast between the paler coverts of the inner forewing and the rest of the wing (cf. Greater Spotted Eagle), although the area varies in size and shape according to age and state of moult. The bases of the inner-most primaries are whitish above, forming a clearly visible patch to mid-hand and the uppertail coverts are whitish or buffish forming a pale U at the base of the tail. In juve-niles and subadults the pale band along the tips of the greater coverts can be seen from afar.

Perched Often appears very long-legged (unlike e.g. Steppe) when it walks around on the ground or when perching briefly. At rest sits more upright and hunched, like other eagles.

Juvenile easily separated from other species by chocolate brown body-feathering with ochre nape-patch (beware of aberrant Greater Spotted Eagles!) and rows of yellowish spots to upperwing coverts, with only the greater coverts band prominent and formed by large spots, and by irregular yellowish streaking to breast, belly and thighs.

Adults and subadults very difficult to tell from faded Greater Spotted Eagles and some adults are virtually impossible to identify, although pale iris of Lesser often distinct. Both spotted eagles have roundish nostrils separating them from e.g. Steppe Eagles with oval nostrils (note that, depending on the angle of light, the shadow of a round nostril can appear oval!).

Bare parts Iris in juveniles dark greyish brown to dark brown, in adults pale yellowish brown, amber or yellow. Timing of change unknown. Iris colour of Greater Spotted Eagle apparently never becomes as pale as in Lesser Spotted, though old adults may show medium-brown irides. As a rule of thumb, if the pupil is discernible on a spotted eagle in the field it should be a Lesser, whereas the Greater Spotted Eagles (and younger Lessers!) appear dark-eyed.

Cere and feet yellow at all ages. Tarsi long and appear rather narrow and feathered down to the toes, but with short and shaggy trousers (see Perched).

Variation: Some juvenile Lesser Spotted Eagles show largely whitish tips to their greater underwing coverts forming a prominent white band across the underwing. From a distance these birds superficially resemble juvenile Steppe Eagles. Such birds should always be identified by using other characters, such as the width of the pale trailing edge and the width of the upperwing bands (narrow in Lesser Spotted, broad in Steppe) and by the wing-formula and the type of barring of the remiges.

The Lesser Spotted Eagle occurs, at least in juvenile plumage, in a very rare pale form. The upperparts of the bird are more or less normal but, on the underparts, the normal brown colour of the body-feathers and underwing coverts is replaced by a pale rufous or buffish colour. The pale areas can also occur just as irregular patches on underwings and breast. The greater coverts, as well as the flight-feathers, however, remain normal in both colour and barring.

Confusion species: Usually very difficult to tell from Greater Spotted and Steppe Eagle, apart from the most typical individuals.

Greater Spotted Eagle (page 332) Adults best told from Lessers from a distance by more uniformly dark brown upperparts with a faint and greyish primary patch, and from below by solidly dark carpal area with just one white and prominent crescent at the bases of the outermost primaries (juvenile Greater Spotted frequently show, however, two pale and rather indistinct pale crescents).

Juveniles and subadults are, on average, darker than the corresponding plumages of Lesser and show broader upperwing bands and more extensive spotting in juvenile plumage.

Steppe Eagle (page 348) Subadults almost identical in plumage to Lesser Spotted Eagles and are best told from latter by mostly greyish and coarsely and sparsely barred remiges, with barring extending to the bases of the outermost primaries (being uniformly greyish or dark on Lesser and Greater Spotted) and the wings are comparatively longer (especially the arm) with a squarer tip (protruding outer rear corner = 7th primary counted ascendantly) and more deeply splayed fingers. Greater underwing coverts also show more extensive pale markings, which may be retained until the adult plumage.

MOULT

Juveniles (first moult) Start to moult body-feathers in spring of 2nd cy, when dark brown feathers appear amongst very faded and pale feathers on mantle and scapulars. The first primary can be moulted in the winter quarters (one with replaced p1, Romania, 2 May), but moult probably more normally commences in Jun–Jul on breeding grounds (Turkey, 19 Jul, p1 half-grown). Before autumn migration up to six (normally three to five) innermost primaries, one or two secondaries (s1 and/or s5) and the tertials are moulted, as well as a few rectrices, often the central pair. Birds on autumn migration show largely juvenile underbody, or a mixture of old and new feathers, whereas mantle and scapulars are largely moulted.

The remex moult is suspended for the autumn migration but resumed in the winter quarters, where between Nov and Jan some additional remiges are moulted. In 3rd cy spring one to four outermost primaries still juvenile, worn, pointed and faded brown. These are lost during second moult in 3rd cy summer together with some inner primaries, as moult gradually adjusts to the pattern of the adults.

Adults (subsequent moults) Start to moult flight-feathers during breeding, but the timing varies considerably, as does the number of feathers replaced in the breeding areas. The moult is suspended for the autumn migration, as majority of birds are seen on migration with intact wings. The moult resumes in the wintering grounds, from *c*. Nov, and is completed in Feb, just before northbound passage. Owing to the two annual moulting periods, the adults seem capable of replacing most of their flight-feathers in one year.

AGEING AND SEXING

Juveniles and adults are rather straightforward to age, whereas older immatures require ideal conditions, and are hence often just classed as 'subadults'.

Ageing summary: Ageing straightforward in fresh juveniles with intact plumage. Pale trailing edge to wing and tail and chocolate brown lesser and median upperwing coverts contrast with blackish greater coverts and remiges. Usually just one complete and distinct wing-band on upperwing along the tips of the greater coverts. From 2nd cy spring and onwards all birds resemble each other greatly and can be aged only by retained juvenile characters, such as pale undertail coverts, spotting of upperwing and underwing coverts, tertials and scapulars, and streaking of underbody. Barring of remiges below lost with age. Adult plumage attained in approximately 4–5 years. The Lesser Spotted Eagle differs from many other large raptors in that it moults both in the breeding season and in the winter quarters. Hence the plumage changes more or less constantly.

Juveniles differ from older birds by their clearly slimmer silhouette, with narrower wings and narrower, longer tail. The trailing edge of the wing is smoothly S-curved and the seventh primary (counted ascendantly) is short and not distinctly fingered. Older birds have broader and squarer wings, and a shorter and broader tail. The wings are nearly parallel-edged and the seventh primary is clearly fingered.

Juvenile (1st cy autumn – 2nd cy spring)   Plates 390–397

Autumn juveniles are readily identifiable by their rather constant plumage features in combination with their typical silhouette. If seen together with older birds the juveniles look clearly narrower-winged with smoothly S-curved trailing edge, and the shape difference may, after training, be reliably used on single birds. Wing-tip looks narrower and less clearly fingered than in older birds, as the seventh primary (counted ascendantly) is short and normally just barely fingered. Tail appears longer and narrower and shows a pale tip, often wider than the pale trailing edge to the wing.

Upperparts are constant, medium chocolate-brown with blackish greater coverts, remiges and rectrices. The contrast between the brown lesser and median coverts and the blackish greater coverts and secondaries is very sharp and visible from afar. There is only one clear wing-band formed by the pale tips of the primary and greater coverts, but often a second, less complete, band can be seen along the tips of the outer median coverts. The inner three primaries are clearly paler than the rest, with pale shafts and darker barring, together forming a large pale area to the inner hand, at times not different from the window of a juvenile Eastern Imperial Eagle. The pale primary covert tips merge with this patch and form a white patch basally to the inner primaries. The nape has an ochre patch, which can be difficult to note on a flying bird. It is best seen when a soaring bird turns towards the observer, as it flashes for a short while against the bird's dark shoulder and mantle.

From below, the body is rather dark brown with contrastingly pale buffish vent and undertail coverts crossed by the dark 'trousers'. The lesser and median underwing coverts are either rather darkish brown, normally somewhat mottled, or they may also be paler, more uniformly sandy brown. The former type of underwing can be very similar to the underwing of younger Greater Spotted Eagles. The greater underwing coverts have, in most cases, pale spots to their tips forming a distinct pearl-band to the underwing. The spots can be small and inconspicuous and hardly discernible in the field, but on rare occasions they can also be large, covering almost the entire feather and forming a wide band rather similar to juvenile Steppe Eagle. Remiges are greyish, varying from pale grey to blackish, depending on how light is reflected from them, but generally appear dark. In good light and at close range one can see the barring on the remiges (always barred, cf.

Greater Spotted), especially on the translucent inner primaries. *The barring is regularly spaced over the entire length of the feather extending to the pale tip and the dark bars are about equal in width to the paler interspaces* (cf. Greater Spotted). The trailing edge to the wing shows a pale even band, well visible if the bird is seen against a coloured background.

A small percentage of juvenile Lesser Spotted Eagles show notably different underparts, with highly variable, irregular creamy or ochre yellow patches in their body-feathering, which at the most may cover a major part of their underparts. In most cases these patches are confined to the axillaries and inner median coverts and on the body they are usually restricted to streaks on the upper breast at times forming a pale breast-band. Some individuals may be ochre over most of the underbody, except for a darker head, neck and upper breast and a few dark lesser underwing coverts.

By 2nd cy spring the birds already greatly resemble the adult plumage-type, with pale and faded upperwing coverts. This sudden change from the distinctly patterned juvenile plumage to the drab and faded adult-like plumage over just 5–6 months is a result of the extreme wear of the plumage on the wintering grounds.

The 2nd cy spring birds are best told from older birds by the remaining juvenile features. The silhouette is still juvenile, as no wing moult has occurred, with typical narrow wings with S-curved trailing edge. The pale trailing edge to the wing, as well as the pale tip of the tail are mostly worn off, but may still show on soaring birds in favourable light. Upperparts are incredibly adult-like and practically all pale spots and other juvenile characters are lost from wear. The head is extremely pale being often the palest part of the whole bird. Only the greater coverts and the outer median coverts are slightly darker than the rest of the coverts, but the areas blend smoothly into each other. The pale area on the upperwing coverts is larger and more uniform than in older birds, where it is always reduced by darker, moulted feathers. 2nd cy spring birds lack all the clear-cut margins between the differently coloured areas typical of adults, such as the dark 'saddle' or the pale straw coloured triangle of the forearm. In flight and under favourable conditions, a faint wing-bar along the tips of the greater coverts can be seen, but as the pale tips are regularly retained only on the more protected inner vanes, the spots are not usually seen on perched birds. As a rule the uppertail coverts are worn to the shaft, which explains the narrow and inconspicuous whitish tail-base.

Second plumage (2nd cy autumn)   **Plates 398–399**

2nd cy birds still largely retain their juvenile plumage, although it is extremely worn and faded. The birds resemble adults more than juveniles but can be aged by their uniformly pale undertail coverts and vent, as in juveniles, and by the moult pattern of the remiges. The primary moult has reached p4 or 5, with moulted feathers being black above with a rounded tip, whereas the retained juvenile outer primaries are browner and comparatively shorter with pointed tips. The new inner three primaries still have narrow pale tips and largely whitish bases above, forming a rather distinct white and roundish patch on the upper inner hand. The extent of the partial body moult varies individually, but embraces mostly the scapulars and mantle feathers, being darker brown and forming a 'saddle' on the upperparts. The dark saddle contrasts strongly with the still juvenile and extremely faded upperwing coverts, which form a larger pale area to the upperwing than in any subsequent plumage. New median upperwing coverts, if any, with an irregular paler spot near the tip, are seen only at close range. Remiges and rectrices blackish brown above and, under favourable conditions, a narrow translucent trailing edge to tail and wings can be seen. The fresh uppertail coverts are buffish, forming a whitish U at the base of the tail, but in other individuals they are worn to the shaft and hence inconspicuous. The majority of birds still carry the juvenile feathers on head, nape and throat, which are extremely pale and worn and among the palest areas on the whole bird. Only a few individuals moult the crown and nape, showing a darkish head with a clear rusty nape-patch, as in juveniles.

On the underparts even less has changed compared with previous spring. Some birds have moulted some lesser coverts and the carpal-patch, which together form a darker band close to the leading edge of the wing. The majority of birds show, however, unmoulted and very faded pale brown lesser and median underwing coverts, probably paler than in any subsequent plumage. Also, the greater coverts are retained juvenile feathers with smaller or larger whitish spots. The birds also retain the uniformly pale vent and undertail coverts of the juvenile plumage. If any tail-feathers are moulted they differ by being longer and broader with a wider pale tip than the retained juvenile rectrices. Also, the new innermost primaries are longer and broader than the juvenile ones and do not seem to fit in with the outline of the wing. The secondaries are mostly retained juvenile feathers and the few possible new secondaries are clearly longer than the others protruding from the otherwise even trailing edge.

(3rd cy spring) Not depicted

The birds still show a number of juvenile characters, but ageing becomes more difficult because of the increasing number of adult characters attained during the previous winter's moult.

The shape of the bird is closer to adult than to juvenile, but the trailing edge of the wing is typically irregular. *Usually one to four outer primaries are still juvenile*, pointed, comparatively short and faded brown. *Many of the secondaries are still juvenile showing as deep indentions in the trailing edge, usually at s3–4 and s8–10 (7–11)*. The replaced secondaries are broader, longer and less clearly barred than the retained juvenile feathers. Some of the earliest moulted secondaries still have narrow whitish tips, but from now on new feathers as a rule lack pale tips. The tail is mainly moulted, new feathers still showing narrow pale tips.

Upperparts worn and rather faded and evenly brown. Head and neck are palest, still with pale nape-patch, whereas mantle and scapulars are slightly darker and do not contrast notably with the upperwing coverts. Lesser and median upperwing coverts are partly moulted, hence all upperwing being slightly darker than in 2nd cy autumn. Greater coverts dark.

Underparts darker and more uniform than in 2nd cy autumn, as body largely moulted during winter and now mostly darker than the underwing coverts. Lesser and median underwing coverts only partly moulted, slightly darker than in 2nd cy autumn. Carpal area and lesser coverts of leading edge often darker than rest. Greater coverts worn, still with paler spots. Undertail coverts either largely unmoulted and pale, or ochre with darker spots and bars.

Third plumage (3rd cy autumn)   **Plates 400–402**

Most birds still possible to age exactly if seen close. Some still retain one or two outermost juvenile primaries, which are short, abraded with narrow, pointed tips and very faded brown. More advanced birds show very dark moulted p2–4 and the outermost, while the median primaries are paler and slightly shorter. One or two juvenile secondaries may be retained in each wing (mostly s4 and s8).

Upperparts largely moulted and darkish mid-brown, similar to fresh adult, lacking strong upperwing contrasts, but often showing extensively pale-spotted upperwing coverts. Diffuse and faint greyish bar along tips of greater coverts possible to see only at close range. May still show solid ochre nape-patch, at least elongated nape feathers showing paler tips. Uppertail coverts buffish with darker mottling, not forming distinct U of younger birds.

Underparts mainly moulted and rather darkish brown, but general impression often untidy and variegated with scattered pale unmoulted feathers retained on throat, breast and among underwing coverts. Worn greater coverts still show pale spots but newly moulted feathers appear more or less uniformly brown. Undertail coverts buffish with darker mottling, pale and dark appearing in roughly equal proportions.

(4th cy spring to autumn)   **Plate 403**

Not possible to age with certainty. Birds lacking juvenile flight-feathers, but retaining a trace of a paler nape-patch, spotted greater underwing coverts and streaked breast, belly and 'trousers', are probably in their 4th cy spring. Undertail coverts as in 3rd cy autumn. Most of these birds also show pale but irregular markings on the large scapulars and tertials. Head and neck worn and faded, whereas mantle and scapulars are rather fresh and darkish brown contrasting with slightly paler upperwing coverts. After summer moult, pale spots may theoretically be lost altogether and bird becomes indistinguishable from adult, but more probably birds retain some spotted underwing coverts until next winter's moult.

From this age onwards the new greater underwing coverts begin to show greyish barring on the paler outer webs as the feathers with uniform pale spots are replaced.

Adult (from 4th cy late autumn/winter and older) Plates 404–409

Upperparts of adult Lesser Spotted Eagles are in general slightly darker and more uniformly coloured than in birds of 2nd cy spring and autumn. The colour of different plumage tracts varies individually, however, depending on state of moult and wear of plumage. Some birds can show paler brown upperwing coverts and a darker brown 'saddle', whereas others at the same time appear rather uniformly mid-brown above. Correspondingly, the head can be either faded and pale, or fresh and darker brown in colour, but the nape lacks the ochre patch of juveniles and subadults. The upperwing coverts area is normally two-toned, with a paler triangle on upper forearm close to the body and darker greater coverts and outer median coverts. The pale patch at the base of the inner primaries is formed by greyish outer webs to the three innermost primaries, looking from a distance pure white and rounded (rather grey and diffuse in some), but may extend to the trailing edge of the wing along the innermost primary. The tail is coloured like the secondaries, but may at times show faint greyish barring and paler tip. The uppertail coverts are normally buffish or greyish with brown mottling, forming a paler U at the tail-base, which, however, is less conspicuous than on juveniles and young subadults.

Underwing coverts appear normally paler and more warm in colour, sandy to rufous brown, compared with the dark greyish to blackish flight-feathers. Many individuals with fresh underwing coverts show darker and duller brown underwing coverts, which do not differ markedly in shade from the remiges and thus may come very close to the appearance of adult Greater Spotted Eagle. Greater coverts are either uniformly dark or show barring to paler outer webs, and the carpal area normally stands out as mottled but darker than the rest of the covert area. *Adults have uniformly coloured remiges* (or show only faint barring at the bases), a character usually impossible to discern in the field (cf. subadult Steppe Eagle). The innermost three primaries tend to be dark in adults, and the underwing thus lacks the pale window of younger birds. There are normally two pale crescents around the carpal area, with a fainter one at the bases of the primaries and a clearer and wider one at the bases of the greater primary coverts. The latter is often also longer, encircling the whole carpal area (cf. Greater Spotted and Steppe Eagles). Body is either darker than the underwing coverts or the same colour, depending on state of moult. Throat may be paler than the rest of the body, much as in Steppe Eagle, and the undertail coverts are brown as the rest of the body, though some pale barring may be left from the subadult stages.

Old subadults (?) are similar to adults, but may show paler mottled undertail coverts and some pale markings to the greater underwing coverts as well as narrow pale tips to rectrices and inconspicuous barring to secondaries.

Sexing: Usually not possible to sex in the field, unless male and female e.g. in a pair are seen together, when male appears smaller and narrower-winged with a comparatively larger head.

References: Brooke et al. 1972; Forsman 1988, 1989, 1990, 1991, 1996b; Mebs 1989; Meyburg et al. 1995b; Olsen 1990; Sladek 1957; Svensson 1975, 1987; Tucker & Heath 1995

Plate 390   *Juvenile. A rather average individual showing diagnostic barring to remiges and short 7th finger (counted inwards). Aged by uniform plumage with pale trailing edge to wings and tail and pale vent and undertail coverts. 6 Oct 1995, Israel (Dick Forsman).*

Plate 391   *Juvenile. A rather uniformly dark individual. Note characteristic barring of secondaries, typical wing-formula and double-crescent at carpal. 28 Sep 1992, Israel (Dick Forsman).*

Plate 392   *Juvenile, with sandy brown underwing coverts while upperwing shows diagnostic contrast between brown lesser and median coverts and black greater coverts with white tips. Note double-crescent of underwing. 11 Oct 1988, Israel (Dick Forsman).*

Plate 393   *Juvenile, showing diagnostic barring and wing-formula, with six prominent fingers only (cf. juvenile Greater Spotted Eagle). Autumn, Israel (Hadoram Shirihai).*

Plate 394 *Juvenile (same as Plate 393). Note pale nape-patch, brown body plumage and distinctly contrasting black greater coverts with pale-spotted tips. Autumn, Israel (Hadoram Shirihai).*

Plate 395 *Juvenile. Note ochre nape-patch, brown body plumage, typically barred secondaries and only one distinct row of spots on upperwing. 5 Oct 1987, Israel (Dick Forsman).*

Plate 396 *Juvenile. This rather more spotted individual is very similar to the brown juvenile Greater Spotted Eagles that occur regularly. Best identified by type of barring to secondaries, not visible here. Note rounded head and small, buzzard-like bill. 14 Oct 1996, Israel (Annika Forsten).*

Plate 397 *Juvenile in worn plumage (2nd cy spring). By spring juveniles are faded and worn and have lost the spotting above. Aged by uniform plumage, with uniform, narrow pale trailing edge to wings and tail. Spring, Israel (Hadoram Shirihai).*

Plate 398 *Second plumage (2nd cy autumn). Much like juvenile from below but told by freshly moulted p1–4, one new rectrix and newly moulted head and forebody, while rest of plumage is still juvenile. Oct 1993, Israel (Klaus Bjerre).*

Plate 399 *Second plumage with typically moulted p1–4, s1 and s5 and part of underbody, while rest of flight-feathers and all underwing coverts are juvenile. 26 Sep 1997, Israel (Dick Forsman).*

Plate 400 *Third plumage (3rd cy autumn). Resembles second plumage, but shows fresh inner and outer primaries, often also irregular trailing edge to arm. Underbody variegated with largely pale vent. 27 Sep 1987, Israel (Dick Forsman).*

Plate 401 *Third plumage. Note pale nape-patch and vent and extensively pale-spotted body, while remiges show feathers of different age, with fresh outer and inner primaries, and no retained juvenile feathers in this individual. Autumn, Israel (Hadoram Shirihai).*

Plate 402 *Third plumage still showing pale spots to underparts but with narrow, diffuse pale tips to greater coverts and irregular trailing edge of wing. 1 Oct 1997, Israel (Dick Forsman).*

Plate 403 *Subadult, probably 4th cy autumn owing to barred remiges and retained shorter secondaries creating irregular trailing edge of wing, but no juvenile remiges left. 27 Sep 1997, Israel (Dick Forsman).*

Plate 404 *Young adult showing pale markings to greater coverts and some barred remiges. Note double carpal-comma. 28 Sep 1992, Israel (Dick Forsman).*

Plate 405 *Adult. Lacks pale markings below except for variably distinct pale carpal crescents. Note uniformly dark flight-feathers. 6 Oct 1995, Israel (Dick Forsman).*

Plate 406   *Adult with typically uniformly dark remiges and dark greater coverts. This bird has a rather pale body plumage. 26 Sep 1997, Spain (Dick Forsman).*

Plate 407   *Adult. A dark bird, very similar to adult Greater Spotted Eagle from below, including identical carpal comma in this individual, but note different wing-formula and pale iris. When identifying difficult birds like this the characters of the upperparts are essential. 30 Sep 1987, Israel (Dick Forsman).*

Plate 408   *Adult from above showing sharp upperwing contrast and distinct pale patch to upper hand. Note also pale uppertail coverts. 13 Jan 1997, S Africa (Annika Forsten).*

Plate 409   *Young adult, still showing pale streaks on neck. Note pale iris, long feathered tarsus and distinct upperwing contrast typical of this species. Jun 1991, Greece (Alfred Limbrunner).*

GREATER SPOTTED EAGLE *Aquila clanga*
Plates 410–429

Subspecies: Monotypic.

Distribution: From E Europe across Asia in a wide zone to China and the Pacific coast.

Habitat: Breeds in forests near wetlands, where it mainly hunts. Winters mostly close to different types of wetlands: deltas, lakes, marshes and fishponds.

Population: European population totals about 860–1100 pairs, of which 800–1000 breed in Russia and the rest in the Baltic states, Belarus, Poland, Ukraine, Moldova and Romania. Data scanty about recent population changes, but occurs in European part of range in much lower densities than the Lesser Spotted Eagle; probably some retreat in northern part of range in the twentieth century.

Migration: Mainly migratory, but less pronounced long-range migrant than Lesser. Leaves breeding grounds on average later than Lesser and turns up at the major flyways around the Mediterranean end of Sep–early Oct. Always present in small numbers, mainly singly or at the most a few together. Migration period protracted and lasts well into Nov. Some birds reach E Africa, down to Kenya, but bulk of population winters further north, from Sudan and Egypt to the Middle East. Small numbers winter in S Europe, mainly in the Balkans. In winter often found several together at favourable feeding sites. Spring passage from mid-Feb, with peak in late Mar and early Apr. Breeding adults reach breeding grounds from Mar, whereas young non-breeders can be seen on passage as late as in May.

Hunting and prey: Hunts either on the wing, scanning the ground from moderate height, or from elevated perch in tree or on the ground. Also walks around on the ground when hunting. Food consists mainly of different vertebrates, depending on local supply. Rodents, especially water vole, and medium-sized waterfowl and their young are frequently taken; locally, fish from fishponds are the most important source of prey, especially during winter. Also uses carrion.

SPECIES IDENTIFICATION

Length 59–63 cm

wing-span 164–181 cm (*n*=3; W.S. Clark, unpubl.); 159–176 cm (Noakes 1990); 160–185 cm (Mebs 1989)

A dark and compact eagle, in size between Lesser Spotted and Steppe Eagle and partly overlapping with both. Adults often extremely similar to adult Lesser Spotted Eagle and adult Steppe Eagle in the field and positive identification requires seeing several plumage characters. Juveniles and immatures are easier to identify, although certain individuals may resemble the two aforementioned species. Juveniles more lightly built than adults, with narrower wings and proportionately longer and narrower tail.

Identification summary: A generally dark and compact eagle with broad wings and short tail and with head and body appearing comparatively large for the wing-area (cf. Steppe and Eastern Imperial Eagles). Very similar to Lesser Spotted Eagle, and possible to identify only by plumage details, although adults especially are, on aver-age, broader-winged with squarer wing-tips than adult Lesser Spotted. Also soars and glides on more arched wings than Lesser with wider 'broom' of splayed fingers at wing-tip in head-on views. Greater Spotted Eagles are relatively easy to identify in juvenile and younger immature plumages, being generally dark below with distinctly darker underwing coverts than flight-feathers, and with a prominent outer whitish crescent at the base of the outermost primaries. Upperparts are blackish or dark brown and lack the distinct contrast of the upperwing typical of Lesser Spotted. Depending on age, upperwing coverts show a variable number of pale wing-bands, at least one broad and distinct at the tips of the greater coverts. Older immatures and adults are much more difficult to identify and can be mistaken for both Lesser Spotted and Steppe Eagles. Adult Greater Spotted best told from Lesser Spotted by more uniform upperwings and by one prominent whitish carpal crescent below and from Steppe Eagle by uniformly dark flight-feathers above and below, and by the distinct whitish crescent basally on the uniformly coloured outermost primaries.

In flight, distant Active flight lighter than in e.g. Steppe and Imperial, but not as light and *Buteo*-like as often in Lesser Spotted and wings kept typically arched during flapping flight. When gliding, wings held diagnostically deeply arched, with hand drooping and primary-tips sharply bent upwards, more so than in Lesser, forming wide 'broom' at tip. When soaring, wings remain more bowed than in other *Aquila*-species.

Distant Greater Spotted Eagles usually have to be identified by the characters of the upperparts since the dark underparts are difficult to assess. Juveniles are usually readily distinguished by blackish ground-colour and several distinct pale wing-bands above. Adults are more difficult to tell from Lesser Spotted but are usually possible to identify by slightly darker and more uniformly brown upperparts with diffuse greyish primary patch. Distant adults often not possible to tell from adult Steppe.

In flight, closer Adults are, on average, slightly bulkier in silhouette than Lesser Spotted, with broader and squarer wing-tips (rather prominently fingered 7th primary counted inwards = more distinct hind corner to hand than in Lesser) and a comparatively shorter and broader tail, but juvenile Greater Spotted has a more similar wing-formula to adult Lesser.

Plumage normally looks dark from below and Greater Spotted is usually easily picked out from a flock of Lesser on this feature. The whitish crescent at the base of the outermost primaries is, on average, broader and shorter and more distinct than in Lesser Spotted, which usually shows two narrow and more diffuse crescents tending to curve around the primary coverts. Upperparts duller brown lacking Lesser's contrasting and clearly defined paler areas on upperwing coverts. From above, the pale area of the upper hand in adults is formed by white feather shafts only, resulting in a diffuse greyish patch, not a round and whitish area as in Lesser, while juveniles and subadults may show a rather prominent and whitish patch rather similar to typical Lesser.

Perched Juveniles and younger immatures mostly identified by multiple rows of spots on blackish or dark brown upperwing coverts, whereas subadults and adults are rather uniformly brown and can be practically identical to corresponding plumages of Lesser. Greater Spotted is, on average, darker brown than Lesser, although some adults may be as faded and greyish brown as typical adult Lesser. Appears bigger and more powerful than Lesser because of slightly deeper and heavier bill and shorter legs, but these differences are only average and by no means exclusive. Adult Greater Spotted told from adult Steppe by lack of ochre nape-patch and lack of latter's diagnostic sparse barring to tertials and tail.

Bare parts Feet and cere yellow; bill black in juveniles and immatures, turning grey from the base in adults. Iris dark brown in juveniles and in most older birds, too; may turn medium brown in adults, but probably not as pale yellowish brown as in many adult Lesser Spotted Eagles.

Variation: The Greater Spotted Eagle occurs at all ages in a rare pale colour morph called '*fulvescens*', which seems to be more frequent in the eastern part of the species' range. These birds vary considerably in paleness and colour. Some birds are very pale and uniformly yellowish buff, resembling pale Tawny Eagles *Aquila rapax* causing confusion in areas where both species may occur together, as in India, S Arabia and N Africa. Others are slightly darker, sandy yellowish brown, with diffuse darker streaking on breast, somewhat resembling immature Eastern Imperial Eagle; yet others appear in a fox-red plumage, varying somewhat in paleness individually, with irregular brownish streaking below. Regardless of paleness of body plumage *'fulvescens'* show normal flight-feathers and distinctly dark greater underwing coverts (often also darker carpal area), leaving the pale forearm of the underwing rather narrow (the lesser coverts often appear slightly darker than the median coverts, as is the general tendency also in normally coloured birds). Flight-feathers appear dark underneath enhancing the diagnostic whitish carpal crescent. Chin, throat and cheeks are often slightly darker than the rest of the head, giving some birds an almost Golden Eagle-like look. Upperparts vary like the underparts, but juveniles and immatures show generally broader pale wing-bars than birds in normal plumage (not formed by spots as in normal plumage). The flight-feathers are also normal above.

See also under 'Juveniles' for brownish, Lesser Spotted-like birds.

Confusion species: Very similar to Lesser Spotted Eagle and Steppe Eagle and the identification of these three species probaly poses one of the most difficult field identification problems of the region.

Lesser Spotted Eagle (page 316) Identified by combination of double crescent to carpal area of underwing, contrasting upperwing with distinctly paler coverts than remiges and with distinct whitish patch to inner primaries, lack of broad upperwing band in all except juvenile plumage and by more rounded wing-tip (shorter p4) and marginally narrower wings (in most individuals).

Steppe Eagle (page 348) Adults may be very dark and practically impossible to separate from adult Greater Spotted from a distance. On average, Steppe shows longer wings (because of longer arm) with even more square-cut tips and longer 'fingers' and, in good light, the remiges appear greyish below (uniformly black in adult Greater Spotted), with sparse barring visible from closeup. From above, most adult Steppe separated from adult Greater Spotted by rusty nape-patch, greyish and diffusely barred uppertail and secondaries, and by much wider and barred greyish bases to the primaries often covering all of the upper hand except for the fingers. Some adult Steppe Eagles are, however, very dark, with unbarred flight-feathers below and above, thus being very similar to adult Greater Spotted Eagles. The distinct whitish underwing crescent of Greater Spotted and the rusty nape of Steppe are sometimes the only plumage differences between the species.

MOULT

The moult is annually incomplete as in other *Aquila*-eagles, but the Greater and Lesser Spotted Eagles are both capable of replacing more flight-feathers during one moult cycle than are larger species of the genus.

Juveniles (first moult) Start to moult their flight-feathers in 2nd cy May–Jun. Moult may continue until late Oct–Nov, when birds can still be seen with growing primaries. In late autumn there are still juvenile remiges left: the outermost four or five primaries and usually also a large group of central secondaries (e.g. s3–4 and s7–11). Tail sometimes completely moulted, but normally shows a few retained juvenile rectrices. Moult often (regularly?) resumed in the winter quarters and a few additional flight-feathers are replaced. On spring migration the outer two or three primaries and a group of median secondaries are still retained juvenile feathers. They are shorter, narrower and more pointed, hence giving the trailing edge and tip of the wing a ragged outline.

Adults (subsequent moults) Primaries are moulted serially descendant. Seem capable of moulting more or less all flight-feathers and rectrices during one moult cycle. The extent of the annual moult, however, varies individually. Moult starts during breeding (adult male, Poland, 25 May, moult recently commenced; non-breeding subadult, Finland, 17 Mar, with moult initiated). Moult in adults suspended in late autumn (Oct–Nov), but resumed later, as actively moulting birds are frequently seen in mid-winter between Dec and Feb.

AGEING AND SEXING

In all, five age-classes can be recognized. Ageing immatures and subadults usually requires close and prolonged views, while juveniles and adults are mostly rather easy to age even from a distance. When ageing Greater Spotted Eagles pay attention to moult of flight-feathers and greater upperwing coverts and note the feather-pattern of the flight-feathers and of the coverts of upperwing, underwing and undertail.

> **Ageing summary:** Juveniles show an even pale trailing edge to wing and tail-tip and the undertail coverts are uniformly buffish. Second plumage resembles the juvenile, but the trailing edge is uneven, the inner primaries are moulted and the upperwing coverts are browner with only one prominent wing-band. In the third plumage the upperwing band and the pale trailing edge start to dissolve (latter still uneven), while the underparts are still rather juvenile-like, but with darker remiges. The fourth plumage differs from the uniformly brown adult plumage by pale vent and undertail coverts and by (partly) retained pale tips to the underwing coverts.

Juvenile plumage (1st cy autumn – 2nd cy spring)   Plates 410–417

Normally very strikingly patterned and rather easy to identify species and also easy to age. Best age character is the even and white, S-shaped trailing edge of the wing and the regular pattern of pale spots on the upperwing. Main variation in plumage caused by variation in number and size of pale spots in plumage. Birds with chocolate brown body-feathers occur rarely, superficially resembling juvenile Lesser Spotted Eagle, though usually duller in colour and more spotted above (for details see below).

Normally blackish ground-colour to upperparts, with a purple sheen in fresh plumage separates juvenile Greater Spotted from any Lesser Spotted. Pale ochre to buffish tips to secondaries, three innermost primaries and to tail-feathers, broader and more prominent below than above. Spots of same colour to most upperwing coverts, forming wing-bands, visible at great distance, at least the ones on the greater and larger median coverts. Extensively spotted birds also show more wing-bands and, in the most extensively spotted birds, the individual drops merge into each other to form a large pale area to the central upperwing. Secondaries and tail-feathers appear blackish with paler tips. The three innermost primaries are pale, the others dark with white shafts and basally greyish outerwebs. The *c.* seven inner primary coverts are tipped white, forming a band merging with the pale primary-bases. The paler parts on the upper hand combine to form a rather large, rectangular and almost whitish area at the bases of the inner primaries. Depending on the viewing angle, e.g. on a soaring bird, the patch varies from pure white and distinct to a wider and pale, shiny area. As a whole the impression of the patch is not much different to the patch of a Lesser Spotted Eagle in corresponding plumage. Uppertail coverts are pale buffish and form a distinct whitish U to the base of the uppertail and often there is another pale patch on the lower back, partly hidden by the scapulars. The lanceolated feathers of the hindneck are normally tipped buffish but only rarely create a solid nape-patch typical of younger Lesser Spotted Eagles.

The ventral parts are more variable in colour because of great individual variation in the amount of pale streaking. The darkest birds are practically blackish brown underneath, except for pale buffish vent and undertail coverts. The majority of birds are streaked buffish to ochre on belly and thighs, with streaking blending softly with darker breast. The palest of the 'normal' birds are streaked all over the underbody, leaving only the throat dark. The lesser and median underwing coverts are usually black and, in good light, appear clearly darker than the greyish and shiny flight-feathers, but some individuals show more variegated underwing coverts, with variable ochre spots or patches. The greater underwing coverts are dark grey and shiny, with or without whitish spots, but they may look either blackish or paler grey depending on the angle of light. In certain light they may seem to form a paler diffuse band to the underwing. The white spots on the underwing greater coverts are, in some birds, large and clear forming a broad band of spots, while other birds show small spots or lack spots completely. The remiges are greyish from below, with inner three primaries often distinctly paler. The tips of the secondaries are widely pale, but still the shining trailing edge is normally narrower than in Imperial and Steppe Eagles, being more similar to Lesser Spotted. In normal light the flight-feathers appear dark and uniform but in extremely good light or at close range one can see the characteristic barring, separating younger Greater Spotted Eagles from other *Aquila*-species: *the dark barring is fine and sparse, the bars being much narrower than the grey interspaces and ending some 5–10 cm before the tips.* The barring is best seen on the inner and translucent primaries (which may be unbarred!). Rarely juveniles may also show uniformly dark secondaries, as adults. The fingered primaries are always uniformly greyish basally (as in Lesser Spotted), lacking the barring of Steppe and Imperial, with narrowly white bases of the outermost forming a diagnostic carpal comma or crescent. In Greater Spotted it is typically confined to the outer three primaries, being rather short but wide and almost pure white in colour. Juveniles normally also show a second, less distinct comma at the bases of the greater primary coverts, which is normally lacking in adults (cf. Lesser Spotted). The outer crescent is less conspicuous in juveniles than in adults because of paler greyish primary-bases and may hence resemble the normal pattern of Lesser Spotted Eagle.

Spring birds are still rather similar to autumn juveniles, although somewhat browner from wear. The pale spots are most liable to wear and may be lacking completely from inner arm, but are usually retained on outer wing. Wing-bands of upperwing appear regular, although narrower and less distinct than in fresh plumage. The trailing edge of the wing is still pale, but narrower than in fresh plumage. Underparts are much as in fresh juvenile plumage.

Brown morph Juveniles occur in a rare brownish morph, with brown body-feathers instead of purplish black. Apart from the ground-colour the birds are normally patterned. These birds can easily be mistaken for juvenile Lesser Spotted Eagles. They can, however, be identified by their wing-formula, with distinctly fingered seventh primary (counted inwards; not distinctly fingered in juvenile Lesser), their diagnostic carpal crescent and by the diagnostic barring of the flight-feathers. However, since some of the few recorded brownish juveniles have shown Lesser Spotted Eagle-like (or intermediate) wing-formula, wing-barring and a distinct pale nape-patch, these individuals may be hybrids between the two Spotted Eagle species.

Second plumage (2nd cy autumn – 3rd cy spring)   Plates 418–423
Still resembles the juvenile plumage, and in fact comprises largely juvenile feathers. Best told from juveniles by broadly white-tipped inner primaries (and one or two secondaries) contrasting with the majority of retained juvenile secondaries, being shorter and lacking white tips (or just showing narrow pale fringes to tips). The trailing edge is straighter than in juveniles, because the shorter inner juvenile primaries have been replaced by longer

feathers. Depending on the extent of body moult the plumage may appear either brown or more blackish brown.

From late summer individuals can be aged by the state of moult with freshly moulted four or five inner primaries in combination with unmoulted, short juvenile secondaries and largely juvenile-like plumage. The upper median coverts are usually completely replaced and the new feathers may have large spots or may be uniformly dark, depending on the amount of spotting of the individual bird. The greater coverts are, however, never completely moulted, showing a number of retained, extremely worn and white-spotted juvenile greater coverts in the middle of the row, while the moulted greater coverts show prominent white spots similar to the juvenile plumage. In some advanced birds the latest replaced greater coverts show, not a distinct roundish spot, but a narrower pale tip with darker marbling. Also, the moulted inner primary coverts show distinct white tips, similar to the juvenile plumage. The few freshly moulted secondaries show broad pale tips, while the pale tips of the retained juvenile secondaries are largely worn off.

Underparts very similar to juvenile, except for the moulted remiges and a tendency for the lesser and median coverts to show a distinctly brownish tinge.

Distant 2nd cy autumn birds look much like juveniles (or Lesser Spotteds!) above, with usually two distinct wing-bars, but with clearly brownish upperwing coverts. The new inner primaries show distinct pale tips in contrast to largely worn juvenile secondaries with abraded and only narrowly pale-fringed tips. The whitish area at the base of the inner primaries is conspicuous and forms an extension to the greater coverts wing-band. The white U of the uppertail coverts may be either fresh and whitish or worn and rather inconspicuous.

In 3rd cy spring, second plumage birds can be difficult to separate from spring juveniles, as both show worn spots on the upperparts. The uneven trailing edge as well as the squarish shape of the wing differ, however, from the more slender-winged juveniles with nicely S-curved and even trailing edge. In closer views the few remaining outer juvenile primaries (shorter and brownish) as well as the remaining central secondaries (shorter) should also be obvious. The ragged and uneven greater coverts bar of the upperwing is also diagnostic.

Third plumage (3rd cy autumn – 4th cy spring)   Plate 424

Difficult to age unless seen close enough for detailed study of the plumage, which still shows extensive pale spotting to the upperparts (scapulars), belly and thighs. The upper lesser and median coverts lack pale spots in many individuals, but there are still pale markings to the tips of all greater upperwing coverts, including the most freshly moulted. However, the fresh coverts no longer show rounded pale spots but narrowly greyish tips with discrete dark marbling. The most recently moulted greater coverts may even lack marbling altogether, being uniformly dark brown as in adults. The wing-band is more distinct on the inner arm, becoming diffuse further out. All juvenile remiges have been replaced now, and the third generation inner primaries are darker, lacking pale tips. Also, the newly moulted secondaries are darker below than those of previous generations.

Fourth plumage-type (4th cy autumn – 5th cy spring)   Plate 425

After the third plumage, Greater Spotted Eagles have at least one more subadult plumage before the final adult plumage is attained. From a distance this plumage appears very similar to the final adult plumage, and the upperparts appear identical. The underparts mostly still show a pale vent and undertail coverts, while the greater underwing coverts are often still pale-spotted, forming a broken band on the underwing. In closer views a few remaining pale-tipped upper greater coverts can be seen as well as paler tips to some scapulars. May still show barring to some of the remiges of the underwing.

Adult plumage (from *c.* 5th cy autumn and older)   Plates 426–429

Adult Greater Spotted Eagles are generally very uniformly medium to dark brown. Perched birds seem to lack identification characters completely, being very similar to perched adult Lesser Spotted and adult Steppe Eagles. In flight, adults appear very uniformly coloured and the few important identification characters are found on the upperwing and underwing.

Upperparts vary with the stage of moult and can be either very uniformly dark brown or pale chocolate brown, in fact very similar to adult Lesser Spotted Eagles. The paler patch at the base of the inner primaries is the most important single identification character above. In adult Greater Spotted Eagles this patch is rather inconspicuous and formed solely by the white feather-shafts of the inner seven or eight primaries, and, in some birds, also by the slightly grey-tinged primary bases and primary covert tips. From a distance the patch is either very indistinct or appears as a greyish sheen on the otherwise uniform upper hand (not as a solid whitish patch as usually in Lesser). In closer views the effect of a greyish area is lost and only the white feather-shafts are apparent. The rest of the upperparts are more variable and the head, neck and mantle, but also some wing coverts, may, in some birds, be as pale as in adult Lesser Spotted. The general impression is, however, that the whole head (including the crown) appears darker than in adult Lesser Spotted. It is normal in Greater Spotted Eagles for the upperwing to look very uniform, lacking distinctly paler and sharply contrasting covert areas. A darker 'saddle' is, however, often seen contrasting with the slightly paler upperwing coverts. The uppertail coverts can be pale forming a distinct U at the tail-base, but they can also be brown like the rest of the upper parts.

Underparts vary less in colour and generally look rather uniformly dark including the vent and undertail coverts. The most reliable underwing character separating adult Greater and Lesser Spotted Eagles seems to be the difference in the shape and brightness of the carpal crescents. In adult Greater there is only one crescent, which is broad and white and extends only over the few outermost primary-bases, whereas in Lesser Spotted there are two narrow crescents often reaching around the carpal area and with the inner being paler and more distinct. The crescent of the adult Greater is normally very conspicuous between the uniformly dark carpal area and dark primary-bases. All remiges, including the inner three primaries, are uniformly blackish and lack barring completely. The underwing coverts vary from medium brown to dark brown, with the lesser coverts and the carpal-patch being frequently somewhat darker than the rest. Darker birds appear very uniform on the whole underwing and only favourable lighting shows any difference between the shades of coverts and flight-feathers. In adults with paler brownish coverts the underwing looks very similar to older Lesser Spotted Eagles, and the two species cannot be separated by this character. The underbody is normally dark, often distinctly darker than the underwing coverts and the trailing edge of the wing lacks the pale border of younger immatures, while the tail sometimes shows a translucent greyish tip.

Adult Greater Spotted Eagles do not seem to acquire a pale yellowish brown iris, which seems to be normal for adult Lesser Spotted.

Sexing: Normally not possible to sex in the field unless male and female are seen together. Females are slightly bigger, heavier and broader-winged than males.

References: Clark 1990; Forsman 1984, 1988, 1989, 1990, 1991, 1996a; Mebs 1989; Meyburg et al. 1995b; Noakes 1990; Olsen 1990; Svensson 1975, 1987; Tucker & Heath 1995

Plate 410 *Juvenile. Note uniform plumage and pale tips to remiges and rectrices, as well as marked contrast between darker coverts and pale remiges. Nov 1996, Oman (Lasse J. Laine).*

Plate 411 *Juvenile. A browner bird with typically greyish remiges and intact pale trailing edge to wing. Winter, Israel (Hadoram Shirihai).*

Plate 412 *Juvenile. Note diagnostic fine barring of secondaries with largely pale and unbarred tips. Dec 1996, UAE (Markku Huhta-Koivisto).*

Plate 413 *Juvenile* fulvescens. *Body-plumage uniformly yellowish buff with dark greater coverts, but flight-feathers normal. Note white comma at bases of outer primaries. 10 Nov 1994, Oman (Hanne & Jens Eriksen).*

Plate 414 *Juvenile from above showing dark plumage and typically spotted upperwing coverts and scapulars. Dec 1996, UAE (Tom Lindroos).*

Plate 415 *Juvenile. A sparsely spotted individual with upperparts typically blackish brown lacking contrast between greater and median coverts (cf. juvenile Lesser Spotted Eagle). 22 Dec 1994, Oman (Hanne & Jens Eriksen).*

Plate 416 *Juvenile. A paler and more richly spotted individual. Birds like this often have a largely pale belly and, as here, uniform, pale trousers. Dec 1993, Israel (Markus Varesvuo).*

Plate 417 *Juvenile fulvescens. The upperwing coverts lack the typical spotting of normal birds. The face and throat are often darker than the rest of the head and underbody. 16 Dec 1994, Oman (Hanne & Jens Eriksen).*

Plate 418   *Second plumage (2nd cy autumn). Greatly resembles juvenile, but note moult in wings with irregular trailing edge and retained juvenile p6–10. The new remiges show a juvenile-like barring. 27 Oct 1995, Oman (Hanne & Jens Eriksen).*

Plate 419   *Second plumage (3rd cy spring) in late winter moult. Similar to juvenile, but aged by three retained outer juvenile primaries. 14 Feb 1995, UAE (Annika Forsten).*

Plate 420   *Second plumage (3rd cy spring). Aged by retained juvenile p9–10 and s4 and s8. The white mottling to underwing comes from missing coverts because of moult. Mar 1997, UAE (Markus Varesvuo).*

Plate 421   *Second plumage* fulvescens. *Told from juvenile by typical moult-pattern showing retained juvenile outer primaries. Note uniformly dark appearance of remiges. Dec 1996, Oman (Lasse J. Laine).*

Plate 422 *Second plumage* fulvescens *from above. Aged by typical moult-pattern of remiges. Note that* fulvescens-*type birds do not show the normal spotted upperwing coverts, hence the more irregular upperwing-pattern in worn plumage. Nov 1994, UAE (Hannu Kettunen).*

Plate 423 *Second plumage (2nd cy autumn). Superficially resembles juvenile but differs by showing coverts and remiges of different age. Aged more exactly by extremely abraded central greater coverts with worn-off white spots. Note that the new coverts still show juvenile-like markings. 4 Nov 1994, Oman (Hanne & Jens Eriksen).*

Plate 424 *Non-juvenile immature, possibly second or third plumage. Irregularly patterned upperwing coverts suggest a* fulvescens-*type bird, not possible to age exactly from this image. Note roundish nostril (cf. Steppe Eagle). 28 Mar 1996, Oman (Hanne & Jens Eriksen).*

Plate 425 *Fourth plumage-type. Remiges uniformly dark, as in adult, but partly pale greater underwing and undertail coverts suggest a younger bird. 30 Oct 1986, Israel (Dick Forsman).*

Plate 426 *Adult showing all dark underparts including dark remiges. Note the diagnostic pale crescent basally on the outer primaries. The white spots in the coverts are due to missing moulted feathers. 29 Oct 1986, Israel (Dick Forsman).*

Plate 427 *Many older birds show brown underwing coverts, distinctly paler than the blackish remiges. Note distinct white comma on outer primaries. Nov 1986, Israel (Markku Huhta-Koivisto).*

Plate 428 *Older Greater Spotted Eagle. A paler brown bird, which could easily be mistaken for a Lesser Spotted Eagle. Note broader wing-tip (long p7), dark carpal-patch and distinct pale comma at outer primary-bases. 18 Oct 1988, Israel (Dick Forsman).*

Plate 429 *Adult showing typical upperwing, with slight contrast between marginally paler coverts than remiges and with diagnostic white primary-shafts only. 31 Oct 1986, Israel (Dick Forsman).*

STEPPE EAGLE *Aquila nipalensis*

Plates 430–460

Subspecies: *A. n. orientalis* in European and western parts of Asian range (to Kirghizia in the east) wintering in Africa; slightly bigger *A. n. nipalensis* from E C Asia (western Altai Mts.) to Mongolia, wintering especially in Indian subcontinent but some probably also reaching Arabia and Africa. Subspecies differ mainly in size.

Distribution: From E Europe (where now practically extinct) eastwards to Mongolia and Lake Baikal.

Habitat: At all times of year confined to open terrain. Breeds in treeless steppe, plains and foothills and winters mainly in African highlands and savanna.

Population: Marked contraction of western part of European range and numbers declining because of agricultural development of virgin steppe. Some 15 000–25 000 pairs still remain in European part of Russia, with a handful of pairs remaining in Ukraine and Turkey.

Movements: Migratory. Main part of population winters in E and S Africa, with smaller numbers locally in the Middle East. Adults winter in Somalia, Kenya and Tanzania, on average further north than younger birds, which venture into Zimbabwe, Zaire and Namibia. Leaves nesting grounds from late Aug. Autumn migration peaks in the Middle East in late Oct, with peak numbers of 7295 birds passing Eilat, Israel on 23 Oct 1980 and 8240 at Suez, Egypt on 25 Oct 1981. Regular spring passage recorded through the region between Jan and Apr, with peaks for adults in late Feb and for younger age-classes a month later. Spectacular passage at Eilat, where 75 053 counted in spring 1985, with 14 164 on 6 Mar.

Hunting and prey: Hunts either from moderate heights where hangs motionless against the wind stooping down on its prey or sits and waits on elevated post or on the ground. In breeding area specialized in hunting small ground-dwelling rodents (such as sousliks). In winter quarters adults hunt mainly singly, relying on carrion and live vertebrates, whereas juveniles congregate in flocks at abundant food resources, such as swarming termites or breeding colonies of weaver-finches, *Quelea*.

SPECIES IDENTIFICATION:

Length 59–66 cm

wing-span 163–193 cm (*n*=11; Israeli migrants; W.S. Clark, unpubl.)

Identification of typical juveniles straightforward, but birds lacking white band of under-wing (rare) may resemble immature Eastern Imperial Eagle. Subadult Steppe may be very similar to subadult/adult Lesser Spotted Eagle and adults can be very similar to adult Greater Spotted Eagle, especially if seen in difficult lighting conditions or when viewed from difficult angles.

Identification summary: Younger immatures are best identified by the diagnostic, broad and whitish band of the greater coverts of the underwing. Older birds have typically grey remiges below and the sparse barring and the dark trailing edge are often easily seen. The greater underwing coverts of older immatures and subadults often show traces of the broad wing-band of the younger birds. The head appears comparatively smaller and slimmer for the body and also more protruding than in the spotted eagles with their big, round heads. The wings are longer because of a longer arm and the fingers are more deeply splayed than in the spotted eagles.

In flight, distant Adults and subadults may be extremely difficult to tell from Spotted and Lesser Spotted Eagles as plumage may appear identical from a distance. With increasing experience slightly different silhouette may render some help, but this character should always be used with extreme caution: Steppe has longer wings with a broader and more square-cut wing-tip, with more deeply splayed and longer fingers, than the spotted eagles.

There is also a marked difference in the flight silhouette between juveniles and older Steppe Eagles. Juveniles have narrower wings with a prominently S-curved trailing edge and the tail is narrower and longer. Adults typically show rather rectangular wings with parallel edges and a square-cut wing-tip, while the tail is broader and shorter, often wedged.

The active flight of the Steppe Eagle is heavier and more laboured and the wing-beats are slower than in the shorter-winged spotted eagles. The Steppe Eagle soars on flattish wings, with level arm but drooping hand, appearing rather similar to the spotted eagles. The long wings, however, appear elastic and flexible, compared with the shorter and stiffer wings of the spotted eagles. When gliding, arms are kept more or less level and hands are clearly drooped, with a distinct angle at the carpal bend in head-on views (angle further out on wing than in the spotted eagles). Because of the longer fingers the 'broom' at the wing-tip of approaching birds is wider and more obvious than in smaller *Aquila*-eagles, the difference being especially pronounced in comparison with the Lesser Spotted Eagle. In head-on views the body looks heavy and appears as if hanging below the wing-level, and when soaring the Steppes show a hunched back and a vulture-like lowered head.

In flight, closer In good light the diagnostic sparse and coarse barring to the flight-feathers is the most reliable character for separation from the spotted eagles. Note the colour and barring of the bases of the outermost primaries: in Steppe the bases are greyish with darker barring and they *usually* lack the prominent white crescents typical of the spotted eagles.

In most cases juveniles and young immatures are readily identified by the broad white underwing band in the greater coverts, while the subsequent age-classes still show a rather prominent pale wing-band formed either by partially retained all-white greater coverts or by partly white greater underwing coverts. Subadults closely resemble Lesser Spotted Eagles, but are identified by their greyish and distinctly barred remiges below, lacking prominent white carpal crescents and by their, on average, more extensive white markings to their greater underwing coverts and the different flight silhouette. Adults resemble Greater Spotted Eagles but from below are identified by mostly distinctly barred greyish remiges, lacking the distinct pale carpal crescents and from above by the greyish tinge and coarse barring to the remiges and rectrices and the ochre nape-patch.

Perched A medium-sized eagle, which prefers to perch on the ground adopting a horizontal posture. Lacks pale spots on breast, belly and upperparts shown by most non-adult spotted eagles. Juveniles and younger subadults further differ from spotteds by broader pale wing-bands and greyish brown colour to upperparts. Adult Steppe differs from older spotted eagles by rusty nape and also by coarsely barred tertials and tail-feathers. The legs appear thicker and shorter than in spotted eagles, the nostril is oval not round and the gape is fleshy and yellow and reaches the centre of the eye or even behind it.

Bare parts Feet, cere and gape yellow at all ages. Iris brown, darkest in juveniles, paler in subadults and adults. Bill blackish in juveniles, becoming gradually paler and greyer at base with increasing age. Nostrils oval in Steppe compared with roundish in spotted eagles. Note, however, that a roundish nostril may create an oval-shaped shadow!

Confusion species: Depending on plumage confused with several other eagles. The underwings generally provide the most reliable identification characters.

Pre-adult plumage birds may be confused with Eastern Imperial and Lesser Spotted Eagles.

Eastern Imperial Eagle (page 374) Immature identified by streaked breast contrasting with uniformly pale rear body (pale trousers diagnostic). Largely streaked underwing and upperwing coverts. Greater underwing coverts usually greyish, inner primaries forming rather contrasting pale window against dark secondaries, but these characters sometimes overlap with young Steppe.

Lesser Spotted Eagle (page 316) Some immature individuals show a rather conspicuous white underwing band, which, however, is narrower than Steppe's with white confined to the tips of the greater coverts and normally formed by a row of spots. Also shows different proportions and flight (note wing-formula) and the remiges generally appear very dark underneath with dense barring if discernible. Typically shows one or two distinct narrow pale crescents at carpal.

Adult Steppe Eagles may be confused with Greater Spotted, Golden and Eastern Imperial Eagles.

Greater Spotted Eagle (page 332) Adult has below uniformly blackish flight-feathers and mostly shows a broad, white crescent at the bases of the outermost primaries. Steppe Eagles with nearly uniformly dark remiges lacking barring also occur, although rare.

Golden Eagle (page 390) Adult separated in all plumages by its much longer and bi-coloured tail and its typically shaped wings, which are broadest at the carpal and taper towards the tip and base, and which are kept lifted when soaring. Also shows typical pale patch on upperwing formed by worn coverts and diagnostic head-pattern with golden shawl.

Eastern Imperial Eagle (page 374) Adult has Golden Eagle-like head-pattern and distinctly bi-coloured tail above whereas the remiges are generally dark from below, with slightly paler bases of remiges only (be aware of certain subadult Eastern Imperials, which may show more Steppe Eagle-like underwing pattern). The Eastern Imperial can be quite similar in outline to Steppe but the head and tail are more protruding, while the hand is more rounded and does not appear as square as in adult Steppe. The species also differ in wing-attitude when gliding. The uniformly dark upperwing, pale straw-coloured nape and neck, very dark underwing and clearly two-coloured upper tail are usually enough to separate the species.

MOULT

Moults remiges annually, but as in other *Aquila*-eagles some body plumage and flight-feathers always left unmoulted. Last juvenile feathers are normally retained until the third moult (4th cy summer), at the age of 3 years, though some rapidly moulting birds may replace them during the previous winter. Plumage moulted mainly in breeding season with additional flight-feathers being moulted in winter. Because of their serial moult old immatures and adults are capable of replacing the majority of their flight-feathers in 1 year.

Juveniles (first moult) Start to moult flight-feathers in May–Jun of 2nd cy; rectrices occasionally earlier in spring or even during first winter. By Oct of 2nd cy innermost four or five primaries are replaced as are a third to one half of the secondaries (on average s1 and s5 and a few innermost, including the tertials, but in more advanced birds s1–2, s5–6 and the innermost 5). Also some rectrices are moulted, usually the central and outer pairs. In the winter quarters a few additional primaries (often p5–6) and also some secondaries are regularly replaced.

Second moult Commences in 3rd cy May where previous waves suspended, but also starting with a new descending wave from p1. In most advanced birds remaining juvenile feathers are lost in this moult, but often one or two of the outermost primaries and some secondaries (s4 and a few around s10) are retained. The tail is usually moulted nearly completely.

Adults (subsequent moults) Plumage replaced nearly completely annually, which is possible because of the serial moult of the flight-feathers and the two moulting periods, in summer and winter. Moult starts during early breeding and is suspended for the autumn migration but is resumed upon arrival in the winter quarters, where some additional remiges are moulted.

AGEING AND SEXING

Ageing juveniles, second-plumage birds and adults is rather straightforward, but ageing older immatures and subadults (third–fifth plumage) always requires favourable viewing conditions. Ageing also confused by individual variation in when adult plumage characters are acquired. Notable difference in flight silhouette between juveniles and older birds.

Ageing summary: Juveniles identified by pale and S-shaped trailing edge to wing. Second-plumage birds similar to juveniles but show moulted inner primaries and a few secondaries, resulting in uneven pale trailing edge to wing. Third plumage still resembles juvenile by large but trailing edge darker with only a few retained narrow pale fringes and underwing band either complete and juvenile-like or broken but distinct. In fourth plumage starts to show adult-type remiges below with almost complete dark trailing edge, but the greater underwing coverts still show partly pale fringes, forming an irregular wing-band, and the undertail coverts are still largely or at least partly pale. Adult plumage lacks pale vent and undertail coverts and pale underwing band, while the remiges are grey with coarse dark barring and broadly dark tips.

Juvenile (1st cy autumn – 2nd cy spring) **Plates 430–436**

The normally coloured juvenile Steppe Eagles are among the easier *Aquila*-plumages to identify. Although the plumage colour varies from dark brown to a paler sandy greyish brown, there are always some constant field-marks making both identification and ageing easy.

The basic colour of juvenile Steppe always appears uniform and is clearly greyish in tone in contrast to the warm tone of e.g. Lesser Spotted Eagles. In certain light the body-feathers of the upperparts may show a pearly grey tone, which is unique among *Aquila*-eagles. In fresh autumn plumage the trailing edge of the wing and the tail-tip are broadly buff, broader than in Lesser Spotted Eagle, and well visible both from above and below. On the upperparts there is a wide buffish band along the tips of the greater coverts and many individuals show another broad band in the outer greater median coverts. Some birds may even show a short band in the outer lesser median coverts. Less patterned birds may show only the distal half of the greater covert band, while the inner greater coverts and all median coverts are uniformly brownish. Uppertail coverts whitish, forming a distinct U at the tail base. Secondaries as well as the distal part of the fingered primaries look dark, whereas the innermost primaries are paler, often with visible darker barring. The pale patch on the inner primaries may extend over most of the primary bases and appears from a distance much like the 'window' of the juvenile Eastern Imperial Eagle, but its size and shape vary individually. In closer views juvenile Steppe show clearer bands to the upper secondaries more frequently than any other *Aquila*-species, with a similar tendency for the rectrices.

Underparts of juvenile Steppe Eagles show one of the bird's most striking field-characters: the broad white wing-band formed by the white greater coverts. It is, however, not rare for juveniles to show darker centres or darker mottling to some greater coverts (e.g. white primary coverts but grey greater secondary coverts) and in some birds (less than 5% of all juveniles) all greater coverts are uniformly grey, causing risk of confusion with Eastern Imperial or Lesser Spotted Eagle. Underbody, however, is very uniform in colour, lacking mottling or streaking to breast, belly and underwing coverts, with only vent and undertail coverts buffish and contrasting with the rest of the underparts (lacks pale trousers of young Eastern Imperial). Flight-feathers dark greyish with sparse and rather broad dark barring extending to the outermost fingered primaries, which are clearly grey and barred basally with darker fingers, thus differing markedly from the uniform outer primaries of the spotted eagles. However, very rarely juvenile Steppes with more or less uniformly dark remiges also occur.

On the wintering grounds the juveniles are exposed to extensive wear and bleaching and some of the plumage characters change dramatically in the course of the winter. The white tips to the flight-feathers as well as the upperwing bands may be extremely difficult to see on perched 2nd cy spring birds, although they are still prominent in flight, albeit narrower than in autumn. The wear of the white trailing edge to the wing makes the wing look narrow but emphasizes its S-curved profile. The white band of the under-wing is normally well preserved.

Second plumage (2nd cy autumn – 3rd cy spring) Plates 437–442

The birds in this plumage still look very much like juveniles with only comparatively small changes in the plumage. A diagnostic character against juveniles is the trailing edge of the wing, which is still pale, but mostly narrow and frayed, except for the *replaced inner primaries and a few secondaries, which are clearly longer with broad pale tips*. The most often replaced secondaries are s1 and s5 and some of the innermost, but advanced birds may have as many as half of the secondaries replaced (s1–2, 5–6 and the innermost 5). Greater upperwing coverts show an irregular wing-band, where those corresponding to the moulted secondaries are widely tipped whitish or tawny, whereas coverts corresponding to retained juvenile secondaries are extremely worn and lack practically any white at the tip. Many birds have also replaced their median coverts, which can be either white-tipped or dark. Tail shows worn feathers lacking the pale tips alongside a few pale-tipped fresh rectrices (often central and outer pairs). On the upperparts the replaced inner primaries are pale, forming a large window, and their corresponding coverts show white tips, as in juveniles. Also, the broad underwing band is still similar to the juvenile's. The body plumage is variably moulted but at least the mantle and scapulars are fresh in most birds, being darker than the rest.

In 3rd cy spring birds are still possible to age by their white-tipped inner primaries and a few secondaries (although already worn), which contrast with an otherwise very worn trailing edge to wing. One or two recently moulted secondaries may have distinct and broad pale tips. The white band of the underwing is broad and fresh distally but narrower and frayed towards the body (still juvenile feathers!). The underbody and also the lesser and median underwing coverts similar to juvenile.

Third plumage (3rd cy autumn – 4th cy spring) Plates 443–448

By the third autumn birds already start to show certain subadult characters, though some individuals may still be surprisingly juvenile-like in their general appearance. The best ageing characters are found in the wings where the first adult-type remiges with wide black tips appear. The innermost three or four primaries are moulted for the second time and p1–2/3 still show narrow white tips, but p3 or p4 are of adult type with a black tip. Also the outer primaries (*c*. p6–9 or p7–10) are moulted and fresh. On the upperparts the hand darkens as usually only the innermost primary is distinctly paler, making the pale patch on the upper hand smaller and more distinct (Lesser Spotted-like). Upper greater secondary coverts dark with rather narrow pale tips. Outer median coverts may, however, still be extensively whitish or tawny, forming a pale patch on the outer arm. On the upperparts, the mantle and scapulars are largely moulted and darker than the lesser upperwing coverts. Head and upper breast are usually fresh and darker than the belly.

Below, a few worn and short juvenile secondaries remain in autumn (usually s9–10), whereas the most recently replaced ones already have dark tips (often s1, 5, 8, 11 and 13), although not as broad and distinct as in adults. The dark tips are, however, still too few to form a continuous black trailing edge. Tail largely moulted showing dark feathers with fine white tips. Uppertail coverts fresh and white and undertail coverts still largely pale. Underwing coverts are largely replaced and often show a mixture of rich tawny and blackish feathers on the carpal. Greater underwing coverts fresh and individually variable. Some birds still grow white coverts, as in the juvenile, while others start to grow greyish feathers with white margins, and yet others show a mixture of white and grey feathers. Females at least are known to breed in this plumage in 4th cy spring (BMNH, pers. obs).

Fourth plumage-type (4th cy autumn – 5th cy spring)   Plates 449–452
By now most of the juvenile plumage characters are lost and the general appearance of the bird can be very similar to Lesser Spotted Eagles in non-juvenile plumages.

Lesser and median upperwing coverts mainly faded brown and lack clear whitish or tawny markings, whereas the tips of the greater coverts form a diffuse and quite narrow pale band. The pale patch above at the bases of the primaries is small and rather distinct and confined to the very bases of the feathers; the innermost primary is by now a dark adult-type feather. Tail-feathers and remiges look dark from a distance but closer looks reveal a grey cast to some of them. The uppertail-coverts are still white.

On the underparts, the lesser and median underwing coverts are usually sandy brown with darker carpal-area and the greater coverts are generally greyish with extensive white fringes and markings. The wings show, for the first time, a broken dark trailing edge, with the broadest dark tips on the most recently moulted secondaries (usually on s1–3, on c. s10 and on the innermost). Vent and undertail coverts still paler than the rest of the body, but often show some darker markings. The body is the same colour as, or darker than, the underwing coverts.

Fifth plumage-type (5th cy autumn – 6th cy spring)   Not depicted
Probably not always possible to separate from adults, but adult-type birds showing extensive white margins to some of the greater underwing coverts, partly pale vent and undertail coverts, and a variably broad but complete dark trailing edge to the underwing may be called 'fifth plumage-type'.

Adult plumage (from c. 6th cy autumn and older)   Plates 453–460
The adult Steppe Eagle is generally a dark bird varying from dark tar-brown or almost blackish brown to a dusky grey-brown showing very few striking characters. It is easily mistaken for an older Spotted or Eastern Imperial Eagle.

Most birds have a paler, rusty-coloured nape-patch, which varies from almost non-existent in some birds to covering almost all of the crown and nape in others. The rest of the upperparts are dark brown with very slight or no contrast between the coverts and the flight-feathers of the upperwing. Uppertail coverts either pale, forming a U at the tail-base, or dark. Tail usually appears dark but in some birds is clearly grey with a dark tip and appears slightly paler than the upperwing. Upperwing pattern of the darkest individuals (probably not full adults?) closely resembles that of adult or near-adult Greater Spotted Eagles and shows only a faint and smallish grey patch at the base of the inner primaries. Others (full adults?) show a larger and clearly grey patch, even extending to the primary coverts in some, with darker barring visible on practically all primary-bases. These birds usually also show greyish barring on secondaries, tertials and rectrices, as if the characteristic underwing pattern would show through.

Many of the important characters of the underparts are visible only in good light and usually the bird appears all-dark if not strongly underlit. When seen from a distance in good light the underwings appear uniformly greyish with a darker carpal-patch and darker fingers and the body appears darker than the underwings except for a paler throat. The deep yellow feet contrast with the dark vent and undertail coverts. The colour and barring of the flight-feathers is perhaps the most important identification character. They are grey with a coarse but rather sparse dark barring and a broad blackish tip forming a wide dark trailing edge to the wing, the latter varying individually in conspicuousness. Rarely the remiges can be all-dark. Lesser and median underwing coverts appear in two colour types, a warm sandy brown and a darker brown to nearly blackish. Normally the underwing coverts appear slightly mottled with the darker carpal area standing out, especially in the paler type.

Sexing: Not possible to sex by plumage. Males smaller than females but size difference difficult to judge unless the two are seen together.

References: Bijlsma 1983; Brooke et al. 1972; Clark 1996b; Forsman 1988, 1989, 1990, 1991; Svensson 1987; Tucker & Heath 1995

Plate 430 *Juvenile. Broad and uniform pale trailing edge to wings and tail diagnostic of fresh juvenile plumage. Body more uniformly coloured than in juveniles of confusion species. 25 Nov 1994, Oman (Hanne & Jens Eriksen).*

Plate 431 *Juvenile. Individual with partly grey greater coverts and dark remiges. Pale vent and undertail coverts typical of immatures. 17 Nov 1994, Oman (Hanne & Jens Eriksen).*

Plate 432 *Juvenile. By 2nd cy spring the trailing edge is worn and less conspicuous, but still uniform. Note lack of white wing-band of this bird owing to grey greater coverts. Apr 1987, Israel (Paul Doherty).*

Plate 433 *Juvenile from above. Note broad and uniform wing-bands typical of fresh juvenile. Body plumage more uniform in colour compared with confusion species. 4 Feb 1994, Oman (Hanne & Jens Eriksen).*

Plate 434 *Juvenile (2nd cy) from above showing uniformly worn plumage with uniform wing-bands. Note greyish barring of remiges in many birds. Mar 1985, Israel (Dick Forsman).*

Plate 435 *Juvenile in fresh plumage. Note uniformly mint condition of plumage including pale feather-tips. 16 Oct 1993, Oman (Hanne & Jens Eriksen).*

Plate 436 *Juvenile in worn plumage (2nd cy spring). Aged by uniformly worn plumage, in particular by uniform greater coverts and secondaries with extremely worn pale tips. Note the first few freshly moulted median coverts. Apr 1987, Israel (Paul Doherty).*

Plate 437 *Second plumage (2nd cy autumn). Best aged by faded juvenile outer primaries contrasting with moulted inner while most of the secondaries are still juvenile (s1 and s5 moulted). Underbody moulted but underwing coverts mostly juvenile. Oct 1995, Israel (Tom Lindroos).*

Plate 438 *Second plumage (3rd cy spring). Moult of remiges identical to Plate 437, but now also underwing coverts and tail moulted. 2 Apr 1996, Israel (Dick Forsman).*

Plate 439 *Second plumage showing rather advanced moult. Note juvenile outer four primaries and median secondaries (s4 and s6–9) and rather scruffy-looking underwing coverts and body. Apr 1994, Israel (Tom Lindroos).*

Plate 440 *Second plumage. This individual, lacking the prominent mid-wing-band of most immatures, is best aged by its faded outer juvenile primaries and median secondaries. 2 Apr 1996, Israel (Dick Forsman).*

Plate 441 *Second plumage. Aged by retained juvenile outer primaries and median secondaries and their coverts. Note that the difference in wear is often easier to assess from the coverts than from the remiges. The pale tips to the median coverts form a pale-spotted area similar to the Spotted Eagles. Jan 1994, Yemen (Matti Rekilä).*

Plate 442 *Second plumage (3rd cy spring). Rather similar to third plumage (cf. Plate 448), but aged by its worn and brown juvenile median secondaries and their coverts. Spring, Israel (Hadoram Shirihai).*

Plate 443 *Third plumage (3rd cy autumn). The body plumage is mostly fresh and the general appearance can be very similar to juvenile, with prominent white wing-band and pale vent and undertail coverts. Note, however, lack of uniform pale trailing edge to wing, worn median primaries and fresh median secondaries. 26 Sep 1996, Oman (Hanne & Jens Eriksen).*

Plate 444 *Third plumage. This individual shows an unusually juvenile-like plumage with complete white wing-band and broadly pale-tipped secondaries. Aged by typical moult-pattern, with worn median primaries and fresh s4 and s8–9. Jan 1994, Yemen (Matti Rekilä).*

Plate 445 *Third plumage (4th cy spring). A more adult-looking bird, with partly grey greater coverts. Note juvenile-like body with pale undertail coverts and lack of dark subterminal wing-band, which separate them from older birds. Mar 1985, Israel (Dick Forsman).*

Plate 446 *Third plumage showing how juvenile-like distant birds may appear. Told from younger birds by fresh underwing coverts and worn median primaries, while the secondaries are rather fresh with narrow pale tips. Mar 1982, Israel (Dick Forsman).*

Plate 447 *Third plumage from above. Very similar to some second plumage birds, but told by worn median primaries contrasting with fresh inner and outer (cf. Plate 441), while the fresh secondaries are greyish with barring distally. 8 Oct 1988, Israel (Dick Forsman).*

Plate 448 *Third plumage. Resembles second plumage, but note fresh median greater coverts and fresh greyish secondaries, both with white tips. Mar 1993, Israel (Lars Jonsson).*

Plate 449 *Fourth plumage-type (5th cy spring). The undertail coverts are still variably pale whereas the greater coverts band becomes less distinct, with white confined to the feather-edges. The flight-feathers lack prominent white tips and the darkest, most recently moulted secondaries show a broadly dark tip, as in adults. Mar 1985, Israel (Dick Forsman).*

Plate 450 *Fourth plumage-type. The underwing-band is still discernible in most individuals while the remiges and rectrices start to show dark tips creating an incomplete dark trailing edge. 15 Mar 1995, Israel (Dick Forsman).*

Plate 451 *Fourth plumage-type from above (same as Plate 450). Distant birds greatly resemble Lesser Spotted Eagle, but the wings are longer. 2 Apr 1986, Israel (Dick Forsman).*

Plate 452 *Fourth plumage-type. General plumage characters rather similar to Lesser Spotted Eagle, but the greater coverts show a narrow wing-band while the flight-feathers show the diagnostic coarse barring. Mar 1985, Israel (Dick Forsman).*

Plate 453 *Adult with typically dark vent, no wing-band and coarsely barred remiges. 15 Mar 1995, Israel (Dick Forsman).*

Plate 454 *Adult, with some pale edges left on greater coverts. The general impression is rather Lesser Spotted Eagle-like, but note sparsely barred remiges. Mar 1996, Israel (Markus Varesvuo).*

Plate 455 *Adult. A rather average-looking darker individual, with diagnostic barring to remiges. Mar, Israel (Urban Olsson).*

Plate 456   *Adult. The darker individuals are easily confused with Greater Spotted Eagles if the underwing barring is not seen. Oct 1995, Israel (Tom Lindroos).*

Plate 457   *Adult from above. Note generally dark plumage with large grey area on inner hand and darker tips and bars to greyish remiges and rectrices. Spring 1986, Israel (Hadoram Shirihai).*

Plate 458   *Adult. Note large grey flash with barring on upper hand with greyish barring continuing onto the secondaries. Mar 1985, Israel (Dick Forsman).*

Plate 459 *Adult. A paler bird in a typically drab-looking plumage lacking diagnostic features. Note oval nostril and thick powerful legs compared with the Spotted Eagles. Mar 1985, Israel (Dick Forsman).*

Plate 460 *Adult, a darker bird. The size of the ochre nape-patch varies individually and cannot be seen from this angle. Mar 1985, Israel (Dick Forsman).*

SPANISH IMPERIAL EAGLE   *Aquila adalberti*

Plates 461–464

Subspecies: Monotypic. Until recently, considered a subspecies of Imperial Eagle *(A. heliaca)*. Hybrid pair between Spanish Imperial Eagle and Golden Eagle in NE Spain known to have produced young in 1994 and 1995.

Distribution: Now solely confined to Spain, and not found breeding in Portugal since 1977. Formerly also occurred in N Africa (Morocco and Algeria) but now thought to be extinct, although recently one pair found breeding in 1995.

Habitat: A bird of sparsely wooded flat or hilly country. Probably better adapted to more wooded areas than Eastern Imperial Eagle.

Population: Population small and dwindling and species considered one of the most threatened eagles in the world. Total European and world population estimated to be 150–160 pairs (in 1993), showing recent slow increase in numbers and range extension.

Movements: Resident, but juveniles and non-breeding subadults dispersive. Mostly keeps within breeding range, but some movements further afield recorded. Exceptionally crosses Strait of Gibraltar into Africa.

Hunting and prey: Food depends on local supply but rabbit important in S Spain, while medium-sized birds more important in C Spain. Hunts from the air and stoops down on prey, approaching in cover of trees and scrub.

SPECIES IDENTIFICATION

Length 74–85 cm

wing-span 177–220 cm (del Hoyo et al. 1994)

Adults and subadults told from similar-looking Golden Eagle by more rectangular wings and proportionately longer neck and shorter tail. Juveniles most similar to pale Tawny Eagle *Aquila rapax* and *'fulvescens'*-variety of Spotted Eagle.

Identification summary: Rather similar to Eastern Imperial Eagle (which see) but adults recognized by white leading edge to wing, and juveniles by more tawny and generally unstreaked plumage. Subadult plumages similar to Eastern Imperial Eagle. Plumage development from juvenile to adult seems to proceed faster than in Eastern Imperial Eagle.

In flight, distant Adults soar on flat and horizontal or marginally lifted wings, but with wings typically smoothly curved (cf. Golden). Wings rectangular but slightly tapering towards hand; does not show bulging trailing edge or pinched-in base of arm like Golden. Head more protruding and tail shorter, about three quarters of width of wings, compared with Golden (see Fig 51, p 392). Juveniles generally pale with dark upper greater coverts and flight-feathers, except for pale inner three primaries; distant birds separated with difficulty from similar species (see above) by diagnostic wing-attitude when soaring and gliding.

In flight, closer Adults are largely black with pale straw-coloured nape-shawl, grey tail with broad black tip, and variably broad white forearm and white epaulettes on scapulars. In good light the remiges are more greyish basally contrasting with black underwing coverts and broad black trailing edge to wing. Juveniles are deep tawny in fresh plumage, fading during winter to pale buffish. Second-plumage birds and juveniles differ from juvenile Eastern Imperial by lack of prominent streaking to breast, wing coverts and upperparts. Older immatures and subadults are more similar to corresponding plumages of Eastern Imperial Eagle, until the white feathers start to appear on the leading edge of the wing.

Perched Rather similar to Eastern Imperial Eagle, but shows proportionately shorter wings and longer tail, with wing-tips usually falling short of tail-tip. Adults told by white marginal coverts of forearm, juveniles by unstreaked breast, upperwing coverts and mantle.

Bare parts Toes and cere yellow at all ages; iris dark in juveniles but gradually becoming paler yellowish brown, turning pale yellow or whitish grey in some adults. Bill proportionately larger than in Eastern Imperial Eagle, pale horn-coloured or grey with slightly darker tip.

Confusion species: The most likely confusion species for adults is the sympatric Golden Eagle, for juveniles and younger subadults the pale phase of the Tawny Eagle or *'fulvescens'* Greater Spotted Eagle. Older subadults are practically identical to Eastern Imperial Eagle in corresponding pied plumage.

Golden Eagle (page 390) Longer tail and less protruding head. Wings diagnostic in shape, with narrower and rounded tips and pinched in at the base leaving broad arm with bulging trailing edge. Soars on wings lifted in shallow V.

Tawny Eagle Pale tawny to buffish individuals very difficult to separate from juvenile Spanish Imperial Eagle, but remiges of underwing more uniform lacking Spanish Imperial Eagle's distinctly paler inner primaries.

Greater Spotted Eagle 'fulvescens' (page 332) Normally shows pale crescent at base of outermost primaries below and the greater underwing coverts are blackish; remiges dark below with inner three primaries only slightly paler than the others. Pale birds also often show slightly darker throat and chin than rest of head.

Moult

Juveniles (first moult) Moult between May and Oct and replace the innermost four or five primaries, a few secondaries and rectrices before moult is suspended.

Second moult Replaces p5–7 and most of the secondaries retaining juvenile p8–10 and s7–10.

Third moult Replaces most of the remaining juvenile remiges, but one or two median secondaries may still be retained. Normally starts a second moult wave from the innermost primary (unless already started the year before) reaching e.g. p4 before suspending moult.

Adults (subsequent moults) Moult during breeding but are not capable of replacing all remiges in one season.

Ageing and sexing

Adults and juveniles are easy to separate and usually two additional plumage-types can be recognized from a distance: younger immatures (second and third plumages) and older immatures or subadults (fourth–fifth plumages). Exact ageing is rather difficult and requires close and detailed views.

Ageing summary: Adults are predominantly black, with a pale nape-shawl, white leading edge of wing and white feathers on scapulars and grey bases to remiges (below) and rectrices. Juveniles are tawny with blackish flight-feathers and a pale even trailing edge to wings and tail. Second plumage resembles juvenile but the trailing edge is uneven, showing mixture of broadly and narrowly white-tipped remiges. Third plumage duller and browner above and the first black marks may appear on breast and upperwings. Fourth plumage is a mixture of pale straw-coloured and black feathers and the head starts to appear adult-like. Fifth plumage differs from adult plumage by retained pale markings to body and wing coverts.

Juvenile (1st cy – 2nd cy spring) **Plates 461–463**

Body plumage uniformly rich tawny (fresh) to buff (worn) with darker flight-feathers, greater coverts and greater scapulars only. Inner three primaries are distinctly paler than the rest of the remiges forming a conspicuous pale window on the inner hand. Broad buff tips to greater upperwing coverts and flight-feathers. Head all-pale merging in colour with mantle and breast.

During winter, plumage fades considerably adding to contrast between flight-feathers and body plumage and bird becomes practically identical in colour to pale Tawny or *fulvescens* Greater Spotted Eagle.

Second plumage (2nd cy autumn – 3rd cy spring) **Not depicted**

General impression rather like juvenile, but identified by partly moulted remiges, rectrices and upperwing coverts: median upperwing coverts and scapulars appear a mixture of tawny and greyish feathers contrasting with pale head. Greater coverts band of upperwing and trailing edge of wing and tail show variably pale tips, as retained juvenile greater coverts and remiges have lost the pale tips from wear but the moulted ones show broad, juvenile-like pale tips. Some individuals also show faint greyer or deep ochre streaking across upper breast, rather similar to Eastern Imperial Eagle, but far less distinct.

Third plumage-type (3rd cy autumn – 4th cy spring) **Plates 462–463**

Still rather juvenile-like but upperparts becoming increasingly browner because of moult and wear, and breast showing diffuse brownish streaking, with the whole plumage being rather similar to Eastern Imperial Eagle in third plumage; more advanced birds may show some fine black streaks to breast and throat. Underwing coverts ochre; rectrices still largely of juvenile-type, uniformly greyish-brown.

Fourth plumage-type (4th cy autumn – 5th cy spring)   **Not depicted**

Head like adult, but rest of body plumage appears blotchy because of mixture of retained pale juvenile-type feathers and newly moulted largely dark and adult-type feathers. Up to 50% of rectrices may show dark subterminal spot, others still uniformly greyish brown juvenile-type feathers. Mantle and scapulars ochre with black arrowheads. Rump appears blotchy, with equal amount of black and ochre. Leading edge of wing pale straw or whitish with black spots, lesser and greater coverts turning dark, but large ochre patch retained in median coverts. Underwing coverts appear pied showing equal proportions of ochre and black. New secondaries of adult-type, greyish with dark subterminal band but still showing narrow ochre tips. Throat and chin 80% black, breast ochre with black markings covering c. 50%. Thighs largely ochre with some black markings; vent and undertail coverts pale ochre.

Fifth plumage-type (5th cy autumn – 6th cy spring)   **Not depicted**

Much like adult, but still shows pale feathers among underwing coverts and inner median upperwing coverts and pale tips and fringes to some greater coverts and secondaries. Also odd pale feathers on belly, legs and upperparts. Secondaries and rectrices may still show odd feathers which are largely uniformly brownish, but most show a dark subterminal band.

Adult plumage (from 6th cy autumn)   **Plate 464**

Appears black from a distance. Plumage predominantly uniformly black, showing in closer views paler crown and hind neck, pale grey tail with broad black subterminal bar and with white leading edge to wing and white braces among scapulars. Vent and undertail coverts ochre. Underwing coverts black contrasting with slightly greyer bases to remiges, latter occasionally showing barring to inner primaries and outer secondaries. Upperwing coverts sometimes showing dark brown (worn) inner median coverts, but never appearing as contrasting as in Golden Eagle.

Younger adults may still show a rather prominent black trailing edge to greyish and barred remiges, but with increasing age the feathers become overall darker and more uniform and the grey area is restricted to the bases of the outer secondaries and inner primaries.

Sexing: Not possible to sex by plumage, but females are bigger than males when seen together, although size difference useless without direct comparison.

References: del Hoyo et al. 1994; Meyburg & Meyburg 1991; Suetens 1989; v.d. Berg & Sangster 1995

Plate 461 *Juvenile in captivity. Note unstreaked tawny upperparts and broad tawny tips to greater coverts and remiges. 27 Jan 1988, Spain (Dick Forsman).*

Plate 462 *Juvenile on the right (same as Plate 461) and a third plumage-type individual (4th cy spring) in captivity. Plumage overall pale straw with first black markings appearing on underbody and throat and among the upperwing coverts. 27 Jan 1988, Spain (Dick Forsman).*

Plate 463 *Third plumage-type bird (same as Plate 462) with juvenile (right). 27 Jan 1988, Spain (Dick Forsman).*

Plate 464 *Adults at nest showing diagnostic blackish plumage and white on leading edge of arm. Note variation in amount of white markings to forewing and scapulars. Spain (Brian Hawkes/Aquila).*

EASTERN IMPERIAL EAGLE   *Aquila heliaca*

Plates 465–486

Subspecies: Monotypic. Spanish Imperial Eagle *Aquila adalberti* (former *A. heliaca adalberti)* here regarded as a full species and hence treated separately (page 367).

Distribution: Breeds in a wide zone from Slovakia and Hungary in the west through the forest steppes of southern Russia to Lake Baikal and N Pakistan. Eastern populations especially are migratory, wintering far south of breeding range.

Habitat: A raptor of open or semi-open habitats. Nests in semi-open terrain with scattered trees or open woodland, often close to open areas. Also found in wooded and mountainous areas at moderate altitude, but is not attracted to high mountains and precipitous cliffs like Golden Eagle. Winters mainly on open plains or steppes with single trees.

Population: European population totals only some 350–600 pairs in eastern Europe, with the majority breeding in Ukraine, Hungary, Slovakia, Romania and Bulgaria.

Movements: Migratory, or partly migratory, with adults often wintering close to breeding grounds, even within Europe. Juveniles and subadults, but also some adults, migrate to the Middle East and N Africa. Autumn migration in the Middle East from Sep through Nov, with a peak in late Oct–early Nov. Younger birds move earlier than adults. During migration survey at Suez, Egypt, between 4 Sep and 5 Nov 1981 a total of 556 was counted with a marked peak during the last 10 days. Spring migration at Eilat, Israel from Feb to early May, with adults peaking in late Feb–early Mar and subadults and juveniles in mid-Mar–early Apr; highest spring total 95 from 1977.

Hunting and prey: Feeds mainly on smaller mammals and medium sized birds relying in SE Europe largely on sousliks. Hunts mostly by hanging against the wind and scanning the ground below, then stooping on prey directly from above, or by hunting from perch and then approaching prey in a long flat glide low over the ground.

SPECIES IDENTIFICATION

Length 68–74 cm

wing-span 191–215 cm (*n*=6; W.S. Clark, unpubl.)

Adults and juveniles/younger immatures differ greatly in plumage, juveniles also in silhouette. Adults resemble adult Golden Eagles in plumage but differ in silhouette and in head-on profile when gliding; younger birds can be confused with Steppe Eagle.

Identification summary: A large eagle, almost as big as a Golden Eagle, holding its wings horizontal or slightly lifted when soaring and gliding, but showing a diagnostic arched wing-profile compared with Golden. Adults are best told by nearly black plumage with Golden Eagle-like head and greyish tail with broad black band at tip. Compared with Golden the wings are rectangular, the tail is shorter and the underwing coverts are blackish. Juveniles and immatures are pale sandy coloured with a darker-streaked breast-band separating pale head from uniformly pale rear-body, including trousers. Subadults are very mottled, showing a largely pale ground-colour, as in juvenile, but with an amount of black spotting increasing with age, while the head and tail start to show adult characters.

In flight, distant Soars on sometimes rather flattish, but mostly slightly bowed, wings and glides on bowed or arched wings; wings may be kept either horizontal with slightly drooping hand or they may be lifted above body-level, approaching wing-attitude of Golden. The neat and rounded arch at the carpal is retained both during soaring and gliding and separates Eastern Imperial from Golden, which shows straighter and more angled profile. Wing-beats are slow, powerful and shallow resembling the wing-action of White-tailed Eagle, which it also resembles in side views, owing to long neck and shortish tail; in adults and old immatures length of neck almost same as length of tail (see Fig 51, p 394), whereas juveniles show more normal proportions with proportionately longer tail.

Adults appear uniformly blackish with a pale crown and neck and a bi-coloured uppertail. Underparts are black, with slightly greyer bases to remiges, conspicuous yellow feet and ochre undertail coverts.

Juveniles and immatures may resemble Steppe Eagles of same age but thighs are pale, and pale underbody clearly divided by darker breast-band. Inner three primaries are often (not always) distinctly paler and the rump is extensively pale especially in juveniles. Subadults mottled and may recall both Steppe and Golden Eagle, but told from former by Golden-like head and pied underparts and from Golden always by pied underparts but also by smaller tail, rectangular wings and different wing-attitude when gliding and soaring.

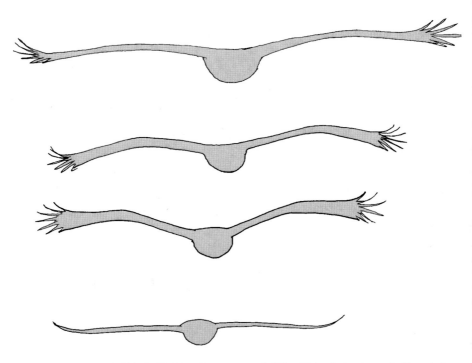

Fig 49 *Eastern Imperial Eagle. Various wing-postures of gliding birds all showing typically arched wings with conspicuous 'broom' at tip. Soars and sometimes also glides on flattish wings (adults especially) with up-turned primaries (bottom).*

In flight, closer Adult Imperials appear overall blackish brown, with all-black underwing coverts and white braces (sometimes minute) on shoulders. Crown and hindneck often very pale, appearing nearly whitish, although birds in fresh plumage may appear as deep ochre as Golden Eagles. Upperwings appear dark, sometimes with a slightly paler faded patch on inner wing coverts but never anything as pale and contrasting as on Golden. The bi-coloured tail may be very distinctive, pale grey with a prominent black band at the tip in some, while others have a darker grey tail with less conspicuous tail-band. Underwing coverts appear uniformly dark in adults, whereas the remiges vary from nearly uniformly black (old birds) to more distinctly barred with a broad black tip (younger adults).

Juvenile and younger immature Imperial Eagles are best identified in flight by their clearly three-coloured underbody, with pale throat, darker streaked breast and diagnostic pale belly, vent and thighs. Other eagles do not show a similar pattern. The generally streaked appearance, both above and below, is another typical trait of Eastern Imperial Eagles in their first three plumages: upperwing coverts and scapulars show narrow pale streaks while the head, body and underwing coverts are more distinctly streaked. The tail is dark, the uppertail coverts are whitish and the pale rump may extend far up between the scapulars on flying juveniles. The remiges are darkish except for the inner three primaries, which often form a distinct pale window to both upperwing and underwing. This is not, however, a fool-proof character, since slightly darker brown immatures often show a window similar to e.g. Steppe Eagles. Subadults show characters intermediate between younger immatures and adults with a generally rather blotchy plumage, with irregular black blotches on otherwise pale underparts. The head-pattern is the first adult feature to appear, followed by adult-type rectrices and remiges. The pale belly and vent are the last areas to darken and in subadult plumages these contrast sharply with darker forebody.

Perched Adults identified by largely black plumage and Golden Eagle-like head-pattern with pale crown and hindneck and white braces to scapulars. Juveniles and young immatures are told by generally sandy appearance in combination with distinctly streaked upper breast, pale throat, pale belly and thighs and pale-streaked upperwing coverts. Subadults show a more or less adult-type head but a unique pied body plumage, with a mixture of pale and black feathers on both upperparts and underbody. Wing-tips reach tail-tip.

Bare parts Bill bluish grey with a darker grey tip, appearing paler than in other large *Aquila*-eagles. Iris greyish or brown in juvenile but changes over the years and may become extremely pale in adults. Cere and feet yellow at all ages.

Variation: Some juveniles have a browner ground-colour instead of the normal pale straw and may therefore be mistaken for immature Steppe Eagles. They can be told by pale thighs and pale throat contrasting with darker and streaked upper breast. The underwing greater coverts band in juveniles and young immatures varies from pale grey to darker grey, and may in the palest cases be rather similar to the underwing band of similarly aged Steppe Eagles. See page 368 for identification of the Spanish Imperial Eagle.

Confusion species: Adults are mostly mistaken for adult Golden or Steppe Eagles.

Golden Eagle (page 390) Adult may be rather similar to older subadult Eastern Imperial, but identified by shorter neck and definitely longer tail. Golden always shows clearly pinched-in wing-bases and a narrower and more rounded wing-tip. Has pale upperwing coverts patch, typical curved trailing edge to arm, with wings clearly tapering both at body and towards tips, and held in an angular V when soaring.

Steppe Eagle (page 348) Adult plumage generally browner and ochre of head restricted to nape. Underwing coverts mostly distinctly brown with slightly darker carpal-patch, remiges grey with distinct barring and distinct dark trailing edge. Tail shorter and more uniformly coloured above, not distinctly two-toned as in Eastern Imperial and Golden.

Greater Spotted Eagle (page 332) Adult plumage, including tail and head, uniformly dark brown. Glides with wings prominently arched, with bowed arms and drooping hands. Wings broad and tail very short and broad.

Juveniles and younger immatures are easier to identify than adults, but can be confused with certain pale Steppe and Greater Spotted Eagles and with Lesser Spotted Eagle. At closer range the diagnostic streaking should rule out other species.

Steppe Eagle (page 348) Immature identified by dark thighs and belly and unstreaked body feathers. These characters also separate Steppe Eagles lacking the broad, white underwing bar from darker than average immature Eastern Imperials, which otherwise may be rather similar.

Greater Spotted Eagle, 'fulvescens'-variant (page 332) Identified by lack of distinct streaking to plumage (may show diffuse streaking on breast), throat usually darker than rest of head and underbody and dark greater underwing coverts.

Lesser Spotted Eagle (page 316) May appear streaked in immature plumages, but the streaking is much more irregular, consisting of pale drop-markings, and the body does not show the regular pattern of differently coloured tracts as in immature Eastern Imperial.

MOULT

Juveniles (first moult) The first moult starts in May of the 2nd cy (Turkey first week of May p1 missing; pers. obs.) and comprises p1–4/5 before suspended in Oct–Nov. Some inner and usually also a few outer (usually s5) secondaries are replaced, as well as some 25–50% of the tail.

Second moult Starts in Apr (4 May growing p6; in both wings; BMNH) comprises p4/5–9/10 and most of the secondaries. Moults p1–3 for the second time. After moult finished in Oct–Nov may still show a juvenile outermost primary and some juvenile secondaries, but may as well have replaced them all.

Adults (subsequent moults) Start to moult in Mar–Apr and complete by Oct–Nov. Occasional remiges are replaced in the winter quarters. Takes two moults to replace the entire plumage.

AGEING AND SEXING

The plumages can be divided into three main classes: the sandy immature plumages (first–third plumage), the pied subadult or transitional plumages (fourth–fifth/sixth plumage) and the adult plumage (sixth/seventh plumage and older), which are also easily separated in the field. Exact ageing requires favourable conditions. Because of individual differences in moult and plumage development, subadults from 4th plumage and onwards are better referred to as plumage-types.

> **Ageing summary:** The plumage develops gradually, from streaked sandy brownish in the juvenile to almost black in the adult. The second and third plumages (resulting from incomplete moults) are still rather juvenile-like and pale. In the subsequent two to three transitional plumages, adult characters are gradually acquired, starting from the head, which becomes darker on chin and throat, with a rustier hood. The adult plumage is acquired at the age of about 6–7 years.

Juvenile (1st cy autumn – 2nd cy spring)   Plates 465–470

Plumage sandy brown with upperparts distinctly streaked pale, varying individually in intensity. Upper greater coverts, primary coverts, remiges and rectrices dark with a wide pale tip, forming clear, white bars (greater coverts bar being of about same width as pale trailing edge). Some birds show a few nearly whitish outer median coverts, instead of normal brownish, forming a paler patch close to bend of wing. Bases to innermost primaries largely pale, whitish to pale grey, forming a large pale area, 'window' on upperwing, which varies in brightness between individuals. Uppertail coverts and rump are pale creamy-white, extending on to back, but latter difficult to discern in flight as mainly hidden by large scapulars.

From below, body clearly divided into pale chin and throat, darker and streaked upper breast and flanks, and pale belly, vent and thighs. Though the streaking is not visible from afar, the clear division into differently coloured 'segments' can be seen over long distances. Rectrices dark with a wide pale band at the tip. Underwing clearly two-toned, with paler coverts and darker remiges. Smaller and median underwing coverts pale sandy brown with darker streaks, like the breast, whereas greater coverts appear rather uniformly grey, appearing either slightly paler or darker depending on the width of the pale margin. Outer greater primary coverts frequently darker, forming a dark comma. Innermost primaries pale with faint barring, while the rest of the primaries are blackish with greyer and somewhat barred bases (cf. spotted eagles). Secondaries appear dark at a distance but when seen from close up show a faint barring to the bases especially of the outermost. The trailing edge of the wing is broadly pale, even and neatly S-curved.

Second plumage (2nd cy autumn – 3rd cy spring)   Plates 471–475

Very similar to juvenile, since plumage consists largely of unmoulted juvenile feathers. Mantle and scapulars appear more uniformly greyish brown than in juveniles, owing to wear of juvenile feathers, which abrades especially the pale streaking of the upperparts.

Mantle frequently shows a pale triangle not found in juveniles. Upper greater coverts and secondaries have lost their wide pale tips from wear but still show regular pale bands on upperwing (greater coverts bar now clearly narrower than the pale trailing edge). Median coverts are partly moulted and the outer and bigger ones especially are nearly whitish, forming a large pale patch, whereas the other moulted median coverts are more tawny in colour. The three innermost greater coverts (sometimes also the outermost) and inner secondaries are freshly moulted and show a wide buffy or tawny tip, best seen on perched birds or in flight from behind. Inner primaries are moulted, forming a pale window, and their broadly whitish tips stand out from the otherwise evenly worn and narrow pale trailing edge of the wing, providing a reliable ageing character. Owing to these longer replaced primaries, the S-curve of the juvenile wing is lost and the wing-profile is squarer. The new replaced inner primary coverts are white-tipped, contrasting with rather worn and uniform outer ones. The pale window on the upperwing formed by the inner primaries resembles that of the previous plumage, but there is a tendency towards a smaller and more rounded patch, at times not different from the patch of a Lesser Spotted Eagle. Tail looks uniform but the tip is normally uneven with some fresh tawny tips protruding beyond the abraded juvenile feathers. Uppertail coverts, rump and lower back are still largely pale as in juvenile.

Underparts are much as in juvenile but the overall impression is often of a slightly paler and more tawny coloured (less brownish) bird. The best separating characters against juvenile are the worn trailing edge of the arm with the contrasting, widely white-tipped inner primaries, the squarer wing-shape and the uneven tail-tip. Many birds also show partly moulted underwing coverts, having replaced some of the juvenile, brownish and streaked outer median underwing coverts with paler and more uniform, tawny-coloured coverts.

Third plumage (3rd cy autumn – 4th cy spring)   Plates 476–477
The overall impression of the bird is, especially at a distance, still rather juvenile-like, but the first few blackish feathers start to appear on the breast and throat and among the upper- and underwing coverts.

Head still very pale yellowish buff, often appearing as the palest part of the whole bird. Many individuals show an emerging blackish malar stripe, as a first sign of the adult plumage, and may also show narrow blackish streaks on throat. Mantle and scapulars are paler than in earlier plumages because of more tawny feathers. Upperwing coverts look 'untidy' and mottled and are mainly tawny, buffish and pale brownish in different shades but the first blackish or partly dark median coverts can be seen, while the lesser coverts look brownish, forming a darker area on the forearm. Greater coverts mainly fresh, dark with whitish margins forming an inconspicuous wing-bar. Innermost three primaries only basally pale, forming a pale wing-patch, but lack the wide whitish tips of the second plumage. The most recently replaced secondaries (usually s3 and/or s4 and s8/s9) and primaries (about p2 and p3) of advanced birds are barred and may show a wide blackish tip well visible in the field. The pale rump shows a dark patch in the middle separating the white uppertail coverts from the pale lower back. Rectrices still mainly uniformly brownish, as in juveniles, but most birds show greyish barring to some feathers, with dark tips in the most advanced individuals.

From a distance, the birds appear very pale below, yellowish buff or pale tawny with darker remiges and tail. Upper breast in most birds is still streaked as in juveniles, but advanced birds can appear more uniform and paler. In closer view one can see the first dark markings appear among otherwise rather pale and uniform underwing coverts and blackish stripes also emerge on the upper breast and throat. Head appears pale, though advanced birds with wide blackish moustache and dark chin-streaks may, at a distance, look darker below with paler crown and nape. Vent, belly and thighs all still appear very pale, yellowish straw. The pale window of the underwing is no longer striking and the innermost primaries lack broadly pale tips.

Fourth plumage-type (4th cy autumn – 5th cy spring)   Plates 478–479

This is the first of the mottled, transitional plumages. From above, the bird appears rather chequered darkish brown on upperwing coverts, whereas the mantle and lesser scapulars still appear predominantly pale. Head almost as in adult birds, with pale crown and nape and dark cheeks, chin and throat. Tail shows more grey feathers with black tips, but there are always some uniformly brownish feathers left (although these may be extremely worn). Uppertail coverts still form a pale ring at the tail-base.

From below, the bird is mainly dark on throat and upper breast, whereas flanks, belly and vent are mainly pale yellowish with dark mottling, especially on belly. Thighs are still pale. Underwing coverts appear pale at a distance, but at closer range one can see black-ish mottling on the underwing, covering about 30% of the coverts. Remiges darkish grey and barred, with a nearly complete, black trailing edge to wing.

Fifth plumage-type (5th cy autumn – 6th cy spring)   Plate 480

The second mottled, transitional plumage is largely dark with reduced pale markings. Head as in the adult, but nape and crown are deeper tawny or rufous instead of pale straw. Upperparts (mantle and scapulars) turn brown, but are still mottled and the white 'braces' become evident. Upperwing coverts also become browner, but there is still a paler area in the inner median coverts. Tail mainly as in the adult but a few uniformly coloured feathers lacking the black tip are often still present.

From below, the bird is mainly dark with pale markings confined to armpits, lower belly and vent. Thighs mottled, becoming increasingly darker. Underwing coverts also mainly dark, with pale feathers comprising less than 50%. Remiges appear dark grey with a wide black trailing edge, whereas the finer barring is visible at close range only.

Sixth plumage-type (6th cy autumn – 7th cy spring)   **Plates 481–482**

There is still one plumage before the definite adult plumage showing some immature features, although the bird resembles an adult in most respects. The inner upperwing coverts are paler than the rest and odd pale feathers are still visible among the underwing coverts, sometimes appearing as a tawny forearm (as in adult Golden!). Some of the older secondaries are still rather pale grey underneath with distinct barring and a distinct black subterminal bar, while more recently moulted secondaries are overall darker with less contrasting pattern.

Adult plumage (from *c.* 7th cy autumn onwards)   **Plates 483–486**

Adults are very dark birds, appearing black from a distance except for the pale crown and nape and the distinctly grey tail with a black band. Feet yellow. Undertail coverts paler. At closer range in flight the black underwing coverts contrast distinctly with the grey bases to the remiges, which in many individuals show a finer dark barring basally. Upper scapulars show a variable number of white feathers forming distinct patches in some individuals, whereas others show only a few hardly discernible white markings.

Sexing: Not possible to sex by plumage. In direct comparison females are bigger and heavier than males.

References: Bijlsma 1983; Forsman 1988, 1989; Gensbøl 1995; Shirihai & Christie 1992; Tucker & Heath 1995

Plate 465 *Juvenile. Aged by uniform white trailing edge to wing and tail. Note uniformly pale head, trousers and rear body and distinctly streaked breast and underwing coverts. 25 Nov 1994, Oman (Hanne & Jens Eriksen).*

Plate 466 *Juvenile. Jan 1994, Yemen (Matti Rekilä).*

Plate 467 *Juvenile from above. Aged by white trailing edge to wing and tail and broad and uniform pale tips to greater coverts. Uniformly streaked forewing and mantle are diagnostic. Dec 1996, Israel (Hadoram Shirihai).*

Plate 468 *Juvenile. Aged by uniform condition of plumage with broad white tips to secondaries and greater coverts. Note diagnostic pattern of upperwings and mantle. Nov 1986, Israel (Dan Zettersröm).*

Plate 469 *Juvenile in worn plumage. Note diagnostic pale head and trousers. 17 Apr 1991, Saudi Arabia (Arnoud van den Berg).*

Plate 470 *Worn juvenile of a darker brownish plumage-type, showing diagnostic pale trousers and uniform streaking. 3 Mar 1993, Oman (Hanne & Jens Eriksen).*

Plate 471 *Second plumage (2nd cy autumn). Much like juvenile, but lacks broad pale trailing edge to wing, except for moulted inner primaries. Half of primaries and most of secondaries and rectrices are still retained juvenile feathers. Nov 1986, Israel (Dan Zettersröm).*

Plate 472 *Second plumage. Differs from juvenile by lack of broad pale trailing edge to wings and tail and by moulted p1–5 while s1 and s5 are growing. Dec 1991, UAE (Tom Lindroos).*

Plate 473 *Second plumage (left) with juvenile. Note moult-wave proceeding at p5 while s1 and s5 are new. 9 Oct 1996, Israel (Annika Forsten).*

Plate 474 *Second plumage from above. Like juvenile, but pale tips to greater coverts and secondaries mostly worn with prominent tips only on the moulted feathers. Nov 1991, Israel (Markku Saarinen).*

Plate 475 *Second plumage (3rd cy spring). Told from juvenile by mostly worn tips to greater coverts and secondaries, except for the inner moulted ones. 5 Mar 1988, Pakistan (Magnus Ullman).*

Plate 476 *Third plumage (3rd cy autumn). General appearance still juvenile-like and this individual lacks the first dark body-feathers shown by many birds of this age. Told from younger birds by dark-tipped inner primaries and by moult-pattern, showing retained juvenile outer primaries and most recently moulted and dark s2–3 and s8–9. Dec 1993, Israel (Markus Varesvuo).*

Plate 477 *Third plumage from above. Note the first grey remiges with adult-like barring and the dark tips to p2–3. Outer median coverts often form a pale patch, as here. 29 Nov 1991, Israel (Annika Forsten).*

Plate 478 *Fourth plumage-type (4th cy autumn). Dark feathers have appeared on upper breast and among the underwing coverts, and the chin and throat have started to darken. The majority of remiges have distinct black tips forming a dark trailing edge to wing. 1 Dec 1988, Israel (Sampsa Cairenius).*

Plate 479   *Fourth plumage-type. Note mottled general appearance with adult-like head and with adult-type tertials and tail-feathers. Jan 1995, Hong Kong (Ray Tipper).*

Plate 480   *Fifth plumage-type (5th cy autumn). The proportion of dark body-feathers has increased and the forebody especially appears nearly adult. Nov 1986, Israel (Dan Zetterström).*

Plate 481   *Sixth plumage-type (7th cy spring). Like adult, but remiges are greyer and distinctly barred and the underwing coverts show some pale feathers. 27 Mar 1996, Israel (Dick Forsman).*

Plate 482   *Sixth plumage-type. 15 Mar 1995, Israel (Dick Forsman).*

Plate 483 *Adult. All-black body and underwing coverts are diagnostic of adults. 6 Feb 1996, Israel (Dick Forsman).*

Plate 484 *Adult. Note wing-shape and compare with Golden Eagle. In good light the coverts are clearly darker than the remiges and the vent is pale. 17 Feb 1997, Israel (Dick Forsman).*

Plate 485 *Adult. With age the markings of the remiges become more and more diffuse and the underwing darkens. Feb 1990, Israel (Lars Jonsson).*

Plate 486 *Adult from above, showing dark upperwing, Golden Eagle-like head and diagnostic white scapular-patches. 20 Jan 1995, Israel (Dick Forsman).*

GOLDEN EAGLE *Aquila chrysaetos*

Plates 487–507

Subspecies: Nominate *chrysaetos* from W Europe to W Asia, *A. c. homeyeri* in Spain, N Africa and the Middle East, *canadensis* in N America and *daphanea* and *japonica* in Asia.

Distribution: European population scattered over large area, with local populations restricted mainly to mountainous areas. More evenly distributed over N Europe.

Habitat: Mostly confined to remote mountainous areas. In N Europe also on lower ground breeding in coniferous forests. Migrants found also in other habitats, such as coastland and open farmland.

Population: Total population of Europe is *c.* 5000–7000 pairs with most in Spain, Scandinavia and the Alps. Population is generally considered fairly stable with small-scale fluctuations.

Movements: Immatures of N European populations migratory, adults mostly resident, more southern populations non-migratory but immatures dispersive. Autumn migration peaks in late Sep–late Oct, spring passage Feb–Apr. At Falsterbo, S Sweden only up to four birds seen per autumn in 1986–1994, indicating that few leave Scandinavia. Finnish birds migrate largely SE wintering in Russia, while others migrate SW to Scandinavia, with up to ten birds seen from one post on peak days.

Hunting and prey: Wide variety of prey taken, with rabbits, hares, grouse and marmots being the most important depending on local supply. Hunts either from elevated perch on top of rock or tree or hangs on motionless wings against the wind scanning the ground below. Capable of impressive stoops and may take birds in flight, although most prey taken on ground.

SPECIES IDENTIFICATION

Length 80–93 cm

wing-span 187–219 cm (*n*=14; Finnish migrants; D. Forsman et al., unpubl.)

Typical shape of wings and longish tail diagnostic among European *Aquilas* as is habit of soaring and gliding on wings lifted in shallow V. Note also golden shawl, colour and pattern of remiges and rectrices and faded patch on upperwing coverts. Most easily confused with subadult/adult Imperial Eagles.

Identification summary: A large and powerful eagle with a characteristic shape in flight. The long wings become narrower towards the base with a clearly bulging trailing edge to the arm, while the wing-tips are narrower and more rounded than those of other *Aquila*-eagles. Tail clearly longer than in any other *Aquila*, giving the Golden Eagle a characteristic silhouette. When soaring, Golden Eagles hold their wings in a shallow V, sometimes also when gliding, but, depending on wind and angle of glide, wings may also be kept arched with a drooping hand. The golden crown and hindneck are usually visible from afar and contrast strongly with the dark face and underparts. Immatures are easily identified from afar by the white wing-patches and the white tail with prominent black tip. Juveniles have uniformly brown upperwing coverts, whereas all older birds show a variable, pale area diagonally across the upperwing coverts. Adults are darker, lacking the white areas in wings and tail, and are not as easy to identify as the immatures. From below they usually appear just dark, as the rusty forearm, the greyish bases to the flight-feathers and the dark trailing edge are obvious only in good light. The upperparts are easier to see, and the grey black-tipped remiges and greater coverts, and the faded brown area across the upperwing coverts, create a rather contrasting pattern. At a distance tail appears grey with a broad black band at the tip but some birds have a darkish tail. The barring in the tail is usually seen only at close range.

In flight, distant Appears generally dark, but the characteristic shape and wing-carriage are obvious from afar. Underparts usually appear dark, even in the more brightly patterned immatures, but the upperparts catch the light better and the main characters are visible from afar. Tail usually clearly two-coloured, with black tip and a whitish or grey base. Upperwings dark in juveniles, except for the prominent white patch at the base of the inner primaries in most birds. Immatures show a similar tail and wing-patch but the upperwing coverts show a faded straw-coloured patch, which varies in size and shape according to stage of moult. Adults are darker, with a similar faded patch on the upperwing and

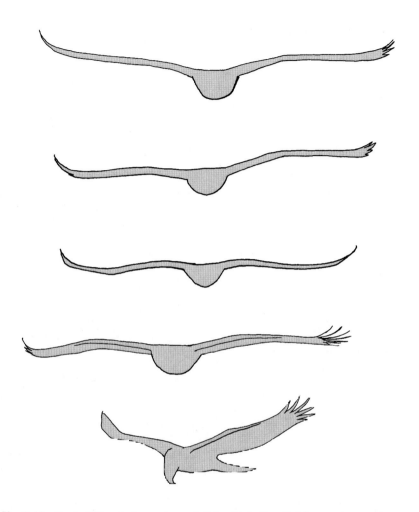

Fig 50 *Golden Eagle. Different wing-postures of gliding birds. Note kink between inner and outer wing as well as strongly up-bent primary-tips.*

with largely grey remiges above bordered by a broad black trailing edge. Tail similarly grey with a broad black band at the tip.

In flight, closer At close range the focus should be on the pattern of the flight-feathers and the typical silhouette. The wing-formula differs from most other *Aquila*-eagles in showing a more rounded wing-tip, with p6–8 being longest. Juveniles and immatures are easily identified by the white tail with a broad black band at the tip and by the variable white patches to the bases of the remiges on the underwing. Non-juveniles and adults show a pale faded area of bleached upperwing coverts diagonally across the arm and adults have grey flight-feathers with broadly dark tips and with variably coarse dark barring or marbling further in.

Perched Can sit either horizontally or upright, but always retains its majestic appearance. The golden crown and hindneck vary in colour from pale straw to deep rufous depending on plumage wear but always contrast with the dark face, throat and foreneck. Juveniles are uniformly dark brown above with a broad black tip to the white tail. The 'socks' are white. Immatures and adults show a paler area of worn upperwing coverts varying in paleness, size and shape according to state of moult. The white socks of the juvenile turn rufous over the next 2 years, but the juvenile tail-pattern remains until the fifth–sixth winter, after which the tail gradually acquires the adult pattern over the next years.

Bare parts Feet, cere and gape yellow at all ages. Iris dark brown in juveniles, but gradually turns paler and brighter during the 2nd–4th year of life and is rufous brown to amber in adults. Bill largely black with a grey base in juveniles but becomes paler with age with the dark restricted to the tip.

Variation: The size of the white wing-patch in juveniles and immatures and the width of the black tail-band vary between individuals and cannot be used for ageing.

  Birds belonging to the subspecies *homeyeri* of S Europe, N Africa and the Middle East are smaller and darker than nominate birds, with smaller or no white wing-patches in immatures and with darker body plumage and less distinctive pale patches on the upperwing coverts in adults (Plates 505–507).

Confusion species: May be confused with other dark eagles, especially other *Aquila*-eagles, but mostly identified by typical silhouette, wing-carriage and wing- and tail-pattern. The adult Imperial Eagle is the most likely confusion species as it has a rather similar plumage.

Imperial Eagle (pages 367 and 374) Adults and near-adults are practically black on the underbody and underwing coverts with no rufous. Upperwing coverts very dark, blackish, often with a restricted browner patch on the inner arm. Flight silhouette is different, with rectangular square-tipped wings and a shorter tail, which is often kept folded when soaring. Wings mostly kept flat when soaring, sometimes lifted, but even then with smoothly arched wing-profile in head-on view. (see Fig 49, p 376)

MOULT (*A. c. chrysaetos*)

Complete moult annually, but some flight-feathers and body plumage always left unmoulted. In first two/three moults only about 30% of flight-feathers are replaced

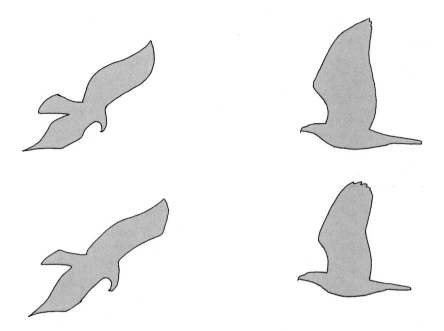

Fig 51 *Golden Eagle (upper two) and Eastern Imperial Eagle (lower two). Note narrow wing-base, longer tail in relation to head and more rounded wing-tip of Golden Eagle and compare with more rectangular wings and shorter tail/longer neck of Eastern Imperial Eagle.*

annually, in later moults more than 50%, enabling replacement of full set of remiges during two successive moults. Body plumage takes 2 years to replace. Non-migratory populations of the Alps and Scotland may moult differently from the Fennoscandian birds, and at least the smaller and largely resident *A. c. homeyeri* of S Europe seems to moult faster.

First moult Starts in 2nd cy Jun and is completed in Sep–Oct. During this moult the inner three or four primaries and some tertials and rectrices are replaced. Of the body plumage the mantle, scapulars and lesser and median upperwing coverts are moulted partially but e.g. the juvenile underwing coverts are retained.

Second moult In 3rd cy starts earlier than the first moult, moulting from Mar–Apr to Sep–Oct. Moults p3/4–6/7 and roughly half of the secondaries and tail. Upperparts are largely moulted and underwing coverts are moulted for the first time.

Third moult In Mar–Oct of 4th cy moults p6/7–9/10 and the remaining juvenile secondaries, but usually one median secondary (mostly s9) and the outermost primary (still juvenile feathers) are retained. Also moults some of the inner primaries and tertials for the second time.

Subsequent moults Moults from Mar to Sep–Oct replacing more than 50% of plumage annually, extent possibly depending on food supply and whether individual is breeding or not. Moult proceeds faster than in immatures because of several simultaneously active moult fronts in wings.

AGEING AND SEXING (*A. c. chrysaetos*)

In the field usually four different plumage-types can be recognized: juveniles, young immatures (second–fourth winter), old immatures (*c*. fifth–sixth/seventh winter) and adults (seventh winter and older). Ageing younger immatures exactly is often possible since the plumage develops gradually, but requires good views, individual plumage variation is considerable. Older immatures (subadults) are not possible to age exactly because of plumage variation and are therefore better referred to as plumage-types. Signs of moult waves, colour and pattern of flight-feathers as well as shape of worn upperwing coverts patch are of importance when ageing Golden Eagles.

> **Ageing summary:** Juveniles have uniformly dark brown upperwing coverts, while all older birds show a faded patch on the upperwing formed by worn and bleached coverts. Young immatures still show a juvenile-like tail and large white underwing-patches, while older immatures show gradually diminishing white areas in wings, and the tail starts to show grey feathers with black tips and white bases. Adults do not show white markings in the flight-feathers, which are grey with broad black tips, and dark bars or marbling further in.

N.B. This account is based on studies of skins and free-living birds of the migratory population in Fennoscandia. It is possible, perhaps even likely, that the moult and plumage sequence in more southern and non-migratory populations differs from this.

Juvenile (1st cy autumn – 2nd cy spring)   Plates 487–489
Both when perched and in flight best identified by uniformly dark chocolate brown upperwing coverts. Inner primaries (often also outer secondaries) show solid white bases, forming an individually variable wing-patch, which is clearly smaller above than below. The white patch may be missing on the upperwing, but in birds from S Europe, N Africa and the Middle East the wings may have no white at all. Tail is always white with a variably wide black terminal band, sometimes narrow and almost broken centrally, sometimes broad and covering the distal half of the tail. Underbody and underwing coverts typically darkish brown, the latter often showing pale, pearl-like feather-tips. At close range the trailing edge of the wing is clearly indented. The socks are white.

The plumage wears during the winter and the upperparts gradually fade to medium brown towards the spring. Although late-spring birds already resemble older birds they never show feathers of different age and the upperwing coverts still look uniform.

Second plumage (2nd cy autumn – 3rd cy spring)   Plates 490–492, 505

In second winter, perched birds have very faded and pale brown upperwing coverts, but some new median and lesser coverts, which are notably darker, can be seen. Only 50% of the birds have replaced the odd inner greater covert or tertial, all the others are uniformly worn juvenile feathers. The eye still looks dark brown as in the previous plumage.

In flight, upperwing coverts look distinctly paler than in juveniles, but compared with older birds they appear rather uniform and the colour differences between different rows of coverts are subtle and gradual. Mantle and scapulars are mostly largely moulted and look dark against the faded upperwing coverts. Tail similar to the juvenile's, although the central pair, which are usually moulted, tend to show narrower and greyer tips. In flight from below very similar to juvenile, but with few innermost primaries moulted and fresh. Secondaries still show rather pointed tips. Plumage of underbody still consists mainly of juvenile feathers, although a few rufous breast-feathers start to appear.

Third plumage (3rd cy autumn – 4th cy spring)   Plates 493–496

Perched birds can be identified by their unmoulted central greater coverts and secondaries, which are very worn and frayed and faded brown in colour. The rest of the upperwing coverts are largely moulted, fresh and dark, with the occasional very worn and faded covert. Newly moulted secondaries and greater coverts show greyish bases with dark tips. The majority of the tail-feathers have been moulted once but the tail still appears 'juvenile'. Eye paler brown with the iris being paler than the pupil.

Underparts become increasingly rusty on the breast, while the lesser and median underwing coverts are more or less rusty brown contrasting with darker greater coverts. The white areas on the underwing are still very uniform and similar to the juvenile's, although the most recently moulted feathers show adult-type barring distally.

Fourth plumage (4th cy autumn – 5th cy spring)   Plates 497–498

Rather similar to second plumage, with largely worn upperwing coverts. The central greater coverts are freshly moulted and dark, whereas the median coverts especially are very worn and bleached. The bleached area is thus more restricted compared with second plumage. Most birds still retain at least one juvenile secondary centrally and many also an outermost juvenile primary, which are extremely worn and light brown in colour. Tail is still rather juvenile-like, whitish with a dark terminal band. In flight from below the birds still show large white wing-patches, but the primary patch is now split from the secondary patch by three or four largely adult-type inner primaries, which may still have partly white bases.

Fifth plumage-type (5th cy autumn – 6th cy spring)   Plate 499

When perched, similar to third plumage with largely fresh upperwing coverts, but lacks latter's row of extremely worn central greater coverts and secondaries. Tail still largely black and white, but some feathers have largely grey outer vanes. The black-and-white rectrices frequently show bold dark bars just inside the dark subterminal band. Underwings show less white than in previous plumages, now mainly as white spikes confined to the bases of some inner primaries but with more white to the bases of the secondaries.

Sixth plumage-type (6th cy autumn – 7th cy spring)   Not depicted

When perched, similar to previous plumage but coverts now largely worn. Tail shows at least some adult-type feathers but the white colour is still visible basally on most feathers. Underwing still shows irregularly scattered white 'spikes' basally on some primaries and secondaries. The fifth and sixth plumages are usually not possible to separate in the field and are better referred to as old immatures or sub adults!

Adult plumage (earliest from 7th cy autumn and older)   Plates 500–504, 506–507

Theoretically the earliest age when the adult plumage is acquired, although many birds known to be of this age have still showed extensive white markings to both tail and underwings. Perched adults are best identified by their flight-feathers, which are grey with a broad dark terminal band and additional broad bars basally. The tail of some adults may show odd white feather-bases until a later age. Iris amber or light brown, sometimes even yellowish.

In flight from above, adults show grey bases and dark tips to flight-feathers, greater coverts and primary coverts making the whole upperwing appear rather greyish and well-marked. Upperwing coverts show a worn patch varying in size and shape according to the bird's state of moult. Underwing shows a rufous leading edge, a dark central band and grey-based and dark-tipped flight-feathers, with individually variable dark barring or marbling.

Sexing: Sexing normally not possible in the field unless the birds in a pair are seen together. Males are clearly smaller and lighter than females in direct comparison. Adult males also tend to be darker on the throat, foreneck and underbody than females and seem on average to have a darker uppertail with finer grey bars.

References: Bortolotti 1984; Forsman 1980, 1984, 1993b; Jollie 1947; Kjellén 1995; Spofford 1946; Tjernberg 1988; Tucker & Heath 1995

Plate 487 *Juvenile. The juvenile remiges are unbarred and more pointed than remiges of later generations resulting in an indented trailing edge to the wing. Underwing coverts are dark. 22 Oct 1989, Finland (Tomi Muukkonen).*

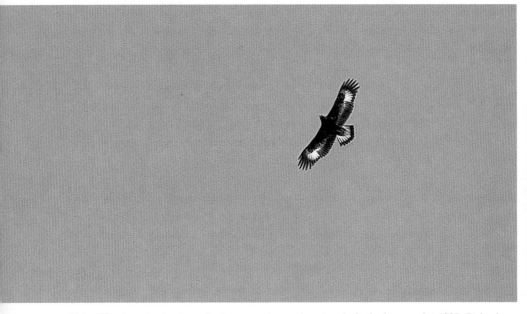

Plate 488 *Juvenile showing pale tips to rectrices and remiges in fresh plumage. Oct 1995, Finland (Tom Lindroos).*

Plate 489   *Juvenile. Note uniform plumage with upperwing coverts of same age. 9 Dec 1993, Finland (Dick Forsman).*

Plate 490   *Second plumage. Much like juvenile with darkish underwing coverts, but p1–4 moulted, while most secondaries are retained juvenile feathers. Oct 1992, Finland (Markus Varesvuo).*

Plate 491   *Second plumage. Upperwing consisting of uniformly worn juvenile feathers with some fresh coverts and tertials only. Head and mantle largely moulted. 9 Dec 1993, Finland (Dick Forsman).*

Plate 492   *Second plumage. Apart from the inner few, all greater coverts and secondaries are retained juvenile feathers. 16 Nov 1993, Finland (Dick Forsman).*

Plate 493 *Third plumage. Still largely juvenile in appearance. Note tawny lesser underwing coverts and diagnostic moult pattern in the remiges. 1 Oct 1987, Finland (Björn Ehrnstén).*

Plate 494 *Third plumage from above (same as Plate 493). Note retained juvenile s3–4 and s7–12, being longer and browner than moulted secondaries as well as diagnostic sequence of retained median greater coverts. 1 Oct 1987, Finland (Björn Ehrnstén).*

Plate 495 *Third plumage. Upperwing coverts largely moulted but a group of median greater coverts are still juvenile. 12 Jan 1978, Finland (Dick Forsman).*

Plate 496 *Third plumage. Diagnostic retained median greater coverts correspond to similarly retained median secondaries. Feb 1993, Finland (Tino Laine).*

Plate 497 *Fourth plumage. Combination of juvenile-type tail and split white underwing patch, owing to adult-type inner primaries, are diagnostic of this age-class. Many birds still retain a juvenile outermost primary (like here) or a median secondary in this plumage. Apr 1996, Finland (Martti Rikkonen).*

Plate 498 *Fourth plumage. Upperwing coverts largely worn, but central greater coverts fresh. Tail still juvenile-like but secondaries of adult type, often with one retained juvenile feather (mostly, as here, s9). 9 Feb 1993, Finland (Dick Forsman).*

Plate 499 *Sub-adult. Juvenile-type tail and extensive white markings to remiges indicate a younger subadult (possibly moulting to fifth plumage). 10 May 1989, Finland (Dick Forsman).*

Plate 500 *Adult male. The remaining white stains to the remiges indicate a younger adult. Apr 1996, Finland (Martti Rikkonen).*

Plate 501 *Adult male from above (same as Plate 500). Note diagnostic pattern of remiges and pale coverts area. White bases to rectrices indicate a young adult. Apr 1996, Finland (Martti Rikkonen).*

Plate 502 *Adult female. Note broadly dark-tipped flight-feathers typical of adult. The washed-out barring of the remiges probably indicates a great age. Winter, Finland (Jorma Luhta).*

Plate 503 *Adult from above with Raven (same as Plate 502). Note greyish flight-feathers with broad dark tips and similarly patterned tail. Winter, Finland (Jorma Luhta).*

Plate 504 *Adult male. Note small bill, rounded head and dark tail indicating male. Feb, Finland (Antti Leinonen).*

Plate 505 *Second plumage ssp.* homeyeri. *Note more advanced moult compared with nominate of same age and also that retained juvenile p7–10 lack white bases. Dec 1990, Morocco (Harri Muukkonen).*

Plate 506 *Adult female ssp.* homeyeri. *Smaller and darker than nominate birds, with proportionately narrower wings and longer tail. 1 Apr 1996, Israel (Dick Forsman).*

Plate 507 *Adult of ssp.* homeyeri. *Darker above than nominate adults with more rufous-brown nape. 2 Feb 1995, Oman (Hanne & Jens Eriksen).*

BONELLI'S EAGLE *Hieraaetus fasciatus*

Plates 508–521

Subspecies: Nominate *fasciatus* in W Palearctic, extralimital *H. f. renschi* in Indonesia.

Distribution: In Europe strictly a Mediterranean species occurring on the Iberian peninsula, in S France, Sicily, Croatia and Greece. From N Africa, Asia Minor and the Middle East to China and India.

Habitat: Prefers sparsely vegetated mountainous areas, with gorges and steep cliffs. Outside breeding season descends to lowlands, particularly young birds.

Population: Total European population *c.* 820–1000 pairs, with 675–751 pairs in Spain in 1990, numbers slowly declining over most of range.

Movements: Non-migratory, but young birds move around before settling to breed. Adults remain faithful to breeding territory throughout the year. Crosses Strait of Gibraltar on rare occasions.

Hunting and prey: Adults often hunt in pairs flying close to each other along cliffs and mountain ridges. Also hunts from perch on rock or cliff-face or may soar high above hunting grounds. Capable of tremendous stoops, similar to Booted Eagle, especially when hunting birds, which are often taken in flight. Main prey consists of Rock Doves, Chukars, Partridges and rabbits, but also smaller birds, mammals and lizards.

SPECIES IDENTIFICATION

Length 58–60 cm

wing-span 145–164 cm (*n*=5; Israeli birds; W.S. Clark, unpubl.)

Best identified by combination of plumage characters and diagnostic shape in flight, with pattern of tail and underwings and colour of underbody important, as are uniform upperwings and white mantle-patch of adults.

> **Identification summary:** A fairly large raptor with a diagnostic silhouette, with rather short but broad and rounded wings and a longish tail. Soars on rather flat and level wings. Adults dark above, with two-coloured tail and white mantle-patch, whitish below, with darker head, thighs and underwings. Juveniles even more uniformly dark brown above, tawny below, with body becoming paler towards rear, and with underwings rather inconspicuously patterned with regular, fine barring to remiges and an inconspicuously darker greater coverts band and wing-tip. Subadults are streaked like adults below, but the underwings appear rather pale with a dark subterminal band and a dark band on mid-wing from the axillaries to the carpal.

In flight, distant Silhouette in flight rather similar to adult Honey Buzzard, with fairly broad and rounded wings when soaring, with a bulging trailing edge, and a fairly long tail. When gliding, carpal pressed forward but trailing edge rather straight, as in Honey Buzzard, but with broader wing-tip. Active flight when hunting slightly similar to Goshawk, with a few powerful wing-beats followed by glides on gently arched wings. Powered level flight with series of rather high and slow wing-beats, not unlike huge Booted

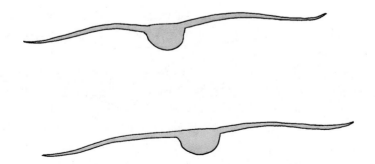

Fig 52 *Bonelli's Eagle. Glides and soars on rather flat wings, with slightly more drooping hand when gliding. Comparatively big-bodied in relation to wing-span e.g. when compared with Short-toed Eagle.*

Eagle, interspersed by regular glides. Soars on flattish wings held horizontally or gently lifted. Juveniles have a different silhouette to adults, with narrower and longer-appearing wings, with a distinctly S-curved trailing edge because of narrower hand. The tail is shorter and opened more frequently when soaring than in adults.

Adults appear fairly dark brown above with a whitish mantle-patch and a greyish tail with broadly dark tip. Underparts show a white body contrasting with darker head and generally dark underwings. Some birds show a conspicuous white forearm from a distance. Juveniles appear uniformly dark above but fairly pale below, with a strong tawny wash to forebody and forearm, darker fingers and generally pale underwings, with slightly darker secondaries than primaries. Lacks prominent dark trailing edge to wing. Subadults are intermediate between adults and juveniles, with wings and tail still rather pale but with a dark trailing edge and a prominent dark mid-wing bar and with dark streaking on breast.

In flight, closer Adults show a rather dull and dark greyish brown upperwing, with fractionally paler median and lesser coverts, a faint greyish wash to the bases of the remiges and primary coverts (variable) and dark tips to the remiges. Head appears dark, but often shows a paler face. Mantle has white mottling, but the amount varies considerably between individuals. Tail distinctly two-coloured, greyish with fine dark bars and a broad, black subterminal band. From below the body and forearm are white variably streaked dark. The trousers are dark showing as dark patches on the rear flanks and the undertail coverts are pale with broad dark barring. Undertail pale with a prominent black subterminal band. On the underwings the carpal area and the greater coverts are dark, forming a broad, dark wing-bar contrasting with greyer and paler remiges. Secondaries and primaries vary according to age, but appear mostly darkish with paler barring confined to inner sections of feathers leaving a broad dark trailing edge and broadly dark wing-tip. The bases of the outermost primaries often show a pale patch, the palest part of the remiges. Younger adults show paler and more distinctly barred underwings with a distinct but rather narrow dark trailing edge.

Juveniles are similarly dark above with a slightly paler and finely barred tail. They can also show white mottling on the mantle, but on average less than in adults. Head dark tawny with a pale throat. Underparts uniformly tawny varying in intensity between individuals and bleaching during winter. Breast and forearm more deeply coloured than the rear body and the median underwing coverts. Greater underwing coverts are partly black and form a narrow and often inconspicuous dark wing-bar, which is usually darkest halfway out fading towards the carpal and the body. Flight-feathers distinctly barred, with uniform and rather fine and dense bars. Tail and secondaries fractionally darker, contrasting with paler and partly translucent primaries, with barred and darker fingers. As in adults, the bases of the outer primaries are the palest area of the underwing.

Birds in transitional plumage are intermediate between juveniles and adults. The body is largely as in adults, although with less distinct streaking on the breast, and the flight-feathers are more similar to juvenile but differ in having a distinct black trailing edge to wings and tail.

Perched Alert birds perch horizontally with legs appearing extremely long, but at rest adopt buzzard-like upright posture, with extremely powerful legs tucked into body plumage. Wings appear rather short, with wing-tips reaching only halfway down the tail. Head only slightly more powerful than in buzzard, with bill somewhat longer and deeper. Adults identified by rather uniform, dark upperparts, greyish tail with broad subterminal band, whitish underparts with dark streaking and by dark trousers and whitish socks. Head often shows darker crown and ear coverts spot, but a pale face with a dark malar stripe.

Juveniles are uniformly brown above with paler grey and finely barred tail. Upper breast is deep tawny becoming gradually paler towards belly. Trousers and socks are pale. Subadults in transition are similar to full adults but the upper breast looks smudgy with rather broad and indistinct dark streaks on a dirty buffish-white ground-colour. Upperwing coverts are paler brown than in full adults.

Bare parts Bill pale grey with darker tip. Feet and cere yellow. Iris pale in adult, varying from amber to yellow, darker and brownish in juvenile.

Variation: Adults vary as to amount of white on forearm of underwing and to pattern of remiges from below, juveniles as to general darkness of body plumage below and distinctness of dark underwing bar.

Confusion species: Usually not confused with other species owing to diagnostic shape and characteristic plumages. Subadults may resemble Long-legged Buzzard (page 391), with dark trailing edge and darkish carpal area, but similar Long-legged lacks prominent dark tail-band and usually shows a diagnostic grey or whitish flash on upper primaries and glides and soars on kinked wings, with lifted arms and level or drooping hand.

MOULT

Complete annually. In first moults some remiges are regularly left unmoulted.

Juvenile (first moult) First moult starts in 2nd cy Mar (Morocco Apr p1–2 already full-grown; Provence 1 Apr p1 missing in both wings; Cyprus 29 Mar still no signs of remex moult; BMNH). Moult arrested in Sep–Oct, when three or four outer primaries and five to seven median secondaries still unmoulted, juvenile feathers. Tail moulted more or less completely in first moult.

Second moult 3rd cy bird from Spain initiated moult on 2 Feb; BMNH. Remaining juvenile remiges lost during 3rd cy summer, Jun–Jul.

Adults (subsequent moults) Moults primaries serially descendant, often showing two waves. Breeding pair in Israel not yet started remex moult by 26 Mar (pers. obs.).

AGEING AND SEXING

Normally three age-classes separable in the field: juveniles, transitional or first-adults and adults. Focus on underwing and uppertail pattern and also on colour of body plumage below.

> **Ageing summary:** Juveniles are best identified by rather uniformly pale rufous buff underparts, with fine but rather dense barring to flight-feathers. Upperparts appear uniformly dark brownish, with slightly paler greyish tail. Adults are white on underbody and forearm (variably), with rest of underwings dark. They also appear uniformly dark above except for pale grey tail with black subterminal bar and white patch on mantle. Birds in transitional plumage resemble adults but from below show a broad and distinct (and broken) dark trailing edge to otherwise rather pale flight-feathers and a dark wing-band along the greater coverts.

Juvenile (1st cy autumn – 2nd cy spring)   Plates 508–514

Silhouette longer- and narrower-winged and shorter-tailed than adult, with prominently S-shaped trailing edge.

From above, rather uniformly dark brown with slightly paler tail and inner hand, often with some white speckling on mantle. Head rufous brown. From below, uniformly tawny, deepest on upper breast becoming gradually paler towards rear. Lesser and median underwing coverts tawny, darker towards leading edge, greater coverts with black markings, forming usually narrow and inconspicuous dark mid-wing bar. From below, all remiges with rather fine, dense and regular barring and with slightly darker secondaries than inner hand. Fingers are rather pale basally with dark barring but darken gradually towards the tips; they form the darkest part of the underwing on a distant bird contrasting with the pale primary-bases. Perched juveniles show diagnostic long pale legs in contrast with rufous upper breast.

By spring, when plumage is worn, upperparts may contrast with pale uppertail, coverts are distinctly paler than rest of upperwing (greater coverts darker), while the underparts bleach to tawny buff.

Transitional plumage (2nd cy autumn – 3rd cy spring)   Plate 515 and Fig 53

Perched birds are often difficult to tell from adults but the breast pattern looks tattier, especially on upper breast, with a dirtier yellowish background colour.

Fig 53 *Bonelli's Eagle, second plumage. Note retained juvenile remiges with pale tips, buffish breast with smudged markings, broad black wing-band and pale ochre forearm. Owing to dark carpal-area and dark trousers may be confused with Long-legged Buzzard, but identified by broad dark subterminal tail- and mid-wing-band, darkish head and different silhouette and flight.*

In flight, upperparts already resemble the adult, with white mottling on the mantle and a greyish tail with a wide, dark subterminal bar, but birds can still be aged by remaining brownish juvenile flight-feathers in tail and wings (see Moult) and the upperwing coverts are often paler brown than in full adults. From below, they are easily identified by the dark line on the underwing, formed by moulted greater and median coverts, sometimes forming a darker carpal-patch. The remiges are also diagnostic, rather as in *Buteos*, finely barred with a distinct but often incomplete dark trailing edge. Lesser underwing coverts are buffish white, irregularly streaked dark. Underbody looks dirty white, with less sharply defined dark streaking than full adults. Trousers are distinctly dark.

Adult (3rd cy autumn and older)   Plates 516–521

Upperparts dark brownish grey, with an individually variable white patch on the mantle, sometimes difficult to see on a perched bird. Crown and ear coverts mostly darker than the rest of the head. Tail grey, with rather faint darker barring and with a broad, black subterminal band at the tip. Underparts white, with black streaking on breast and belly, and with dark trousers. Perched birds look typically long-legged and short-winged but long-tailed.

At a distance adults in flight appear rather contrastingly coloured. Body looks white underneath and contrasts with dark underwings and head. Upperparts look very uniformly dark with a pale grey and black-tipped tail. The white mantle-patch is often visible from afar. At closer range the generally uniform upperparts show a slight contrast between dark remiges and greater coverts and browner median and lesser coverts, while some birds show a distinctly darker trailing edge to wing and dark tips to primary coverts from above. Tail grey with a broad black band close to the tip and with additional finer barring in some individuals. Head appears dark, often with paler face and white throat.

From below, the white breast shows prominent black streaking and the diagnostic dark trousers are conspicuous on the rear flanks. Tail pale with a broad dark subterminal band. Underwing variable: some appear to have more or less all-dark underwings, while others show a prominent white forearm. The white lesser and median underwing coverts are variably streaked in accordance with streaking on the body. The remiges also vary from nearly all-dark, with faint greyish marbling confined especially to the outer primary-bases (old birds), to paler and more clearly barred feathers with a distinct black trailing edge (younger adults).

Older birds are more finely streaked below, show less barring on the uppertail and have more uniformly dark remiges below than younger adults.

Sexing: Sexing normally not possible in the field, although male is slimmer and smaller than female when seen together. Adult males are on average whiter and more finely streaked below than females of similar age.

References: Tucker & Heath 1995

Plate 508 *Juvenile. Tawny body plumage and finely barred flight-feathers with paler hand are diagnostic. 1 Nov 1986, Israel (Pekka Komi).*

Plate 509 *Juvenile (same as Plate 508) showing diagnostic shape with rather long tail and broad wings with S-curved trailing edge. 1 Nov 1986, Israel (Pekka Komi).*

Plate 510 *Juvenile in full soar. Uniform body plumage and dense, fine barring of flight-feathers are diagnostic. Note also dark outer greater coverts. Nov 1992, Morocco (Markus Varesvuo).*

Plate 511 *Juvenile. Upperwing coverts are dull brown and only slightly paler than the finely barred remiges. 5 Nov 1986, Israel (Dick Forsman).*

Plate 512 *Juvenile. Rather uniform-appearing upperparts are diagnostic. Note grey and finely barred tail and small white patch often visible on upper back. 1 Nov 1986, Israel (Pekka J. Nikander).*

Plate 513 *Juvenile. By 2nd cy spring plumage wear adds to upperwing contrasts. Note moulting inner primaries and central tail-feather. 11 Mar 1997, UAE (Antti Below).*

Plate 514 *Juvenile (same as Plate 513) in bleached plumage. Note long and pale legs with huge feet and short wings in relation to tail-tip. 11 Mar 1997, UAE (Antti Below).*

Plate 515 *Transitional plumage (3rd cy spring). Distinct dark tips to flight-feathers form narrow dark bands to wings and tail, but note diagnostic retained juvenile outer primaries (p9–10) and median secondaries (s4 and s8–9) lacking dark tips. Feb 1990, Morocco (Tom Lindroos).*

Plate 516   *Young adult. Differs from older adults by largely barred remiges below with distinct dark trailing edge to wing. Nov 1990, Morocco (Harri Muukkonen).*

Plate 517   *Adult. Note largely dark remiges of adults with paler patch proximally on outer primaries. Amount of white on forearm varies individually. Nov 1992, Morocco (Markus Varesvuo).*

Plate 518 *Old adult. Note almost all-dark remiges of this adult female. Tail-pattern and dark thighs are diagnostic, well visible in flight. 3 Apr 1996, Israel (Dick Forsman).*

Plate 519 *Moulting adult. 28 Sep 1987, Israel (Henry Lehto).*

Plate 520   *Adult from above. Note white mantle patch, grey tail with broad subterminal band and slightly paler coverts than remiges. Mar 1993, Israel (Antti Below).*

Plate 521   *Adult female on nest with nearly fledged young. Note long legs of both and short wings in relation to tail. Jun 1984, India (Rishad Naoroji).*

BOOTED EAGLE *Hieraaetus pennatus*
Plates 522–539

Subspecies: Nominate *pennatus* in Europe, Africa and W Asia, *H. p. harterti* in SW and C Asia.

Distribution: Widely distributed from SW Europe to Lake Baikal and Manchuria, but subpopulations scattered with large uninhabited areas in between. In Europe widespread in Iberia and European part of Russia, more scattered in France, eastern Europe and the Balkans.

Habitat: Confined to partly wooded areas interspersed with more open slopes with scrub, pastures and farmland. Nests in woods but hunts mainly over open areas, including open woodland.

Population: European population approximately 3000–6000 pairs, with an estimated 2000–4000 in Spain. Populations of other European countries much smaller, ranging from a few to some hundred pairs.

Movements: Summer visitor to Europe but winters occasionally in the Mediterranean basin. W Palearctic birds winter in the savannas of sub-Saharan Africa from Sahel to S Africa.

Autumn migration from late Aug to Oct, peaking mid-Sep to early Oct. Mostly uses routes over Bosporus–Levant and Gibraltar, like other large raptors, but also crosses Sicilian Channel, and frequently observed on Mediterranean islands. Autumn passage by far most intense over Gibraltar with daily maxima of nearly 2000 at end of Sep–beginning of Oct and an autumn total of 15 137 birds counted in 1972. Numbers along eastern route smaller, with autumn totals of 530 at Bosporus (1971), 2000 N Israel (1986) and 1100 at Suez, Egypt (1984). Usually migrates singly or in groups of two or three, often on their own but also mixes with e.g. flocks of buzzards.

Spring passage more protracted, from early Mar to late May, with peak period at Gibraltar and Eilat during first half of Apr. In spring 450 counted on passage at Suez and 600 over W Israel, but only 175 at Eilat. Immatures return later than adults.

Hunting and prey: Hunts mainly on wing soaring high and scanning the ground below. Stops every now and then to hang against the wind. When prey is spotted stoops at great speed with folded wings and long legs stretched forward during final stage.

Bulk of prey consists of medium-sized birds, big lizards and small mammals. Birds range in size from warblers to domestic chicken, with preference for thrush- and partridge-sized birds, depending on local supply.

Species identification

Length 42–49 cm

wing-span 113–134 cm (*n*=30; Israeli migrants; W.S. Clark, unpubl.)

Pale morph unmistakable but dark morph superficially resembles e.g. Marsh Harrier and Black Kite. However, pattern of upperparts diagnostic, as well as typical wing-carriage in head-on views and wing-beats in active flight. Hunting behaviour also diagnostic.

Identification summary: A small eagle, like a long-tailed and square-winged buzzard. Occurs at all ages in two distinct colour morphs, pale and dark. Pattern of upperparts diagnostic and similar in both morphs, with distinctive pale patches across upperwing coverts and scapulars and with pale uppertail coverts. Tail greyish with narrowish darker subterminal band. Seen well, pale morph unmistakable from below, with white underparts contrasting sharply with dark remiges. Dark morph more or less uniformly brown below but undertail pale with dark subterminal bar; barring of underwing usually visible only on translucent inner three primaries. Individuals vary in darkness of underbody and underwing coverts. Dark birds best told from similar Black Kite by diagnostic upperparts, 'head-lights', wing-attitude and diagnostic head coloration.

In flight, distant Typical shape, with rather short, rectangular and blunt-tipped wings (six fingers) and fairly long square-tipped tail, together with distinctive coloration of upperparts can often be assessed from afar. The Booted Eagle appears slightly shorter-winged and longer-tailed than e.g. a buzzard, having a distinct shape of its own. When soaring the wings appear more rectangular than in any buzzard, with fuller hand and more ample wing-tip, latter due to six well-developed fingers in Booted, instead of five in buzzards. Juveniles differ from adults in having slightly narrower wings with white S-curved trailing edge. Tail is comparatively longer than in buzzard and is mostly kept closed or only half-open adding to long image. The active flight is very different from a *Buteo*, more recalling Honey Buzzard, with high and rather stiff yet relaxed wing-beats, but differs from Honey Buzzard by more pronounced downstroke than upstroke. When gliding, wings kept distinctly arched with marked 'broom' at wing-tip; when soaring, only slightly bowed, but again with more curved primary-tips than in other raptors of similar size. When comparing head-on silhouettes with rather similar Black Kite, Booted Eagle appears shorter-winged and larger-bodied with more arched wings and clearly more curved primary-tips.

Even from a distance easily identified by diagnostic head and upperparts. Underparts are much more difficult to assess as even pale birds may appear dark below in strong sunlight.

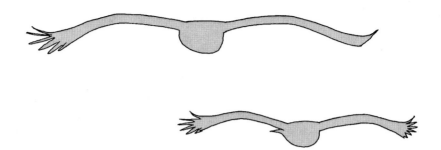

Fig 54 *Booted Eagle. When gliding shows clearly arched wings with wide 'broom' at wing-tip. Note also big body in relation to wing-span.*

In flight, closer The colour and pattern of the upperparts are diagnostic excluding virtually all other species. The bird is basically brown with nearly blackish brown flight-feathers and primary coverts, but has conspicuous pale areas diagonally across the upperwing coverts and scapulars. Head typically two-coloured with paler crown and nape and a darker face contrasting in pale birds with the whitish throat. Uppertail coverts are pale, forming a distinct band at the base of the greyish tail, which shows a darker subterminal band. Only certain autumn juvenile Honey Buzzards may at times come very close to the characteristic upperparts of Booted Eagle.

Seen head-on the white 'head-lights' at the base of the forewing are typical, although they are easily overlooked if not especially looked for and similar head-lights may also occur in e.g. juvenile Honey Buzzards and Bonelli's Eagles.

From below, the tail is pale with a darker diffuse band close to the tip and the tarsi are feathered, leaving only the toes yellow. Remiges very dark and the rather dense and uniform but broad barring is mostly difficult to see in the field. It is usually visible only on the somewhat paler inner three primaries. Outer primaries frequently show narrow pale bases forming a pale crescent at the leading edge. Secondaries have whitish tips in fresh plumage, but these wear down rather soon. Pale birds are practically white underneath, with sparse and variable brown or rufous streaking on the upper breast, sometimes turning into barring on the 'trousers'. Underwing coverts also white, but show variable dark spotting, sometimes forming lines of spots along the tips or concentrated to form a carpal crescent. Dark birds are variably brown below, ranging from uniformly blackish brown to a more variegated medium brown. The birds may be either streaked or uniformly coloured on the body and the underwing coverts vary from uniform to streaked to richly pale-spotted. The so called intermediate or rufous morph just represents the pale end of the variation in dark birds (see under 'Variation').

Perched Perches in an upright posture resembling a Common Buzzard. Head often appears large because of raised nape-feathering, creating eagle-like crown, and shows darker cheeks

and face contrasting with straw-coloured crown and nape giving impression of Golden
Eagle. Feet strong with feathered tarsi, excluding all hawks (save for Rough-legged
Buzzard). Wing-tips fall slightly short of tail-tip. Pale morph easy to identify by whitish
body with contrasting darker head. Dark morph uniformly dark brown below or medium-
brown with darker irregular streaking. Pale areas of upperwing coverts and scapulars, so
distinctive in flight, are much less conspicuous on perched birds.

Bare parts Cere and feet yellow at all ages. Iris dark, greyish brown, in juveniles, brighter
coloured, orange-brown to dark rufous-brown in adults.

Variation: The ratio between the two colour morphs is different in W and E Europe with
a higher percentage of pale birds in the west: in Spain 509 pale and 139 dark birds
(*c.* 80% pale birds) compared with 213 pale and 149 dark (*c.* 60% pale birds) in counts
from Turkey, Greece and Israel (unpubl. data).

The recently described rufous (or intermediate) morph of the Booted Eagle represents
the pale extreme within the variation of the dark morph, which is far more variable than
generally appreciated. These birds, both adults and juveniles, are characterized from below
by tawny to rufous brown body and forearm contrasting with normally coloured dark
greater coverts, while flight-feathers and upperparts are normal.

Confusion species: Often confused with other birds of prey, dark birds mostly with Black
Kite and Marsh Harrier, pale birds with pale juvenile Honey Buzzard (being the trickiest
confusion species) or pale Common Buzzard. Other pale or partly pale raptors, such as
Egyptian Vulture, Osprey, Short-toed Eagle and male harriers, etc. are all easily told from
Booted Eagle by different silhouette and upperparts.

Head-on silhouette, with arched wings and prominent 'broom' at wing-tip, as well as
high, powerful wing-beats in active flight differ from potential pitfalls, such as Black Kite,
Marsh Harrier, Common Buzzard and juvenile Honey Buzzard.

Marsh Harrier (page 167) Females/juveniles have different flight and head-on silhouette
and narrower wing-tip (five fingers). The pale areas on the upperwing are on the leading
edge of forearm and the uppertail coverts are brown, not white.

Black Kite (page 65) Active flight slower, with shallow and more gentle wing-beats; glides
on gently arched wings with no noticeable 'broom' at wing-tip. Slimmer with comparatively longer wings, smaller body and longer, forked tail. Shows pale upperwing
coverts patch but lacks pale scapulars and pale uppertail coverts and head-lights of
Booted.

Common Buzzard (page 266) and Honey Buzzard (page 30) Pale birds are from below always separated from superficially similar looking pale Booted Eagle by pale centre of hand, contrasting markedly with dark fingers and darker secondaries, and from above by darker and more distinctly patterned tail and by darker and more uniform upperwing coverts and scapulars. Pale juvenile Honey Buzzards, which are the most likely pitfalls, mostly also have a pale head with the diagnostic dark 'sun-glasses'.

MOULT

Complete annually starting during breeding and suspended for autumn migration, to be completed in the winter quarters. In contrast to most other eagles the Booted Eagle seems able to replace the entire plumage in one year.

Juveniles (first moult) Moult commences in 2nd cy late May–early Jun (Turkey, 16 Jun missing p1–2 in both wings) but is suspended for the autumn migration. By Sep–Oct four or five outermost primaries and most of the secondaries and tail still comprise juvenile feathers. In winter quarters most of the remaining juvenile remiges and rectrices are replaced retaining (in some only?) one or two juvenile outermost primaries and some median secondaries until 3rd cy summer. When retained, the shorter and pointed and very faded brown juvenile feathers are important ageing characters in 3rd cy spring.

Adults (subsequent moults) Starts moulting in May or Jun, with great individual differences in timing (sex-dependent?). In five birds from Apr none had commenced moulting, while in three from 5–6 May two were moulting inner primaries (BMNH). Moult is suspended for the autumn migration but resumed upon arrival in the winter quarters, where it is completed. May replace all flight-feathers in one year.

AGEING AND SEXING

Juveniles and adults are very similar in plumage, hence ageing requires ideal conditions. Best aged by different wing-shape and by condition of white trailing edge of wing and tail-tip and by moult pattern.

Ageing summary: Juveniles are narrower-winged than adults with a markedly S-curved trailing edge. Wings and tail have an even, neat white or evenly worn trailing edge and show no signs of moult. Adults have broader and more rectangular wings with a broader and more square-cut hand, while the trailing edge of the wing and the tail-tip show irregular white tips, broad on fresh feathers and narrow on worn feathers (the difference in abrasion can be difficult to see unless the bird is viewed at close range or seen against a blue sky or a dark background).

Juvenile (1st cy – 2nd cy summmer)   **Plates 522–528**

During autumn fresh juveniles are best aged by their perfect plumage, neatly S-curved trailing edge to the wing showing an unbroken and even white line, and a similarly neat pale tail-tip. Plumage more worn in spring but juveniles still possible to age using the same characters, although the pale tips to remiges and tail are narrower.

Pale morph Underparts very distinctive with largely white body plumage contrasting with very dark, from a distance even black, flight-feathers. Tail appears pale grey from below with a suffused darker subterminal band next to the tip, usually visible only when tail is spread. Head rufous brown with a whitish throat contrasting well with the rest of the body. Underwing coverts usually spotted black, varying in extent between individuals, but usually with at least prominent black spots forming a band along the greater coverts. Underbody may be more or less streaked but in juveniles the streaks are, on average, more concentrated on the upper breast and are more diffuse than in adults. Secondaries are very dark contrasting with the paler inner three or four primaries, forming a typical window. Outer primaries are more or less uniformly dark, while barring of inner is visible only in best possible conditions. Pale trailing edge to wing and tip of tail even and unbroken are the best characters for ageing.

Upperparts of juveniles are tidy with clearly marked wing- and uppertail coverts. Juveniles also have pale-tipped greater upperwing coverts forming a narrow band, still visible in 2nd cy spring.

Dark morph Juveniles appear very uniformly dark below, with only the inner three or four and the base of the outermost primaries paler than the rest of the plumage. Body plumage of the underparts is dark brown to almost blackish brown, somewhat paler towards the vent and undertail coverts in some birds. Paler birds show distinctly paler, rufous brown forearm to underwing contrasting with blackish greater underwing coverts. In good light the flight-feathers, which are practically identical to those of the pale morph, are clearly paler than the body and the greater underwing coverts. Juveniles are, on average, more evenly coloured below than adults, which more frequently show pale-spotted underwing coverts, a blotchy or streaked underbody and more distinctly barred secondaries.

Upperparts are quite similar to those of the pale morph, with the same distinctive pattern on back and upperwing coverts, but the overall colour is somewhat darker with slightly less contrasting pale areas, such as the uppertail coverts and wing coverts patch. Dark morph juveniles also show the pale tips to their greater coverts, forming a band on the upperwing.

Transitional plumage (2nd cy autumn – 3rd cy summer)   **Plates 529–531**

When seen close up and in good conditions first-adults are possible to identify and to tell from older birds. In 2nd cy autumn they are still much like juveniles with a rather neat trailing edge to wing, with only a few, if any, newly moulted secondaries. However, the five to seven innermost primaries are moulted and the inner show broadly white tips, being blacker, longer and more rounded at the tip than the retained outer juvenile primaries fingers. In 3rd cy spring more difficult to age as usually only a few (if any) juvenile feathers are left, mainly some outer primaries and some median secondaries, which are very worn and pointed, faded brown and clearly shorter than the new ones.

Adult (3rd cy autumn and older)   Plates 532–539

Adults best told from juveniles by signs of wing and tail moult, easiest to see in the trailing edge of the wing and in the tip of the tail. These look ragged, with shorter and worn feathers standing next to fresh, longer and pale-tipped feathers. The finer tail-bars, inside the broader subterminal bar, seem to be more numerous and more distinct in adult, and the secondaries are greyer with more distinct barring.

Pale morph Very similar to pale morph juvenile and difficult to separate by plumage. Adults are, on average, more streaked below with more distinct streaks which often reach lower down on the body than in juveniles, to lower breast or belly. Upperparts quite similar to juvenile, but the paler upperwing covert areas are less clearly marked merging more into each other. Lacks distinct pale band of juvenile along tips of greater upperwing coverts.

Dark morph Adults are, on average, slightly paler and more mottled below than more uniformly coloured juveniles. Underwing coverts are frequently spotted pale and the body shows darker streaking. Upperparts are similar to adult pale morph, but with slightly less contrast between the pale and dark areas of the upperwing.

Sexing: Sexing normally not possible in the field, although females are slightly bigger and heavier than males.

References: Clark 1987a, 1989; Conzemius 1996; Cramp & Simmons 1980; Shirihai & Christie 1992; Svensson 1976; Tjernberg 1989; Tucker & Heath 1995; Ullman & Undeland 1985

Plate 522 *Juvenile, pale morph, showing diagnostic underwings of the species. Aged by uniform white trailing edge to wings and tail. 9 Nov 1988, Morocco (Jyri Heino).*

Plate 523 *Juvenile, pale morph. Note uniform condition of wings and tail of this individual with a tawny hood. 19 Oct 1987, Israel (Tom Lindroos).*

Plate 524 *Juvenile, pale morph. By spring the pale tips of the flight-feathers are worn away but the wings still show a nicely S-shaped trailing edge of uniformly worn tips. Spring, Israel (Hadoram Shirihai).*

Plate 525 *Juvenile, dark morph. Note typically arched wings with deeply splayed and upbent fingers and white position lights at wing-base. Mar 1986, Israel (Dick Forsman).*

Plate 526 *Dark juvenile, aged by uniform pale trailing edge to wings and tail. Note pale tail and paler inner primaries with barring, typical of the species, while uniform underwing coverts indicate a juvenile. 12 Sep 1997, Spain (Dick Forsman).*

Plate 527 *Dark morph juvenile from above, aged by uniform plumage and pale band to greater upperwing coverts. Note the diagnostic upperparts of the species, including white headlights at wing-base. 10 Sep 1997, Spain (Annika Forsten).*

Plate 528 *Juvenile. Note uniformly worn upperwing of this dark morph bird (so-called rufous morph). Apr 1986, Israel (Esa Sojamo).*

Plate 529 *Dark morph in transitional plumage (2nd cy autumn). Has replaced p1–4 (p5 still growing) and s1 and s5, while the other remiges are juvenile. Note worn and brownish juvenile fingers and distinct white trailing edge to inner hand. 10 Sep 1997, Spain (Dick Forsman).*

Plate 530 *Transitional plumage (2nd cy autumn), dark morph (so-called rufous morph). Aged by predominantly juvenile, uniformly worn secondaries (s5 moulted) and by retained outer four juvenile primaries. 19 Nov 1996, Ethiopia (Dick Forsman).*

Plate 531 *Pale morph in transitional plumage. Aged by diagnostic even, white trailing edge to inner hand, while all secondaries, except for left s5, are worn juvenile feathers. 10 Sep 1997, Spain (Dick Forsman).*

Plate 532 *Adult, pale morph, showing irregular white tips to secondaries. 4 Apr 1995, Israel (Tomi Muukkonen).*

Plate 533 *Adult, pale morph. Note characteristic irregular trailing edge to wings and tail. Adults also tend to be more streaked on breast than juveniles. (Dan Zetterström).*

Plate 534   *Adult, pale morph. 23 Sep 1987, Israel (Dick Forsman).*

Plate 535   *Pale morph adult showing diagnostic upperparts of the species. Differs from juvenile by irregular white tips to remiges and greater coverts. 9 Sep 1997, Spain (Dick Forsman).*

Plate 536   *Adult, pale morph. Aged by rufous-brown iris and variably worn greater coverts and secondaries. May, Turkey (Alfred Limbrunner).*

Plate 537   *Adult, dark morph. Aged by uneven trailing edge of wings and tail. Mar 1993, Israel (Markus Varesvuo).*

Plate 538 *Adult, dark morph, showing irregularly white-tipped flight-feathers. Note diagnostic silhouette and wing-formula, pale grey tail with darker subterminal band and pale inner primaries and compare with confusion species. 4 Oct 1986, Israel (Pekka J. Nikander).*

Plate 539 *Adult, dark morph, moulting. 3 Nov 1989, Yemen (Magnus Ullman).*

LESSER KESTREL *Falco naumanni*

Plates 540–558

Subspecies: Monotypic.

Distribution: In Europe mainly in the Mediterranean basin and in E and SE Europe. Occurs from N Africa and Levant through C Asia to Siberia and China.

Habitat: Prefers open and dry areas such as steppes, semi-deserts and cliffs. Often found breeding around human settlements, in villages and towns, nesting colonially on old buildings, ruins and cliffs.

Population: Dramatic and rapid decline over much of Europe, with 95% drop in numbers in Spain between 1950s and 1990s (from 100 000 pairs in 1950s to 20 000–50 000 pairs in 1980s and down to 4200–5100 pairs by 1990), but Spain still holds great majority of European breeding population. The population of the entire W Palearctic is estimated at 12 500–18 000 pairs.

Movements: Long-range migrant wintering in E and S Africa. Disperses from breeding grounds by late Jul–Aug and seen on migration from Aug onwards, with a peak during Sep–Oct. Migrates on broad-front like other falcons and does not congregate along major flyways. Usually not seen in greater numbers during autumn migration but joins parties of Red-footed Falcons and Kestrels. Forms huge flocks on wintering grounds with thousands of birds. A few adults winter in Spain, Morocco and Turkey. Spring migration more noticeable, with birds returning in small parties of up to some ten together, reaching S Europe during Mar and Apr. At Eilat, Israel, passes in spring between early Feb and mid-May, with peak in early Apr and in autumn from late Aug to early Nov, with total of 20 in 1980.

Hunting and prey: Hunting habits very similar to Red-footed Falcon. Perches openly on poles or wires from which drops down on prey on ground. Also hovers frequently when hunting ground prey, or alternatively, snatches flying insects in flight like Hobby and Red-footed Falcon. On migration often seen hunting together with Kestrels and Red-footed Falcons. Prey consists of various small vertebrates, such as rodents and lizards, but mainly large insects.

Species identification

Length 25–31 cm

wing-span 66–71 cm (*n*=21; Israeli migrants; W.S. Clark, unpubl.)

Apart from Kestrel, told from all other small raptors by largely rufous upperparts. Females and juveniles very similar to Kestrel and identification requires seeing several characters, preferably wing-formula, head-pattern, feather-pattern of upperparts and pattern of remiges and coverts of underwing.

Identification summary: A small falcon with size and shape of Red-footed Falcon. Most difficult to separate from Kestrel, the two sharing almost identical plumages. On perched birds the wing-tips reach, or nearly reach, the tip of the tail in Lesser Kestrel, but fall mostly well short in Kestrel and the claws are pale (black in Kestrel). In direct comparison with Kestrel size difference obvious.

Adult males readily identified by spotless upperparts with partly grey upperwing coverts and mostly unbarred remiges below with broad but diffuse grey trailing edge and tip to underwing. Females and juveniles very similar to Kestrel in corresponding plumage, but identified by plainer head with prominent moustache-mark only, lack of dark eye-line, narrow chevron-shaped barring above and by pale and nearly unmarked bases to remiges below, contrasting with distinctly patterned underwing coverts and with diffuse but broadly grey tip and trailing edge to hand.

In flight, distant Very similar to Kestrel, although flight silhouette of Lesser Kestrel on average slightly different, with shorter tail and more rounded wings, being more similar to Red-footed Falcon. When soaring, wings appear shortish and rounded and the appearance of a distant male may even be reminiscent of a Levant Sparrowhawk! In profile,

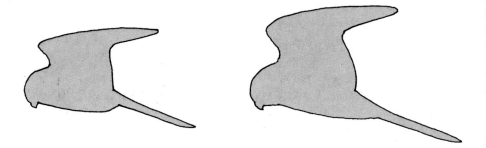

Fig 55 *Lesser Kestrel (left) and Kestrel hovering. Note proportionately shorter tail and more plump rear-body of Lesser.*

when seen soaring or hovering Lesser Kestrels appear typically chubby, with a short and rounded body ending suddenly at the vent.

Adult male possible to tell from adult male Kestrel even from afar by whitish underwing with widely dark tips, deeply coloured breast contrasting with whitish underwings and pale throat, and by diagnostic wide and triangular tail-band. Note, however, that southern Kestrels are deeper coloured on underbody than northern birds.

Juveniles and adult females not possible to separate from Kestrels by plumage from a distance, but difference in flight silhouette may be helpful as tentative character (see above).

In flight, closer Adult males fairly easily separated from adult male Kestrels by whitish underwing with contrasting widely dark wing-tips, rather deep coloured underbody with contrasting whitish throat, and by clearly wider and more triangular black subterminal bar to tail (about one third to one quarter of tail-length in Lesser and one fifth to one sixth in Kestrel). Tail and head are more bluish grey in Lesser but this, as well as unspotted upperparts and blue-grey wing-patch, discernible only at surprisingly short distances. Underwing coverts variable, probably individually rather than with age, from uniformly white to white with extensive black spotting.

Apart from the slight difference in shape there are also several plumage characters separating juveniles and females of the two kestrel species when seen well. Lesser Kestrel has a 'plain' face, lacking the dark eye-stripe of Kestrel thus showing only a dark moustache below the eye. The remiges of Lesser are proximally paler below with less prominent barring, but with distinctly darker wing-tips and a faint darker trailing edge (in Kestrel secondaries and primaries distinctly barred and primary-tips show only narrow darker tips to outermost). The pale underwing with contrasting darker wing-tips is most striking in adult males and considerably less pronounced in juveniles, which may be rather like Kestrels. The juveniles differ from Kestrels, however, by their heavily spotted underwing coverts, which contrast strongly with the generally pale bases to the remiges. In Kestrel the underwing looks very uniformly patterned with no marked difference between coverts and remiges. Be aware of 2nd cy birds in spring, with moulted, longer tail-feathers creating a more Kestrel-like silhouette. The different feather-pattern of the upperparts is rarely seen in flight. The tail is similar in shape to Kestrel (see Moult); juvenile and female Lesser Kestrels frequently show a reduced or irregular barring in tail, but there is much overlap in this character.

Perched Similar to Kestrel, but distinguished by longer wings, reaching tip of tail or nearly so. Note, however, that 2nd cy birds in spring may have replaced their tail with longer feathers and that they are hence more similar to Kestrels. (Kestrels may also sometimes appear rather long-winged, with wing-tip reaching close to tail-tip.) Claws pale or greyish, never black.

Adult males identified by spotless red upperparts with partly grey upperwing coverts and tertials. Head mostly uniformly bluish grey but may show faint moustache (especially in 2nd cy spring), but not distinctly paler cheeks, as in Kestrel. Underparts deep ochre or tawny, either uniformly coloured or with dark spots. Throat paler than rest of underparts.

Females and juveniles best identified by head-pattern and feather-pattern of upperparts. Head looks plain and featureless, apart from dark moustache below the eye, with pale cheek-patch reaching to lateral crown (no dark posterior eye-line). Head may be either rufous or greyish, varying individually but also according to age, sex and state of plumage wear. Upperparts are more finely barred than Kestrel, with dark barring considerably narrower than rufous interspaces and with individual bars shaped like arched chevrons instead of transverse bars.

Bare parts Iris dark brown at all ages. Feet yellow, cere and orbital skin yellow, deeper in adults than juveniles. Claws pale, whitish or greyish, not black as in Kestrel.

Confusion species: Apart from Kestrel all other small raptors can be excluded by the largely rufous brown upperparts.

Kestrel (page 443) Shorter wings and longer tail when perched, black claws and head more distinctly patterned, with a dark posterior eye-line and a smaller and more distinctly bordered pale cheek-patch. The wing-formula is different between the two, with p10=p7 in Kestrel (p10 distinctly longer than p7 in Lesser). The remiges are more distinctly barred below, creating an evenly patterned underwing. The dark tip of the hand is narrow and inconspicuous, compared with Lesser Kestrel. In profile when hovering shows a longer tail and a smoothly tapering vent.

Fig 56 *Wing-formula of Lesser Kestrel (left) and Kestrel. Note distinctly longer p10 than p7 in Lesser, while in Kestrel p10 and p7 are roughly equal in length.*

Adult males are spotted above and greyish head shows distinctly paler cheeks. Females and juveniles have, apart from a different head-pattern, more heavily patterned upperparts, with transverse dark bars.

MOULT

Juveniles have a partial body moult in their first winter. The annual complete moult starts during breeding, earlier in females than in males, and is suspended for the autumn migration but resumed and completed in the winter quarters. At least some birds also suspend remex moult during the late nestling period.

Juveniles (first moult) Undergo a rather extensive partial body moult, similar to Red-footed Falcon, starting from Nov–Dec, when the first adult-type feathers appear on mantle and rump. By 2nd cy Mar males have moulted most of their body-feathers and wing coverts, retaining only the juvenile remiges, greater coverts and outer median and lesser coverts. The tail can be completely moulted, but some juvenile feathers are usually retained. Females moult less than males, normally only part of mantle, scapulars and rump, leaving the bird looking moth-eaten in its extremely worn juvenile plumage. The juvenile tail is normally retained or shows replaced longer central pair (being an explanation for the 'diagnostic Lesser Kestrel tail with protruding central tail-feathers').

The first complete moult starts in May–Jun, sooner than in adults, so that 2nd cy birds on average show a greater number of moulted primaries than adults at any one time. In a colony in N Greece on 27 Jun 1989 2nd cy females showed one to five, mostly two to three moulted primaries whereas second year males showed zero to three (mostly one or two). Many birds had already suspended their moult showing a complete wing with one or two freshly moulted primaries. The moult is suspended for the autumn migration, to be resumed in the winter quarters, where it is finished in Nov–Dec (pers. obs.).

Adults (subsequent moults) Start to moult like the juveniles in May–Jun, females earlier than males, and on average slightly later than 2nd cy birds. In Greece, by 27 Jun 1989, adult females had replaced up to three, mostly one or two primaries (p4–5), whereas males had up to two moulted primaries but most had not yet started. Moult thus (regularly?) suspended during the late nestling period and certainly suspended for the migration (in Kazakhstan 8 Sep 1993 ad male with p4–5 and ad female with p2–6 moulted; on 9 Sep ad male with p3–6 moulted and p2 and p7 growing). Moult is resumed and completed in the winter quarters (pers. obs.).

AGEING AND SEXING

Two separable age-classes in the field, although ageing in spring requires good views. In spring look for signs of moult, such as differently worn and differently patterned feathers, in males for barred juvenile upperwing coverts, secondaries and rectrices. To separate females and juveniles in autumn also look at breast pattern and colour of feather-tips above.

Ageing and sexing summary: Adult males unmistakable, with unmarked upperwing coverts and very pale remiges below. In autumn juveniles separated from adult females, like Kestrels, by pale tips to remiges, upperparts and upperwing coverts and by streaked rather than spotted underbody. Juveniles also lack any signs of moult. In spring 2nd cy males resemble adults, but are identified by retained juvenile barred secondaries (barring difficult to discern from below) and upperwing coverts and often also by some retained juvenile rectrices. Females are more difficult to age, but 2nd cy birds show partial body moult, with contrast between worn upperwing and fresh scapulars and mantle, whereas adult females appear more uniform and the plumage is fresh.

Juvenile (1st cy autumn until partial winter moult)   Plates 540–543

Fresh autumn juveniles on average have more bleached colours on upperparts compared with more deeply rufous adult females. Head often washed-out and colourless compared with rest of upperparts. Juvenile Lesser Kestrels are, however, frequently more rufous on upperparts than juvenile Kestrels. Ageing reliable by broad pale tips to upper primary and greater coverts and remiges, as in juvenile Kestrel, and by neatly streaked breast.

Juveniles are difficult to sex, but males show various amount of grey on rump, upper-tail coverts and tail-feathers, whereas juvenile females have these parts rufous brown, but this character may not be consistent, since more rufous males occur. The amount of tail-barring varies in juvenile males and some individuals may have almost unbarred, greyish or rufous-grey tail-feathers (yet retaining the broad subterminal band). Tails of juvenile females are more regularly and more heavily barred. The barring of scapulars and wing coverts is finer and sparser in juvenile males (recalling adult female) compared with more heavily barred juvenile females.

In winter, juveniles undergo a partial body moult, which varies individually in extent. In this moult the body-feathers are largely replaced, and even tail-feathers and lesser and median (and some greater) coverts can be replaced. Thus 2nd cy birds in spring generally appear very similar to adults in the field and are usually possible to age only by unmoulted juvenile upperwing coverts and tail-feathers (if left).

Transitional plumage (2nd cy spring – 2nd cy autumn)   Plates 544–549

Males Tend to moult more than females but are always possible to age by unmoulted and barred juvenile upperwing coverts and secondaries, whereas rest of plumage normally moulted into adult plumage by early 2nd cy summer. The most advanced birds retain only juvenile primaries, primary coverts, alula and outermost secondaries and greater coverts while the rest of the plumage is moulted and adult-like. The juvenile feathers are best seen on perched birds as the lack of grey on inner wings is very difficult to discern on a flying bird from a distance. Wings not as white below nor as uniformly coloured as in adult males, with less striking contrast between white bases to primaries and darker tips. 2nd cy males also frequently show bolder pattern to their axillaries, forming a darker area in the armpit.

Females Practically impossible to tell from older females in the field, except when seen well (preferably perched). Normally only mantle and scapulars moulted and the central pair of tail-feathers, which clearly protrude beyond the abraded juvenile feathers. This character is, however, useless on birds with a retained juvenile tail and loses its value in others as tail-moult proceeds. Upperwing coverts very worn and faded and contrast with recently moulted feathers of mantle and scapulars. The barring on e.g. greater coverts is broader than on adult females, with dark bars about as wide as rufous bars. Remiges not as pale and uniform below as in adult females, but faintly barred and with less distinct dark wing-tips, at times rather similar to Kestrel. Underwing coverts, however, are usually very heavily spotted and contrast strongly with pale bases to remiges, as opposed to Kestrel, where the whole underwing appears rather uniformly patterned.

Adult (from 2nd cy late autumn/winter and older)   Plates 550–558

Males Very colourful with deep bluish grey head, tail, rump and wing-patch (wing-patch varies individually but greater coverts, tertials and outer median coverts normally grey), deep chestnut-red mantle, scapulars and lesser coverts. Breast deep salmon contrasting with paler throat and turning gradually paler towards vent and undertail coverts. Wings whitish below with contrasting dark tips and often also with wide darker trailing edge. Amount of dark spotting on breast and underwing coverts vary independently of each other and also individually. Tail shows a broad black subterminal band, widest at centre, becoming gradually narrower towards the edges, thus forming a flat black triangle at the tail-tip, with white tip accordingly growing in width from centre to corners. Many males show a faint darker moustache and (very rarely) some individuals even show a paler cheek, reminiscent of adult male Kestrel. Lesser Kestrels, however, never show the prominent dark eye-line of Kestrel. The grey area on upperwing is surprisingly difficult to discern on flying birds, as red and grey of upperparts blend with each other. Also be aware of more brightly coloured Kestrels in S Europe showing Lesser Kestrel-like colours on under-body.

Females More reddish-brown above than younger birds, with finer and sparser chevron-like bars on mantle, scapulars and upperwing coverts. The dark bars of the greater coverts are finer than the rufous interspaces (cf. juveniles and 2nd cy). Head in many birds bright russet, with large pale cheek-patch continuing up to sides of crown. Dark moustache variable, but always the most prominent feature of the head which lacks dark eye-stripe of Kestrel. Breast and underparts usually with russet tinge, not pale buff as in juveniles, and with distinctive black spots instead of more diffuse streaks of juvenile. Rump either rufous or grey (no consistent difference compared with Kestrel), rectrices rufous, often with grey admixed, with fine dark barring and broad subterminal band and pale tip. In fresh plumage tail shape not different from Kestrel. Wedge-shaped tail, formerly believed to be diagnostic for Lesser Kestrel, mainly resulting from fresh and longer central tail-feathers in 2nd cy spring or from largely worn away pale tail-tip.

Sexing: Adults differ in plumage, whereas juveniles are rather similar and often not possible to sex in the field (see under Ageing and Sexing).

References Bijlsma et al. 1988; Clark 1996a; Gensbøl 1995; Tucker & Heath 1995

Plate 540 *Juvenile. Note distinctly marked underwing coverts contrasting with proximally pale and unmarked primaries with broadly dusky tips. 14 Sep 1993, Kazakhstan (Dick Forsman).*

Plate 541 *Juvenile showing typical featureless head, but rather prominently barred underwings. Note broader dark trailing edge to hand and paler primary-bases than in Kestrel, as well as different wing formula. 10 Sep 1997, Spain (Dick Forsman).*

Plate 542 *Juvenile male. Note the largely unbarred, white bases to the primaries and the broadly dark wing-tip. This character is usually less distinct in juvenile females, which are often more similar to Kestrels. 12 Sep 1993, Kazakhstan (Dick Forsman).*

Plate 543 *Juvenile male (same as Plate 542) showing typical head-pattern with distinct black moustache-spot but lacking dark eye-line behind the eye. Note also long wings in relation to tail-tip. 12 Sep 1993, Kazakhstan (Dick Forsman).*

Plate 544 *Transitional (2nd cy) male. Note barred juvenile greater coverts and inner secondaries while mantle is moulted and unmarked and adult-like. Jun 1991, Turkey (Markku Huhta-Koivisto).*

Plate 545 *Transitional (2nd cy) male. Note barred juvenile upperwing coverts and remiges in contrast to freshly moulted body plumage. 23 Jun 1991, Turkey (Tom Lindroos).*

Plate 546   *Advanced transitional (2nd cy) male with entire plumage moulted apart from retained juvenile remiges and tertials and inner greater covert. 22 Apr 1994, Oman (Hanne & Jens Eriksen).*

Plate 547   *Transitional male in autumn identified by retained barred inner secondaries. 9 Sep 1993, Kazakhstan (Dick Forsman).*

Plate 548   *Transitional (2nd cy) female. The generally worn upperwing with broadly barred greater coverts and short wings in relation to new, long tail are typical characters of transitional females. Note plain head and lack of dark eye-stripe and compare with Kestrel. 23 Jun 1991, Turkey (Tom Lindroos).*

Plate 549   *Transitional (2nd cy) female with suspended moult aged by extremely worn juvenile p9–10 and s1–3. 27 Sep 1996, Oman (Hanne & Jens Eriksen).*

Plate 550 *Adult male. Amount of spotting to underwing coverts and body varies individually. Note unbarred remiges, grey sides to head and broad tail-band of adult male (cf. Kestrel). 15 Apr 1994, Oman (Hanne & Jens Eriksen).*

Plate 551 *Adult male. Note broad dusky margin to pale underwing and contrasting pale throat. 14 Apr 1994, Oman (Hanne & Jens Eriksen).*

Plate 552 *Adult male from above showing grey greater coverts and unspotted mantle. Black tail-band is broader than on Kestrel. June 1991, Turkey (Tom Lindroos).*

Plate 553 *Adult male. Note unmarked upperparts with grey tertials and greater coverts band and long wings reaching close to tail-tip. A faint moustache is not rare in males. 25 Mar 1986 (Dick Forsman).*

Plate 554   *Female. Females in spring are practically impossible to age from below, but here sparsely marked underwing coverts indicate adult. Note wing-formula with p10 longer than p7 and compare with Kestrel. 15 Apr 1994, Oman (Hanne & Jens Eriksen).*

Plate 555   *Female. Note diagnostic wing-formula and head-pattern. 1 Apr 1993, Oman (Hanne & Jens Eriksen).*

Plate 556 *Female (2nd cy?) showing heavily marked underwing coverts contrasting with paler remiges. 27 Jun 1989, Greece (Dick Forsman).*

Plate 557 *Adult female showing rather well preserved and uniformly worn plumage with narrow barring to greater coverts and tertials (cf. juveniles). Note chevron-like bars to median coverts and typical head-pattern and compare with Kestrel. Jun 1991, Turkey (Markku Huhta-Koivisto).*

Plate 558 *Female. Note flat face, owing to small bill, long wings and chevron-like markings to scapulars and coverts compared with Kestrel. 25 Mar 1986, Israel (Dick Forsman).*

KESTREL   *Falco tinnunculus*

Plates 559–573

Subspecies: Nominate *tinnunculus* from Europe to NE Asia, *F. t. canariensis* and *dacotiae* on the Canary Islands, *neglectus* and *alexandri* on the Cap Verde Islands and *F. t. rupicolaeformis* in Egypt and S Arabia. Another five extralimital subspecies in Africa and Asia.

Distribution: Common and widespread throughout the region.

Habitat: Prefers open areas from agricultural fields and pastures to moors, steppes, semi-deserts and tundra, but also occurs in towns and villages.

Population: Probably decreased during this century, certainly so during pesticide era in Europe in 1950s and 1960s. One of the most common raptor species of Europe, with a total population for the W Palearctic of about 320 000–490 000 pairs.

Movements: Northern populations migratory, birds from further south resident or partly migratory, with juveniles being more dispersive than adults. Birds from N Europe migrate south and winter in S Europe, N Africa and the Middle East, sometimes even in sub-Saharan Africa. Northern migrants start to move in Aug with a peak around mid-Sep, after which the migration levels off and ceases in early Nov. At Falsterbo, S Sweden, between 312 and 609 were counted on passage in the autumns of 1986–1994, with 71 on 8 Sep 1989 and 66 on 21 Sep 1991, with other peak days between late Aug and late Sep. Spring migration starts from late Feb and peaks in the north during Apr, but birds are seen on passage throughout May.

Hunting and prey: Hunts voles and other small rodents, but also preys on small birds and insects, depending on local supply. Hunts either from perch, such as a fence post or telegraph pole, or in flight, quartering fields 20–50 m above the ground and every now and then stopping to hover against the wind. Stoops from hovering position, often after a step-wise descent, with folded wings to brake just before contact with the ground. Also hunts insects (even gregariously) in the air in similar fashion to Lesser Kestrel, Red-footed Falcon and Hobby and small birds by same technique as Sparrowhawk and Merlin.

Species identification

Length 29–35 cm

wing-span 68–78 cm (*n*=60; Israeli birds; W.S. Clark, unpubl.)

Colour and pattern of upperparts and tail diagnostic against most other raptor species except for Lesser Kestrel, where juveniles and females extremely similar to Kestrel. To identify from Lesser Kestrel, wing-formula, details of underwing and pattern of upperparts and head are all important characters. When identifying perched kestrels the different wing to tail ratio is important.

Identification summary: In all plumages the rufous brown or rufous sandy upperparts of Kestrels rule out all other raptor species apart from Lesser Kestrel. Adult males are recognized by their brick-red upperparts with dark spots (cf. 2nd cy spring Lesser Kestrel males), bluish grey rump and uppertail with a broad black subterminal band and whitish tip, and a grey head with a faint moustache and a paler cheek. Females and juveniles are sandy or rufous brown above with dark barring to upperparts and the tail has dense and fine barring and a broad black subterminal band. They are very similar to Lesser Kestrels in corresponding plumage and are best identified by a combination of characters. Perched Kestrels have shorter wings/longer tails than Lessers and the wing-tips fall well short of the tail-tip. The head shows a more contrasting pattern as the pale cheek is bordered not only by a darker moustache, but also by a dark posterior eye-line and darker ear coverts. In flight Kestrels are longer-tailed with an evenly attenuated rear body. The underwing is more distinctly barred and shows a narrow but distinct dark tip.

In flight, distant The Kestrel is a typical falcon, but shows a slightly longer tail than other European falcon species. In active flight the wings appear fairly broad at the base and pointed at the tip, but may appear rather broad with a rounded tip when soaring, at times even resembling Sparrowhawk in silhouette. The flapping flight consists of a series of wing-beats interrupted by frequent glides, not unlike straight-flying Sparrowhawk, and the wing action is looser than in other small falcons. When hunting, it quarters at moderate height above the ground, stopping every now and then to hover against the wind with fluttering wing-beats and fanned tail. Among smaller raptors the habit of frequent hovering is shared only by the Lesser Kestrel and the Red-footed Falcon (and the Black-shouldered Kite).

From a distance identified from most small raptors by red-brown upperparts contrasting with darker hands and the habit of frequent hovering while hunting. Head and tail are either

Fig 57 *Kestrel. Glides on flattish wings with slight kink between arm and lowered hand.*

pale grey, contrasting with rest of upperparts, or of same colour as the mantle and inner wing. Underparts look generally pale and the underwings especially appear pale in good light. In practice impossible to tell from Lesser Kestrel if plumage details are not seen.

In flight, closer Adult males differ distinctly from adult females and juveniles, but, regardless of sex and age, all Kestrels share the following characters. Upperparts rufous with black spots in adult males and dark barring in females and juveniles, and the hands contrast as darker. The long tail has a prominent black subterminal band and a pale tip and is either finely barred or more or less uniformly coloured grey or sandy. Head-pattern rather inconspicuous in flight. Underparts generally appear rather pale, with streaked or spotted body and with distinctly spotted underwing coverts. Remiges completely barred, with rather distinct grey bars and the outer primaries show narrow but distinct dark tips (both diagnostic characters against Lesser Kestrel). Wing-formula differs from most other falcons in showing p9=p8 and shorter p10=p7 (see Fig 56, p 432). Tail-pattern rather indistinct from below apart from the diagnostic wide subterminal band.

Perched Kestrels appear very long-tailed and the wing-tips fall clearly short of the tail-tip, reaching about three quarters down the tail. This character alone excludes Hobby, Red-footed Falcon and Lesser Kestrel. Only in Sparrowhawk and Merlin do the wings clearly fall short of the tail-tip, but these can easily be separated by different colour and pattern to upperparts. In close views Kestrels always show blackish claws, whereas Lesser Kestrels have pale or greyish claws.

Adult males are easily told by their brick-red upperparts with dark spots. Adult females and juveniles show a typical head-pattern, with a dark eye-line behind the eye (often the darkest marking of the head) and a darker diffuse moustache and streaked ear coverts bordering the pale cheek. Upperparts show rather transverse bars, with the outermost bar to each feather shaped like a flattened triangle.

Bare parts Feet, orbital skin and cere yellow, deeper in adult and more greenish tinged in juvenile. Bill pale greyish, darkening towards tip; claws black (cf. Lesser Kestrel) and iris dark brown in all ages.

Variation: Birds from S Europe tend to have a deeper ochre breast than birds from further north. This may cause confusion especially in adult males, which then show a marked contrast between deep rufous ochre underbody and pale underwings, appearing rather similar to male Lesser Kestrels from a distance.

Confusion species: The Kestrel is usually easy to identify by its rufous upperparts from other small raptors, leaving the Lesser Kestrel as the only true confusion species.

Lesser Kestrel *(page 429)* Always have pale or greyish claws, not black as in Kestrel and usually (not always!) the wing-tips reach close to the tail-tip on perched birds, although some birds may appear rather Kestrel-like. These are usually first-summer birds (2nd cy spring and summer), which have replaced their juvenile tail feathers with longer adult feathers during the winter but which still retain the shorter juvenile primaries.

In flight, p7 is much shorter than p10, while they are of equal length in Kestrel. Adult male Lesser Kestrels are best identified by their unspotted mantle and scapulars, partly grey upperwing coverts and by the uniformly grey cheeks. From below, the differently patterned primaries, with uniformly whitish bases (or just faintly barred) and broadly but diffusely darker (grey) tips seem the best characters. Adult females and juveniles are very difficult to tell from Kestrels in corresponding plumage. The face is paler and less distinctly patterned and usually shows only a dark moustache, but lacks the prominent eyeline and also the darker ear coverts of Kestrel, leaving the sides of the head pale and featureless. The upperparts also show narrower and more rounded bars. From below, the bases to the primaries are paler because of narrower or incomplete and fainter barring and the wing-tip is broadly and diffusely grey. Owing to basally paler remiges, the dark spotted underwing coverts contrast more with the rest of the underwing than in Kestrel. Some juvenile Lesser Kestrels (females?) do have more distinctly barred underwings than average, but the difference in the wing-tip pattern still remains. In profile, e.g. when hovering, Lessers also show a more rounded body, a proportionately shorter tail and more rounded wing-tips.

MOULT

Annually complete during breeding.

Juveniles (first moult) Body-feathers, especially on mantle and rump, are replaced starting from 1st cy autumn. In S Finland 16 out of 92 juveniles trapped on migration in Aug–Oct already showed moulted feathers. In Britain 40% of birds showed at least some adult-type feathers by Sep and by Jan nearly all birds did. By 2nd cy spring most birds have moulted, either partially or completely, their mantle and scapulars, others also rump, uppertail coverts and breast, and can, as in adults, be reliably sexed by pattern of mantle feathers. Some tail-feathers are occasionally replaced during the winter. The juvenile remiges and their greater coverts are, nevertheless, retained and not moulted until the first complete moult starting in 2nd cy May–Jun. The complete moult is finished in Aug–early Oct. The scanty material suggests, that 2nd cy birds start and finish their moult somewhat before the adults.

Adults (subsequent moults) Complete moult between May–Jun and Sep–Nov. Females start some days to some weeks after laying first egg, males on average 1–3 weeks later (one Finnish male had not yet started its primary moult by 26 Jun). A captive male took 130 days to replace its primaries completely, while free-living birds took 136 days in females and 122 days in males.

Breeding birds may suspend the moult during the late nestling period; in Britain 36% of the males and 11% of the females showed suspended primary moult.

AGEING AND SEXING

Two sometimes three separable age-classes in the field. Adult males are mostly straight-forward to recognize, whereas adult females and juveniles have to be seen well to enable ageing and sexing. Colour of feather-tips of scapulars, upperwing coverts and flight-feathers and pattern of underparts are important characters to note when ageing female-type birds. In late summer adults show active wing moult. Some adult females resemble juvenile and even adult males, showing a predominantly greyish rump, tail and head.

Ageing and sexing summary: Adult males are easy to recognize by brick-red upperparts with dark spots and grey head and tail, whereas female-type birds need a closer scrutiny for ageing. Pale tips of remiges and upperwing coverts and streaked underparts are diagnostic for juveniles, whereas adult females lack pale tips above and are spotted rather than streaked below. Adults usually show primary moult in summer–early autumn, whereas juveniles have complete wings. In spring juveniles identified by mixture of partly worn and partly fresh upperparts while adults show uniformly worn feathers. From a distance first-adult males (2nd winter) may be difficult to tell from adult females.

Juvenile (1st cy – 2nd cy spring)   **Plates 559–563**

In fresh plumage juveniles show broad buffish tips to upperwing coverts and remiges, from a distance giving the whole upperparts a sandier colour compared with deeper rufous brown in adult females. Breast streaked rather than spotted and the streaks are rather diffuse compared with the distinct spots of the adults. Ageing flying birds is difficult unless the aforementioned characters are seen. Perhaps the single most important character visible over any longer distance is the pale line formed by the tips of the upper primary coverts, together with the translucent trailing edge of the wing. Juveniles never show signs of wing moult during 1st cy. Many juveniles can be sexed in the field given good views of preferably perched birds.

Juvenile males More finely and more sparsely patterned above, with more of the ground-colour showing through and making them altogether slightly redder above than juvenile females. In many males the pattern on the mantle is very similar to that of the adult female and may even approach that of the adult male, with just one visible subterminal triangle-bar to each feather. The dark bars on the median and greater coverts are usually clearly narrower than the rufous interspaces. A distinctly greyish rump and inner tail (both may also be rufous!) strongly indicates a male in juveniles (50% of trapped juvenile males in Britain had greyish inner tail and rump). The rump is often either sparsely or faintly barred (can even appear unbarred) and the tail-barring is often incomplete, with thin or broken bars gradually dissolving towards the base.

Juvenile females More coarsely barred above and therefore appear darker and browner from a distance. Mantle feathers often show multiple broad dark bars and the median and greater wing coverts show equally wide dark and rufous bars. Rump and tail usually of the same colour as the rest of the upperparts (not greyish) with rather broad complete, regular and distinct barring.

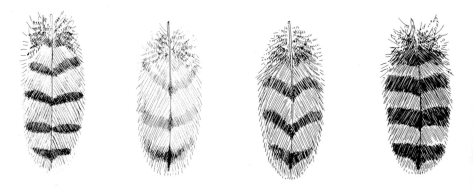

Fig 58 *Kestrel. Longest uppertail coverts of juveniles and adult females. From left, types 1–3 are common in adult female and juvenile male, whereas type 4 is typical of, and type 3 less common in, juvenile female. The ground-colour of types 1–3 varies from sandy brown to brownish grey and pure grey, whereas type 4 is sandy or rufous but not grey.*

During winter the pale tips of the upperparts gradually wear off making ageing more difficult, but broad buffish tips are usually retained on the inner primaries, which are protected from wear by the secondaries. At the same time the fresh mantle feathers provide a means for ageing, as they contrast slightly with the worn upperwing coverts. This is often the only notable difference between young and adult females in spring. Juvenile males show the spotting of adult males in the fresh feathers of the upperparts, which contrast with the duller and barred juvenile upperwing coverts.

Adult male (2nd cy autumn – older)   **Plates 564–567**

Perched adult males can be identified by their brick-red upperparts with variable dark subterminal spots to each feather. Head greyish with a faint dark moustache and paler cheek; tail grey with a whitish tip and a broad black subterminal bar. Primaries appear blackish above. Underbody varies from pale buff to deep salmon (deeper coloured in S Europe) with variable dark spotting.

In flight, adult males are easy to recognize from above by grey head contrasting sharply with reddish upperparts and arms. The dark spotting of the upperparts is visible usually only at close range. Hands appear blackish and the rump and tail are uniformly grey, the latter with a broad black subterminal band and a whitish tip. From below, males usually appear rather pale, but the body may be more richly coloured, variably spotted dark. Remiges show distinct grey bars with distinctly but narrowly dark-tipped outer primaries. Tail-pattern is obvious from below. The plumage remains much the same between the moults.

Males in their first-adult plumage cannot usually be told from older males with certainty, but they show, on average, a more rufous tinged crown, the spots of the upperparts and breast are bigger and the tail tends to show dark barring on the inner vanes (usually visible only from below when tail fanned). Birds showing all these characters can at least tentatively be called first-adult males (2nd cy autumn–3rd cy spring), whereas birds with tiny dark spots to upperparts and breast and with a pure grey head are likely to be at least a year older.

Adult female (2nd cy autumn – older)   **Plates 568–573**

Perched adult females resemble juveniles and are often difficult to separate from them. Mantle feathers and upperwing coverts lack the pale tips that juveniles show, while the tips of the primaries and primary coverts have finer pale tips. The dark barring on the upperparts is finer, with dark bars being narrower than the rufous interspaces, thus resembling the pattern commonly found in juvenile males. The ground-colour of the upperparts is deeper rufous than in juveniles, but the colour can be difficult to assess without direct comparison. Rump either rufous or greyish, usually with faint dark barring and tail either rufous or more or less greyish, either with regular and complete, or with incomplete dark barring. In a study in Britain the amount of grey in rump and tail increased with age in females: in first-adult plumage 40% showed grey against up to 75% of birds in subsequent age-classes. Underparts distinctly patterned with drop-shaped spots, not streaked as in juveniles.

In flight, adult females are usually difficult to tell from juveniles, and particularly from juvenile males. The greyish rump and tail-base as well as the finer barring of the upper-parts and the more rufous ground-colour above are often shared by both. In late summer and early autumn the most reliable characters of the adults are the dark upper hands, lacking the pale primary covert-tips of juveniles, and the distinctly spotted breast. During breeding and until mid-autumn adults can also be identified by their moulting primaries. After the moult is finished in adults, and as the wear and the partial body moult of the juveniles proceed, ageing becomes increasingly difficult by winter. By then close views are required to see the difference in plumage condition between the age-classes: adult females still show fairly fresh upperparts whereas first-winters have worn upperwing coverts contrasting with at least partly fresh scapulars and mantle.

Some old females may, from a distance, greatly resemble adult males in having a greyish head and a greyish rump, while showing a tail with incomplete barring (sometimes even lacking the finer bars completely) and sparsely patterned rufous upperparts. They are best identified by barred secondaries, wing coverts and scapulars of the upperparts.

Sexing: Males are only fractionally smaller than females and the size difference cannot be used for sexing in the field. Adults differ significantly in plumage; most juveniles are possible to sex if plumage details are seen.

Fig 59 *Kestrel. Outer tail-feather of juvenile (left) and adult female. Note rounded feather-tip and half moon-shaped subterminal spot of juvenile and compare with more squarish tip and squarish subterminal band of adult female (After Forsman 1980).*

References Forsman 1980, 1984, 1993b; Gensbøl 1995; Glutz et al. 1971; Kjellén 1992b, 1995; Piechochi 1955b; Village 1990; Village et al. 1980

Plate 559 *Juvenile. Note streaked breast and no signs of moult. Primaries barred to the base and narrower dark wing-tip compared with female plumage Lesser Kestrel. Sep 1989, Turkey (Esa Sojamo).*

Plate 560 *Juvenile. Ageing by pattern of outer tail-feather. Note wing-formula, complete primary-barring and clear-cut dark primary-tips and compare with Lesser Kestrel. 6 Apr 1996, Israel (Dick Forsman).*

Plate 561 *Fresh juvenile. Note more sandy colour of juvenile and prominent pale tips to coverts and primaries compared with adult female. Narrow dark markings above indicate male. Aug, Finland (Tapani Räsänen).*

Plate 562 *Juvenile male showing typical adult-like triangular spots to the median upperwing coverts and finer bars to the greater coverts and tail compared with juvenile female. This male has already moulted in some adult-type scapulars, which are brick-red with a black spot and lack the worn, pale tip of the juvenile feathers. Sep, Germany (Alfred Limbrunner).*

Plate 563 *Juvenile first winter male. Mantle and scapulars are moulted while upperwing still mostly juvenile. Note worn primaries lacking pale tips of fresh juvenile. Dec, Israel (Hadoram Shirihai).*

Plate 564 *Adult male. Wing-formula and pale cheeks diagnostic against Lesser Kestrel, while underparts may appear rather similar to especially transitional male Lesser Kestrels. 20 Feb 1997, Israel (Dick Forsman).*

Plate 565 *Adult male from above showing diagnostic black-spotted mantle and inner wing and grey tail with broad subterminal band. 1 May 1996, Oman (Hanne & Jens Eriksen).*

Plate 566 *Adult male showing distinct dark moustache and pale cheeks (cf. Lesser Kestrel). 6 Jul 1990, Finland (Dick Forsman).*

Plate 567   *Adult male with typical brick-red upperparts with distinct black spots and grey tail with black subterminal band. Jan, Germany (Alfred Limbrunner).*

Plate 568   *Adult female showing the diagnostic silhouette of the species and generally pale underparts with a distinct black subterminal tail band. 8 Oct 1988, Israel (Dick Forsman).*

Plate 569 *Adult female. Note complete barring and narrow and distinct dark tips to primaries compared with adult female Lesser Kestrel. 28 Jun 1990, Finland (Pekka Helo).*

Plate 570 *Adult female (same as Plate 569). 28 Jun 1990, Finland (Pekka Helo).*

Plate 571 *Females are very difficult to age in spring. Here, worn upperwing contrasting with fresher scapulars indicates a 2nd cy juvenile. Apr, Finland (Tapani Räsänen).*

Plate 572 *Adult female. Some birds show almost a male pattern on scapulars and upperwing, but note barred greater coverts. Birds from southern populations are also more rufous than further north. 15 Dec 1991, Morocco (Dick Forsman).*

Plate 573 *Adult female. The breast is distinctly spotted and the scapulars and upperwing show a uniform wear. Note also adult-type outer tail-feather. Jan, Germany, (Alfred Limbrunner).*

RED-FOOTED FALCON *Falco vespertinus*

Plates 574–591

Subspecies: Monotypic.

Distribution: From E Europe to Mongolia and Lena river in the east. *F. amurensis* of E China and Manchuria earlier considered subspecies of *F. vespertinus*.

Habitat: Breeds in open areas including cultivated fields, meadows, steppe, marshes and bogs. Nests in an old nest of tree-nesting birds (e.g. Corvids) and thus depends on trees or small woods. On migration on fields and plains; on wintering grounds confined to savanna and grasslands.

Population: European population 18 000–44 000 pairs, with most in Russia; only 2000–3000 pairs outside the CIS countries, with majority in Hungary. Population reduced dramatically since nineteenth century, mainly as a consequence of habitat destruction and pesticide use. Where abundant breeds in colonies.

Movements: Long-range migrant, with total Eurasian population wintering in S Africa. The migration route describes a loop, the southward migration being more easterly. Disperses from breeding grounds from Aug, but autumn migration in Levant and the Middle East does not peak until early Oct. Migrates on broad front and does not concentrate along major flyways. Largest concentrations found in Levant and eastern parts of Mediterranean basin, where in early Oct flocks of hundreds of birds can be seen, either on passage or at stop-over sites. Reaches African wintering grounds from late Oct. Winters mainly in S and SW Africa, where congregates in huge flocks of several thousands around profitable food resources. Spring migration through W Africa along a more westerly route, crossing the Mediterranean further west than in autumn, explaining the more frequent spring occurrence of the species in W Europe, where mainly 2 cy birds are involved. Reaches the Mediterranean from mid Apr, with a peak during first half of May. Most observations from W and N Europe refer to late Apr–early Jun and late Aug–Oct.

Hunting and prey: Hunts either in flight or from perch. Hovers persistently against the wind and swoops down to take prey from ground but also hunts like Hobby, flying directly on prey, which is grabbed with the feet and then dismembered and eaten in flight. Hunts at different heights, from low over the ground to considerable heights depending on occurrence of swarming insects. Also hunts from perch such as telegraph wires and poles or dead tree-tops, from where it glides down to catch prey on ground. Also hops around on the ground in search of insects. Unlike Hobby frequently hovers when hunting, e.g. when scanning fields for prey. Feeds mainly on different kinds of insects, but small vertebrates (lizards, mammals and birds) are also taken. Wintering flocks concentrate in open areas rich in insects.

SPECIES IDENTIFICATION

Length 28–29 cm

wing-span 74–75 cm (*n*=2; Israeli migrants; W.S. Clark, unpubl.)

Head-pattern, upperparts and tail-pattern diagnostic in all plumages. Adult males and females easily identified, whereas juveniles more similar to other falcons. Juveniles best identified by characteristic underwing, head and tail.

Identification summary: A small falcon, identical in size and proportions to Lesser Kestrel, being clearly smaller than Kestrel in direct comparison. Size, however, difficult to assess in the field without direct comparison with other species. Adults show different silhouette and flight-action compared with similar species, but flight silhouettes of juveniles and adults differ. Characteristic plumage of older birds make these readily identifiable. Adult males from below are coloured in different shades of greys and black, appearing uniformly dark from a distance. Upperparts are dark with distinctly paler outer hands. Females are identified by generally pale head contrasting with greyish upperparts and dark hands, while the underbody is either pale yellowish buff or more deep orange. From below, the remiges appear basally pale with a broad black trailing edge to the wing. Juveniles are best identified by greyish brown upperparts contrasting with darker hands and with pale rump and rather pale and completely barred tail. Underwings are distinctly patterned as in females. Transitional males (2nd cy) in spring are like adult males but still retain their barred juvenile remiges; by autumn they show some uniformly black remiges, creating a diagnostic underwing pattern.

In flight, distant The shape of a distant Red-footed is something between a Hobby and a Kestrel. The wings are comparatively shorter and blunter-tipped than in Hobby, but the tail appears slightly longer. Juveniles resemble juvenile Hobbies or even Merlins because of slightly different silhouette than the adults. In head-on views the wings appear shorter and the body bigger than e.g. Hobby. The head also appears bigger in Red-footed than Hobby. In active flight (on migration) wing-beats are slightly faster, lighter and looser, while the tips describe a wider amplitude, with more pronounced upstrokes and deeper downstrokes than the more powerful and stiffer wing-action of Hobby.

Fig 60 *Red-footed Falcon. Note rather plump body and shortish, slightly down-pressed wings when gliding.*

Distant adult males appear very uniformly coloured but from below show black underwings and a paler grey body, often with a darker face. Upperparts are generally dark, but the head and tail appear black and the outer hand is distinctly paler, almost silvery white in fresh plumage in spring.

Adult females are more colourful with grey upperparts and tail in contrast to darker hands and a distinctly pale head. Underbody is rusty yellow and the underwings show paler bases to the remiges and a contrasting black trailing edge.

Autumn juveniles show a similar contrast above to adult females, albeit less distinct. Head appears darker than in adult female but usually features a white neck-band, a pale forehead and a dark face-mask. Underwings show the same diagnostic pattern in the remiges as the adult females with a broadly black tip and trailing edge and proximally pale but distinctly patterned primaries.

In spring 2nd cy males are variable and some may resemble Hobbies, with rather similar head-pattern and darkish upperwings. They are identified by the characteristic underwing pattern of the juvenile and often also by a mixture of uniformly black and barred greyish rectrices in the tail. Distant females are not possible to age in spring.

In flight, closer Adult male and female are unmistakable if seen well (see under Ageing and sexing); immatures are more difficult. Juveniles show a rather contrasting head, with black eye-mask and short moustache, pale forehead and supercilium, white throat and cheeks and a pale neck-band. Upperparts appear greyish with a rufous cast, but the colour varies with changing light conditions. Rump and tail paler greyish, latter with complete and fine darker barring and a wider subterminal bar. The tip of the tail is white. The dark hand contrasts clearly with the rest of the upperparts and the white tips to the primary coverts and the remiges form narrow wing-bands.

Underbody appears rather pale with variably distinct brown streaking on breast. Underwing-pattern is diagnostic when separating from similar species: the remiges are distinctly patterned, with black barring on white ground and with broadly black tips. Underwing coverts variably patterned but often appear slightly darker than the remiges. Tail appears pale from below, but against the light the complete barring (including central pair) can easily be seen.

In spring 2nd cy males are identified by the striking underwing-pattern of the juveniles, although the body plumage may be extremely variable. The most likely confusion risk is with Hobby, as the head-pattern may be superficially similar, but the Red-footed never shows a similarly heavily streaked underbody, although it may vary from uniformly grey to largely grey with orange breast.

Perched Red-footed Falcons are very long-winged and the wing-tips reach at least to the tip of the tail, even beyond it. They appear small-headed with a flat face (because of the small bill), the body is small and rounded and the stern is long. Adults are easily identified by their diagnostic plumage (see under Ageing and sexing), but juveniles may resemble several other falcons in plumage. Kestrel and Merlin can easily be excluded by the longer wings and shorter tail of Red-footed. The characteristic head-pattern, with a distinct yet short black moustache and eye-mask, a pale forehead and supercilium, a chestnut hindcrown and a nearly complete pale neck-band excludes the other falcons, including Hobby. Upperparts of juvenile Red-footed are diagnostic, greyish with darker barring and with rufous and buffish tips to wing coverts and scapulars.

Bare parts Iris dark brown at all ages. Claws white or pale. Cere, orbital skin and feet orange-yellow to deep orange in juveniles and adult females, reddish orange to orange-red in adult males. Base of bill same colour as cere.

Confusion species: Adults usually unmistakable but males may be confused with adult Eleonora's and Sooty Falcons and females with adult male Merlins. Habit of hovering when hunting excludes most other falcons but not the kestrels.

Eleonora's Falcon (page 470) Adult dark morph shows uniformly dark upperwing, while underwing has paler bases to outer primaries (skua-flash). Compared with 2nd cy spring male Red-footed, adult Eleonora's shows less pale to bases of remiges on underwing, 2nd cy more mottled underbody.

Sooty Falcon (page 485) Adult usually shows paler underwing than body from below; from above, outer hand clearly darker than rest of upperwing and mantle (both opposite in Red-footed). Feet and cere yellow and lacks red trousers and vent.

Merlin (page 495) Adult male identified by dark crown and diffuse face pattern and lack of fine barring to upperparts and tail. Wings fall well short of tail-tip.

Juvenile Red-footed may be confused with Hobby, Eleonora's and Sooty Falcons, Merlin and Kestrel.

Hobby (page 505) Unbarred upperparts, uniformly black central tail-feathers, darker and more solid head-pattern and underparts boldly streaked in black. Underwings appear uniformly patterned and darkish, lacking distinctly paler bases to remiges and dark trailing edge of Red-footed.

Eleonora's Falcon (page 470) Juvenile and light morph adult show underbody more distinctly streaked in black and upperparts darker and unbarred. Tail like Hobby's. Underwing may resemble juvenile Red-footed's, but is usually darker with less pale on primary bases and with darker wing-coverts. The head of juvenile Eleonora's may appear rather similar to a juvenile Red-footed, but the moustache is longer and more distinct and there is no pale supercilium and neckband, and the crown is frequently paler than the eye-mask.

Sooty Falcon (page 485) Juvenile has more deep ochre underbody with diffuse dark streaking concentrated on upper breast. Head and upperparts much as in juvenile Hobby, also tail rather similar, but with extremely broad dark subterminal band. Underwings appear darkish with slightly paler rufous, not white barring to bases of outer primaries.

Merlin (page 495) Females and juveniles always identified by short wings when perched. Upperparts dark brown with bold rufous spots and bars, tail shows sparse and broad barring. Underwing appears rather dark and uniformly patterned and head appears more uniform, with diffuse markings. Flight behaviour diagnostic.

Kestrel (page 443) Females and juveniles identified by rufous upperparts (and tail) with dark barring. Head-pattern inconspicuous. Tail reaches mostly well beyond wing-tips.

MOULT

Complete annually. As in other long-range migrants moults mainly on the wintering grounds. First remex-moult begins earlier than subsequent moults, starting on the breeding grounds.

Juveniles (first moult) Juveniles attain adult-type body-feathers by late autumn; by 2nd cy spring practically all body plumage is moulted and birds greatly resemble adults. Remiges and primary coverts are not moulted in the winter and the juvenile greater coverts are retained with a few exceptions (some inner may be replaced), as are most of the underwing coverts. The tail may be completely moulted, but usually a variable number of (sometimes all) juvenile rectrices are retained. Males tend to replace more tail-feathers than females. First remex-moult starts in 2 cy summer earlier than in adults, but is later suspended for the autumn migration (1 Aug, Hungary, male with p4–5 moulted and p3 and p6 growing). By late Sep–early Oct migrants in Israel showed four to nine new primaries (6,6,8 and 9 new primaries in four females and 4,4,5 and 8 in four males). The last juvenile remiges and rectrices are moulted in the winter quarters, where moult is completed earlier than in adults (one male from Nov (no exact date) with p1 and p9–10 still juvenile, as well as two secondaries and two rectrices; a female had completed moult by 2 Jan; BMNH).

Adults (subsequent moults) Starts complete moult on average clearly later than 2nd cy birds (1 Aug, Hungary, most adult females and males with old primaries but some had dropped p5 and one female was missing p4–5). Autumn migrants show, on average, fewer moulted primaries than 2nd cy birds and many adults have not even started to moult before migrating, while others show one or two rarely three to four new primaries (in late Sep–early Oct, Israel, six adult males had moulted 0,0,0,1,1,1 primaries, and five adult females had replaced 3,4,4,4,5 primaries, respectively). The moult is suspended for the migration and resumed on the wintering grounds, where the late-moulting birds commence their moult. The moult is completed by Feb–early Mar (latest: adult male with p10 growing on 25 Feb; BMNH), i.e. 1–2 months later than birds completing first moult (pers. obs.).

AGEING AND SEXING

Ageing Red-footed Falcons is straightforward and one can separate juvenile (summer–first autumn), transitional (from first to second autumn/winter) and adult plumages (from second winter on). There are thus two age-classes in spring and three in autumn. The most difficult problem is to separate 2nd cy and adult females in spring and early summer. For the more difficult plumages focus should be on tail, under- and upperwings, with special reference to details in feather-patterns, moult and plumage wear.

> **Ageing summary:** Juveniles are streaked below, show distinct rufous fringes and tips to upperparts and have more or less completely chestnut hindcrown. Adult males are uniformly grey and black, whereas females are grey with dark barring above and buff to orange below and the head is predominantly pale. Birds in transitional plumage are identified by mixture of adult and juvenile feathers especially in wings and tail.

Juvenile (to Dec of 1st cy)   **Plates 574–578, 591**

Head often appears pale at a distance but appearance varies individually. Short moustache and eye-mask dark and contrasting. Throat and cheeks white, with white from latter extending up and behind the dark ear coverts almost reaching nape. Hindneck largely white with dark central band connecting crown and mantle and with darker spots on each side of it. Forehead and forecrown invariably pale joining with pale supercilium, hindcrown more variable pale to deep chestnut. Palest birds show almost whitish crown with only slight rufous cast on hindcrown, whereas more pigmented individuals are rather dark-headed, with a russet crown and a paler supercilium between crown and eye-mask.

Upperparts are rather constant in colour and pattern, brownish grey, but with hue changing from more greyish to more rufous depending on the light. Scapulars and wing-coverts with rusty-buff tips giving upperparts a somewhat scaly appearance. Remiges show distinct white fringes to tips.

Tail greyish and densely barred, with darker and paler bands of approximately equal width, with the exception of a broader dark subterminal band. On a flying bird the greyish rump and uppertail are usually the palest tract on the entire upperparts. The tail-tip is pale, as is the trailing edge of the wing. In flight the wings are clearly two-toned from above, with a dark hand and a paler greyish-brown arm. The pale tips of the greater coverts, especially conspicuous on the primary coverts, form a clear whitish band to the upperwing.

Underparts vary from buffish white to more deep buff. The streaking of the underparts can be either rather fine and pale brown in paler birds to heavier and darker brown in more pigmented individuals. The pattern of the underwing coverts follows the same general rule: less prominent dark barring on paler birds and heavier barring on more pigmented ones. Underwing remiges show a diagnostic contrasting pattern with black barring on white ground. The trailing edge of the wing is normally broadly black and contrasting, which is a good character against the Hobby from a distance.

Cere and feet differ in colour from other falcons, being deep yellow to almost orange.

Transitional plumage (2nd cy spring – 2nd cy late autumn)   Plates 579–584
After the partial moult in 1st cy winter the birds resemble the adults.

Males 2nd cy males in spring are variable. Some birds are extremely adult-like in their body plumage, whereas others show immature characters such as dark moustache and paler cheeks and throat, and a large orange breast-patch. All 2nd cy spring males, regardless of the state of body moult, have retained their, from below, distinctly barred juvenile remiges, which separates them instantly from older males with all-black remiges. Tail varies individually and may either be completely moulted, or, more normally, show a variable number of retained, barred juvenile feathers. The new tail-feathers are blackish grey with a broad black subterminal band, but in the field they appear all-black. From above, 2nd cy males can be difficult to separate from Hobbies, as the upperwing appears rather uniformly dark, lacking the silvery primaries of the older males. Particularly difficult are males with a Hobby-like head-pattern, and these birds should be identified by the reliable characters of underwing and tail.

During early summer only minor changes take place in the plumage of 2nd cy birds, but once the remex moult commences it affects the appearance more dramatically. The new central primaries are black underneath but silvery grey above, forming a black wedge to the underwing but a pale wedge on the upperwing. Through the autumn 2nd cy males are easily told from adults by their diagnostic wing-pattern with partly adult-type and partly juvenile remiges. Underwing coverts are still partly juvenile and barred.

Females 2nd cy females are often impossible to separate from adult females at a distance, unless the plumage can be studied in detail. The body plumage is extremely similar to adult females and ageing is based on the retained juvenile feathers, especially primaries, tail and under- and upperwing coverts. Practically all females retain most of their juvenile tail through the partial moult and the juvenile rectrices are clearly shorter (*c.* 2 cm) than the moulted feathers and also show a different colour and barring. The juvenile feathers have almost equally wide dark and pale bars (often broader subterminal bar), whereas the moulted feathers are pure grey with fine dark bars and a Kestrel-like wide black subterminal band. The pale tips of the juvenile feathers are worn off, whereas the recently moulted feathers show broad pale tips. Underwing coverts are mainly retained juvenile feathers showing dark barring in contrast to uniformly coloured coverts in adult females. Upperwing coverts can be partly moulted, but worn and dull juvenile coverts are found among the greater and outer lesser and median coverts. Upperwing coverts are most easily studied on perched birds, when the abraded and dull brown primaries are also quite obvious.

In autumn 2nd cy females are still difficult to tell from older females, although ageing is slightly easier than in spring. In late summer and autumn 2nd cy birds show, on average, more moulted primaries than adults at the same time, something that is visible from a fair distance. The new four to five central primaries are clearly longer and show a broader and darker black tip than the retained juvenile primaries, creating a clear 'bulge' in the trailing edge of the hand. From above, the new feathers differ in being grey and black instead of dull and uniformly brownish like the juvenile primaries. Adult females are less advanced in their moult or they still show a complete set of unmoulted remiges and the trailing edge lacks the bulge. The difference in colour and pattern between old and new feathers is much more difficult to note in the adults. The remaining barred juvenile underwing greater and primary coverts can be difficult to discern, as are possibly retained juvenile rectrices and upperwing coverts, but when seen they are reliable ageing characters. Some 2nd cy females may appear rather like juveniles with pale brown-streaked breast (finer and more distinct streaks than in juvenile) and a rather juvenile-like head-pattern, but they can always be aged in flight by the characters mentioned above and perched birds by lacking rufous and white tips to upperparts and remiges.

Adult (from *c.* 2nd cy Dec and older) Plates 585–591
Males Adult males are coloured in different shades of grey with brick-red vent, thighs and undertail coverts. The red colour can be surprisingly difficult to see in the field and favourable conditions are needed. On the upperparts the head is blackish, mantle and upper-

wing coverts are dark grey, and uppertail coverts and tail are black, the latter being the darkest of all upperparts. Primaries and outer secondaries are silvery grey above, being the palest part of the whole bird. The primaries are palest in spring, when the plumage is fresh, and they may appear almost whitish from a distance. During summer the 'frosty' shine gradually wears duller and the hand acquires a darker trailing edge, but some of the silvery touch is retained throughout the year as a character for adult males. From below, the bird looks dark with black face, underwing and tail, whereas the greyish underbody often stands out as being paler. The red on the rear body is normally inconspicuous in flight unless it catches the direct sunlight. In good light the underwing coverts appear darker than the shinier flight-feathers, but normally the whole underwing looks black.

In autumn, perched non-juvenile males can be aged by colour and number of moulted primaries. The adults have, at the most, a few new primaries which are nearly white above even though they are surrounded by silvery feathers. The 2nd cy males show four to six moulted feathers, but they never appear as pale and silvery, although they are surrounded by dull and brownish juvenile primaries.

Females Adult females are colourful birds with barred greyish upperparts and orange-tinged underbody and head. Head and underparts vary from almost whitish buff to deep rusty ochre and the amount of fine, black streaking on the breast varies individually (possibly more streaking in younger birds?). Cheeks and throat are always palest, nearly white, and the eye-mask is blackish with a small dark moustache-mark below the eye. Upperparts greyish with dark barring, neck and upper mantle being darkest. The primary projection on perched birds is blackish with some grey visible towards the base. In flight, the pale orange head is usually distinct from afar and contrasts with generally darkish upperparts, with dark mantle, greyish tail and inner wings, and dark hands. From below, the orange body and the distinctly patterned underwing with uniformly orange coverts, wide black trailing edge and otherwise distinctly white-spotted remiges make the bird unmistakable. Tail is grey with numerous fine black bars and a wider subterminal bar just inside the pale tip.

Sexing: Adults differ significantly in plumage; juveniles are not possible to sex in the field until first-adult-type feathers are attained in late 1st cy.

References Forsman 1980, 1984, 1993b, 1995a; Small 1995; Tucker & Heath 1995

Plate 574 *Juvenile. The distinct, black-and-white barring of the remiges is diagnostic, as well as black face-mask and pale neck-band. Sep 1978, Turkey (Lars Jonsson).*

Plate 575 *Juvenile showing typically chequered remiges with diagnostic broad, black trailing edge to underwing. Note rather pale and completely barred tail. Aug 1992, Hungary (Tom Lindroos).*

Plate 576 *Juvenile showing diagnostic underwing pattern. Oct 1990, Cyprus (Esa Sojamo).*

Plate 577 *Juvenile. Streaking of breast is normally less distinct than in Hobby. Note complete pale tail-bands and pale claws of this rather dark-headed bird. 3 Aug 1992, Hungary (Tom Lindroos).*

Plate 578 *Juvenile. When fresh, upperparts are distinctly fringed rufous. Note barring on central tail, tertials and greater coverts ruling out Hobby. 3 Aug 1992, Hungary (Tom Lindroos).*

Plate 579 *Transitional male (2nd cy spring). Underbody moulted, with orange breast-patch shown by many, while underwings are completely juvenile. Tail shows mixture of black and barred feathers. May 1989, Turkey (Martti Siponen).*

Plate 580 *Transitional male (2nd cy autumn). Note diagnostic mixture of barred and black remiges. 6 Oct 1987, Israel (Dick Forsman).*

Plate 581 *Transitional male (2nd cy autumn). 6 Oct 1988, Israel (Dick Forsman).*

Plate 582 *Transitional male (2nd cy autumn). Told from adult male by retained barred rectrices and worn and brownish juvenile remiges. Oct 1990, Cyprus (Esa Sojamo).*

Plate 583 *Transitional female (2nd cy spring). Very similar to adult female, but told by retained and worn brownish upperwing coverts and dark remiges and by partly juvenile, partly moulted tail. 7 Jun 1981, Finland (Dick Forsman).*

Plate 584 *Transitional female (2nd cy autumn). Note more distinctly patterned and longer moulted flight-feathers compared with bleached, retained juvenile feathers. 2 Oct 1990, Turkey (Kari Soilevaara)*

Plate 585 *Adult male. The underbody usually appears distinctly paler than the dark underwings and head, while the red vent is conspicuous only in favourable lighting. 16 Jul 1997, Hungary (Dick Forsman).*

Plate 586 *Adult male showing diagnostic silvery outer upperwing and uniformly dark underwings. 16 Jul 1997, Hungary (Dick Forsman).*

Plate 587 *Adult male. In summer adult males become rather dark from wear but are told from 2nd cy males by uniformly silvery remiges above. 1 Aug 1993, Hungary (Dick Forsman).*

Plate 588 *Adult female with distinctly patterned remiges and uniform underwing coverts and body. 16 Jul 1997, Hungary (Dick Forsman).*

Plate 589 *Adult female showing suspended moult (fresh p3–6), with old remiges also being grey adult-type feathers. Oct 1987, Israel (Markku Huhta-Koivisto).*

Plate 590   *Adult female showing unmistakable plumage, with orange underbody and crown and barred, grey upperparts. 16 Jul 1997 (Dick Forsman).*

Plate 591   *Adult female (right) with juvenile. Adult females are on average more uniformly coloured below, whereas 2nd cy females are more or less streaked. Oct 1990, Cyprus (Esa Sojamo).*

ELEONORA'S FALCON   *Falco eleonorae*

Plates 592–608

Subspecies: Monotypic.

Distribution: Breeds on islands in the Mediterranean, on the Canary Islands and off the coast of Morocco. Winters mainly in Madagascar and its surroundings in southern Indian Ocean.

Habitat: Breeds between Aug and Oct on islands with steep coastal cliffs but may also nest locally on more accessible sites on small rocky islands. Hunts the air-space above different kinds of terrain from open sea and coast-line to inland mountains, woods and marshes. In summer before breeding may range far inland and reach localities not normally associated with this species.

Population: Practically the whole world population (4500 pairs) nests in the Mediterranean, with main concentrations in Greece (2500–3000 pairs) and Spain (*c.* 600 pairs). Situation considered fairly stable with local increase in e.g. Spain. Vulnerable, owing to colonial nesting with restricted number of breeding sites.

Movements: Migratory, spending winter in Madagascar and surrounding islands of Indian Ocean but also frequents coastal SE Africa. Leaves breeding area during a long period in Oct–Nov depending on timing of nesting. First individuals reach wintering grounds in early Nov (2nd cy bird and pale adult, Aldabra Islands 1 Nov and 17 Nov, respectively; BMNH), when others still in breeding area. Some juveniles may spend 2nd cy summer in wintering areas. Little is known about passage itself and routes taken, but birds seen regularly along eastern coast of Mediterranean and also in inland Israel. Usually seen singly or a few together on passage. Spring migration is rather late and many birds are still found in the wintering grounds in Apr, by which time the vanguard reappear at breeding sites. Arrives at nesting localities through May. Disperses widely before settling to breed in late summer and vagrants occur nearly annually in W Europe up to the Baltic.

Hunting and prey: Feeds mainly on insects for most of the year, except during autumnal breeding, when specialized in catching migrant songbirds. Prey always taken on wing either after long dives, vertical stoops or after horizontal pursuit in powered flight. When hunting shows unsurpassed aerial skills, often performing masterly team-work where several birds hunt together.

SPECIES IDENTIFICATION

Length 36–40 cm (Cramp & Simmons 1980)
wing-span 84–103 cm (Noakes 1991)

Easily identified at breeding localities, but when seen singly, e.g. on migration, identification difficult with risk of confusion with especially Hobby, Red-footed and Sooty Falcon.

> **Identification summary:** A medium-sized falcon falling in size between Hobby and Peregrine. The largest member of the group of 'smaller, distinctly patterned, moustached or dark falcons' comprising Eleonora's, Hobby, Red-footed and Sooty. Wings are long and pointed, showing in full soar a 'bulge' at the outer secondaries when seen head-on, and the tail of adults is notably longer than in other similar species. Juveniles and adults differ in silhouette. Although adults actually (and absolutely) have longer tails than juveniles, latter appear longer-tailed because of shorter wing-span. Juveniles thus do not fully correspond to the classic 'Eleonora's-shape', but have shorter and comparatively broader, more triangular wings and resemble juveniles of the aforementioned species. Body appears long and slim in flight, being widest at upper breast and tapering evenly towards vent and tail, while the head appears notably small.
>
> Upperparts generally uniformly dark, mostly showing diagnostic coffee-brown hue, with slightly darker outer tail and wing-tips, and with marginally paler and greyer inner tail and rump. Dark morph adults uniformly dark below, only with restricted greyer area to bases of outer primaries. Pale morph adults variable, but identified by dark underwing coverts contrasting with proximally paler remiges and by rufous of belly often reaching to breast and even higher; breast often with diffuse streaking. Juveniles more similar to other falcons, but identified by darkish underwing coverts and by head-pattern lacking pale supercilium and nape-patches, as well as by proportions and flight.

In flight, distant Wings are long and appear rather powerful and stiff, yet flexible and elegant at the same time. Often easy to identify on flight alone when seen leisurely flying or hunting insects, when gives impression of elegance and masterly flying skills. But when hunting birds, or when just gliding by or diving on motionless wings, can be very difficult to tell from Hobby. Juveniles especially, which lack the true 'Eleonora's shape' and which are not as skilful fliers as the adults, frequently cause identification problems. The silhouette of a soaring Eleonora's is rather distinctive, showing small head, long and narrow tail, and long and slim wings with pointed tips, very straight trailing edge and well-marked angle at carpal on leading edge. Upperparts appear mostly uniformly dark, whereas underparts show diagnostic paler 'skua-flash' on outer primaries even from a fair distance. Distant juveniles probably very difficult to tell from juvenile Sooty, if plumage details are not seen.

Fig 61 *Eleonora's Falcon. Viewed head-on appears very long-winged and small-bodied.*

In flight, closer Dark morph adult easily identified by very uniformly dark brown to dark greyish brown plumage, with small paler area on bases to outer primaries below. Readily told from other dark falcons of the region by clearly brownish tinge to plumage. Pale morph adult more variable and most likely to be confused with Hobby, but shows dark underwing coverts contrasting with paler bases of remiges and often also differs by more diffuse streaking to breast and by rufous colour to much of underbody. Juveniles show similar upperwing contrast to juvenile Red-footed, owing to extensively pale-fringed upperparts when fresh, but folded tail appears uniformly dark from above with pale tip only. Underparts also resemble juvenile Red-footed superficially, but differ by darker underwing coverts, darker and more Hobby-like head-pattern and by Hobby-like tail, with uniformly dark central-pair, best seen when tail is fanned. The distinct streaking of underparts often turns into bolder spot-marks on flanks.

Perched Slim and long-winged falcon with wings protruding well beyond tip of tail (by several cm). Head appears comparatively smaller than in the group of similar falcons (Hobby, Red-footed and Sooty), thus giving impression of slightly larger size. Adults are rather uniform above with typical brownish tinge to plumage. Dark morph adult also uniformly dark brown underneath, pale morph more variable but shows Hobby-like head-pattern (although with more regular rounded cheek-patch) and finely or diffusely streaked breast with rufous colour from vent and belly often extending to upper breast. Juveniles are extensively pale-fringed above with prominent pale tips to primaries and greater coverts. Head usually shows Hobby-like pattern, but crown is ochre with black face-mask thus becoming more prominent, causing head-pattern not unlike juvenile Red-footed, but with longer moustache and lacking prominent supercilium and pale neck-band of latter.

Bare parts Iris dark brown at all ages. In adults, sexes differ in colour of cere and orbital skin: pale (chalky) blue in female and yellowish in male. Legs yellow. Juvenile has bluish bill with darker grey tip, cere and orbital skin pale blue, legs pale greenish yellow.

Variation: About 25% of the adults belong to the sharply defined dark morph. Juveniles are much more similar and the two morphs can be separated only in close views (see Ageing and sexing).

Confusion species: Easily confused with other smaller falcons with similar basic plumage characters.

Hobby (page 505) Always has more uniform underwing, while red to rear underbody of adult is always restricted to trousers, vent and undertail coverts. The head-pattern regularly shows a second 'tooth' behind the eye as well as pale nape-spots, both normally lacking in Eleonora's.

Sooty Falcon (page 485) Has narrower wings and comparatively shorter tail. Adults are much paler grey than dark morph adult Eleonora's, from below with rather pale underwings and from above with distinctly darker tail- and wing-tips than rest of upperparts. Juveniles more difficult to tell apart, but Sooty shows deeper colour to underparts, more ochre or rusty-tinged, while the streaking is more diffuse and often concentrated on to upper breast; the underwing is also less contrasting than juvenile Eleonora's and the tail has a diagnostic, very broad dark subterminal band. Although smaller than Eleonora's, size difference of little use in the field.

Red-footed Falcon (page 456) Juveniles differ by diagnostic head-pattern and by completely barred uppertail. Adult males have silvery primaries above and uniformly black underwings. They also lack the typical brownish colour of dark adult Eleonora's, being more bluish grey with orange or reddish feet, orbital ring and cere. Size and hunting behaviour in flight are also different.

MOULT

As in other long-range migrant raptors Eleonora's Falcons moult mainly in winter, following much the same moult strategy as e.g. Hobby, Sooty and Red-footed Falcon. The first complete moult commences in the breeding area, whereas adults do not normally start until after reaching the wintering grounds.

Juveniles (first moult) During their first winter, juveniles undergo a partial body moult, which varies in extent. Some birds replace hardly any feathers, whereas others moult most of their body plumage. Most birds moult at least the upperparts partially (mantle and scapulars). Wings are normally left unmoulted.

By 2nd cy summer the plumage is more or less worn. During late summer and autumn most birds start to replace their remiges and a few rectrices, which can be seen as gaps, particularly obvious in the primaries. By the time of the autumn migration birds have replaced up to three (0–3) primaries, often also some secondaries and the central tail-feathers (the Cyclades, on 15 Aug, one with fresh p4, BMNH; of four 2nd cy birds from Mallorca in mid-Oct, one had replaced two to three primaries, another two, the third had shed its first but the fourth had not yet started (pers. obs.). One from Aldabra Islands, on 1 Nov, showed complete set of old primaries; BMNH. Moult is suspended for the migration and resumed in the winter quarters, where it is completed earlier than in adults, probably during Jan.

Adults (subsequent moults) A complete annual moult is delayed until birds arrive in the winter quarters, although some adults may replace a first primary (p4) on the breeding sites. Owing to later start, the adults do not complete the moult until Mar–Apr, just prior to their migration north (in two individuals collected in Madagascar on 14 Mar and in 'April' p10 still growing; BMNH).

AGEING AND SEXING

Eleonora's occur at all ages in two morphs, a more common pale and a rarer dark, latter comprising about 25% of the population. Juveniles are, however, rather similar and the two morphs are difficult to separate in the field. Up to four age-classes can be separated in autumn.

> **Ageing summary:** Juveniles identified by scaling to upperparts and by pale buffish underparts with distinctly streaked breast and distinctly barred remiges and rectrices. Transitional plumage (2nd cy) is identified by retained and worn juvenile feathers and by partly adult, partly juvenile plumage characters and first-adult plumage (3rd cy) by some retained characters of immaturity to underwings and underbody. Adults are uniformly coloured above, the underwing coverts are uniformly dark and the flight-feathers show only diffuse, if any, barring below.

Juveniles (1st cy autumn)   **Plates 592–596**

Juvenile Eleonora's resemble juvenile Red-footed Falcons in plumage. The head-pattern however, is different to all other species of the group: mask black with a distinct and rather long moustache; no 'second' hook down from the ear coverts, as in other species; cheek-patch roundish with even edges; nape and neck uniform, lacking the distinct pale spots of Hobby and the pale collar of Red-footed; crown slightly paler than the eye-mask, ochre-brown. Upperparts are coloured much as in juvenile Red-footed, with ground-colour changing from greyish to brownish depending on the light, and each feather showing an ochre or buffish margin. In flight from above, the hand appears darker than rest of upperparts with pale tips to inner primaries and a pale band formed by pale primary covert tips. When folded, tail appears dark with a distinct pale tip, but when fanned or seen from below shows distinct and narrow rufous bands over the entire length of the feather, similar to juvenile Hobby. When spread, tail shows a wide buffish tip and a darker subterminal bar, 1–2 cm wide. From a distance the tail looks brownish-grey with a wide pale tip. The overall impression of the bird is very similar to juvenile Red-footed Falcon. Colour morphs of juveniles are similar from above.

From below, juveniles resemble juvenile Red-footeds, differing mainly in details of underwing. Body pale buffish with narrow dark streaks, narrower than in Hobby and darker than in Red-footed. The streaks are finer at mid-breast widening towards the lower flanks where they change to arrow-heads or chevrons. Belly and vent pale. Underwing coverts heavily barred and appear clearly darker than the adjacent, pale-mottled bases to the remiges. Remiges widely dark distally, creating a broad dark trailing edge to wing, similar to juvenile Red-footed. The pale pattern of the remiges is pale ochre in Eleonora's (white in Red-footed).

The two colour morphs differ mainly in pattern of underwing coverts and undertail coverts. In the pale morph the underwing coverts are clearly paler, appearing mottled or barred and the undertail coverts are uniformly pale buffish, whereas in the dark morph the underwing coverts appear more or less dark and the undertail coverts show distinct dark barring. The dark morph is also, on average, more heavily streaked on the breast, being more similar to Hobby than to juvenile Red-footed and shows more heavily mottled and darker flanks and trousers.

Transitional plumage (2nd cy spring – 2nd cy late autumn/winter)   Plates 597–599
After the first partial body moult in winter, juveniles may look very different in spring, depending on both the extent of the moult and the colour morph. They can best be aged by their retained juvenile flight-feathers, which show distinct paler barring from below, tail when spread also from above, and the remains of the wide pale tail-tip, now extremely worn on the central tail but still visible towards the corners. The remains of the pale tips to the upper primary coverts often show surprisingly well in flight. The body plumage varies from worn and nearly completely juvenile to almost entirely moulted, but always appears partly rugged and untidy compared with the fresh plumage of adults. The pale juvenile feather-margins of the upperparts are all lost and the appearance is rather uniformly tar-brown, whereas freshly moulted feathers have a greyish tinge. Generally, the birds appear a lot darker above than adults. The upperparts of the two colour morphs are rather similar.

It is often possible to tell the colour morph by the underparts, especially on advanced birds. The pale morph resembles Hobby, with distinct blackish streaking on a pale, buffish-white ground-colour, whereas dark morph birds appear darker and soiled and unevenly mottled on the breast and show a paler vent. The least moulted birds can be identified to morph in the same way as juveniles or by combining juvenile and transitional plumage features.

By autumn it becomes easier to identify the colour morph of the birds because of progressing body moult. In 2nd cy autumn birds still retain their juvenile, barred rectrices and also most of their juvenile remiges, while some of the central primaries are moulted or still growing. The moulted primaries (and rectrices) are clearly longer and darker than the nearby retained juvenile feathers. From above, 2nd cy birds are usually readily identifiable by their extremely worn inner wing coverts and tertials, which, together with the worn rectrices, form a rusty brown area to the otherwise dark but tatty upperparts. Some dark morph birds may, by autumn, already show surprisingly dark underwing coverts from wear.

First-adult plumage (3rd cy spring – 3rd cy autumn)   Plate 600

Some birds are still possible to age after their first complete moult with some characters intermediate between juveniles and adults. Upperparts are much as in adults, but are slightly darker and browner, lacking the greyish hue of old adults. The underparts differ more. Regardless of colour morph all birds show juvenile-like pale mottling to underwing coverts, more extensively in pale morph birds. The rectrices also differ from full adults by their more distinct and more juvenile-like barring reaching closer to tail-tip than in adults. The rectrices still show narrow pale tips. Pale morph birds are still rather distinctly streaked on the breast and usually show only small amounts of rust on the belly and lower breast. Dark morph birds usually show paler mottled cheeks and throat and are still somewhat unevenly coloured on breast and belly, with paler feather-margins showing through. They also frequently show some barring on the remiges below, which full adults lack.

Definite adult plumage (4th (or 3rd cy; see above) spring and older) Plates 601–608

Pale morph Adults are uniformly dark greyish brown over the entire upperparts, with a specific dark brownish hue different from otherwise similar falcon species. Head slightly darker with a long and distinct moustache and a 'closed', roundish white cheek-patch lacking the 'second' hook at the ear coverts found in Hobby, juvenile Red-footed and juvenile Sooty. Distal part of the tail and wing-tips dark and more brownish than the rest of the upperparts, with mantle and scapulars slightly greyish; the rump and inner tail are usually the greyest and palest area of the entire upperparts. Underparts vary individually, but are usually rufous to rusty-brown on undertail coverts, vent, belly and lower breast, merging softly with paler upper breast. The amount of rufous-brown and the amount and type of streaking on the breast vary, birds probably becoming increasingly rusty and more suffusely streaked with increasing age. The outer half of the tail is practically uniformly greyish, slightly darker above than below. The suffused banding on the rectrices is confined to the basal parts of the feather, becoming visible only when the tail is fully spread, from above barely visible even when spread.

Dark morph Upperparts even darker and more evenly coloured than in pale morph with wing-tips darkest, but with same diagnostic coffee-brown hue to entire upperparts. Tail appears, even when spread, uniformly dark, lacking any notable barring. Underparts appear very dark, with faintly paler area at primary-bases the only exception.

Sexing: Sexes differ significantly in colour of cere and orbital ring as adults. In adults, males are slimmer with narrower wings and tail and the upperparts are greyer than in females.

References F. Spina (1992); Walter 1979; Wink et al. 1987

Plate 592 *Recently fledged pale morph juvenile showing rather juvenile Red-footed Falcon-like underparts, but note darker underwing coverts and ochre, rather than white barring to remiges. 9 Oct 1997, Spain (Dick Forsman).*

Plate 593 *Pale morph juvenile showing general resemblance to both juvenile Hobby and juvenile Peregrine, but note more prominent dark trailing edge to wings. 12 Oct 1997, Spain (Dick Forsman).*

Plate 594   *Dark morph juvenile. Note diagnostic darker underwings, especially coverts, and more extensively blotched underbody compared with pale morph juveniles. 9 Oct 1997, Spain (Dick Forsman).*

Plate 595   *Dark morph juvenile from above showing typically prominent pale tips to upperparts, especially to greater scapulars. Also note Hobby-like tail with dark central feathers, but with diagnostic faintly darker subterminal band. 7 Oct 1997, Spain (Dick Forsman).*

Plate 596 *Recently fledged juvenile. Note diagnostic head, distinct pale fringes of upperparts and sawtooth pattern of tertials and inner greater coverts. Autumn, Italy (Pierandrea Brichetti).*

Plate 597 *Pale morph in transitional plumage (2nd cy autumn). Can be very Hobby-like in appearance, like here, but mostly told by more distinctly marked remiges below. This bird also told by more finely marked and rufous underbody and by moulted all-dark p4 in each wing. 10 Oct 1997, Spain (Dick Forsman).*

Plate 598   *Dark morph in transitional plumage (2nd cy autumn). Told from older birds by distinctly barred remiges and rectrices and by mostly pale and blotchy rear underbody, and from similar Sooty Falcon by narrow subterminal tail-band. 7 Oct 1997, Spain (Dick Forsman).*

Plate 599   *Pale morph in transitional plumage (2nd cy autumn) from above. Aged by pale rufous and barred uppertail and by tatty upperwings. Dark morph similar but show dark cheeks. 10 Oct 1997, Spain (Dick Forsman).*

Plate 600 *First-adult plumage (3rd cy autumn), pale morph. Note barring of tail and remiges being quite distinct, but not as clear-cut as in the juvenile flight-feathers and not reaching as close to the tip. Note also moulting primaries. 17 Oct 1987, Spain (Dick Forsman).*

Plate 601 *Dark morph adult female. Note underwing contrast with darker coverts than remiges and compare with other dark falcons. 7 Oct 1997, Spain (Dick Forsman).*

Plate 602 *Dark morph adult female (same as plate 601). Note uniformly coloured upperparts with diagnostic coffee-brown hue. 7 Oct 1997, Spain (Dick Forsman).*

Plate 603 *Definite adult plumage, dark morph. Practically uniform flight-feathers with faint barring on inner tail only. 8 May 1991, Greece (Martti Siponen).*

Plate 604   *Pale morph adult male. Note underwing contrast and distinct white throat and cheeks and compare slim silhouette with heavier females (eg. plate 601 and 605). 12 Oct 1997, Spain (Dick Forsman).*

Plate 605   *Pale morph adult female. Note heavier build and broader wings compared with males. 11 Oct 1997, Spain (Dick Forsman).*

Plate 606   *First-adult plumage, pale morph female (sex by bluish cere and eye-ring). Note rather brownish and worn upperparts, but not as faded and abraded as in 2nd cy autumn and with darker and more uniform tail and tertials. Aug/Sep, Greece (Alfred Limbrunner).*

Plate 607   *Adult, dark morph female. The worn and brownish plumage indicates a first-adult plumage bird, with a fledged juvenile to its left. Italy (Alberto Badami).*

Plate 608   *Adult, pale morph male (sex by yellow eye-ring and cere). Note more greyish and better preserved upperparts compared with Plate 606. Aug/Sep, Greece (Alfred Limbrunner).*

SOOTY FALCON *Falco concolor*

Plates 609–619

Subspecies: Monotypic.

Distribution: Breeds in the deserts of N Africa (from Libya in the west) and the Middle East (Sinai, Israel, Arabian peninsula to Persian Gulf) and on islands in the Red Sea. Little known about subpopulation of continental Africa and knowledge stems mainly from studies in the Middle East.

Habitat: During breeding confined to barren deserts, arid coastal areas and rocky islands. Little is known about habitat preferences during migration. Winters in Madagascar and adjacent coasts of continental Africa, preferring open areas such as marshes and dryer savannas.

Population: Total world population estimated to be roughly about 10 000–20 000 birds, mainly based on sample counts of wintering birds on Madagascar, where more numerous than Eleonora's Falcon. In Israel *c.* 200 pairs. Status presumed stable.

Movements: Migratory, although some may winter close to breeding grounds. Leaves breeding areas in Middle East from Oct and Nov, returning from late Apr. No large concentrations known en route to or from wintering grounds, but seen singly or in small groups through much of interior E Africa. Winters mainly on Madagascar and adjacent coasts of E Africa, but also found further inland in S Africa.

Hunting and prey: Nests in late summer and autumn, like Eleonora's, feeding like latter mainly on migratory passerines and other smaller birds. Prey taken on wing after stoop or tail-chase. According to studies in the Middle East, swifts, swallows, bee-eaters and songbirds comprise bulk of prey. In winter mainly insectivorous.

SPECIES IDENTIFICATION

Length 33–36 cm (Cramp & Simmons 1980)
wing-span 73–84 cm (Noakes 1990)

Adults mostly easy to identify but juveniles are easily confused with other similar small-ish falcons, especially Hobby, Red-footed Falcon and Eleonora's Falcon. Wing and tail-pattern diagnostic in all plumages and also flight silhouette unique.

Identification summary: Slender falcon with proportionately big head and extremely long wings, reaching well beyond tip of tail. Central pair of tail-feathers slightly elongated and pointed, hardly discernible in juveniles and normally only visible at close range in adults. Adults bluish grey, with contrasting blackish primaries above (females slightly darker and contrast less striking). Many individuals show paler chin and/or darker moustache. Feet, cere and eye-ring strikingly deep yellow. Juveniles look much like juvenile Red-footeds or Eleonora's, but differ by suffused blotching/streaking on breast and by more vividly rufous-buff ground colour below (paler and more yellowish buff in Red-footed and Eleonora's). Juveniles have two pale patches on hind-neck, similar to Hobby, but lacking in Eleonora's.

In flight, distant Smallish falcon, size between Eleonora's and Hobby, with females averaging slightly larger and heavier. Shape in flight diagnostic, with, even among falcons, extremely long and narrow, scythe-like wings (hand especially long and narrow) and a rather short tail, giving impression of wing-tips reaching beyond tail-tip in flight (character somewhat less pronounced in shorter-winged juveniles). In flight appears relatively large-headed compared with e.g. Hobby and especially Eleonora's.

In flight, closer Adults most easily confused with dark adult Eleonora's or adult male Red-footed Falcon. Despite some variation in colour of adults (females darker), most Sootys are pale, bluish ashy-grey, while the wing-feathers from below are generally only slightly paler than the wing-coverts, with a somewhat darker wing-tip. Body appears clearly darker in flight than the rather pale underwings. This separates adult Sooty from adult male Red-footed, where underwings appear solidly black compared with clearly paler body. From above, adult Sooty Falcons are bluish grey, with hand and tail gradually darkening distally.

Juveniles resemble both juvenile Eleonora's and juvenile Red-footed Falcons. Juvenile Sootys are best separated by the dusky and more diffuse breast-streaking, with streaks melting into each other and often forming larger, suffused dark patches on sides of upper breast. Undertail-pattern of Sooty diagnostic with *c.* 5-cm-wide dark subterminal band, the widest on any juvenile W Palearctic falcon, while tail appears all-dark from above with pale tip only, as in juvenile Hobby. Underwing of juvenile Sooty appears rather dark-ish because of rufous ground-colour and broadly dark tips and trailing edge, but typically shows a paler centre, as in juvenile Red-footed, although much less distinct.

Perched A very slim and elegant bird with long and narrow wings reaching well beyond tip of tail in adults and juveniles. Adults look uniformly grey, either paler bluish grey or duller ash grey with darker projecting primaries and often with a paler chin and a slightly darker moustache. Juveniles look much like juvenile Hobbies, especially above, but dif-fer by their more rufous ochre and diffusely streaked underparts. In adult, feet almost orange yellow, cere and eye-ring deep yellow, while in juveniles, these are pale bluish or greenish.

Bare parts Adult: legs, cere and orbital skin of males are a bright chrome yellow, almost orange yellow in some, whereas colour of cere and orbital skin in females is closer to lemon. 2nd cy birds: cere and orbital ring a dirty/dusky greenish yellow, not as bright as in adults. Juveniles: legs pale greenish yellow or even pale bluish, cere and orbital skin pale bluish. Iris at all ages dark brown.

Variation: A previously recognized dark phase was rejected by Frumkin & Clark (1988). Some second-year birds (probably only females), however, do grow nearly black feathers to all upperparts and breast and belly and thus appear black in the field. Identification on the breeding grounds, however, usually easy because of favourable viewing conditions with lots of reflected light from below.

Confusion species: Possible to confuse with other smaller falcons, juveniles especially with juvenile Hobby, juvenile Red-footed and juvenile Eleonora's, and adults with adult male Red-footed Falcon and dark phase Eleonora's Falcon.

Eleonora's (page 470) Adult dark morph darker, browner and more uniformly coloured above, with darker underwing coverts contrasting with paler bases to primaries.

Eleonora's (page 470) Juvenile may appear rather similar from above, but underbody pale buffish with distinct dark streaking and underwings distinctly patterned with marked con-trast between darker coverts and distinctly barred remex-bases.

Red-footed (page 456) Adult male separated by all-black tail and silvery primaries above. From below, the body often appears paler grey than the black underwings, whereas the opposite is normally true with adult Sooty Falcon.

Red-footed (page 456) Juvenile has greyish but distinctly barred tail from above, a paler head and a whitish neck-band. From below, underbody paler buffish with more distinct brownish streaks and remiges show a very contrasting black-and-white pattern and broad black tips, while the coverts often appear somewhat browner with a duskier pattern.

Hobby (page 505) Shows evenly patterned underwing, appearing rather uniform from a distance and the breast is pale with distinct black streaks. Adults show rufous vent, thighs and undertail coverts, whereas the juveniles lack the broad dark subterminal tail-band diagnostic of juvenile Sooty.

MOULT

Annually complete. A long-range migrant, moulting largely in the winter quarters.

Juveniles (first moult) Begin to moult their body-feathers early in winter. Moult starts from mantle, rump, head, upper breast and thighs, but extent and timing of moult varies individually, creating a wide variety of plumages. Juvenile remiges and rectrices, as well as underwing coverts and greater upperwing coverts, however, are always retained. Birds showing least moult have not replaced any feathers (e.g. by 3 Apr), or may show only a few bluish grey feathers to the upperparts. The most advanced birds have shed most of their body plumage, but retain some juvenile upperwing coverts.

First complete moult, including remiges and rectrices, begins in 2nd cy late summer–early autumn, shedding p4 or p5 (2nd cy male still with old set of remiges and rectrices on 6 Aug). Before departure only a few (up to four) primaries are moulted, new feathers being of uniformly dark adult-type (female from 11 Oct in active moult with three fresh primaries). By this time 2nd cy birds show, on average, more moulted primaries than adult birds. Rest of plumage moulted on wintering grounds where moult is completed during Feb (–early Mar). Rarely some secondaries (e.g. s1) may be left unmoulted and retained until the following summer.

Adults (subsequent moults) Moult commences in females during nestling period, when the first primaries are shed. Only a few primaries are moulted before moult is suspended for the migration. Breeding males seen late in the breeding season (mid-Oct) have all still had their old primaries. This may indicate that males do not start to moult until on the wintering grounds. Adults complete their moult in (late Feb–) Mar, when the outermost primaries and secondaries are fully grown. Females probably complete moult earlier than males. Moult thus completed on average 1 month later than in first moult.

AGEING AND SEXING

Juveniles and adults easily separable. Transitional plumage (in 2nd cy) identified by retained juvenile feathers.

Ageing summary: Juveniles are rather similar to juvenile Red-footeds or Eleonora's. Second cy birds are transitional, with partly juvenile, partly adult plumage. After plumage completely moulted, at age of about 18 months (3rd cy spring), looks like adult. Ageing not difficult, provided good views. Distant juveniles may resemble adults from above, with clearly two-toned upperparts, but can be safely aged by patterned underwings and body. 2nd cy birds are told from adults by retained juvenile-type remiges.

Juveniles are shorter-winged and therefore appear comparatively broader-winged and longer-tailed than adults. They thus resemble other smaller falcons in silhouette more than the extremely long- and slender-winged and short-tailed adults.

Juvenile (1st cy autumn)   **Plates 609–612**

Head-pattern most resembles Hobby with pale dots to hindneck and a small 'double' moustache. Mantle, scapulars and wing coverts dark with pale rufous fringes. The folded tail is uniformly dark with a pale tip, especially obvious in flight. When tail is fanned or seen from below shows diagnostic barring concentrated on inner vanes, but with diagnostic, extremely broad dark subterminal band (*c.* 5 cm). Upperwings appear greyish-brown, as rest of upperparts, changing from more grey to more brown depending on angle of light. At a distance the whole upperparts may appear shining pale greyish with slightly darker wing-tip. In closer view the pale tips to the upper primary coverts stand out against the dark primaries, as does the pale trailing edge when the bird is viewed against a darker background.

Underparts rufous-buff, slightly darker in colour and colder in tone than in similar small falcon species. The streaking is dark greyish-brown and appears dusky and diffuse; it varies individually and the dark centres often dominate over the ground-colour on the upper breast, at times forming a darker breast-band. Throat and lower breast to undertail coverts are uniformly pale (rufous) buff. Underwing may appear pale from a distance (in strong light) with only wing-tip and trailing edge to hand clearly darker, and the body frequently appears darker than the underwing. In closer view one can discern the same type of underwing pattern as in juvenile Red-footed, with widely dark trailing edge and tip, paler remex-bases and a slightly duller covert-area. In Sooty falcon, compared with Red-footed, these different areas are softer in tones and pattern, melting with each other to form a more uniform general impression.

Transitional plumage (2nd cy spring – 2nd cy autumn) **Plates 613–614**

In winter, juveniles become extremely abraded and their appearance changes whether body-feathers are moulted or not. All the pale margins to the upperpart are lost, except for visible traces remaining on outer tail-feathers and the primary coverts. The birds thus become much darker and more uniform above and distant birds become more difficult to separate from e.g. Hobby. Underparts become equally darker, partly because of worn away pale fringes, but also because new dark feathers appear on breast.

The majority of birds moult the body partially during winter, while others do not start until in 2nd cy summer, explaining the individual variation found in autumn birds. Some individuals have moulted almost the entire body plumage by Jan, while others have not even started by Apr. New feathers appear first on upperparts, head and upper breast. The average bird in spring seems to have moulted head, upper breast and most of the upperparts, while the belly and the lower parts of underbody and wing coverts, remiges and rectrices are still juvenile feathers. Consequently the wings appear darker than the rest of the upperparts. Even the most advanced birds still show a faint juvenile head-pattern with pale throat and cheeks and a pale wash on lower breast. The replaced upperparts feathers are in most birds pale bluish grey, as in adults, but at least some females (only females?) grow entirely blackish new feathers, which differ markedly from the colour of the adults. Darker individuals can be very tricky and difficult to tell from dark morph Eleonora's, especially as the shape is not yet typically long-winged as in adults, but closer to a 'normal' falcon. In such cases one should focus on pattern of underwing coverts, remiges and rectrices, if possible, since these feathers are juvenile, showing diagnostic characters.

Adult (from 3rd cy spring and older) **Plates 615–619**

Extremely long- and narrow-winged and short-tailed, with silhouette in flight unlike any other species. In active flight shaped like a huge Sand Martin *Riparia riparia*, with sharp bend at carpal joint and with extremely long hand (but short arm) appearing to reach beyond tip of tail. Appears surprisingly pale both above and below when seen in good light. From above, mantle, wing coverts and inner half of tail are pale bluish grey, with darker head, wing-tips and outer tail. From below, wing coverts only slightly darker than pale greyish remiges, with primary-tips and tail darkest. Usually the body appears clearly darker grey than the underwings. Moulting autumn birds show slightly darker wedge to central primaries formed by fresh feathers. In closer views yellow feet and cere are apparent as well as the slightly elongated and pointed central tail-feathers. Dark grey, almost blackish birds with adult-type, from below uniformly coloured, remiges and rectrices, are probably birds (females?) in their 3rd cy.

Sexing: Adult females are on average darker and less bluish grey than males and also differ in colour of bare parts (see above). Sexes not known to differ in juvenile plumage, but males smaller and slimmer with narrower wings, however, apparent only when both sexes are seen together.

References: Cade 1982; Clark et al. 1990; Frumkin 1984, 1988; Frumkin & Pinshow 1983; Frumkin & Clark 1988; Noakes 1990; Shirihai 1995

Plate 609 *Recently fledged juvenile. Underwings appear generally dark, body typically deep rufous ochre with diffuse dark streaking, often forming collar around upper breast. 21 Oct 1994, Oman (Hanne & Jens Eriksen).*

Plate 610 *Recently fledged juvenile. Note diffusely marked underwing coverts and diagnostic pattern of remiges, with pale barring confined to feather bases only. Nov 1996, Oman (Jan-Michael Breider).*

Plate 611 *Recently fledged juvenile. Resembles juvenile Hobby, but ground-colour below deep rufous ochre and breast-markings more diffuse and spot-like. Oct 1986, Israel (Hadoram Shirihai).*

Plate 612 *Recently fledged juvenile. Note juvenile Hobby-like upperparts, with diagnostic tail-barring visible only from below. Head-pattern like Hobby and fringes to upperparts more diffuse than in juvenile Eleonora's Falcon. Oct 1986, Israel (Hadoram Shirihai).*

Plate 613 *Transitional plumage (2nd cy autumn). Note diagnostic barring of juvenile tail, with pale barring ending far from the tip leaving a broad black subterminal band. Underwing juvenile except for moulted p4–5. Head and body moulted, but not uniformly grey. 27 Sep 1996, Oman (Hanne & Jens Eriksen).*

Plate 614 *Transitional plumage (2nd cy autumn) showing retained juvenile greater upperwing coverts and blotchy underparts and cheeks. 11 Oct 1989, Israel (Markus Varesvuo).*

Plate 615 *Adult. Note uniform plumage with bright yellow cere and feet. 27 Sep 1996, Oman (Hanne & Jens Eriksen).*

Plate 616 *Adult showing diagnostic silhouette with very long wings and relatively short tail and uniform appearance from below. 11 Oct 1989, Israel (Tomi Muukkonen).*

Plate 617 *Adult. In neutral light the underwings are slightly paler than the body, with tail and wing-tips darkest. The pale throat indicates a (young?) female. Aug 1995, Egypt (Klaus Bjerre).*

Plate 618 *Adult showing uniformly grey upperparts with darker hands and outer tail only. 28 Sep 1996, Oman (Hanne & Jens Eriksen).*

Plate 619 *Adult. Uniformly grey plumage and yellow cere and feet are diagnostic. 18 Oct 1996, Oman (Hanne & Jens Eriksen).*

MERLIN *Falco columbarius*

Plates 620–632

Subspecies: From N Europe to W Siberia as *F. c. aesalon*, on Iceland as *F. c. subaesalon* (larger and darker; birds from Britain and Ireland intermediate between *aesalon* and *subaesalon*, but sometimes regarded as *subaesalon*). *F. c. insignis* (larger and paler than *aesalon*) from N and E Siberia east of *aesalon*, winters regularly in the Middle East. *F. c. pallidus* from steppes of N Kazakhstan and SW Siberia larger and paler than *insignis,* occurs as a rare winter visitor to the Middle East. Extralimitally four more subspecies in Asia and N America.

Distribution: A Holarctic species breeding in Europe from Iceland, Britain and Ireland through Fennoscandia, the Baltic states and northern Russia.

Habitat: Breeds in open terrain on the ground on moors and open tundra. In N Europe also in coniferous forest, in old nests of Corvids, often near shores, open bogs or villages. Outside breeding season prefers flat, open areas such as plains, fields, shores and moors.

Population: The total population of the W Palearctic estimated at 35 000–55 000 pairs, with 75% breeding in Russia. Main populations in Europe in Fennoscandia (8000–18 500 pairs), Iceland (500–1000) and Britain (550–650).

Movements: Northern populations are migratory, wintering in W and S Europe, NW Africa and in the Middle East, whereas birds from Britain and Ireland are mainly resident but disperse after the breeding season. Migration starts in Aug and peaks during Sep. At Falsterbo, S Sweden between 155 and 272 birds were counted on autumn passage in 1986–1993, with 10–20 birds on peak days. Return passage from early Mar, peaking in Apr. Migrates on broad front, mostly seen singly on passage.

Hunting and prey: Feeds almost exclusively on small birds of open habitats, such as larks, pipits, wagtails and small waders. Takes prey by surprise, approaching in a fast, rocket-like flight low over ground. Sometimes follows escaping birds up in the sky chasing and stooping like Hobby.

SPECIES IDENTIFICATION (*F. c. aesalon*)

Length 25–30 cm

wing-span 52–64 cm (*n*=7; Finnish migrants; D. Forsman, unpubl.)

Flight observations of Merlins are mostly very brief and plumage details are difficult to see. The flight identification thus often relies on shape, jizz and the typical flight-behaviour and wing-action of the species, with tail-pattern and bold primary barring being the most striking plumage features.

Identification summary: Merlins are mostly identified by their typical flight, darting at full speed just above the ground on fast, spinning wings. When soaring the silhouette is characterized by fairly short, basally broad but pointed wings and a rather long and full tail. Plumage of adult male unmistakable with bluish grey upperparts, blue-grey tail with broad black subterminal band and rather inconspicuous head-pattern, with darker crown, pale supercilium and faint moustache. Females and juveniles are generally dark brown above, often with conspicuously pale-spotted primaries above. The tail shows four or five equally wide pale and dark bars and the head is characterized by dark crown, pale supercilium, faint moustache and a darker auricular patch behind the pale cheek.

In flight, distant A small yet powerful falcon, the male being the smallest of all European raptors. The flight silhouette is characterized by rather short wings, which are broad at the base but narrow and pointed at the tip, and by a relatively long tail. The silhouette of soaring birds is reminiscent of larger falcons, e.g. juvenile Peregrine or Gyrfalcon, because of broad arm and rather rounded wing-tip and full tail. Usually seen in rocket-like pursuit of small birds low over ground, with extremely fast working wings. Longer distances, as on migration, covered in powered flight with long series of fast wing-beats interrupted by occasional short glides. Soars less often than other small falcons and does not hover when hunting, but is capable of hovering for short periods in strong wind. When approaching prey often switches to thrush-like undulating flight during the final stages prior to the terminating stoop.

Distant females and juveniles appear fairly dark underneath and also dark above with sparsely but distinctly barred tail. Adult males are recognized from afar by their bluish upperparts with a broad black band at the tail-tip and blackish outer hands. The underwings appear dark but the ochre or buffish body may be apparent from afar, depending on the light.

In flight, closer Adult males are easily identified by their diagnostic plumage: blue-grey upperparts with darker hands and black tail-band, pale ochre underparts and darkish, rather coarsely patterned underwings with row of pale spots inside of dark trailing edge of hand. Females and juveniles appear generally dark brown above, with diagnostic, sparsely barred tail, showing only four or five equally broad pale and dark bars. The outermost dark bar is often more prominent from below than the others forming a wider subterminal band to the tail. Underwings more coarsely barred than in other small falcons but appear generally dark with a band of pale spots close to the trailing edge of the hand. Wing-tip broader and more rounded than in other small falcons (although appears pointed in most situations in the field), with p8–9 longest and p10 and p7 slightly shorter and of equal length.

Perched Perched Merlins are short-winged, with a wing-tip to tail-tip ratio separating them from most other small raptors (see, however, Kestrel and Sparrowhawk). The wing-tips fall well short of the tail-tip reaching about three quarters down the tail. Adult males are easily identified by their blue-grey upperparts, their yellowish buff underparts and their typical rather faint head-markings. Females and juveniles are dark brown above, variably spotted/barred rufous, and the head-pattern is diagnostic showing dark crown and pale supercilium, whereas the face-pattern is usually rather inconspicuous. Moustache faint compared with the dark eye-line, while the pale cheek reaches up behind the eye with a dark auricular patch bordering it from behind. Perches frequently on the ground when looking for prey.

Bare parts Iris dark brown at all ages. Feet and cere yellow, greenish tinged in juveniles, deeper yellow in adults.

Confusion species: Possible to confuse with other small falcons or Sparrowhawk, although flight of Merlin typical. Distant soaring birds may also resemble larger falcons, when size is not apparent. The bluish grey upperparts of perched adult male may recall adult female Red-footed Falcon or adult male Sparrowhawk. Juveniles and females may from a distance appear similar to juvenile Red-footed Falcon, Kestrel or Hobby.

Sparrowhawk (page 245) Short, rounded wings, with rounded tip, and much longer tail. Flaps and glides at a slower tempo than Merlin. Perched Sparrowhawk has shorter wings and longer tail, with three or four broad bars and very long and thin legs. Underparts barred, not streaked.

Kestrel (page 443) Longer wings, which fall slightly short of tail-tip when perched. Upperparts rufous with prominent dark barring. In flight from above, primaries considerably darker than rest of upperparts; from below, wings generally pale. Tail of females/juveniles from above rufous or greyish with fine barring and a broad black subterminal bar. Frequently hovers.

Hobby (page 505) Always shows distinct head-pattern, with white cheek surrounded by black moustache, ear coverts and sides of neck. When closed, tail appears uniformly dark above and wing-tips reach tip of tail. In flight shows narrower and more pointed wings and shorter tail. Hunts mostly in the sky and feeds largely on insects.

Red-footed Falcon (page 456) Wing-tips reach tail-tip on perched birds. In juveniles the distinct black face-mask stands out as the darkest part of the head. Adult females have a pale or orange crown and a black face-mask and the tail is grey with Kestrel-type barring. In flight, females and juveniles show contrasting black-and-white underwing pattern with broad black trailing edge. Frequently hovers and feeds mostly on insects.

MOULT

Annually complete during breeding.

Juveniles (first moult) Juveniles undergo a partial body moult in winter, sometimes starting in Sep, but normally from Feb to May. This moult usually comprises scapulars and rump, sometimes also the occasional tail-feather. The complete moult, including the flight-feathers, between early Jun and Sep.

Adults (subsequent moults) Adults have a complete moult between early Jun and Sep/Oct, starting earlier in females than in males. The moult of the remiges takes about 4 months.

AGEING AND SEXING

Two separable age-classes: adult males are easily recognized, whereas adult females and juveniles are rather similar, especially in flight. During summer–early autumn adult females are in active wing moult.

> **Ageing and sexing summary:** Adult males are readily identified by their bluish grey upperparts. Autumn juveniles are dark brown with rufous markings above, whereas adult females are more greyish brown and more patterned above with a distinctly paler, greyish rump.

Juveniles (1st cy autumn – 2nd cy spring)   **Plates 620–624**

In fresh plumage dark brown above with rufous tips and fringes, but ground-colour varies depending on angle of light from vinous to almost greyish. Remiges, greater coverts and scapulars show individually variable rufous bars, which, in juveniles, often appear as oval spots on the upperparts, not as regular bars as they often do in adult females. Underparts yellowish buff with rufous brown streaking, changing to wider mottling and cross-bars on flanks. The pale bars on the outer tail-feathers (best seen from below) appear regular compared with the pattern of adult females (Fig 62).

By spring, juveniles are worn and greyish brown and even more difficult to tell from adult females. If seen close up, many of them can be aged by their partially fresh upperparts, with newly moulted feathers on scapulars and rump, which are bluish grey in males.

Autumn juveniles are difficult to sex in the field despite the considerable size difference. In most males the pale bars of the uppertail are greyish on inner tail, whereas all bars are rufous in females. However, exceptions occur, and juvenile males with no grey in the tail are not rare.

Fig 62   *Merlin. Outermost tail-feather of juvenile (left) and adult female. Note narrower and more pointed tip of juvenile with regular barring and compare with squarer tip and irregular pattern of adult female (From Forsman 1980).*

Adult males (2nd cy autumn and older)   Plates 625–627

Upperparts bluish grey with darker primaries and the bluish grey tail has a broad black subterminal band, well visible from below. Underparts vary from off-white to deep rusty yellow, with variably strong dark and distinct streaking on breast. From below, the remiges are rather contrastingly barred in white and dark, but this is rarely seen in the field and the underwing mostly appears rather dark and uniformly patterned. Head-pattern shows a faint moustache, a dark crown and a narrow, pale supercilium.

Adult females (2nd cy autumn and older)   **Plates 628–632**

Adult females are generally very difficult to tell from juveniles by plumage. In autumn they appear more greyish brown above, with a distinctly paler and greyer rump and with, at least on average, more cross-barred scapulars and wing coverts. Tail-pattern shows less regular barring, especially on the outer rectrices. Underparts whiter and spotted rather than streaked and the markings are more distinct. Adults in late summer–early autumn also show moult gaps in wings and tail.

In spring adult females are even more similar to young birds because of extensive plumage wear, but still appear more barred above and show a pale grey rump, paler than the rest of the upperparts. Adult females further show evenly worn upperparts lacking the contrast between partly fresh and partly worn feathers of spring juveniles.

Sexing: Merlins cannot as a rule be sexed in the field unless seen close, despite the rather marked sexual size dimorphism. Adults differ significantly in plumage, whereas juveniles appear similar apart from the difference in tail-barring.

References Forsman 1980, 1984, 1993b; Gensbøl 1995; Kjellén 1995; Temple 1972

Plate 620 *Juvenile. Coarsely patterned primaries to both underwing and upperwing and uniformly brownish mantle and innerwings are typical of the species. Note prominent pale supercilium. Aug, Finland (Markku Huhta-Koivisto).*

Plate 621 *Juvenile showing typical silhouette of the species with rather short but pointed wings and a fairly long tail. 7 Feb 1996, Israel (Dick Forsman).*

Plate 622 *Juvenile. The breast is warm buffish with dark streaks turning to bars towards the flanks and the upperparts are brown with rufous spots and feather-tips. Note short wings in relation to tail-tip. Aug 1978, Finland (Dick Forsman).*

Plate 623 *Juvenile. Note rufous brown tinge to all plumage typical of fresh juvenile. Aug, Finland (Mikko Pöllänen).*

Plate 624 *Juvenile. The whiter and more contrasting underparts of this bird may indicate a more easterly origin. Dec 1987, Israel (Paul Doherty).*

Plate 625 *Adult male. Note pale ochre, nearly unmarked breast, poorly marked head and typical silhouette. 7 Feb 1996, Israel (Dick Forsman).*

Plate 626 *Adult male showing typical bluish upperparts with black shaft-streaks, ochre underparts and poorly marked head. Apr, Finland (Tapani Räsänen).*

Plate 627 *Adult male with typically patterned head and upperparts. Apr, Finland (Tapani Räsänen).*

Plate 628 *Female showing diagnostic wing-formula and coarsely patterned underwings. 11 Jul 1991, Norway (Dick Forsman).*

Plate 629 *Female. Note pattern of head and underwing and darker flanks than breast and compare with other small falcons. 11 Jul 1993, Finland (Dick Forsman).*

Plate 630 *Adult female. Adults are more greyish brown above than juveniles, often also distinctly more barred on scapulars and upperwings. Apr, Finland (Tapani Räsänen).*

Plate 631 *Adult female. The rather greyish upperparts, especially rump, with distinct black shaft-streaks are typical of adult females. Note diagnostic sparse tail-barring and compare with other falcon species. Spring, Finland (Tapani Räsänen).*

Plate 632 *Adult female. The breast shows regular drop-shaped spots and the flanks are more distinctly barred compared with juveniles. Spring, Finland (Tapani Räsänen).*

HOBBY   *Falco subbuteo*
Plates 633–646

Subspecies: Nominate *subbuteo* in W Palearctic and extralimital *F. s. streichi* in China.

Distribution: From W Europe across Asia to the Pacific. Widely but unevenly distributed over Europe. Occurs on passage in areas with no breeding population. Relatively rare in the maritime parts of W and NW Europe, more common in areas with drier continental climate.

Habitat: Usually seen in the air hunting above woods or open landscapes. Prefers wet-lands, bogs, moors and reed-beds when hunting insects. Hunts birds mostly high up in the air but also dashes among bushes and trees in semi-open areas. On migration found in all kinds of open terrain. In winter found in different types of savanna.

Population: W Palearctic population estimated at 55 000–75 000 pairs, but population fig-ures still poorly known for many countries. About 50% of the total population lives in Russia, with the remaining 50% spread evenly over most of Europe. Rare in the west and far north and northwest. For countries where populations are reliably monitored numbers appear stable or increasing with no recent drastic declines.

Movements: Long-distance migrant to tropical and S Africa, where sometimes seen in larger concentrations. Returns to Europe from early Apr, reaching northern parts of range from mid-May, but with 2nd cy birds still arriving during first half of Jun. Departure begins in Aug and peaks during Sep. By mid-Oct most birds have already left Europe. Wintering records for Europe extremely rare. Migrates on broad front crossing seas freely and does not concentrate along specific routes. On passage usually recorded in small numbers, migrating singly or a few birds together. At Falsterbo, S Sweden, autumn numbers varied between 29 and 71 in 1986–1994.

Hunting and prey: Hobbies are mostly encountered over wetlands hunting dragonflies, which form an important part of their diet. When hunting insects, flies with leisurely wing-beats snatching the prey in flight with great ease, devouring it directly from the talons while gliding on stretched wings. When hunting birds, flight more determined and pow-erful. Hunting Hobbies are usually revealed by warning Swallows and House Martins, which immediately start to climb to get above the falcon. Birds are often chased and finally caught high up in the air and long tail-chases are not rare. Hobbies can also appear out of the blue like Merlins, flying at tremendous speed low over the ground trying to seize their victim from below. Hunts mainly birds of open spaces such as hirundines, wagtails and pipits and is often drawn to concentrations of roosting migrants.

SPECIES IDENTIFICATION

Length 29–32 cm

wing-span 74–84 cm (*n*=13; Israeli migrants; W.S. Clark, unpubl.)

Although mostly easy to identify when seen close, juveniles especially may be mistaken for other similar-looking falcon species, especially for juvenile Red-footed Falcon and Eleonora's Falcon.

Identification summary: A small falcon about the size of a Kestrel. Mostly seen in flight hunting smaller birds or insects. Seen perched less often than other small falcons. Uses elevated perches, often dead branches and treetops and only rarely seen on roadside telephone wires and poles. Often active until dark, hunting dragonflies low over reed-beds. Does not hover when hunting, but capable of doing so for short periods in strong wind, e.g. when disturbed at nest.

Upperparts dark grey, often with slightly darker hand and paler grey rump and base to tail. Always contrasting head-pattern with narrow and pointed black moustache, variably dark crown and sides of neck, and shining white cheek and throat. Underbody pale with distinct black streaking, underwings densely patterned appearing generally dark.

In flight, distant Compared with other small falcons appears longer winged and shorter tailed, giving from time to time the impression of a large swift (*Apus*) because of diagnostic wing-shape, with long pointed hand and short arm. Flight fast and agile, with wing-beats appearing stiffer and more powerful than in other small falcons. Often seen hunting high up in the sky, where it may soar freely for long periods. Capable of impressive stoops and frequently takes up a chase on birds seen just as small specks in the distance, kilometres away.

Upperparts appear greyish, in adults and juveniles, with slightly darker hand and paler inner tail; white cheek-patch is often prominent from afar. Underbody appears pale with prominent black streaking; underwings appear mostly uniformly dark.

In flight, closer The distinct long, narrow and black moustache and the white cheek and throat form a distinct head-pattern. The whitish underbody shows distinct black streaks starting below the throat and continuing to the lower breast. Adults have vent, undertail coverts and trousers rusty red, whereas the rear body is buffish in juveniles. Underwing looks densely and uniformly barred lacking any striking features. Seen in good light the darkish coverts with rufous spotting may appear slightly darker than the rufous-barred remiges. Upperparts always appear rather uniformly coloured, with slightly darker primaries and with two pale spots on the sides of the upper neck in all plumages.

Perched Looks slim when perched, with wing-tips reaching to or protruding beyond the tip of the tail. Upperparts look uniformly bluish grey or blackish brown, with slightly darker primaries and uniformly dark tail. The pale breast is boldly streaked in black (dark and pale streaks about equally broad). Crown appears dark (although the forehead can be largely buffish in some juveniles) and the black moustache contrasts from afar with the white cheeks and throat.

Bare parts Eyes dark brown at all ages; cere and legs deep yellow in adults, duller greenish yellow in juveniles; orbital skin lemon in adults, bluish or greenish yellow in juveniles. Bill dark grey to blackish in adults, a shade paler and bluer in juveniles.

Confusion species: May easily be confused with other falcons, most likely with Red-footed and Eleonora's, sometimes also with Peregrine.

Red-footed Falcon (page 456) Juvenile Red-footed Falcons can be very similar to juvenile Hobbies, but also 2nd cy males in spring can cause confusion. Juveniles told from Hobbies by contrasting underwing pattern, barred upper tail and paler head, with contrasting black face-mask. Juvenile Red-footed also show a more complete pale neck-band. In spring 2nd cy male Red-footeds may show a head-pattern recalling Hobby's, but the moustache is usually shorter. They are, however, best identified by their distinctly patterned juvenile underwing remiges and they never show the Hobby's distinct streaking on the breast.

Eleonora's Falcon (page 470) Bigger, with longer wings and tail, although size and silhouette are not always diagnostic. Flight usually more relaxed but, when seen only briefly, the two can appear very similar. Eleonora's Falcon shows a diagnostic underwing pattern in all plumages, darker underwing coverts contrasting with distinctly paler bases to primaries and outer secondaries. Juveniles also show distinct black tip and trailing edge to wings. On pale morph adults the rufous colour of the underparts often reaches to the upper breast and the streaking is less prominent.

Peregrine (page 554) From above shows a distinctly paler rump and inner tail and either finely barred or more thinly streaked underparts than Hobby. Usually told from Hobby by slower and more powerful movements in the air and by heavier proportions, with broader wings and broader base to tail, much heavier body and slower circles when soaring.

Merlin (page 495) Shorter wings with broad bases and a longer tail. They also have faster wing-beats than Hobbies and use different hunting methods. Head-pattern is far less contrasting, the tail is barred above and the primaries often show coarse barring above and below.

Kestrel (page 443) Easily told from Hobby by rufous upperparts with contrasting dark primaries. Underwings appear pale and the head-pattern is faint by comparison.

MOULT

Annually complete, commencing in the breeding areas but suspended for the autumn migration, resumed and completed in the winter quarters.

Juveniles (first moult) Partial body moult in winter. The extent of the moult varies individually, but at least some feathers on rump and mantle/scapulars are moulted and stand out as bluish grey against the blackish brown, abraded juvenile feathers. More advanced birds may moult practically all body-feathers, giving the bird almost an adult appearance. Even some tail-feathers can be replaced but never any remiges or primary coverts. Remex moult starts earlier than in adults, from 2nd cy Jun–Jul, but may be delayed until late Aug. Unlike adults the great majority of migrating juveniles show at least a few replaced primaries, whereas birds with no sign of primary moult are rare.

Adults (subsequent moults) Primary moult starts in some adults on the breeding grounds in late summer, on average later than in 2nd cy birds. Most adults, however, migrate south with old remiges and the moult commences in late autumn on the wintering grounds. Birds starting to moult during breeding suspend the moult for the migration and complete it in the winter quarters. Moult completed by Feb–Mar, just before the spring passage.

AGEING AND SEXING

Separating juveniles and adults is not difficult given good views. Some 2nd cy birds can be rather similar to adults, but pattern of undertail diagnostic. Adults and juveniles differ in silhouette.

Ageing summary: Autumn juveniles best identified by distinctly barred undertail with prominent pale tip, pale trailing edge to wing and yellowish buff vent and undertail coverts. 2nd cy birds best aged by retained juvenile rectrices, as body plumage may be largely moulted and similar to adult. Adults lack pale tip to tail and trailing edge of wing, the undertail shows diffuse greyish barring, and the trousers, vent and undertail coverts are rusty red. The flight silhouette is also different in adults and juveniles, the adults having longer and narrower wings and a shorter tail. Juveniles resemble e.g. juvenile Red-footed Falcons in shape.

Juvenile (1st cy autumn)   Plates 633–638

Blackish brown above with buffish fringes, the amount of scaling varying individually. Usually the rump and uppertail coverts show the most prominent pale fringes, making this area in flight the palest on the entire upperparts. The distinct buffish tip to the tail and the buffish trailing edge to the wing are also diagnostic and conspicuous from afar, when the bird is seen against a dark background or a blue sky. Primary coverts and greater coverts of the upperwing are tipped buffish-white, forming a fine band. Head-markings similar to adults, apart from the sometimes extensively pale forehead, somewhat resembling the pattern of juvenile Red-footed Falcon. Juveniles in fresh plumage may, in flight, appear greyish above with contrasting darker primaries, resembling both adult Hobbies and juvenile Red-footeds.

Underparts buffish, not white, with bold black streaking confined to the breast, while belly, vent and undertail coverts are uniformly pale. Undertail distinctly barred with ochre bars over the entire length of the feather. The closed tail is uniformly dark from above with a pale tip, but when fanned the prominent barring of the inner vanes becomes visible.

Transitional plumage (2nd cy spring – 2nd cy autumn)   Plates 639–641

2nd cy spring birds are variable depending on the extent of the partial body moult in winter. Most birds show at least newly moulted bluish grey feathers on the rump, mantle and scapulars, contrasting with faded and dull juvenile feathers, but some have moulted the entire body plumage, including vent, thighs and undertail coverts, being rufous as in adult. These birds can be separated from adults only by their juvenile tail-feathers, with distinct ochre barring underneath. The pale feather-tips and margins are by now all worn away.

Fig 63 *Hobby. Tail-feathers (r3/4) of juvenile (left) and adult. Note narrower and more pointed tip of juvenile with distinct pale tip and distinct bars, whereas the adult shows more diffuse markings and the feather-tip is blunt and lacks the distinct pale tip (From Forsman 1980).*

By the time of the autumn migration advanced birds may show up to half of the primaries moulted, which is far more than any adult would show.

Adult (from 3rd cy and older)   Plates 642–646

Adults are uniformly grey above with blackish head-markings and darker outer hand. The tail also darkens somewhat towards the tip, which, like the wings, lacks the distinct pale trailing edge of the autumn juvenile. The folded tail looks uniformly grey above, but when fanned a rather subtle and fine, greyish barring can be seen, especially from below. The pale barring becomes more distinct proximally as it softly blends from grey to more rufous.

Underbody white with evenly spaced bold, black streaks over the chest. Thighs, vent and undertail coverts rusty red, with or without dark streaking. The colours are more vivid in spring, when the plumage is fresh, and become gradually duller, upperparts attaining a brownish tinge during summer.

Sexing: As a rule Hobbies cannot be sexed in the field. Seen together the male is clearly slimmer with narrower wings, reminiscent of a Swift in shape, whereas the female is stockier and broader-winged and may at times even resemble a slender Peregrine. Males also tend to be bluer grey above and to show unstreaked trousers, whereas females mostly have streaked thigh-feathers and duller upperparts. Juveniles cannot be sexed in the field.

References Forsman 1980, 1984, 1993b, 1995a; Gensbøl 1995; Kjellén 1995; Stresemann & Stresemann 1966

Plate 633   *Juvenile showing distinct head-pattern, darkish underwings and boldly streaked breast. 27 Oct 1992, Israel (Dick Forsman).*

Plate 634   *Juvenile (same as Plate 633). Ochre ground-colour of remiges separates Hobby from Red-footed Falcon. Juveniles show distinctly barred rectrices with pale tips in fresh plumage. 27 Oct 1992, Israel (Dick Forsman).*

Plate 635   *Juvenile. Note typically darkish underwings with dense barring to both remiges and coverts. Pale vent, distinct tail-barring and pale tips to flight-feathers are diagnostic of autumn juveniles. 14 Sep 1993, Kazakhstan (Dick Forsman).*

Plate 636   *Juvenile from above. The pale tips and fringes of the upperparts of juveniles are well visible at close range. Note greyish sheen to upperparts, which may cause confusion with juvenile Red-footed Falcon. 14 Sep 1993, Kazakhstan (Dick Forsman).*

Plate 637 *Juvenile from above showing unbarred central tail-feathers, which is a diagnostic character against juvenile Red-footed Falcon. 1 Sep 1996, Finland (Sampsa Cairenius).*

Plate 638 *Juvenile. Note buffish underparts including vent and trousers and rufous fringes to feathers of the upperparts. 10 Sep 1993, Kazakhstan (Dick Forsman).*

Plate 639 *Transitional plumage (2nd cy). The distinctive juvenile tail-barring is barely visible on the half-opened tail and the upperparts are dull and dark in colour lacking bluish grey. Jul 1988, Finland (Esa Sojamo).*

Plate 640 *Transitional plumage (2nd cy). Note the colour contrast between nearly completely moulted body plumage, including central tail-feathers, and retained juvenile upperwings and tail. 1 Jun 1980, Finland (Markku Huhta-Koivisto).*

Plate 641   *Transitional plumage (2nd cy). Despite later date has moulted less of body than Plate 640. Note replaced median primaries and secondaries and distinct pattern of retained juvenile rectrices. 12 Sep 1987, Finland (Björn Ehrnstén).*

Plate 642   *Adult showing typical silhouette, being longer-winged and slimmer in build than juveniles. Apr 1978, Turkey (Lars Jonsson).*

Plate 643   *Adult showing typically diffuse tail-barring and red thighs, vent and undertail coverts. Apr 1978, Turkey (Lars Jonsson).*

Plate 644   *Adult. Distant birds appear rather dark below with striking head-pattern. May 1995, China (Markku Huhta-Koivisto).*

Plate 645 *Adult. The upperparts are uniformly greyish with black shaft-streaks. Head-pattern diagnostic. Sep, Finland (Mikko Pöllänen).*

Plate 646 *Adult showing grey upperparts, white ground-colour to underparts and red thighs and vent. 13 Oct 1988, Israel (Dick Forsman).*

LANNER *Falco biarmicus*

Plates 647–663

Subspecies: Polytypic, with five subspecies: *F. b. feldeggii* in Italy, the Balkans and Asia Minor; *F. b. tanypterus* from the Middle East to Libya and Egypt; *F. b. erlangeri* from Morocco to Tunisia and vagrant to Spain; *F. b. abyssinicus* in Africa south of Sahara; and nominate *F. b. biarmicus* in southern Africa. Subspecific differences small and not even all adults possible to identify to subspecies. European *feldeggii* largest, with on average darkest and most streaked crown and dark and clearly barred upperparts. NW African *erlangeri* smallest with palest crown, more uniform upperparts and least patterned underparts and *F. b. tanypterus* intermediate between the two (see Variation).

Distribution: European population largely confined to the mountains of S Italy; now extremely rare in the Balkans. From Asia Minor to Jordan, Israel and Egypt. Birds from NW Africa occasionally straggle to Iberian peninsula as far as C Spain.

Habitat: Typically a bird of arid zones, barren and rocky deserts and semi-deserts. In Europe also in more hospitable Mediterranean environments, but breeds in rocky habitat. Outside breeding season also found on lower ground, plains, steppes and fields.

Population: One of Europe's most threatened birds of prey, with a dwindling population, perhaps not more than 200 pairs in all, with 160–170 in Italy, 10–20 in Croatia and 20–40 in Greece. Turkish population poorly known, estimated at 10–100 pairs. Has declined in Europe during past decades. More common in N Africa.

Movements: Adults mainly sedentary but juveniles straggle within breeding range. European race *feldeggii* recorded on several Mediterranean islands. Some seasonal altitudinal movement from breeding mountains to lowland wintering areas. Alleged wintering of *feldeggii* in the Middle East obscured by dispersion of local populations and problems regarding subspecific identification in the field.

Hunting and prey: Despite its size preys generally on smaller birds than e.g. Peregrine, favouring small to medium-sized passerines, such as larks, up to birds as big as quail and doves. Also takes mammals, reptiles and insects, catching e.g. swarming ants and termites in flight like Hobby.

SPECIES IDENTIFICATION

Length 38–44 cm

  wing-span 90–109 cm ($n=2$ *(tanypterus)*; Israeli birds; W.S. Clark, unpubl.)

Large falcons are notoriously difficult to identify in the field. Attention should be paid especially to head-pattern, underwing contrast and details of underwing coverts, flanks and upperparts. Separating juveniles of Lanner and Saker is one of the most difficult field-identification problems, but Lanners are also frequently confused with juvenile and adult Barbary Falcons. Juveniles, slightly narrower-winged and longer-tailed than adults, are very similar to juvenile Saker in proportions.

> **Identification summary:** Typical Lanners have a contrasting head-pattern, with a straight, rather narrow and pointed moustache and a blackish eye-line, together forming a dark angle through the eye. The dark marking is often the darkest part of the whole bird and the dark eye merges with the dark pattern. Crown either uniformly yellowish buff or whitish to buff with dark streaks, with streaking concentrated on the forehead as a diadem and forming a lateral crown stripe above the pale supercilium.
>
> Juveniles are uniformly brown above and streaked below, while adults are ashy grey and scaly above with darker barring on the rear upperparts, barred flanks and thighs and transverse spots on the sides of the breast.
>
> Compared with Peregrine and Barbary, Lanner has a comparatively slimmer body with longer and more rounded wings and a longer tail, which is narrower at the base. The flight is relaxed with shallow and elastic wing-beats differing from the more hurried flapping flight of Peregrine and Barbary.

In flight, distant Clearly a large falcon with active flight appearing effortless and relaxed, like Saker's. The wing-beats are shallow and the wing is flexible giving the impression that only the hand works. When soaring, arm is held slightly lowered or flat with hand slightly raised, as in Saker. In head-on silhouette body appears smaller and wings noticeably longer than in bulky and rather short-winged Peregrine/Barbary.

In shape very similar to Saker and the slimmer juveniles especially are practically inseparable. Wings appear rather long and big for the body, with a shortish, parallel-edged arm and a long, tapering hand. Body slim; head appears comparatively small and tail longish, being notably narrow at the base and widening slightly towards the tip even when closed.

Although the pale crown is usually prominent even from some distance and the upperparts appear more uniform than e.g. Saker's, there are no reliable ways of separating distant juveniles of the two species unless plumage details are seen. Adult Lanners are, however, distinctly grey above with a uniform and pale grey tail, and their wings often appear pale below, especially in old adults.

In flight, closer Adults are rather easy to identify when seen well. Underwing looks rather uniformly pale, with more coarsely barred greater underwing coverts forming a slightly darker central band to the underwing, the extent of barring depending on age and sex of the bird (see below). Wing-tips are more widely and diffusely tipped dark than in Peregrine/Barbary and the arm shows a dark trailing edge. Upperwings and mantle appear rather uniformly pale ashy grey with outer hand being slightly darker. Tail, the palest part of the bird, is uniformly coloured, pale creamy-grey, with dense and regular dark barring.

Juveniles are much more difficult to identify. Underwing is clearly two-toned, with darker coverts than remiges. Some juveniles may, however, show rather little contrast between coverts and flight-feathers, becoming more difficult to tell from juveniles of the

Fig 64 *Juveniles of Lanner (left) and Saker. Note diagnostic pale vent, trousers and rear flanks of Lanner, while most (not all!) juvenile Sakers are darker, on rear flanks especially. Compare also pattern of head, underwing coverts and remiges, which on average also differ between the species.*

Peregrine-group (note, however, complete dark trailing edge to wing). In separating Lanner and Saker the head-pattern is of great importance, together with details of underbody and underwing. Head-pattern more contrasting than in Saker and rear underbody is largely pale, with pale trousers and unstreaked belly. Juvenile Lanners also show rather conspicuously barred primaries below, whereas Sakers often show indistinct barring or no barring at all on the outer primaries, creating a large pale area on the hand contrasting with darker secondaries ('skua-flash'). The colour of the underwing coverts varies individually in both species, depending on the general darkness of the bird, and cannot as such be used for identification. However, juvenile Lanners show distinct pale spotting to the underwing coverts, whereas Sakers mostly show pale longitudinal markings especially on the carpal area. Although juvenile Lanners show, on average, more mottled and paler forearm than juvenile Sakers, birds with nearly all-dark underwing coverts occur in both species. Upperparts appear greyish brown with slightly darker outer hand and a paler tail, thus being very similar to Saker, but the contrast between paler innerwing and darker tip is less clear-cut in Lanner and runs further out, across the distal part of the hand.

Perched Perched birds show shorter wing-to-tail projection than juvenile Saker, with wing-tips reaching closer to tail-tip.

Adults are mostly easy to identify from diagnostic head-pattern, pattern of underbody, and colour and pattern of upperparts. The orange, pale ochre or yellowish-buff crown and a distinct, long and rather narrow and pointed moustache, and a similarly distinct blackish eye-stripe are typical of adult Lanners. Only very old birds (males only?) may have somewhat suffused head-markings, thus nearing Saker. The central breast is never barred, but spotted or unmarked, with coarse transverse spots or bars on flanks and finer barring on thighs. Upperparts grey with a darker mantle and darker barring discernible on lower scapulars, innerwing coverts and tertials, while the tail is pale grey with fine and complete dark bars.

Juveniles show much the same head-pattern as the adults, but the crown is more streaked and less rich in colour. Some darker birds may even resemble juvenile Barbarys, showing extensive dark pattern on crown, but even then the streaking is concentrated on the forehead and lateral crown, leaving the central crown paler. Upperparts brown as in juvenile Saker and Peregrine with rufous fringes when fresh and the breast is streaked. Vent and undertail coverts uniformly pale (cf. Peregrine/Barbary), trousers pale with fine dark streaking (cf. Saker), and feet yellowish (cf. Saker).

Bare parts Iris dark brown at all ages. In juvenile the cere and eye-ring are bluish grey turning greenish yellow in the autumn and the feet are pale bluish with a greenish tinge at fledging but turning yellow by autumn (cf. Saker). Cere, eye-ring and feet yellow in adult.

Variation: Underbody and head-pattern of juveniles vary in extent of pigmentation with pale individuals showing rather finely streaked breast, rather fine head-pattern and richly spotted underwing coverts, whereas dark birds may appear all-dark on breast and underwing coverts and show very bold and prominent head-markings.

Adults vary in boldness of pattern of underbody and underwing coverts as a function of age. Older birds show finer barring and very old males especially may appear almost unpatterned below. The head-markings also vary with age and old birds show fainter moustache and eye-line than younger adults.

European subspecies *feldeggii* is largest and darkest. Adults show, on average, a more deep rusty or deep orange coloured and more heavily streaked crown, resulting in less striking head-pattern than in ssp. *tanypterus* and *erlangeri*. Some *feldeggii* may even show completely streaked or even uniformly dark crown, creating a head-pattern not very different from some adult Barbary Falcons or even Sakers. *F. b. feldeggii* also have darker upperparts, with a dark mantle and with rather prominent dark barring across the upperparts. Underparts are more coarsely patterned than in the two following subspecies. *F. b. erlangeri* is smaller and generally paler. It is more uniformly and paler grey above and the crown is rather unstreaked and uniformly pale buffish. *F. b. tanypterus* of the Middle East is intermediate between the two, being more similar to *erlangeri*.

Single individuals not always possible to identify to subspecies, except for typical adults such as darkish and strongly patterned, rusty-crowned *feldeggii* or very pale and bleached-out, nearly unpatterned and buffish-crowned *erlangeri/ tanypterus*. Juveniles are even more difficult to separate, but very pale-headed and thinly streaked birds can be regarded as representing the *erlangeri/tanypterus*-type.

Confusion species: Easily confused with other large falcons in juvenile plumage, especially with Saker and juvenile Barbary but also juvenile Peregrine, which may occur together in winter. Identification requires good views, especially when separating juveniles.

Saker (page 529) Does not show grey upperparts and barred flanks like adult Lanner. Sakers differ from juvenile Lanners by mostly darker rear underbody with darkish trousers and streaked belly, by less distinctive head-pattern, with less contrasting eye-line and moustache, the latter often being broken below the eye. Upperwings show darker hand than arm; underwing coverts often show longitudinal pattern and bases to primaries appear white contrasting with greyish secondaries. Feet are bluish in young Sakers at least up to 2nd cy spring (see Fig 64 p 515).

Barbary (page 567) and Peregrine (page 554) Appear big-bodied, big-headed and smaller-winged by comparison, with distinctly faster and stiffer wing-action in powered flight. Underwings are evenly patterned and appear generally rather uniform and dark in juveniles; rump/inner tail paler above than distal half. When soaring, often keep wings slightly raised in a flat V.

MOULT

Moult annually complete. Juveniles have a partial body moult in the autumn–winter.

Juveniles (first moult; *F. b. tanypterus*) Start to moult their head, upper breast and some feathers on mantle and rump during early autumn. This partial body moult, the extent of which varies individually, is then suspended and not resumed before the complete moult starts in (Mar–)Apr of 2nd cy (a 2nd cy falconer's bird with p4 halfgrown in Egypt on 9 Apr; 2nd cy bird in Israel on 21 Mar still with juvenile primaries). Moult is completed by late summer. Moult in European *feldeggii* commences later, partial body moult from Nov, complete moult from May and completed in Sep.

Adult (subsequent moults; *F. b. tanypterus*) Starts complete moult in Mar (breeding adult male (Israel) missing p4 on 27 Mar; breeding females begin to moult before males). Moult completed in late summer, details unknown. Timing in (captive) *F. b. feldeggii* later, primary moult starting in May, and completed in 104–146 days (average 120 days). However, since nesting begins in Feb and early Mar earlier moulting dates would be expected. Adult male from the wild with p9 and p10 growing in Aug (Sicily; ZMH).

AGEING AND SEXING

Ageing normally not difficult as colour and pattern of upperparts and pattern of underparts and underwing differ markedly between adults and juveniles.

> **Ageing summary:** Juveniles are readily distinguished by their uniformly dark brownish upperparts (more greyish in flight) and streaked breast. In flight from below juveniles show a strong contrast between dark, pale-spotted underwing coverts and paler remiges, whereas adults show only slightly duskier, barred median/greater coverts than remiges and forearm.
>
> Adults are grey and barred above and the underbody is distinctly spotted, with finer spotting of mid-breast turning to bigger transverse spots and cross-bars on flanks and underwing coverts.

Juvenile (1st cy autumn – 2nd cy spring)   **Plates 647–655**
Perched birds appear above uniformly dark brown (fresh) to more dull greyish brown (worn). In fresh plumage upperparts are finely scaled, but the rufous fringes wear off

Fig 65 *Lanner, juvenile. Note diagnostic pointed and narrow, solidly dark moustache and solid dark eye-line, merging with dark eye, and isolated dark triangular nape-patch. Dark head-markings as dark as mantle. Crown typically pale with dark band across forecrown and dark lateral crown stripes bordering supercilium from above. After field-sketch, Greece, 18 Jun 1989.*

during autumn/winter. Tail appears uniformly brown when folded, with a conspicuous pale tip when fresh.

Underparts vary from buffish to more whitish with dark streaks increasing in width towards the flanks. Paler birds have narrow streaks, whereas the darkest birds appear more or less dark-breasted. Trousers pale and rather finely streaked (cf. Saker). Vent and under-tail coverts uniformly pale or thinly streaked (cf. Peregrine/Barbary).

Head-pattern varies individually, but most birds show a dark, straight and pointed mous-tache and a prominent black line through the eye. This face-pattern is usually the darkest part of the bird and merges completely with the dark eye (cf. Saker). The crown varies from off white to yellowish buff, either uniformly coloured or with dark streaks concentrated on the forehead and lateral crown just above the pale supercilium. When viewed from behind, the head appears pale with a dark, down-pointing triangle on the nape (cf. Saker). The streaked crown of fledglings is moulted from early autumn and by winter most birds have acquired a more adult-like head, with a plainer *(tanypterus/erlangeri)* and more richly coloured crown. Often this partial moult also includes parts of the upper breast, hindneck and mantle. In juveniles the cere is bluish grey turning greenish yellow in the autumn and the feet are pale bluish with a greenish tinge turning yellow by autumn.

In flight, juveniles are considerably slimmer than adults with narrower wings and longer and narrower tail (especially at base). Upperparts appear rather dark and uniformly brown at close range, with a slight rufous cast when fresh. By autumn upperparts appear grey-ish-brown in flight, similar to juvenile Saker. Remiges are slightly darker than coverts, with outer hand appearing darkest.

Tail appears rather uniformly coloured from a distance (not two-toned as often in Peregrine/Barbary), and slightly paler to the sides. It is paler than the upperparts generally, sometimes with a narrow darker band just inside the conspicuously pale tip. Tail-pattern is variable, being either completely barred, or, more frequently, having the central pair uniformly dark and the rest barred on inner vanes only (oval spots, not round), showing pattern only when tail is spread or from below. Tail has a wide and conspicuous pale tip in fresh plumage, but this wears narrower during winter.

Underwing is clearly two-toned, with distinctly darker coverts than remiges (cf. Peregrine and Barbary), being superficially similar to the underwing of Saker. Coverts can be uniformly dark, but mostly the lesser coverts are paler and the darker median and greater coverts show extensive pale spotting. From a distance the remiges appear rather uniformly pale greyish, with a darker trailing edge to the wing and the dark wing-tip is wider and more diffuse than in Peregrine/Barbary. On average, juvenile Lanners tend to show a more conspicuous dusky trailing edge to the arm than juvenile Sakers, which show more uniformly grey and less barred secondaries, and whiter and less barred primaries, thus showing a slight contrast between hand and arm on the underwing. The underbody streaking is on average more restricted than in juvenile Saker, ending on lower breast, leaving belly, vent and trousers largely pale (see also Fig 64, p 517).

Adult (2nd cy autumn and older)   Plates 656–663

Perched birds are often mistaken for adult Barbary Falcon. Head-pattern in adults basically similar to juveniles, but the crown tends to show fewer and finer dark streaks. In very old birds the normally contrasting moustache and eye-stripe may become suffused and less distinct and the crown becomes uniformly coloured. In flight the pale crown normally contrasts well against the rather dark mantle, especially in ssp. *erlangeri* and *tanypterus*.

Upperparts ashy grey, less blue than in Peregrine and Barbary, with a tendency towards darker barring, depending on subspecies. The barring is often most evident on the lower scapulars, inner greater coverts and inner secondaries. Upperwings appear rather uniformly greyish in flight, with the outer hand slightly darker. Tail paler grey than rest of upperparts, with rather fine and regular dark grey bars and a whitish tip. One or two of the outermost dark bands are normally slightly wider than the rest, but do not form a widely dark distal band as in Peregrine/Barbary.

Underparts whitish with dark spots which grow in size from mid-breast towards the flanks and also vary in size according to sex and age. Old adults have smaller spots than younger adults and males tend to have finer spots than females of the same age. Thus females in first-adult plumage can be very heavily patterned below, whereas very old males may have no noticeable pattern. The flank marks are typically bold cross-bars, which differ from the rounded spots of Saker (see, however, '*saceroides*'-type Saker) and the fine barring of adult Peregrine/Barbary.

Median and greater underwing coverts are rather distinctly barred and form a dusky bar across the underwing. Old birds (of *erlangeri/tanypterus* only?) show very pale and immaculate underwings except for darker tips and trailing edge and faintly barred greater coverts. These birds can appear rather similar to very old Peregrines/Barbarys, which, however, lack the darker wing-band and the complete dark trailing edge and instead show a narrower and more distinct dark wing-tip.

Sexing: Sexing normally not possible in the field, though males are smaller and lighter and more agile in flight than females. Adult males are more finely patterned on breast, flanks and underwing coverts than females of the same age.

References Massa et al. 1991; Mebs 1960; Shirihai 1995; Shirihai & Forsman 1998; Tucker & Heath 1995

Plate 647   *Juvenile* erlangeri. *Distinct dark head-markings, spotted underwing coverts and pale trousers and rear-body are diagnostic of juveniles. Nov 1992, Morocco (Markus Varesvuo).*

Plate 648   *Juvenile (upper) with adult male. This juvenile has already moulted its head but shows the typically spotted greater underwing coverts. Nov 1992, Morocco (Markus Varesvuo).*

Plate 649   *Juvenile. An unusually pale-headed individual. Note diagnostic pale thighs, rear flanks and belly and compare with juvenile Saker. 21 Jan 1995, Israel (Dick Forsman).*

Plate 650   *Juvenile stooping. A rather heavily marked bird showing diagnostic underbody, with streaking ending on lower breast, leaving largely pale rear-body. 8 Oct 1988, Israel (Dick Forsman).*

Plate 651 *Juvenile. Note darker underwing coverts than remiges and distinct dark moustache and eye-line. Note also uniformly barred translucent tail. Dec 1990, Morocco (Harri Muukkonen).*

Plate 652 *Juvenile* feldeggii. *Note typical underwing coverts and head-pattern. 17 Aug 1993, Italy (Roberto Gildi).*

Plate 653 *Juvenile (same as Plate 649) from above. Note diagnostic head-pattern, paler coverts than remiges and pale tail. 21 Jan 1995, Israel (Dick Forsman).*

Plate 654 *Juvenile with freshly moulted head and some scapulars. Dec 1990, Morocco (Harri Muukkonen).*

Plate 655 *Juvenile (2nd cy spring). Head-pattern diagnostic, with distinct, pointed moustache, prominent eye-line and dark band across forehead. Aged by uniformly brown upperparts and streaked breast. 9 Apr 1991, Egypt (Annika Forsten).*

Plate 656 *Adult* erlangeri *showing diagnostic underwing and head-pattern and transverse spots on flanks. Note more dark at wing-tip than Peregrine/Barbary. 9 Nov 1990, Morocco (Annika Forsten).*

Plate 657 *Adult* tanypterus. *Spotted breast, contrasting underwing coverts and uniformly barred tail separate from Peregrine-type birds. Mar 1985, Israel (Dick Forsman).*

Plate 658 *Adult* tanypterus *soaring. Note spotted breast, coarsely barred greater underwing coverts and uniformly barred tail. Head-pattern and silhouette typical of the species. Mar 1985, Israel (Dick Forsman).*

Plate 659 *Adult* erlangeri. *Grey upperparts with evenly barred tail, scapulars and greater coverts and bold transverse spots on flanks are diagnostic. Jan 1990, Morocco (Harri Muukkonen).*

Plate 660 *Adult* tanypterus *male. Note reduced pattern of breast with bars on flanks. The moustache can be rather washed-out in old birds. Apr 1986, Israel (Hadoram Shirihai).*

Plate 661 *Captive adult male* feldeggii *in first-adult plumage (with retained juvenile upperwing coverts). Note all dark crown, which is not rare in this subspecies, barred mantle and coarsely barred flanks. Italy (Andrea Ciaccio).*

Plate 662 *Captive adult female* feldeggii. *Note rather dark head-pattern, deep rufous crown and barred upperparts diagnostic of this subspecies. 18 Nov 1994, Italy (Dick Forsman).*

Plate 663 *Adult female* erlangeri. *More uniform on mantle than adult* feldeggii *and crown more creamy-buff. Dec, Morocco (Göran Ekström).*

SAKER *Falco cherrug*

Plates 664–680

Subspecies: Taxonomy complex with several recognized subspecies earlier now lumped to two: *F. c. cherrug* in Europe and W Russia Yenisey River and Altai Mts to China from N Mongolia E and *F. c. milvipes* in S Central Asia. *Altaicus* from the mountains of C Asia (Altai, Tien-Shan) by some regarded as a full species Altai Falcon *F. altaicus*. The variation is clinal from west to east, as birds tend to become overall paler and the upperparts become increasingly barred. Pale markings on flight-feathers above increase towards east. The easternmost forms are coloured and barred above almost like a female Kestrel.

Distribution: From Austria, the Czech Republic and Hungry in the west through Russia and C Asia to C China.

Habitat: A raptor of vast open spaces, such as steppes, cultivated plains, mountain plateaus and foothills.

Population: Rare, with an estimated *c*. 350–500 pairs breeding in eastern parts of Europe, from Austria (5–10) and the Czech Republic (8–12) to Russia (80–150), Ukraine (120–150) and Bulgaria (20–40), with another 10–100 pairs estimated to breed in Turkey. Despite steady and long-term decline has recently shown increasing numbers in e.g. Hungary (120) and the Czech Republic.

Movements: Adults more or less sedentary in southern part of range but may straggle away from breeding area in winter. Juveniles migratory, leaving breeding grounds in Oct and returning in Mar–Apr. European birds winter in the Middle East and N Africa, regularly crossing the Mediterranean between Italy and Tunisia.

Hunting and prey: During breeding specialized in hunting small mammals, especially sousliks, which are attacked from low flight barely above the ground. May also hunt in a leisurely, harrier-like manner quartering slowly against the wind and may even stop to hover briefly. Also capable of hunting birds up to the size of doves and ducks, occasionally even bigger prey. Wintering birds are often seen robbing prey from other birds of prey, including Kestrel, Sparrowhawk, Merlin, harriers, kites and Long-legged Buzzard.

SPECIES IDENTIFICATION

Length 43–60 cm

wing-span 104–135 cm (Baumgart 1980), 97–120 cm (Noakes 1990)

Large falcons present one of the most difficult identification problems of the region, especially juveniles of Saker and Lanner. Attention should be paid to pattern of head, underwings and underbody and to pattern of individual feathers of upperparts and underparts. Plumage quite variable both individually and geographically.

Identification summary: The moustache and eye-line are usually mottled and less contrasting than in Lanner and young Peregrine, the moustache often being broken below the eye, slightly bent and showing a blunt tip. The dark eye is often conspicuous in the bland face. Wing-tips usually fall well short of tail-tip on perched birds. Underwings show darker coverts than remiges, darker in juveniles than adults, often with longitudinal markings, and a slight contrast between greyer secondaries and pale bases to primaries (more pronounced in juveniles), while the underbody streaking often extends to the rear flanks and thighs.

Lacks grey colour to upperparts and barring to underparts (except for '*saceroides*'-type, see Variation). Adults show rufous margins to upperparts and a tendency for rufous barring especially to inner greater coverts and inner secondaries/tertials, while the underparts show roundish spots; juveniles are more streaked below. Dark trousers and roundish pale spots in tail are diagnostic features of Saker, but these characters are not shown by all birds.

In flight, distant Often impossible to tell from Lanner, and young birds especially appear almost identical from a distance. Upperparts greyish brown with marginally paler tail and upperwings show slightly darker hand than arm, whereas Lanners tend to show darker wing-tips only. In many juveniles the underwing shows basally pale primaries (skua-flash) contrasting with greyer secondaries, the underwing coverts are distinctly darker than the remiges and the underbody appears rather dark. Adults have paler underwings with a darker trailing edge and a darker mid-wing-bar.

When taking off from perch drops considerably before getting properly airborne, with first wing-beats appearing deep and laboured. After gaining speed active-flight looks easy and relaxed, with just hand working. The wing-beats are shallow, slow and elastic and the flight is powerful yet effortless (as if in slow-motion). Wing-tips bend up markedly during gliding. Soars on flattish wings, often with slight kink between level arm and slightly drooping hand. Silhouette in flight slimmer than in other large falcons with longer wings

Fig 66 *Saker. Appears long-winged and small-bodied when gliding. Note up-bent wing-tips.*

(especially arm) and tail, slim shape being especially pronounced in juvenile. Body slender, being widest around chest and tapering markedly towards the rear, with vent and tail appearing long and slim; adults are more compact than juveniles with broader wings and heavier body, more resembling Lanner or Gyrfalcon in shape.

In flight, closer White underneath with variably dense dark spotting/streaking on breast becoming heavier towards flanks. In younger birds especially the breast may appear entirely dark. From below, the outer primaries often show reduced dark barring, making the primary bases look pale in the field and adding to the contrast between pale primaries and greyer secondaries (remiges usually more uniformly barred in Lanner). Underwing coverts distinctly darker than remiges, although juveniles and adults may differ considerably on this point. The pale markings of the median and greater underwing coverts consist mainly of pale margins, giving a streaked effect (pale spotting or distinct barring in Lanner), especially prominent in the carpal area. Most Sakers have darkish trousers forming a dark V when seen from below and the dark on the flanks appears to extend further back than on juvenile Lanners, in which the pale trousers create a pale V to rear body when seen from below (see Fig 64, p 517).

From above, Sakers usually show a slightly darker hand than arm, but apart from this they appear very similar to juvenile Lanners. Tail slightly paler than the rest of the upperparts. Although many birds have identical tail-pattern to juvenile Lanners, round pale spots always indicate Saker. Head-pattern varies considerably and the head does not usually appear as distinctly pale as in Lanner: the crown appears darkish, either streaked or more uniform, and the pale supercilium is prominent. The moustache and dark eye-line are less conspicuous than in juvenile Lanner, but, generally, the head-pattern is mostly difficult to assess on flying birds.

Perched Perched birds are identified by wing-to-tail ratio, head-pattern and pattern of underparts and upperparts.

Appears broad-shouldered, small-headed and long-tailed with tail protruding clearly beyond the wing-tips, about 2–3 cm in adults and up to 5 cm or more in juveniles. Some adults (males only?) show a proportionately shorter tail and approach Lanners in this respect, with tail only marginally protruding beyond the wing-tips.

Head-markings are the same colour as the upperparts, not distinctly darker as in Lanner. Crown darkish and the dark eye is often the most conspicuous feature in the face. The moustache may be dark and distinct but it starts from the gape and is typically disconnected from the eye by a paler area. It is often darkest at the tip, whereas the rest of the moustache, as well as the eye-line, is loosely and finely spotted or streaked. The pattern and colour of the crown is variable showing mostly dark streaking on either pale or rufous ground. The latter variant can at first appear very similar to a Lanner, but in Saker the whole crown is streaked, whereas Lanners show a dark band across the forecrown and above the supercilium.

Fig 67 *Saker, juveniles, showing variation in head-markings. Most individuals identified by uniform crown connected with mantle along hind-neck and by streaked and slightly decurved moustache being often darkest close to tip and broken before reaching the eye. The dark head-markings are often paler than the mantle, which makes the dark eye stand out. After field-sketches, both Israel, 13 Jan 1990.*

Upperparts neatly rufous-fringed in fresh plumage, but first-winter birds look uniformly greyish brown above as early as late autumn, thus being similar to juvenile Lanners. Adults show broader rufous fringes and a tendency for barring to rear upperparts. A distant perched Saker may even give the impression of a Long-legged Buzzard, because of pale head and upper breast contrasting with darker lower breast and flanks. The thighs are mostly hidden in the belly feathers, but when seen, dark trousers indicate Saker, whereas streaked trousers occur in all large falcon species.

Bare parts Iris dark brown at all ages. Feet, eye-ring and cere pale bluish in young birds up to at least 2nd cy spring, bright yellow in adult. Second-winter birds may still show very bleached and colourless, almost whitish bare parts, although colour of cere usually difficult to determine in the field.

Variation: Some adults in Europe occur in a rare plumage type called *'saceroides'*, which may be extremely similar to adult Lanner. These birds are rather greyish above and show (rufous-tinged) barring to lower mantle, wing coverts, rump and tail. As they may also have a rufous (yet streaked) crown and the spots on the breast may change into wide cross-bars towards the flanks, identification can be extremely difficult. *Saceroides*-type birds, however, still retain the typical rufous Saker-margins to most feathers of the upperparts, and the underwing coverts are spotted or streaked rather than distinctly barred. Wing-tip to tail-tip ratio is also an important character on perched birds.

Confusion species: Large falcons are notoriously difficult to identify, and telling Saker from juvenile Lanner, and also from juvenile Gyrfalcon, is a truly difficult field identification problem. Although Sakers and Gyrfalcons are normally allopatric, falconers' escapes have to be kept in mind. In flight most difficult to separate from juvenile Lanner. Also very similar to juvenile Gyr, but latter has bulkier body (weight nearly double) and broader wings (wings therefore appear shorter) making whole silhouette more compact. Adult Lanner and Gyr told by grey upperparts and barred flanks and underwing coverts.

Lanner (page 515) Juvenile has dark moustache and eye-stripe forming a solid dark pattern; crown uniformly pale ochre or tawny buffish with dark band across forecrown and lateral crown (crown may be completely streaked in fledgling until 1st cy autumn). Greater underwing coverts typically show extensive pale spotting, lesser and median coverts often clearly paler and evenly streaked; primaries mostly completely barred below. Trousers pale with narrow dark streaking. Feet yellowish from 1st cy autumn. On perched birds wings reach close to tail-tip.

Gyrfalcon (page 542) Juvenile more greyish brown above with creamy-white spots and tips to upperparts, lacking the narrow rufous fringes of Saker. Underparts more creamy, not white as in Saker and the head-pattern is less distinct with darker and more streaked cheek-patch. As in Saker feet remain bluish through first winter and wing-tips fall well short of tail-tip.

Peregrine (page 554) and Barbary (page 567) Juveniles show uniformly patterned underwings lacking distinct contrast between darker coverts and paler remiges and the tail is often two-coloured above with paler markings on rump and base and darker distal half. The wing-action is more hurried with faster and stiffer wing-beats. Feet turn yellowish from 1st cy autumn. Adults are dark-headed and finely barred below; underwings uniformly barred with dark trailing edge only to hand and the uppertail is distinctly two-toned.

Moult

Annually complete between Apr and Sep.

Juveniles (first moult) A partial body moult commences during 1st cy autumn/winter, in which feathers of head, neck, upper breast and mantle are moulted to a variable extent. Complete moult as in adults, but starting later in spring.

Adults (subsequent moults) The complete moult begins for females shortly upon laying, from early Apr to mid-May, and is completed during late Sep–Oct. (Hungary, 30 Jul, adult female moulting outer primaries; pers. obs.). Adult males begin to moult up to a month later, but moult still completed in time with the females. Captive birds completed their primary moult in 110–128 days.

Ageing and sexing

Normally difficult to age in the field because of early partial moult in juveniles, but also because of considerable plumage variation within each age-class. Attention should be paid to pattern of breast, upperparts and tail, but also to pattern of coverts and remiges of underwing. Colour of bare parts, especially feet, diagnostic.

> **Ageing summary:** Sparsely spotted breast, more distinctly barred secondaries below and more sparsely patterned underwing coverts are typical of adults. Juveniles are darker and more heavily marked on breast and have darker underwing coverts and plainer grey secondaries below. Juveniles are also more uniform above, with narrow but distinct paler margins to the individual feathers, whereas adults show wider and more diffuse rufous fringes and a tendency for rufous cross-bars. Some juveniles and adults (first-adult plumage?) are very similar and are best aged by colour of bare parts.

Juvenile (1st cy autumn – 2nd cy spring)   **Plates 664–670**

Crown appears dark in most, varying from white to deep ochre, with more or less dense dark streaking. Supercilium pale and conspicuous. Eye-stripe variable, usually prominent but not darker than e.g. mantle, mottled or more solid and usually reaching mantle along sides of neck. Dark moustache streaked, usually long and bending around lower cheek and mostly broken below the eye, not straight and pointed as in Lanner. Some birds are very pale headed. Dark eye normally conspicuous in bland face (cf. Lanner).

Upperparts uniformly dark brown with distinct narrow rufous margins to each feather. During winter, margins bleach and gradually wear off. In flight, from a distance, upperparts appear greyish brown with contrasting darker hand. Tail from a distance uniformly coloured, usually slightly paler than rest of upperparts, especially on sides. Tail-barring consists of roundish or oval buffish-white spots, confined mainly to inner vanes, central pair often uniformly brown. Tail thus rather similar to other large falcons; however, round spots diagnostic when present. Pale tail-tip distinct and broad, buffish white, but wears narrower during winter.

Breast whitish with dark streaking extending to belly; vent and undertail coverts uniformly buffish white. Streaking of breast varies individually and least pigmented birds are rather similar to adults, with smallish streaks covering less than 50% of the pale ground-colour, while darker birds may look all-dark on breast showing hardly any light ground-colour. The dark markings grow bolder towards the flanks, which are usually considerably darker than the mid-breast. Trousers vary individually from showing dark streaking to being heavily mottled and practically all-dark, latter being diagnostic against Peregrine and Lanner.

Underwing coverts generally dark with paler margins, creating a typical longitudinal pattern, particularly prominent on the carpal (cf. Lanner). The darkness of the underwing coverts varies with the general pigmentation of the underbody. Thus, birds with a dark breast normally also show dark underwing coverts, whereas average birds usually have paler lesser coverts and darker median and greater coverts. Secondaries uniformly grey with paler barring normally visible only at base of the outer. Primaries have dark tips forming a dark trailing edge to the hand which widens towards wing-tip. Because of reduced barring, the outer primaries of many individuals show a prominent white flash basally (cf. Lanner), contrasting with darker secondaries, while others show more uniform barring similar to juvenile Lanner.

Cere and eye-ring bluish grey, feet pale bluish.

Adult (2nd cy autumn and older)   Plates 671–680

In good views upperparts more vividly fringed and mottled rufous and in many individuals tail is completely barred rather than just showing pale spots. Breast shows usually sparse rounded spots compared with dense streaking in juveniles, but this varies individually and the difference can be marginal, females in first-adult plumage especially may be rather similar to juveniles. Older adults show smaller and sparser round spots on breast with larger rounded spots on flanks and thighs.

In flight, adults are more patterned above and show barring to rear mantle and inner wing and, on average, a less marked contrast between darker hand and paler arm than in juveniles.

Underwing coverts variably patterned and reflect the breast-pattern; birds with pale breast also have pale underwings. Underwing paler than in juveniles with reduced dark markings to coverts and more distinctly barred secondaries. In younger adults the underwing coverts are rather similar to juvenile, but in older birds (especially males) they can appear almost uniformly white. In the palest birds only the greater underwing coverts are patterned, forming an inconspicuous band under the wing; they are streaked or spotted, not barred as in adult Lanner.

The deep yellow colour of the feet in adults is a good ageing character against juveniles in first winter, whereas the colour of the yellow cere can be hard to see in the field.

Sexing: Sakers usually cannot be sexed in the field without direct comparison. Males are smaller and lighter-built than females and they are more sparsely patterned below than females of same age.

References Baumgart 1980; Gantlett 1992; Mebs 1960; Shirihai & Forsman 1998; Stresemann & Stresemann 1960; Tucker & Heath 1995

Plate 664 *Juvenile showing streaked breast, blue feet and greyish secondaries. Nov 1991, Israel (Markus Varesvuo).*

Plate 665 *Juvenile. A rather dark bird showing almost uniformly dark underwing coverts and flanks and heavily streaked underbody. Note pale flash on primaries and pale tail. 7 Feb 1996, Israel (Dick Forsman).*

Plate 666 *Juvenile. A rather dark bird. Note dark trousers and blue feet as well as diagnostic round pale spots in tail. Winter, Israel (Hadoram Shirihai).*

Plate 667 *Juvenile. A rather pale individual with reduced markings on breast. Note white ground-colour to underparts, well marked underwing coverts and typical head-pattern. 16 Mar 1992, Israel (Dick Forsman).*

Plate 668 *Fresh juveniles in captivity showing variation in pattern of upperparts and head. Note rufous feather-fringes to upperparts and tail-pattern and compare with juvenile Gyrfalcon. Jun 1992, Kazakhstan (Krister Mild).*

Plate 669 *Juvenile. An escaped falconer's bird showing a better preserved plumage than juveniles in the wild (cf. Plate 670). Note bluish cere and feet and uniform rufous fringes to upperparts typical of juvenile. Head-pattern typical, with moustache disconnected from peering dark eye. Feb 1997, Israel (Markus Varesvuo).*

Plate 670 *Juvenile showing typically faded and worn upperparts by spring. This bird has a very poorly marked head and shows some newly moulted dark scapulars. 19 Feb 1997, Israel (Dick Forsman).*

Plate 671 *Adult (possibly first-adult plumage) showing heavily spotted underbody, rather dark greater underwing coverts and pale but distinctly barred remiges. 21 Jan 1995, Israel (Dick Forsman).*

Plate 672   *Adult. Note spotted breast of adult. Dark trousers indicate Saker when present. Dec 1993, Israel (Markus Varesvuo).*

Plate 673   *Old adult showing reduced markings to breast and flanks but with retained dark trousers. Only greater underwing coverts with prominent dark markings, while remiges are white with rather distinctive barring. 7 Feb 1996, Israel (Dick Forsman).*

Plate 674 *Captive adult of unknown origin.
Note roundish spots to underbody with more
intensely marked trousers. Head shows uniformly
streaked crown and disconnected moustache.
18 Nov 1994, Italy (Dick Forsman).*

Plate 675   *Adult (same as Plate 674). In adults
the rufous markings above are most prominent at
the feather-tips compared with the juveniles. 18
Nov 1994, Italy (Dick Forsman).*

Plate 676   *Adult. A rather heavily marked
individual showing spotted rather than streaked
underbody and pale yellowish not bluish feet.
20 Dec 1991, Israel (Tomi Muukkonen).*

Plate 677   *First-adult plumage (3rd cy spring)
showing boldly spotted underparts and adult-type
tail but very bleached, almost colourless feet.
7 Feb 1996, Israel (Dick Forsman).*

Plate 678 *First-adult plumage (same as Plate 677). Dark trousers and fine rufous fringes to upperparts are diagnostic of Saker when present. Note also wing-tips falling well short of tail-tip. 7 Feb 1996, Israel (Dick Forsman).*

Plate 679 *Captive adult of 'saceroides'-type of unknown origin. Greyish upperparts with faint barring as well as barred thighs make this form rather similar to adult Lanner. Note streaked crown and distinctly rufous feather margins above. Jan 1983, Britain (Dick Forsman).*

Plate 680 *Adult female at nest showing diagnostic dark trousers and rear flanks and typical head-pattern, with uniformly streaked crown and with dark moustache broken before reaching the eye. May, Turkey (Alfred Limbrunner).*

GYRFALCON *Falco rusticolus*
Plates 681–698

Subspecies: Now widely considered monotypic, but older sources recognize up to nine subspecies.

Distribution: Holarctic, breeding from Iceland and N Fennoscandia east through Asia, N America and Greenland.

Habitat: Breeds in proximity to open tundra venturing along Arctic coasts, although some nest further south in the coniferous zone hunting on nearby mountain slopes and open bogs. Breeds in mountainous areas but hunts and winters in all kinds of open and semi-open areas, avoiding only dense woodland.

Population: The European population is now considered rather stable, although has declined markedly since nineteenth century. The total population for Europe is estimated to be 780–1330 pairs, with an additional 500–1000 pairs breeding in Greenland.

Movements: Resident and dispersive, with adult birds remaining close to breeding area in winter but juveniles dispersing widely. Many young birds winter along the coasts of N Norway while others fly south to winter in S Scandinavia, much rarer in Denmark and N Germany. N Greenlandic birds (white morph) more migratory, wintering in S Greenland and Iceland and some annually reaching W Europe, especially Britain and Ireland. Most observations from outside the breeding range are from late Sep–early Apr.

Hunting and prey: Preys mostly on medium-sized birds, with coastal populations feeding on waders, ducks, gulls and auks while inland birds rely mainly on Willow Grouse and Ptarmigan. Takes rodents in peak vole years.

Species identification

Length 50–60 cm

wing-span 110–130 cm (Mebs 1989), wing-span *c*. males 110–115 cm, females 120–128 cm (Haftorn 1971)

Similar to other large falcons. Identification should always be based on plumage characters, such as head-pattern and pattern of upperwing and underwing coverts and colour of uppertail. More distant birds characterized by uniform upperparts, broad wings, heavy body and longish tail. Adults and juveniles have different flight silhouettes.

> **Identification summary:** Identified by broad yet falcon-shaped wings with rounded tips, fairly long but broad tail and heavy body. Upperparts appear uniformly greyish or greyish brown, with slightly paler tail, and always lacking pure browns and rufous tones; underwings mostly show contrast between darker coverts and paler remiges. Head-pattern less distinct than in other large falcons.

In flight, distant Distant Gyrfalcons appear rather uniform in colour lacking contrasts to upperparts and the flight silhouette is characterized by broad wings and a fairly long and broad tail, which appears to taper towards the tip. In side profile the breast is deep, while the vent is full and continues well under the tail, adding to the characteristic 'barrel-shape' of the body (cf. Saker). Adults are broader winged than juveniles, and show a unique silhouette among falcons, sometimes even recalling Goshawk, but with straighter wings, shorter tail and a very different active flight. Juveniles are somewhat slimmer and closer in build to other large falcons, but the wings are still proportionately broader and the body is broad and heavy.

Although a Gyr always looks ponderous at take-off, its active flight is relaxed and effortless: the wing-beats are shallow and the hand seems to do most of the work. In powered flight long series of wing-beats are interspersed with short glides, during which the wing-tips clearly bend upwards, a feature usually shared only by the Saker among large falcons. During the glides the wings may appear pointed but, when soaring, the diagnostic broad and almost triangular wings with rounded tips become evident. Gyrs soar on flat wings held level, or sometimes with hands slightly bent up from the carpal.

From a distance, adult Gyrs appear just greyish above with tail slightly paler than the rest of the upperparts. Head coloration varies and may be either paler or darker than the rest of the upperparts. Underparts are paler but the contrast between upperparts and underparts is less pronounced than in e.g. adult Peregrine. The pale underwings regularly show a slightly darker mid-wing-bar and darker wing-tips. Juveniles are more brownish grey above, but give a uniform impression with just the tail slightly paler (especially when fanned). The underbody is streaked and the underwings usually show a rather distinct contrast between patterned coverts and rather uniformly greyish remiges.

In flight, closer In closer views the broad wings and bulk of the body are apparent. The wing-formula differs from the Peregrine-group with p8 being longer than p10, whereas the Peregrines have p10 longer than p8 (p9 longest in both).

Adults are grey above with darker barring, except for more uniform and slightly darker wing-tips; tail is slightly paler grey with fine and dense dark barring unlike Peregrine's dark outer tail. Head-pattern may be either inconspicuous, appearing rather pale with a faint moustache, or all-dark and hooded as in Peregrine, although slaty in colour, not black like Peregrine's. The most common type shows a pale supercilium between dark crown and dark eye-line and the moustache is less prominent than in other large falcons because of darker streaking to pale cheeks. Underparts whitish and distinctly patterned, with rounded spots to upper and mid-breast, changing to broad cross-bars on flanks and thighs. Undertail coverts are barred. Underwings appear rather indistinctly patterned, but this varies according to age and sex. Remiges are more distinctly barred than in juveniles but the darkish wing-tip is still the most apparent character, and the underwing coverts frequently show a darker mid-wing-bar formed by distinctly barred greater and median underwing coverts. Tail appears grey but shows fine complete barring when fanned or when seen against the light.

Juveniles are browner above than adults but usually appear greyish in the field with paler spots to all upperparts including the remiges. Depending on the amount of pale feather fringes above, birds may appear overall paler or darker, but generally appear to lack any contrasts to the upperparts. The general impression from above is usually very uniform, although paler birds may show a paler crown and tail than the rest of the upperparts, with extensive pale feather-tips and spotting visible at close range. The pattern of the head and underbody varies with the general amount of pigmentation. Thus birds with extensively pale spotted upperparts also show a relatively pale head, with just a darker moustache and eye-line, and the breast is finely streaked, while birds with darker and more uniform upperparts show a more distinct and complete head-pattern and the underparts are more boldly streaked. The darkest birds lack pale spots above and show only narrow pale fringes to the upperparts. These birds also show dark heads and the breast appears almost dark with broad, dark streaks. The remiges of all juveniles appear uniform and greyish with an indistinct pattern, save for the darker wing-tips, but the underwing coverts mirror the general amount of pigmentation: paler birds have finer dark streaks and correspondingly rather pale underwing coverts, whereas the average and darker juveniles show boldly streaked median and greater underwing coverts, distinctly darker than the remiges. Regardless of type of underwing coverts they mostly contrast with the paler remiges. Undertail coverts finely streaked and tail appears greyish from below, showing incomplete barring when fanned, although paler birds tend to show broader and more complete barring than darker juveniles.

Perched Gyrfalcons look extremely powerful when perched with broad shoulders and a deep chest, and long fluffy feathers forming bushy trousers to flanks. Wing-tips reach to about one half to two thirds down the tail. Adults are grey above with darker barring; tail paler grey with fine dark bars. Underparts whitish with spots on the upper and mid-breast and bold barring on flanks. Juveniles appear uniformly brownish grey above, with a distinctly paler buffish tail-tip. Creamy feather-tips to the upperparts form tiny Vs on scapulars and upperwing coverts which can be seen only at close range. Underparts creamy with variably bold streaking from upper breast to vent often concentrated into darker patches on flanks. Undertail coverts finely streaked. Head-pattern variable, usually showing a pale supercilium, a rather prominent, yet suffused, dark moustache and a pale cheek-patch, but some darker birds have almost complete hoods.

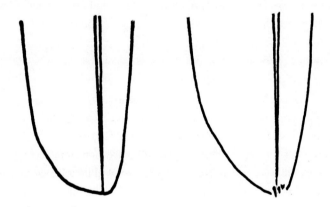

Fig 68 *Gyrfalcon. Outer tail-feather of adult (left) and juvenile. Note different shape with narrower and more pointed tip in juvenile, especially useful when ageing white birds (shape difference applies also to other large falcons; from Forsman 1984).*

Bare parts Cere, orbital skin and feet are bright yellow in adults, pale bluish in juveniles, remaining bluish until at least the next summer. Iris dark brown at all ages.

Variation: The Gyrfalcon occurs in three distinct colour morphs, which to some extent are geographically isolated: a white morph in the high Arctic; a grey morph in the low Arctic; and a dark morph in the sub-Arctic and boreal zones of N America. Intermediates between grey and dark and between grey and white morphs occur. Since the dark morph does not occur in Europe it is treated here rather superficially.

The dark morph is confined to NE Canada as a breeding bird. Dark birds are uniformly dark slate above but the adults show the normal Gyrfalcon-barring on the tail and rump with narrow dark bars on paler grey ground. Juveniles have unbarred tails but show pale tips to rectrices. Underparts are dark slate in both adults and juveniles, with some barring visible on flanks in adults, whereas juveniles are predominantly streaked below and the distinctly dark underwing coverts of both contrast strongly with paler remiges. Head is all-dark with just a paler throat, giving the bird a hooded appearance.

The white morph breeds in the high Arctic of N America, N Greenland and E Siberia, with the frequency of white birds increasing in Asia from west to east. Although it is unmistakable, ageing white morph birds in the field may prove difficult.

The grey morph is the most common of the three and occurs both in N America and in Eurasia and it is the only morph breeding in N Europe. Icelandic birds, formerly separated as ssp. *islandus,* are intermediate in plumage between grey and white birds. They appear generally greyish, but are paler above than Fennoscandian birds, pale milky-grey rather than bluish-grey and with more prominent and more complete barring to the upperparts and paler head with distinct streaking on the crown in adults (mostly uniformly dark in Fennoscandian birds).

Confusion species: Most similar to Saker, but, because of distribution, more likely to be confused with pale juvenile (northern) Peregrines. Confusion risk with Goshawk also possible.

Peregrine (page 554) Juveniles show uniformly patterned and rather dark underwings, with darker and much more distinct barring to remiges than Gyr, and also show yellow feet at fledging. Adults show contrasting black head and distinctly paler rump and inner tail than rest of upperparts.

Saker (page 529) More lightly built than Gyr with narrower and more pointed wings, slimmer body and narrower tail (like comparing flight silhouettes of Pomarine and Arctic Skuas). Saker shows rufous feather-fringes to upperparts and often also rusty crown, while the head-pattern is more contrasting and brighter. Juveniles show clearly darker underwing coverts and hence more pronounced underwing contrast than Gyr.

Lanner (page 515) Adult identified by diagnostic colour of crown and distinct head-pattern; juvenile told from Gyr by distinct head-pattern and in flight as juvenile Saker above.

Goshawk (page 256) Broader and more rounded wings with uniformly pale tips and the tail is longer with a few broad bands. Flies with series of flaps on rather stiff wings interspersed by regular glides, much like huge Sparrowhawk. Head-pattern and eye-colour diagnostic.

MOULT

Annually complete during breeding. Breeding birds may suspend regularly moult during late nestling period.

Juveniles (first moult) Partial body moult starts during the first winter with new feathers appearing on mantle, scapulars and rump. Complete moult from Apr (Norway, 7 May, missing p4–5), probably completed earlier than in adults, although material scanty.

Adults (subsequent moults) Females start to moult during egg-laying/incubation in Apr–early May, males later (Norway, 24 Apr, female on eggs with p4–5 in pin; 2 May, breeding female with p4–5 (–p6 in one wing) in pin (both ZMK); Norway, 13 May, breeding female with p4 growing and p5 missing; Finland, 27 May, ad female in active moult with replaced p4–5, growing p3 and p6 and missing p7 and p2; her mate with p4 growing and p5 missing). At three nests all females suspended primary moult for unknown time starting from mid-Jun, when on average three outermost primaries still unmoulted (pers. obs.). Moult takes *c*. 5 months.

AGEING AND SEXING

Pattern of upperparts and underparts diagnostic. Sometimes also possible to identify first-adult plumage.

> **Ageing summary:** Ageing usually not difficult given good views. Adults are grey above with regular dark barring and the underbody is spotted on mid-breast but barred on the flanks. Bare parts are yellow. Juveniles are brownish-grey above with fine creamy tips and the tail shows incomplete creamy bars. The underparts are heavily streaked with bolder markings on flanks. Bare parts are pale bluish.

Juvenile (1st cy – 2nd cy spring/summer)   Plates 681–689
Cere, eye-ring and feet bluish until at least 2nd cy spring/summer.

Grey morph Upperparts rather greyish brown seen close but appear more greyish in the field. Wing coverts and scapulars with narrow creamy tips, with additional diffuse creamy spots to greater coverts and remiges in many birds. Tail greyish brown with distinct pale tip and incomplete tail-barring formed by buffish ovals rarely reaching across feather; darker birds have more reduced pale spots on tail and uniformly dark central pair, while paler birds have more prominent pale bars, often also on central pair. Underparts creamy buff with individually variable dark streaking, finer in paler birds and bolder in darker birds, growing in width from mid-breast towards flanks. Undertail coverts pale, usually with fine dark streaks.

White morph Unmistakable. Largely whitish ground-colour, although may appear deeper buff from a distance, especially in worn plumage in spring. Upperparts variably patterned in brown, darker when fresh, more chocolate when worn, with more dark arrowheads and broader dark bars above than in adult plumage (pale bars often incomplete, more like marginal spots). In paler birds, with reduced dark markings above and below, retained markings usually as streaks rather than as distinct spots. Pattern of upperparts, underparts and tail extremely variable and depending more on general amount of pigmentation than age or sex.

Adult (2nd cy autumn and older)   Plates 690–698
Cere, eye-ring and feet yellow, even bill largely yellow in white morph.

Grey morph Upperparts grey with darker grey barring, tail paler grey with fine and regular dark bars. Underparts whitish with distinct blackish spots to mid-breast changing to cross-bars on flanks and thighs. With increasing age the underparts become gradually more finely patterned and some old birds may appear nearly white underneath, retaining fine bars on flanks only.

Birds in first-adult plumage (2nd cy autumn – 3rd cy summer) may sometimes be recognized by less distinct pattern of underparts, at times appearing almost soiled, showing yellowish tinge and rather heavy drop-shaped streaking to upper breast, often with diffuse markings, and inconspicuously barred upperparts. Frequently retains odd juvenile upperwing coverts or scapulars.

White morph Unmistakable. Like white morph juvenile, but with blackish rather than brownish markings. Barring of upperparts is finer and more complete and the underparts pattern consists of distinct spots rather than streaks. As in juveniles, adults have highly variable plumages ranging from heavily patterned to almost uniformly white and sometimes with partly white, partly patterned feathers (parti-coloured). First-adult plumage may sometimes be recognized by retained juvenile upperwing coverts and scapulars.

Sexing: Usually not possible to sex in the field without direct comparison. Females are bigger and heavier than males when seen together. Sexes are similar in plumage, although adult males show, on average, a finer pattern below than females, as in other large falcons.

References Clark & Wheeler 1987; Forsman 1993e; Gantlett 1992; Mebs 1960, 1989; Shirihai & Forsman 1998; Tucker & Heath 1995; Wheeler & Clark 1995

Plate 681 *Juvenile. Note greyish brown coloration, contrast of underwing between darker coverts and faintly marked pale greyish remiges and bluish feet. Nov 1995, Sweden (Göran Ekström).*

Plate 682 *Juvenile (same as Plate 681). Softly patterned remiges below, indistinct head-pattern and rather uniform upperwing are typical of juvenile Gyrfalcon. Nov 1995, Sweden (Göran Ekström).*

Plate 683 *Juvenile from above showing uniformly patterned upperparts with paler tail. This bird has a rather pale head. 8 Jul 1991, Finland (Dick Forsman).*

Plate 684 *Juvenile showing pattern and colour of underwings and tail. 8 Jul 1987, Finland (Dick Forsman).*

Plate 685 *Juvenile showing typical upperwing and head-pattern of Scandinavian juveniles. 9 Jul 1991, Finland (Dick Forsman).*

Plate 686 *Juvenile showing typically shortish wings of the species, falling well short of tail-tip. Note dusky cheeks and compare with Saker. Nov 1989, Germany (Axel Halley).*

Plate 687 *Juvenile (same as Plate 686). Plumage greyish brown and whitish buff lacking rufous tones of fresh Saker. Note bluish feet and cere indicating juvenile. Nov 1989, Germany (Axel Halley).*

Plate 688 *Three juveniles showing plumage variation within a brood. 9 Jul 1991, Finland (Dick Forsman).*

Plate 689   *Juvenile white morph. Note rather brownish ground-colour above with whitish spot-marks. 13 Mar 1992, Canada (Bruce Mactavish).*

Plate 690   *Old adult male. Markings of underparts become sparser and smaller with age. 27 May 1991, Finland (Dick Forsman).*

Plate 691   *Old adult male (same as Plate 690). Note broad wings with rounded tips and very heavy body for a large falcon male. 27 May 1991, Finland (Dick Forsman).*

Plate 692   *Adult female with diffuse head-markings and boldly spotted breast with broad bars on flanks. 31 May 1991, Finland (Dick Forsman).*

Plate 693 *Adult female (same as Plate 692). Broad and rounded wings and thick-set body are typical, as well as distinctly barred underwing coverts contrasting with greyer flight-feathers. Note complete and uniform barring of tail. 31 May 1991, Finland (Dick Forsman).*

Plate 694 *Adult female. Note coarse barring of flanks and indistinct head-pattern of this presumably old female. Feet and cere are yellow in adults. May, Finland (Teuvo Hietajärvi).*

Plate 695 *Adult female showing typically completely barred upperparts. Note also uniformly grey rump and tail with regular barring. 30 May 1991, Finland (Dick Forsman).*

Plate 696 *Adult female (same as Plate 695). Note barred upperparts, spotted breast with coarse barring to flanks and trousers and barred undertail coverts. 27 May 1991, Finland (Dick Forsman).*

Plate 697 *White morph, first-adult plumage (3rd cy spring). Note adult-type barring of upperparts, while some lesser upperwing coverts are faded and retained juvenile feathers and the bill appears still bluish. 16 Feb 1992, Canada (Bruce Mactavish).*

Plate 698 *White morph, possibly first-adult plumage. Note pale bluish bill and cere and very pale feet (not deep yellow) indicating immature, while the upperparts show nearly blackish markings with more complete barring than in typical spring juvenile. 2 Apr 1986, Ireland (Anthony McGeehan).*

PEREGRINE FALCON *Falco peregrinus*
Plates 699–720

Subspecies: Nominate *peregrinus* over much of Europe, *F. p. brookei* in the Mediterranean basin and Turkey and *F. p. calidus* on the tundra from NE Europe and further east. Extralimitally another 14 subspecies on all continents except for the Antarctic. For identification of subspecies, see Variation. Barbary Falcon *Falco peregrinus pelegrinoides* sometimes considered separate species.

Distribution: Cosmopolitan with a worldwide distribution except for the Antarctic.

Habitat: Breeds on steep cliffs, in the north also on the ground on wet bogs. Hunts over all kinds of habitats, but prefers open spaces such as coasts, moors and fields.

Population: European population crashed during 1950s because of pesticides, but populations have recovered since in many areas. Total European population now 6200–10 000 pairs (including Greenland), with major populations in Spain, Britain and France.

Movements: Northern populations migratory, while birds of C and S Europe are sedentary or dispersive. Birds from N Fennoscandia leave their breeding grounds from late Aug, with peak late Sep, levelling off during Oct, with late birds still seen in Nov. N European birds winter mainly in France and Spain, but also in NW Africa and the Middle East. In Falsterbo, S Sweden autumn totals in 1986–1994 have varied between 15 and 37. Migrates on a broad front and mostly seen singly on passage and rarely more than a handful even on best days. On passage in the Middle East between mid-Sep and mid-Oct, with some staying to winter. Spring migration in Mar–Apr, with adults moving before juveniles, latter returning as late as May. *F. p. calidus* is a long distance migrant wintering from S Europe and the Middle East throughout Africa.

Hunting and prey: Specialized in catching medium-sized birds in the air. When hunting soars for long periods and often very high up. When suitable prey spotted goes in to a long steep glide, sometimes terminating in an impressive vertical stoop with folded wings. Either knocks out its victim when passing or grabs prey from below and behind while levelling off. Also hunts from perch taking up pursuit after flying birds. Choice of prey depends on local supply, but corvids, pigeons, wildfowl, shorebirds and medium-sized passerines (starlings and thrushes) are usually well represented.

SPECIES IDENTIFICATION

Length 37–50 cm

wing-span 90–115 cm (C & N European birds; Mebs1989) wing-span *c.* males 87–100 cm, females 110–114 cm (Haftorn 1971)

Juveniles and adults differ in flight silhouette, as do males and females, and resident populations are more compact in build than migrants.

> **Identification summary:** Peregrines are best identified by their paler inner tail and rump and their uniformly patterned underwings, with only the hand showing a dark trailing edge. The flight silhouette is robust, with a full chest and vent, a broad-based tail, and the wings have broad bases but fairly narrow and pointed hands when gliding, but appear more evenly broad when soaring, often with a bulging trailing edge to hand and a rounded wing-tip. Adults are typically dark-headed with a white cheek and grey above, while the juvenile head-pattern is more variable, depending on origin.

In flight, distant Distant Peregrines appear heavy and compact compared with other large falcons. Body heavy with a deep chest and a full vent because of huge feet, while the head is big and bull-necked. Body looks almost drop-shaped in side views. Arm broad while the hand appears pointed in powered flight and when gliding, but more rounded with a bulging trailing edge in full soar. Tail broad with a squarish tip and typically appears very broad at the base. Glides and soars on flattish wings, but typically shows slightly raised wings (shallow V-shape) with body appearing heavy as if 'hanging' below the wing-level. In head-on views shows broader body and narrower wing-span than Lanner and Saker. Wing-beats in powered flight are faster and stiffer than in larger falcons, with wings moving from the shoulder.

Upperparts appear greyish or brownish with a notably paler rump and inner tail, while the head looks dark and hooded. Underparts usually show a distinctly paler upper breast contrasting sharply (adults) or gradually (juveniles) with slightly darker lower breast and rather uniformly dark underwings.

Fig 69 *Peregrine. Note broad body in relation to wing-span. Often soars with lifted hands but level arm owing to heavy body in relation to wing-area.*

In flight, closer At closer range adults are bluish grey above, darker on mantle, outer hands and outer tail, with a distinctly paler grey area on rump and inner tail. Head shows a contrasting black-and-white pattern, with a broad and rounded moustache separating the shining white cheek-patch from the white throat. Underbody whitish, often with a salmon wash, and the clean white upper breast contrasts with a finely spotted greyer lower breast and finely barred flanks. Underwings evenly barred and appear very uniformly patterned even at close range. Only the distinct but narrow dark trailing edge to the hand differs from the otherwise uniform appearance.

Juveniles are uniformly dark brown above, but frequently show pale markings on tail-coverts and rump. Tail has a distinct pale tip, but otherwise appears rather dark, with barring difficult to discern. Head-pattern similar to the adult's, although usually less contrasting, with e.g. darker streaking to pale cheeks. Underbody pale buffish and clearly streaked, but tends to show bold cross-bars or arrowheads on the flanks, while the undertail coverts are finely barred. Underwings appear rather uniformly patterned, with only marginally darker coverts than remiges, and only the hand shows a distinct dark trailing edge (cf. Lanner and Saker).

Perched A big-headed and strong falcon with broad shoulders and wing-tips reaching almost to tail-tip. Adults easily identified by distinct black head with broad moustache and white cheeks, bluish grey upperparts and finely barred underparts. Most juveniles identified by typical head-pattern, whereas others resemble more juvenile Lanner/Saker/Gyr in this respect. Juvenile told from juvenile Saker/Gyr by longer wings in relation to tail and by yellow feet, and from all three by finely barred undertail coverts and mostly also by darker head with a broad, rounded and contrasting moustache.

Bare parts Iris dark brown at all ages; cere, eye-ring and feet greenish in late nestling period but turning yellowish during fledgling period, deep yellow in adult. Bill pale grey with a darker tip.

Variation: Although the three European subspecies are distinct, single individuals may be impossible to assign to a certain subspecies, especially *calidus* and northern *peregrinus* (note different moult strategy).

F. p. brookei is small and compact in silhouette, with shortish and broad wings and a stout body recalling Barbary Falcon. Adults are very dark-headed, with a broad moustache and a small cheek-patch, at times appearing completely hooded. Some individuals may show rufous feathers on nape, as adult Barbary Falcon. Lower breast deep salmon, with a sharp division from paler upper breast and the barring of the breast and underwings is broad and distinct. Juveniles are also dark-headed with a broad moustache and a reduced cheek-patch, while the underparts appear fairly dark, with broad dark streaking on ochre ground.

Fig 70 *Peregrine. Typical head-pattern of an Arctic juvenile. Note wide and white cheek-patch, rather narrow but distinct and rounded moustache (often darkest marking of head) and prominent pale supercilium. The forecrown is often pale and the dark eye-line is narrow, which may cause confusion with juvenile Barbary and Lanner. After field-sketch, Israel, 6 Feb 1996.*

F. p. calidus is the largest and palest of the European subspecies and appears long-winged in flight. In N Europe *peregrinus* and *calidus* probably represent a cline from W to E, since many breeding birds from *calidus*' range appear very similar in plumage to *peregrinus* of N Fennoscandia, and vice versa. Adult *calidus* are on average paler bluish grey above and whiter below with finer barring than *peregrinus,* and some old birds may appear completely unbarred below. The moustache is narrower and the white cheek correspondingly wider. Juveniles are whiter below than *peregrinus* and the streaking is finer. Head paler than in typical *peregrinus*, with a prominent pale supercilium, a partly pale (fore)crown, a narrower moustache, and a wide and white cheek-patch. Head-pattern of juvenile *calidus* often bears more resemblance to juvenile Lanner or Saker than to juveniles of normal dark *peregrinus,* but the moustache is broader and darker, often being the most prominent feature in the head while the eye-line may be rather diffuse.

Confusion species: Peregrines may easily be mistaken for other large falcons.

Lanner (page 515) and Saker (page 529) More relaxed wing-action in powered flight. Upperparts more uniformly coloured in all plumages with tail being slightly paler than the rest but lacking Peregrine's pale rump and inner tail. Underwings with distinctly darker coverts than remiges in juvenile but rather uniformly pale or with greyer mid-wing bar in adults, which further show a dark trailing edge to the underwing and more dark at wing-tip. Saker has comparatively shorter wings when perched and never shows fine barring below; juveniles have bluish feet and cere.

Gyrfalcon (page 542) Longer-tailed and broader-winged and the hand is distinctly broader. Powered flight with relaxed wing-beats on flexible wings. Upperparts rather uniform with tail slightly paler than rest. Underwing remiges diffusely patterned. Underwing coverts frequently darker than flight-feathers in juvenile, more variable in adult, but underwing appears generally paler. Perched Gyrs have shortish wings and juveniles have bluish feet and cere.

Hobby (page 505) Much lighter and slimmer with a lighter and more agile flight on faster wings. Hobbies are always streaked on the breast and lack adult Peregrine's distinctly pale rump and inner uppertail.

Eleonora's Falcon (page 470) Much slimmer with narrower wings and much longer and narrower tail and is never barred on breast. Rump and inner tail more or less concolorous with the rest of the upperparts, while the underwings show a contrast between dark coverts and distinctly pale bases to remiges, most prominent on outer hand (skua-flash).

MOULT

Annually complete beginning in females during egg-laying, in males later.

Juveniles (first moult) (C European birds) Start to moult body plumage as early as late winter, beginning with rump, mantle and scapulars. Moult of remiges starts earlier, by Mar, than in adult, and is completed by early autumn.

Adults (subsequent moults) (C European birds) Females start to moult during egg-laying or incubation, males from around hatching. Primaries moulted in 128–185 days and moult completed by Sep–Oct.

  F. p.calidus moults largely in the winter quarters, starting on the breeding grounds in Jun–Jul (in Finnish Lapland breeding females start to moult in late May, coinciding with egg-laying; pers. obs.). The moult is then suspended for the autumn migration, when birds show four (females) or two (males) moulted primaries. The moult is completed in the winter quarters by Feb–Apr. A Finnish adult female, ringed as a nestling 4 years earlier, was found on 7 Oct and showed suspended moult, with p3–6 moulted and p7 growing (pers. obs.). In W Israel, a wintering adult male and two adult females, all showing characters of *calidus*, all had p10 half-grown on 6 Feb. 1996, indicating that the moult was nearing completion (pers. obs.).

AGEING AND SEXING

Adults and juveniles are easily separated by different colour above and by different pattern of underbody. Note also different shape in flight between adult and juvenile.

Ageing summary: Juveniles recognized by brownish upperparts and streaked under-parts. Adults are greyish above and white with dark barring underneath. Juveniles have shorter wings and longer tails than adults, and are hence more similar in sil-houette to other large falcons.

Birds in 2nd cy, until completion of moult, are similar to juveniles but show scat-tered grey feathers on upperparts, especially on rump, mantle and scapulars.

Juvenile (1st cy – 2nd cy summer)   Plates 699–709

Head-pattern more variable than in adult, but most birds show a broad dark moustache, rounded at tip, a darkish crown and a well-defined pale cheek-patch, latter often finely streaked. Paler birds may show a head-pattern more similar to other large falcons, with a prominent paler supercilium, a dark eye-line, a narrower moustache and a partly pale fore-crown and nape. These birds are more common in the north but may also occur in pop-ulations further south. Upperparts dark brown with fine ochre feather margins and broader pale tips to greater coverts and remiges. Rump and uppertail coverts show extensive pale fringes creating a paler rump-patch, which is diagnostic against other large falcons. Uppertail variable, generally darkish when folded, but when spread shows dense ochre barring on hidden inner vanes. Other birds have more completely barred rectrices, includ-ing central pair. Tail-barring typically with pale bars finer than dark ones and with amount of dark in tail gradually increasing towards broadly buff tip. Underparts vary individually in ground-colour from buffish white to yellowish ochre and the dark streaking on breast may be heavier or finer. Typically the streaking turns to bold cross-bars on the flanks (often hidden by the wing on perched birds). Belly, vent and thighs paler and less intensely streaked, whereas the undertail coverts are finely barred, another diagnostic character against other juvenile large falcons. Feet yellow at fledging, separating young Peregrines from juveniles of Saker and Gyr which have blue feet.

By 2nd cy spring and early summer the upperparts are bleached and the pale fringes and feather-tips are lost from wear, whereas the underparts remain much the same. From this time the first blue-grey feathers start to appear on the upperparts.

Adult (2nd cy autumn and older)   Plates 710–720

Head largely black with a broad black moustache and a white cheek-patch and throat. Upperparts grey, with a darker mantle, wing-tips and outer tail, and showing a diagnostic bluish grey rump and inner tail, the latter being the palest area above. Underbody often shows a clear division between shining white upper breast and greyish (barred) lower breast and belly, while the body generally appears paler than the underwings. Closer views reveal sides of breast and flanks to be regularly and finely barred, while mid-breast is spot-ted. Underwings are evenly barred and in more distant views appear uniformly greyish apart from a narrow and distinct dark trailing edge to hand. Underwing coverts are densely barred and do not contrast particularly with evenly barred remiges. Tail is densely barred, with dark bands becoming gradually broader towards the tip, appearing from a distance as a paler base and a darker distal half.

With increasing age the barring of the underparts becomes finer and may almost disappear in old males, whereas females tend to retain a more distinct barring regardless of age.

Sexing: Females are considerably larger than males, but the size is difficult to assess in the field without direct comparison. Males appear bigger-headed in relation to body size and also comparatively narrower-winged than females. In juveniles sexes are similar in plumage; adult males tend to be paler grey above and finer barred below than females of same age.

References Forsman 1980, 1984, 1993b; Haftorn 1971; Kjellén 1995; Mebs 1960, 1989; Shirihai 1995; Shirihai & Forsman 1998; Stresemann & Stresemann 1960, 1966; Tucker & Heath 1995

Plate 699 *Juvenile. Note rather uniformly patterned underwing with distinct dark tips to primaries and barring of tail increasing in width distally. 24 Nov 1996, Ethiopia (Dick Forsman).*

Plate 700 *Juvenile (same as Plate 699). Underwing diagnostic compared with other large falcon species as well as barred undertail coverts. 24 Nov 1996, Ethiopia (Dick Forsman).*

Plate 701 *Juvenile. Underwing and head-pattern typical. Note that streaking of underbody changes to arrowheads on flanks and thighs. 13 Jan 1997, South Africa (Dick Forsman).*

Plate 702 *Juvenile male of Nearctic race* tundrius, *shown because of similarity with juvenile* calidus. *Head-pattern may be extremely similar to juvenile Lanner, but underwing diagnostic. Oct 1995, USA (Jens B. Bruun).*

Plate 703 *Juvenile from above showing paler rump and inner tail. 13 Jan 1997, South Africa (Dick Forsman).*

Plate 704 *Juvenile. Broadly marked flanks and barred undertail coverts are diagnostic for juvenile Peregrines. Note also typically dark head-pattern of this bird. Jul 1984, Turkey (Alfred Limbrunner).*

Plate 705   *Recently fledged juvenile with* calidus-*like head and streaking below. Note yellow feet already at fledging. Jul, Finland (Jorma Luhta).*

Plate 706   *Juvenile* brookei. *Note dark head and deep ochre underparts with dark streaking. 12 Dec 1991, Morocco (Dick Forsman).*

Plate 707   *Juvenile male of Nearctic race* tundrius *(same as Plate 702). Practically identical to* calidus *in plumage. Oct 1995, USA (Jens B. Bruun).*

Plate 708   *Juvenile of* calidus-*type. Note white ground-colour below with fine streaking, as well as pale crown and white cheeks. Note broad spots and bars on flanks and barred undertail coverts both diagnostic of juvenile Peregrine. 21 Dec 1991, Israel (Tomi Muukkonen).*

Plate 709 *Juvenile moulting to first-adult (2nd cy spring). Has replaced most of head, mantle and scapulars while tail and upperwings are still juvenile. 10 Apr 1991, Hong Kong (Ray Tipper).*

Plate 710 *Adult male showing diagnostic head and finely barred underwings and body. 13 Jul 1991, Finland (Dick Forsman).*

Plate 711 *Adult females are more coarsely barred below than adult males.. This bird is in its 5th cy. 19 Jul 1981, Finland (Dick Forsman).*

Plate 712 *Adult female. 12 Jul 1991, Finland (Dick Forsman).*

Plate 713 *Adult from above showing diagnostic pale rump and inner tail. 15 Dec 1991, Morocco (Dick Forsman).*

Plate 714 *Adult breeding female. Note diagnostic head and barring to underparts. Jul, Finland (Jorma Luhta).*

Plate 715 *Adult breeding male. A surprisingly pale individual from the breeding range of* brookei. *Jun, Turkey (Alfred Limbrunner).*

Plate 716 *Captive adult male* brookei. *Dark head and deep salmon chest are typical of this subspecies. Note broad outer tail-bands. 18 Nov 1994, Italy (Dick Forsman).*

Plate 717 *Captive adult female* brookei *showing typically hooded head, deeply coloured chest and heavily patterned lower breast. 18 Nov 1994, Italy (Dick Forsman).*

Plate 718 *Adult Peregrine/Barbary. Many Moroccan birds show intermediate characters between* brookei *Peregrines and Barbary, with darker upperparts and nape, more deeply coloured breast and more distinctly patterned breast and underwings than typical Barbary, but showing narrower moustache, paler cheeks and more sparsely barred underbody than typical adult* brookei. *Apr, Morocco (Göran Ekström).*

Plate 719 *Adult Peregrine/Barbary (same as Plate 718). Note diagnostic paler bluish-grey rump and inner tail compared with other large falcon species. Apr, Morocco (Göran Ekström).*

Plate 720 *Adult male Peregrine/Barbary (see comment to Plate 718). Dec 1991, Morocco (Axel Halley).*

BARBARY FALCON
Falco peregrinus pelegrinoides
Plates 721–737

Subspecies: Taxonomic status confusing and controversial. Forms superspecies with Peregrine *F. peregrinus*, and is either regarded as a desert subspecies *F. p. pelegrinoides* of this (author's preference), or a full species *F. pelegrinoides* in its own right. It is considered a monotypic species by e.g. Howard & Moore (1991), while e.g. Cade (1982) and Gensbøl (1995) also include the Red-naped Shaheen of C Asian deserts in this species (*F. pelegrinoides babylonicus*).

In coastal W Morocco, where Peregrines and Barbarys meet, individuals with plumage intermediate between *F. p. brookei* and *F. pelegrinoides* (pers. obs., see Plates 718–720) occur. Recently, Clark & Shirihai (1995) treat it as a separate species, but found no conclusive evidence (including preliminary results from DNA tests) to validate a split between Peregrine and Barbary. Therefore the Barbary Falcon is best treated as a subspecies of Peregrine pending further studies especially in Morocco, where the two forms meet and are said to breed sympatrically without interbreeding.

The Barbary Falcon is given full treatment here, because most adults are rather easily separable from Peregrines and because of the confusion risk with Lanner where the two occur sympatrically.

Distribution: Scattered over N Africa and the Middle East, but may be more widespread than currently known.

Habitat: Confined to deserts and semi-deserts. Breeds on cliffs, but hunts over all kinds of open areas often ranging far from the nest. Sometimes moves to more cultivated areas outside the breeding season.

Population: Poorly known, but probably more common and widespread than previously thought. About 100 pairs known from Israel, with 2–4 km between known nests in suitable habitat.

Movements: Adults mainly resident, but juveniles disperse or migrate leaving breeding grounds Jul–Sep and returning Mar–May.

Hunting and prey: Specializes in hunting birds in the air, much like Peregrine; being smaller, is even more agile. Takes wide variety of small and medium-sized birds, from larks, swallows and waders to doves, pigeons and sandgrouse.

SPECIES IDENTIFICATION

Length 32–40 cm

wing-span 79–98 cm (*n*=15; Israeli birds; W.S. Clark, unpubl.)

Like a small and compact Peregrine but generally paler above and with different head-markings. Ground-colour and pattern of underparts important in adults, whereas juveniles may be similar to certain Peregrines (especially juvenile *calidus*), hence identification requires combining several characters.

Identification summary: A small and compact Peregrine-type falcon with a heavy body in relation to relatively small wings. Head-pattern similar to Peregrine, but, on average slightly narrower moustache, wider pale cheek-patch and variable cinnamon, rufous or buffish forecrown and nape-patches. Adults generally paler and more ashy grey above than Peregrines and underparts yellowish buff or sandy with fine and indistinct barring, mostly confined to the flanks. Juveniles are similar to Peregrines above but marginally paler; the underparts are pale buffish with finer, sparser and paler streaking than typical juvenile Peregrines.

In flight, distant Heavy-bodied and small-winged, with thick neck and notably thick base of tail, as in Peregrine, thus much more compact than Lanner/Saker. Juveniles, however, are better proportioned with longer tails, being thus more similar in silhouette to e.g. Lanner. Active flight similar to Peregrine and totally different from other large falcons, with rapid and hurried wing-beats on stiff wings working from the shoulder; when soaring, wings are often held in shallow V (cf. Lanner/Saker) owing to relatively heavy body and higher wing-loading. During pursuit of prey, when speeding low over the ground, the wings move extremely fast, especially on smaller male, at times even reminiscent of a Merlin in full acceleration. Adults told from Lanner and Saker of Gyr-group by distinctly paler rump and inner tail contrasting with dark outer tail, juveniles by marginally paler rump than rest of upperparts and by uniformly coloured underwings. Distant birds cannot, as a rule, be separated from Peregrines, unless important plumage details are seen.

In flight, closer Similar in shape to small and compact Mediterranean Peregrine *(F. p. brookei)*, although appears fractionally smaller-winged. Shows wing-formula of Peregrine-group with p10 longer than p8, thus differing from Lanner/Saker, where p8 longer than p10. Most difficult to tell from Peregrine, and juveniles especially are often not possible to identify.

Adults are fractionally paler above than Peregrines but are best identified by the head and underparts. Head-pattern differs from Peregrine in having a slightly narrower moustache and a larger, cinnamon-tinged cheek-patch, but above all by rufous areas on crown and nape, varying in size and shape between individuals. Underbody has a distinctly warm tone, either sandy yellowish or cinnamon, with a paler throat and upper breast. The fine grey barring is mostly confined to the flanks, often greyish themselves, whereas the mid-breast is just finely spotted or may even be unmarked. Underwings appear generally pale, because of the strongly reflected light from the desert environment, and they also appear rather uniform, lacking distinct contrasts. Primaries have narrow and rather distinct dark tips and the carpal shows a faintly darker comma (greater primary coverts). In close views the underwing coverts are barred and, depending on the width of the bars, can appear either fractionally duskier (young adults) or paler (older birds) than the remiges. Tail shows dark bars increasing in width towards the tail-tip, jointly forming a broad subterminal band, but a similar pattern is also frequent in Peregrines.

Juveniles are very similar to *F. p. brookei* in size and proportions, but the head-pattern resembles more that of the larger *F. p. calidus*. Head-pattern varies quite extensively between individuals, especially regarding amount of pale feathering on crown and nape, but usually shows a paler forehead and forecrown and a darker hindcrown and variable pale patches to the sides of the nape, often as irregular bands down the sides of the neck. The pale supercilium is rather variable, normally reaching from the eye to the nape, and the moustache is rather long and narrow with a rounded tip (Fig 71; cf. Lanner). Upperparts are dark brown in fresh plumage with prominent rufous or sandy fringes and feather-tips. The fringes bleach to off-white during the autumn and finally wear off, but the pale tips of the greater coverts are mostly retained. By spring the upperparts become increasingly duller and greyer, through wear. When fresh, rump and uppertail coverts show pale barring, making them the palest area above, but worn spring birds may appear rather uniform above. The tail-barring varies and is rather similar to e.g. Lanner, with narrow rufous bars, often better developed on the inner vanes, and the central pair may either be uniformly dark or show hints of the barring. The tail-tip is broadly buff in fresh plumage, but the tips wear off more or less completely by 2nd cy spring.

Underparts and pale areas of the head are warm buffish or sandy to begin with, but soon bleach to buffish white, approaching *F. p. calidus* in coloration. Fine streaking runs from upper breast to belly leaving much of the ground-colour visible. Thighs are finely streaked and undertail coverts finely barred. Underwings appear darkish and uniform from a distance, showing uniformly barred coverts (cf. Lanner/Saker) and lacking the contrast between coverts and remiges.

Perched A powerful and broad-chested Peregrine-type falcon with comparatively big feet and with wing-tips reaching tip of tail (adults) or close to it (juveniles). Adults identified by rufous areas to crown and nape (may be absent on crown and reduced on nape), rusty-buffish cheeks, and strong and rounded dark moustache. Underparts show a variably deep cinnamon wash, paler on upper breast and throat and with fine barring to underparts, mostly confined to greyer flanks. Upperparts appear pale ashy bluish grey with primaries almost of same colour, but with slightly darker tips.

Juveniles similar to small juvenile Peregrines, but with paler forehead and forecrown, pale supercilium and pale patches to sides of nape; moustache on average narrower and pale cheek-patch wider. Underparts sandier and with finer streaking. Not all individuals possible to tell from Peregrines.

Fig 71 *Barbary Falcon, juveniles. Head-pattern similar to Arctic Peregrines (cf. Fig 70). Note Peregrine-like solid and dark moustache with rounded tip. Supercilium variable, crown pale in front with darker rear crown but details vary. After field-sketches, Israel, 1 Nov 1993 and 10 Oct 1988, respectively.*

Bare parts Cere, orbital skin and feet yellow in adult. In juvenile, cere and orbital skin bluish and feet greenish yellow at fledging, but all turn yellow by first autumn. Iris dark brown at all ages.

Confusion species: Can be difficult to tell from Peregrine in all plumages; juveniles often also confused with young Lanners.

Peregrine (brookei) (page 554) Adults are darker above and more distinctly barred on deeper rufous salmon breast: they have a black crown and nape (some rufous feathers may occur) and, on average, a broader moustache and a smaller cheek-patch; some have an all-black hood. Juveniles are mostly darker, with darker heads (as in adult *brookei*) and the breast is deeper ochre with darker and broader streaks, often with markedly dark flanks. Some juvenile Peregrines may have a superficially similar head-pattern to juvenile Barbary, but the underparts are usually not sandy buff with fine brown streaking, as in Barbary, but are either whiter *(calidus)* or deeper ochre *(brookei)* and the streaks are darker and more contrasting.

Lanner (page 515) Both adults and juveniles are more uniform above, lacking Barbary's paler rump and inner tail. Juveniles show marked underwing contrast between dark coverts and paler remiges, while underwings of adults are generally pale *(erlangeri/tanypterus)* or show a darker mid-wing bar *(feldeggii)*; always more dark at wing-tip than Barbary. Active flight much more relaxed with slower wing-action and body appears smaller in relation to wing-span in head-on views. Soaring birds typically show narrow base of tail.

Saker (page 529) Differs from Barbary as Lanner above.

Merlin (page 495) Clearly smaller and more agile than any Barbary. Lacks prominent moustache and head-markings in all plumages. Adult males show distinct black subterminal band on tail, whereas females and juveniles show sparsely but completely barred upper tails.

MOULT

Annually complete during breeding.

Juveniles (first moult) Juveniles undergo partial body moult in first winter and start to replace some body plumage during 1st cy Oct–Nov, when new adult-type feathers start to appear on upper breast and cheeks, and grey feathers emerge on the upperparts. By 2nd cy spring most birds have moulted head and upper breast complelely. Complete moult, including flight-feathers, starts from early 2nd cy Apr (2nd cy male still with juvenile wings on 17 Mar, Israel; another 2nd cy bird (unsexed) with missing p4 on 8 Apr, Israel). Moult is probably completed by early autumn (2nd cy female completed moult by 1 Oct, Israel).

Adults (subsequent moults) Complete moult between Mar–Apr and Oct–Nov. Commences earlier in females than in males, probably from egg-laying or early incubation (ad male with complete wings on 19 Mar, Israel; ad female missing p4 in Mar, Israel; another ad female missing p4 on 10 Apr, Egypt). One adult male from Israel was still growing p9–10 in Oct (pers. obs).

AGEING AND SEXING

As in Peregrine, juvenile and adult plumages differ significantly and ageing not difficult given reasonable views.

> **Ageing summary:** Adults are bluish or ashy grey above and finely barred below, while the head-pattern is contrasting black and white. Juveniles are brownish above and streaked below with a 'looser' and less distinct head-pattern. With age the barring of the underparts in adults gets gradually finer and finally almost disappears (in both sexes).

Juvenile (1st cy – 2nd cy summer)   **Plates 721–730**

Juveniles are very similar to juvenile Peregrines of the race *F. p. brookei* and the two cannot always be separated. The flight silhouette is more similar to that of other falcons (e.g.
juvenile Red-footed Falcon) than to adult Barbary: the wings appear more evenly broad
and the tail is longer and narrower.

Upperparts are rather dark, yet clearly brownish and often with a slightly rufous cast.
Rump and inner tail are paler and more sandy in colour owing to pale fringes and bars.
Tail shows a prominent pale buffish tip, which wears narrower during winter and may
eventually be lost. Some individuals show a paler area on the upperwing owing to distinctive pale margins to the median coverts.

Underbody always appears pale, sandy to pale buff, bleaching during winter. The streaking is narrow and the individual streaks are finer than the pale areas between them.
Underwing appears uniformly patterned, lacking the striking difference between dark
coverts and pale secondaries of Lanner/Saker, but shows distinct dark tips to the primaries.
During Sep–Oct the first adult-type feathers start to appear on cheeks and upper breast
and differ in being deeper rufous. The partial moult eventually comprises most of the head
and upper breast with some bluish grey feathers appearing on the upperparts. The general
impression is still that of a juvenile, with streaked underparts and largely faded and brownish upperparts and a juvenile tail.

Adult (2nd cy autumn and older)   **Plates 731–737**

Head-pattern always distinct but colour of crown varies considerably. Majority of individuals have a paler forehead, a darker crown and prominent rufous patches on the sides
of the nape, but the darkest individuals are almost completely hooded and show only small
rufous dots on the nape. Moustache always broad, distinct and rounded at the tip (cf.
Lanner), although it may, on average, be slightly narrower than Peregrine's. Upperparts
are pale bluish grey to paler ashy grey, either with faint dark barring or lacking barring
completely. In flight from above, rump and inner tail palest and outer tail and head darkest. Upperwings grey with slightly darker primary-tips.

Underparts appear very uniform and pale. Cheeks, throat and upper breast pale sandy-
buffish, contrasting with deeper colour on lower breast. Flanks and thighs grey and finely
barred, with barring also on those individuals with a uniformly pale lower breast.
Underwing coverts pale grey, with darker barring. Secondaries pale grey and evenly barred
lacking contrast with coverts. Mostly shows a slightly darker crescent at carpal, although
this is shown by some Peregrines, as well. Narrow and distinct dark trailing edge to hand,
widening slightly towards tip. Tail greyish basally with barring becoming gradually more
prominent distally, and outer bars merging to form broad dark subterminal band.

Younger adults (in first-adult plumage) are darker above, often appearing unbarred on
mantle and scapulars, while the underparts show broader bars on flanks, prominent spots

on mid-breast and the underwing coverts are boldly barred (first-adults can be confusingly similar to adult *F. p. brookei*). Older adults are paler grey and more distinctly barred above, whereas the underparts show reduced markings, with fine bars on flanks and with mid-breast either immaculate or with small vestigial spots and the underwings are paler with fine barring on coverts.

Sexing: Females considerably bigger and heavier than males, but size difficult to assess in the field without direct comparison. Females differ slightly in proportions from males, being bigger-bodied and comparatively smaller-headed. As in other large falcons, the underparts tend to be more finely barred in males than in females of same age.

References Baumgart 1989a,b,c; Cade 1982; Clark & Shirihai 1995; Gensbøl 1995; Howard & Moore 1991; Shirihai 1995; Shirihai & Forsman 1998

Plate 721 *Juvenile showing typical tail-pattern, uniformly marked underwings with distinct dark tip and sandy ground-colour below. 31 Oct 1993, Israel (Dick Forsman).*

Plate 722 *Juvenile (same as Plate 721). Note pattern of flanks and barred undertail coverts. 2 Nov 1993, Israel (Dick Forsman).*

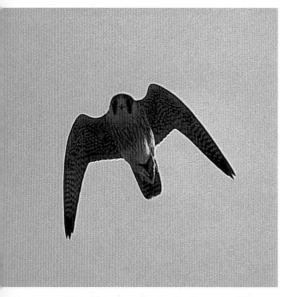

Plate 723 *Juvenile showing Peregrine-like head-pattern and finely streaked underparts. 12 Oct 1988, Israel (Dick Forsman).*

Plate 724 *Juvenile from above in fresh plumage. Note distinct pale tip of tail, barred uppertail-coverts and strong buff wash to head. Jun 1987, Israel (Hadoram Shirihai).*

Plate 726 *Juvenile (same as Plate 725). 1 Oct 1986, Israel (Hadoram Shirihai/IBCE).*

Plate 725 *Juvenile. Has already moulted a few adult-type, uniformly buff feathers on the crop. 1 Oct 1986, Israel (Hadoram Shirihai/IBCE).*

Plate 727 *Juvenile male (2nd cy spring) with moulted head and upper breast, while rest of plumage is still juvenile. Mar 1985, Israel (Dick Forsman).*

Plate 728 *Juvenile (same as Plate 727). Note extreme abrasion of upperparts caused by arid desert climate. Mar 1985, Israel (Dick Forsman).*

Plate 729 *Juvenile female (2nd cy spring) showing moulted head with extensively rufous nape but otherwise still largely juvenile upperparts. Mar 1985, Israel (Dick Forsman).*

Plate 730 *Juvenile in first winter showing moulted head, scapulars and rump, but retaining diagnostic juvenile upperwing and tail. Winter, Israel (Hadoram Shirihai).*

Plate 731 *Adult female. Note sparsely patterned underbody and forewing and fine barring of greater underwing coverts compared with Peregrine. 10 Apr 1991, Egypt (Annika Forstén).*

Plate 732 *Adult males are even less patterned below than adult females. Note diagnostic tail-barring, with bands getting broader towards tip. 19 Mar 1993, Israel (Dick Forsman).*

Plate 733 *Adult male. Small wings in relation to body creates characteristic shape. Note poorly marked underparts with darker carpal crescent and distinct dark primary-tips, big feet and diagnostic head-pattern. Sep 1989, Israel (Markus Varesvuo).*

Plate 734 *Adult male showing typically paler grey rump and inner tail as in Peregrine. Mar 1985, Israel (Dick Forsman).*

Plate 735 *First-adult female (2nd cy). Females show bolder markings to underparts compared with males of same age. 3 Nov 1986, Israel (Hadoram Shirihai/IBCE).*

Plate 736 *First-adult male (same as Plate 737). Upperwings and mantle are darker with less distinct grey barring compared with older birds. 16 Sep 1986, Israel (Hadoram Shirihai/IBCE).*

Plate 737 *First-adult male (2nd cy). Note poorly marked underbody already from first-adult plumage and compare with Peregrine. 16 Sep 1986, Israel (Hadoram Shirihai/IBCE).*

Bibliography

Adam, A. & Llopis Dell, A. 1995: Caracteristicas en Cada Edad del Quebrantahuesos *(Gypaetus barbatus)* y su Proceso de Muda. (Summary of manuscript: Adam, A. & Llopis Dell, A. 1994: Altersmerkmale beim Bartgeier, 1-25.).

Adolfsson, K. & Cherrug, S. 1995: *Bird Identification – A reference Guide*. Skånes Ornitologiska förening, Lund.

Anon. 1995a: European News: Levant Sparrowhawk. *B. Birds* 88:30.

Anon. 1995b: European News: Monk Vulture. *B. Birds* 88:268.

Anon. 1996: European News: Red Kite. *B. Birds* 89:29.

Arroyo, B. 1989: Il censo de Buitreras. *La Garcilla* No. 76:17.

Arroyo, B.E. & King, J.R. In press: Age and sex differences in molt of the Montagu's harrier *Circus pygargus*. *J. Raptor Research*.

Baker, K. 1994: *Identification Guide to European Non-Passerines*. BTO Guide 24. BTO, Thetford.

Balfour, E. 1970: Iris colour in the Hen Harrier. *Bird Study* 17:47.

Baumgart, W. 1980: *Der Sakerfalke*. Wittenberg Lutherstadt.

Baumgart, W. 1989a: Damaszener Wüstenfalken, teil 1. *Falke* 36:6–13.

Baumgart, W. 1989b: Damaszener Wüstenfalken, teil 2. *Falke* 36:54–59.

Baumgart, W. 1989c: Damaszener Wüstenfalken, teil 3. *Falke* 36:91–94.

Bavoux, C., Burneleau, G., Cuisin, J. & Nicolau-Guillaumet, P. 1991: Le Busard Roseaux *Circus aeruginosus* en Charente-Maritime (France) IV Variabilité du plumage juvénile. *Alauda* 59:248-255.

Beaman, M. 1994: *Palearctic Birds*. Harrier Publications, Stonyhurst.

Berg, A.B. van den & Sangster, G. 1995: WP Reports. *Dutch Birding* 17:214.

Bernis, F. 1975: Migración de falconiformes y *Ciconia* spp. por Gibraltar II. Análisis descriptivo del verano-otoño 1972. *Ardeola* 21:489–580.

Bijlsma, R.G. 1983: The migration of raptors near Suez, Egypt, autumn 1981. *Sandgrouse* 5:19–44.

Bijlsma, R., Hagemeijer, E.J.M., Verkley, G.J.M. & Zollinger, R. 1988: Ecological aspects of the Lesser Kestrel *Falco naumanni* in Extremadura (Spain). Rapport 285 Werkgroep Dieroecologie, Katholieke Universiteit Nijmegen.

Bond, R.M. & Stabler, R.M. 1941: Second year plumage of the Goshawk. *Auk* 58:346–349.

Bortolotti, G.R. 1984: Age and sex size variation in Golden Eagles. *J. Field Ornithol.* 55:54–66.

Broekhuysen, G.J. & Siegfried, W.R. 1970: Age and moult in the Steppe Buzzard in southern Africa. *Ostrich* suppl. 8:223–237.

Broekhuysen, G.J. & Siegfried, W.R. 1971: Dimensions and weight of Steppe Buzzards in southern Africa. *Ostrich* suppl. 9:31–39.

Brooke, R.K., Grobler, J.H., Stuart, I.M.P. & Steyn, P. 1972: A study of the migratory eagles *Aquila nipalensis* and *A. pomarina* (Aves: Accipitridae) in southern Africa, with comparative notes on other large raptors. *Occas. Pap. Natl. Museum of Rhodesia*, B5:61–114.

Brown, C.J. 1989: Plumages and measurements of the Bearded Vulture in Southern Africa. *Ostrich* 60:165–171.

Brown, L. & Amadon, D. 1968: *Eagles, Hawks and Falcons of the World*, 1–2. Hamlyn, Feltham, Middlesex.

Brown, L.H., Urban, E.K. & Newman, K. 1982: *The Birds of Africa*, vol 1. Academic Press, London.

Bruun, B. 1981: The Lappet-faced Vulture in the Middle East. *Sandgrouse* 2:91–95.

Bruun, B., Mendelssohn, H. & Bull, J. 1981: A new subspecies of Lappet-faced Vulture *Torgos tracheliotus* from the Negev Desert, Israel. *Bull. Br. Orn. Club* 101:244–247.

Brüll, H. 1977: *Das Leben Europäischer Greifvögel*. Gustav Fischer Verlag, Stuttgart/New York.

Burton, P., Forsman, D. & Lewington, I. In press: *Birds of Prey of Britain and Europe*. Domino Books.

Bährmann, U. 1941: Ein Beitrag zur Mauserweise des Hühnerhabicts, *Accipiter gentilis gallinarum* Br. *Mitt.Ver. Sächs. Ornithol.* 6:126–133.

Bährmann, U. 1969: Einiges über die Flügel- und Schwanzmauser des Mäusebussards. *Beitr. Vogelkde.* 14:330–333.

Cade, T.J. 1982: *The Falcons of the World*. Comstock/Cornell University Press, Ithaca, New York.

Campbell, B. & Lack, E. (eds.) 1985: *A Dictionary of Birds*. T & AD Poyser, Calton.

Christensen, S. 1977: Feltbestemmelse af overgangsdragter af hanner af Hedehøg *Circus pygargus* og Steppehøg *Circus macrourus* (English summary: Field identification of *Circus pygargus* and *Circus macrourus* males in transitional plumages). *Dansk Orn. For. Tidsskr.* 71:11–22.

Clark, W.S. 1987a: The rufous morph of the Booted Eagle. In: *International Bird Identification*, pp. 21–24, IBCE, Eilat.

Clark, W. S. 1987b: The dark morph of the Marsh Harrier. *B. Birds* 80:61–72.

Clark, W.S. 1989: The rufous morph of Booted Eagle. *Dutch Birding* 11:57–60.

Clark, W. S. 1990: Spotted Eagle with rufous nape patch. *B. Birds* 83:397–399.

Clark, W.S. 1996a: Die Unterscheidung des Rötelfalken *Falco naumanni* vom Turmfalken *F. tinnunculus*. *Limicola* 10:57–78.

Clark, W.S. 1996b: Ageing Steppe Eagles. *Birding World* 9:268–274.

Clark, W.S. & Forsman, D. 1990: Plumages of subadult male Marsh Harrier. *Dutch Birding* 12:181–185.

Clark, W.S. & Gorney, E. 1985: *The Eilat, Israel Raptor Migration Banding Project Spring 1985*. IRIC & SPNI, Israel.

Clark, W.S. & Shirihai, H. 1995: Identification of Barbary Falcon. *Birding World* 8:336–343.

Clark, W. S. & Wheeler, B. 1987: *A Field Guide to Hawks of North America*. Houghton Mifflin, Boston.

Clark, W.S., Frumkin, R. & Shirihai, H 1990: Field identification of Sooty Falcon. *B. Birds* 83:47–54.

Conzemius, T. 1996: Hinweise zur Bestimmung des Zwergadlers *Hieraaetus pennatus*. *Limicola* 10:153–171.

Cramp, S. & Simmons, K.E.L. (eds.) 1980: *The Birds of the Western Palearctic*, Vol. 2. Oxford University Press, Oxford.

Danko, S. 1988: Urcovanie Pohlavia a Veku u Mysiaka Severskeho *(Buteo lagopus)* a Niekolko Dalsich Poznamok k Pretahujucej Zimujucej populacii na Vychodnom Slovensku (English summary: Determination of the sex and the age of the Rough-legged Buzzard *(Buteo lagopus)* and some information concerning migrating and wintering populations in East Slovakia). *Buteo* 3:79–106.

Delin, H. 1989: Informellt om stäpp- och ängshökar. *Fåglar i Uppland* 16:173–178.

Dementev, G.P., Gladkov, N.A., Ptushenko, E.S., Spangenberg, E.P. & Sudilovskaya, A.M. 1966: *Birds of the Soviet Union*, Vol.1. The Israel Program for Scientific Translations, Jerusalem.

Dittrich, W. 1985: Gefiedervariationen beim Mäusebussard *(Buteo buteo)* in Nordbayern. *J. Orn.* 126:93–97.

Doherty, P. 1992: Steppe Buzzard morphs at migration. *Dutch Birding* 14:177–178.

Dunne, P., Sibley, D. & Sutton, C. 1988: *Hawks in Flight*. Houghton Mifflin, Boston.

D'Urban, W.S.M. & Mathew, M.A. 1892: *The Birds of Devon*. London.

Edelstam, C. 1969: Ruggologi eller fåglarnas fjäderbyte. *Forskning och Framsteg* 3: 25–29.

Edelstam, C. 1984: Patterns of moult in large birds of prey. *Ann. Zool. Fennici* 21:271–276.

Ekman, B. & Helander, B. 1994: Vita örnar. *Vår Fågelvärld* 53/2:10–12.

Fischer, W. 1983: *Die Habichte*. A. Ziemsen Verlag, Wittenberg Lutherstadt.

Forsman, D. 1980: *Suomen päiväpetolinnut* (In Finnish). Lintutieto, Helsinki.

Forsman, D. 1981: Ruggningsförlopp hos och åldersbestämning av Havsörn *Haliaeetus albicilla* (L.). (In Stjernberg, T. (ed.): *Projekt Havsörn i Sverige och Finland)*. Luonnonvarainhoitotoimiston julkaisuja, Vol. 3 (1981), Helsinki.

Forsman, D. 1983: Åldersbestämning av Havsörn. *Fåglar i Stockholmstrakten* 12:35–39.

Forsman, D. 1984: *Rovfågelsguiden* (In Swedish). Lintutieto, Helsinki.

Forsman, D. 1988: Harvinaisten *Aquila*-lajien määrittämisestä. Osa 1: Kontrastikotkat. *Lintumies* 23:157–164.

Forsman, D. 1989: Harvinaisten *Aquila*-lajien määrittämisestä. Osa 2: Tummat kotkat. *Lintumies* 24:21–26.

Forsman, D. 1990: Fältbestämning av större skrikörn, mindre skrikörn och stäppörn - särskilt äldre fåglar. *Fåglar i Uppland* 17:43–69.

Forsman, D. 1991: Die Bestimmung von Schell- *Aquila clanga*, Schrei- *A. pomarina* und Steppenadler *A. nipalensis*. *Limicola* 5:145–185.

Forsman, D. 1992a: Örnvråk! -bestämning i fält. (English summary: Identification of Long-legged Buzzard). *Fåglar i Uppland* 19:75–81.

Forsman, D. 1992b: Piekanan iän ja sukupuolen määrittäminen (English summary: Rough-legged Buzzards -ageing and sexing). *Lintumies* 27:28–33.

Forsman, D. 1993a: Onko merikotka betonissa? *Tringa* 20:96–99.

Forsman, D. 1993b: *Roofvogels van Nordwest Europa* (In Dutch). GMB Uitgeverij, Haarlem.

Forsman, D. (ed.) 1993c: *Suomen haukat ja kotkat* (In Finnish). Kirjayhtymä, Helsinki.

Forsman, D. 1993d: Hybridising Harriers. *Birding World* 6:313.

Forsman, D. 1993e: Identification of large falcons: Gyr Falcon. *Birding World* 6: 67–72.

Forsman, D. 1993f: Maakotkan iän määrittäminen. (English summary: 'How to age Golden Eagles'.) *Linnut* 28:21–27.

Forsman, D. 1994: Field identification of Crested Honey Buzzard. *Birding World* 7:396–403.

Forsman, D. 1995a: Tunnistatko punajalkahaukan (English summary: Do you know your Red-footed Falcons?). *Alula* 1:8–13.

Forsman, D. 1995b: Field identification of female and juvenile Montagu's and Pallid Harriers. *Dutch Birding* 17:41–54.

Forsman, D. 1995c: Male Pallid and female Montagu's Harrier raising hybrid young in Finland in 1993. *Dutch Birding* 17:102–106.

Forsman, D. 1995d: 2K blå kärrhök eller stäpphök? *Fåglar i Sörmland* 28:18–21.

Forsman, D. 1996a: Identification of Spotted Eagle. *Alula* 2:16–21.

Forsman, D. 1996b: Identification of Lesser Spotted Eagle. *Alula* 2:64–67.

Forsman, D. & Shirihai, H. 1997: Identification, Ageing and Sexing of Honey-buzzards. *Dutch Birding* 19:1–7.

Frumkin, R. 1984: The Sooty Falcon in Israel. *Israel – Land and Nature* 9:138–143.

Frumkin, R. 1988: Biologie und Bestimmung des Schieferfalken *Falco concolor*. *Limicola* 2:83–109.

Frumkin, R. & Clark, W.S. 1988: Is there a dark morph of the Sooty Falcon *Falco concolor*? *Ibis* 130:569-571.

Frumkin, R. & Pinshow, B. 1983: Notes on the breeding ecology and distribution of the Sooty Falcon *Falco concolor* in Israel. *Ibis* 125:251–259.

Gamauf, A. 1984: Einjähriges Wespenbussard ♀ (*Pernis apivorus* L.) brütet erfolgreich. *Egretta* 27:84–85.

Gantlett, S. & Millington, R. 1992: Identification forum: large falcons. *Birding World* 5:101–106.

Gensbøl, B. 1995: *Collins Guide to the Birds of Prey of Britain and Europe.* Collins, London.

Gerdehag, P. & Helander, B. 1988: *Havsörn.* Bonniers, Stockholm.

Ginn, H.B. & Melville, D.S. 1983: *Moult in Birds.* BTO, Tring.

Glutz von Blotzheim, U., Bauer, K.M. & Bezzel, E. 1971: *Handbuch der Vögel Mitteleuropas.* Vol. IV. Akademische Verlagsgesellschaft, Frankfurt a. Main.

Goodman, S.M. & Meininger, P.L. (eds.) 1989: *The Birds of Egypt.* Oxford University Press, Oxford.

Gorman, G. 1996: *The Birds of Hungary.* Christopher Helm, London.

Haftorn, S. 1971: *Norges Fugler.* Universitetsforlaget. Oslo, Bergen, Tromsö.

Harris, A., Shirihai, H. & Christie, D.A. 1996: *The Macmillan Birder's Guide to European and Middle Eastern Birds.* Macmillan, London.

Helander, B., Ekman, B., Hägerroth, J-E. Hägerroth, P-Å. & Israelsson, J. 1989: Dräktkaraktärer hos havsörnar med känd ålder (English summary: Age-specific field characteristics of the White-tailed Sea Eagle, *Haliaeetus albicilla* L.). *Vår Fågelvärld* 48:319–334.

Hollom, P.A.D., Porter, R.F., Christensen, S. & Willis, I. 1988: *Birds of the Middle East and North Africa.* Poyser, London.

Howard, R. & Moore, A. 1991: *A Complete Checklist of the Birds of the World,* 2nd edn. Academic Press, London.

Hoyo, del, J., Elliott, A. & Sargatal, J. 1995: *Handbook of the Birds of the World,* Vol. 2. Lynx Edicions, Barcelona.

Humphrey, P.S. & Parkes, K.C. 1959: An approach to the study of moults and plumages. *Auk* 76:1–31.

Jenni, L. & Winkler, R. 1995: *Moult and Ageing of European Passerines.* Academic Press, London.

Jollie, M. 1947: Plumage changes in the Golden Eagle. *Auk* 64:549–576.

Jonsson, L. 1992: *Birds of Europe with North Africa and the Middle East.* Christopher Helm, London.

Kjellén, N. 1992a: Differential timing of autumn migration between sex and age groups in raptors at Falsterbo, Sweden. *Orn. Scand.* 23:420–434.

Kjellén, N. 1992b: Ålders- och könsfördelning hos sträckande rovfåglar över Falsterbohalvön hösten 1991. *Anser* 31:81–100.

Kjellén, N. 1994: Ålders- och könsfördelning hos sträckande rovfåglar över Falsterbohalvön hösten 1993. *Anser* 33:1–20.

Kjellén, N. 1995: Ålders- och könsfördelning hos sträckande rovfåglar över Falsterbohalvön hösten 1994. *Anser* 34:85–104.

Leshem, Y. 1984: The rapid population decline of Israel's Lappet-faced Vulture *Torgos tracheliotus negevensis*. *Int. Zoo Yearbook* 23:41–46.

Lontkowski, J. 1995: Die Unterscheidung von Korn- *Circus cyaneus*, Wiesen- *C. pygargus* und Steppenweihe *C. macrourus* (English summary: Identification of Hen *Circus cyaneus*, Montagu's *C. pygargus* and Pallid Harrier *C. macrourus*). *Limicola* 9:233–275.

Massa, B., Lo Valvo, F., Ciaccio, S. & Ciaccio, A. 1991: Il Lanario (*Falco biarmicus feldeggii*, Schlegel) in Italia: Status, Biologia e Tassonomia. *Naturalista sicil.* S. IV, XV (1–2), 27–63.

Mather, J.R. 1986: *The Birds of Yorkshire*. Croom Helm, London.

McAdams, D.G. 1994: *Complete Photographic Index to Premier Birding Periodicals and Books*. Privately published, Flensburg.

McCollough, M.A. 1989: Molting sequence and ageing of Bald Eagles. *Wilson Bull.* 101:1–10.

Mebs, T. 1960: Untersuchungen über den Rhytmus der Schwingen- und Schwanzmauser bei grossen Falken. *J. Orn.* 101:175–194.

Mebs, T. 1989: *Roofvogels van Europa*. Thieme, Den Haag.

Meyburg, B-U. & Meyburg, C. 1991: Acquisition of adult plumage in the Spanish Imperial Eagle *Aquila (heliaca) adalberti*. *Birds of Prey Bull.* 4:255–258.

Meyburg, B-U., Scheller, W. & Meyburg, C. 1995a: Zug und Überwinterung des Schreiadlers *Aquila pomarina*: Satellitentelemetrische Untersuchungen. *J.Orn.* 136:401–422.

Meyburg, B-U., Eichacker, X. Meyburg, C. & Paillat, P. 1995b: Migrations of an adult Spotted Eagle tracked by satellite. *B. Birds* 88:357–361.

Miller, A.H. 1944: Molt centers among secondary remiges in the *Falconiformes*. *Condor* 43:113–115.

Morioka, T., Kanouchi, T., Kawata, T. & Yamagata, N. 1995: *The Birds of Prey in Japan*. Bun-ichi Sogo Shuppan, Tokyo.

Moritz, D. & Vauk, G.1976: Der Zug des Sperbers *Accipiter nisus* auf Helgoland. *J. Orn.* 117:317–328.

Mundy, P., Butchart, D., Ledger, J. & Piper, S. 1992: *The Vultures of Africa*. Academic Press, London.

Newton, I. 1979: *Population Ecology of Raptors*. T & AD Poyser, Berkhamsted.

Newton, I. 1986: *The Sparrowhawk*. T & AD Poyser, Calton.

Newton, I. & Chancellor, R.D. 1985: *Conservation Studies on Raptors*. ICBP, Cambridge.

Newton, I. & Marquiss, M. 1982a: Eye colour, age and breeding performance in Sparrowhawks *Accipiter nisus*. *Bird Study* 29:195–200.

Newton, I. & Marquiss, M. 1982b: Moult in the Sparrowhawk. *Ardea* 70:163–172.

Newton, I., Marquiss, M. & Moss, D. 1981: Age and breeding in Sparrowhawks. *J. Anim. Ecol.* 50:839–853.

Noakes, D. 1990: Wing spread of raptors. *Australian Raptor Association News* 11:12–15.

Olsen, K.M. 1990: Spotted and Lesser Spotted Eagles soaring with wings raised. *B. Birds* 83:280.

Olsen, S.F. 1983: Artsbestemmelse av vandrefalk og jaktfalk. *Vår Fuglefauna* 6:15–19.

Opdam, P. & Müskens, G. 1976: Use of shed feathers in population studies of *Accipiter* hawks (*Aves, Accipitriformes, Accipitridae*). *Beaufortia* 24:55–62.

Ortlieb, R. 1996: Die Kleider immaturer Schwarzmilane *Milvus migrans*. *Limicola* 10:105–113.

Palmer, R.S. 1972: Patterns of moulting. In: *Avian Biology*, Vol. II (pp. 65–102). Academic Press, New York.

Picozzi, N. 1981: Weight, wing-length and iris colour of Hen Harriers in Orkney. *Bird Study* 28:159–161.

Piechocki, R. 1955: Über Verhalten, Mauser und Umfärbung einer gekäfigten Steppenweihe (*Circus macrourus*). *J. Orn.* 96:327–337.

Piechocki, R. 1956: Über die Mauser eines gekäfigten Turmfalken *Falco tinnunculus*. *J. Orn.* 97:301–309.

Porter, R.F., Willis, I., Christensen, S. & Nielsen, B.P. 1974: *Flight Identification of European Raptors*. T & AD Poyser, Berkhamsted.

Prevost, Y. 1982: *The wintering ecology of Ospreys in Senegambia*. Ph.D. thesis, University of Edinburgh.

Prevost, Y. 1983: The moult of the Osprey *Pandion haliaetus*. *Ardea* 71:199–209.

Prout-Jones, D.V. & Milstein, P. le S. 1986: Sequential moult with age-class establishment in the African Fish Eagle *Haliaeetus vocifer*. *S.-Afr. Tydskr. Natuurnav.* 16:17–26.

Pöyhönen, M. 1995: *Muuttolintujen matkassa*. Otava, Helsinki.

Rüger, A. & Neumann, T. 1982: *Das Projekt Seeadlerschutz in Schleswig-Holstein*. Kiel.

Saurola, P. 1977: Suomalaisten hiirihaukkojen muuttoreitit (English summary: The migration routes of Finnish Common Buzzards). *Lintumies* 12:45–53.

Saurola, P. & Koivu, J. 1987: *Sääksi*. Kanta-Hämeen Lintumiehet ry., Forssa.

Schmitt, M.B., Baur, S. & Maltitz, F. 1980: Observations on the Steppe Buzzard in the Transvaal. *Ostrich* 51:151–159.

Shirihai, H. 1987: Field characters of the Lappet-faced Vulture. In: *International Bird Identification*. IBCE, Eilat.

Shirihai, H. 1995: *The Birds of Israel*. Academic Press, London.

Shirihai, H. & Christie, D. 1992: Raptor migration at Eilat. *B. Birds* 85:141–186.

Shirihai, H. & Doherty, P. 1990: Steppe Buzzard plumages. *Birding World* 3:10–14.

Shirihai, H. & Forsman, D. 1991: Steppe Buzzard morphs at migration and their separation from Long-legged Buzzard. *Dutch Birding* 13:197–209.

Shirihai, H. & Forsman, D. 1998: Field identification of large falcons in the West Palearctic. *B. Birds* 91:12–35.

Sladek, J. 1957: Prispevok k Nidobiologii a k Postembryonalnemu Vyvoju Orla Kriklaveho (*Aquila pomarina* Brehm). *Prirodovedne Prace Slovenskych Muzei*, Vol. III: 1–10.

Small, B. 1995: Field identification of Red-footed Falcon. *B. Birds* 88:181–189.

Snyder, N., Johnson, E. & Clendenen, D. 1987: Primary moult of California Condors. *Condor* 89:468–485.

Spina, F. 1992: Falco della Regina *Falco eleonorae*. In Brichetti, P., De Franceschi, P. & Baccetti, N. (eds.): *Fauna d'Italia*, Vol. XXIX/ Uccelli I (pp. 658–673). Calderini, Bologna.

Spofford, W.R. 1946: Observations on two Golden Eagles. *Auk* 63:85–87.

Stresemann, V. & Stresemann, E. 1960: Die Handschwingenmauser der Tagraubvögel. *J. Orn.* 103:50–85.

Stresemann, V. & Stresemann, E. 1966: Die Mauser der Vögel. *J. Orn.* 107, Sonderheft.

Suetens, W. 1989: *Les Rapaces d'Europe*. Perron, Liege.

Svensson, L. 1971: Stäpphök *Circus macrourus* och ängshök *C. pygargus* -problemet att skilja dem åt. *Vår Fågelvärld* 30:106–122.

Svensson, L. 1975: Större skrikörn *Aquila clanga* och mindre skrikörn *A.pomarina* - problemet att artbestämma dem. *Vår Fågelvärld* 34:1–26.

Svensson, L. 1976: Problemet att skilja ljus dvärgörn *Hieraaetus pennatus* och ormörn *Circaetus gallicus* från ljusa vråkar *Buteo/Pernis*. (English summary). *Vår Fågelvärld* 35:217–234.

Svensson, L. 1981: Om bestämning i fält av bivråk *Pernis apivorus*- art, ålder och kön - samt jämförelser med ormvråk *Buteo buteo*. (English summary). *Vår Fågelvärld* 40:1–12.

Svensson, L. 1982: Ålders- och könsbestämning av fjällvråk *Buteo lagopus*. *Fåglar i Stockholmstrakten* 11:136–141.

Svensson, L. 1987: Underwing pattern of Steppe, Spotted and Lesser Spotted Eagles. In: *International Bird Identification*, pp. 12–14. IBCE, Eilat.

Svensson, L. 1991: Unterschiede zwischen weibliche Korn- *Circus cyaneus* und Steppenweihen *C. macrourus*. *Limicola* 5:125–128.

Svensson, L. 1992: *Identification Guide to European Passerines*. Privately published, Stockholm.

Sylvén, M. 1977: Hybridisering mellan glada *Milvus milvus* och brun glada *M. migrans* i Sverige 1976. *Vår Fågelvärld* 36:38–44.

Sylvén, M. 1987: Verksamheten inom Projekt Glada 1986. *Vår Fågelvärld* 46:137–143.

Temple, S.A. 1972: Sex and age characteristics of North American Merlins *Falco columbarius*. *Bird Banding* 43:191–196.

Tjernberg, M. 1988: Åldersbestämning av kungsörn *Aquila c. chrysaetos* (English summary: Age determination of Golden Eagle *Aquila c. chrysaetos*). *Vår Fågelvärld* 47:321–334.

Tjernberg, M. 1989: Dvärgörnsliknande ettårig bivråk. (English summary: 2y Honey Buzzard, *Pernis apivorus*, resembling Booted Eagle, *Hieraaetus pennatus*). *Vår Fågelvärld* 48:139–141.

Tucker, G.M. & Heath, M.F. 1995: *Birds in Europe: their Conservation Status*. BirdLife International, Cambridge.

Tyrberg, T. 1994: Fågelrapport för 1993. *Vår Fågelvärld* suppl. nr. 21:51–99.

Ulfstrand, S. 1970: A procedure for analysing plumage variation and its application to a series of South Swedish Common Buzzards *Buteo buteo* (L.). *Orn. Scand.*1:107–113.

Ulfstrand, S. 1977: Plumage and size variation in Swedish Common Buzzards *Buteo buteo* L. (*Aves, Accipitriformes*). *Zool. Scr.* 6:69–75.

Ullman, M. & Undeland, P. 1985: Två intermediärt färgade dvärgörnar *Hieraaetus pennatus* i Skåne 1980. *Vår Fågelvärld* 44:156–158.

Underhill, L.G. 1986: A graphical method to determine the ordering of moult, illustrated with data from the Blackshouldered Kite *Elanus caeruleus. Bird Study* 33:140–143.

Village, A. 1990: *The Kestrel.* T &AD Poyser, London.

Village, A., Marquiss, M. & Cook, D.C. 1980: Moult, Ageing and Sexing of Kestrels. *Ringing & Migration* 3:53–59.

Voipio, P. 1946: Zur Rassenfrage der finnischen Hühnerhabichte. *Orn. Fenn.* 23:3–18.

Walter, H. 1979: *Eleonora's Falcon. Adaptations to Prey and Habitat in a Social Raptor.* Chicago University Press, Chicago.

Weick, F. & Brown, L. 1980: *Birds of Prey of the World.* Collins, London.

Weigeldt, C. & Schulz, H. 1992: Counts of Lappet-faced Vultures *Torgos tracheliotus* at Mahazat As Said (Saudi Arabia), with discussion of the species' taxonomy. *Sandgrouse* 14:16–26.

Welch, G. & Welch, H. 1988: The autumn migration of raptors and other soaring birds across Bab-el-Mandeb Straits. *Sandgrouse* 10:26–50.

Wheeler, B.K. & Clark, W.S. 1995: *A Photographic Guide to North American Raptors.* Academic Press, London.

Wink, M., Scharlau, W. & Ristow, D. 1987: Population structure in a colony of Eleonora's Falcon *(Falco eleonorae).* In: Spagnesi, M. (ed.): *Rapaci Mediterranei* III:301–305. Supplemento alle Ricerche di Biologia della Selvaggina.

Wood, H.B. 1950: Growth bars in feathers. *Auk* 67:486–491.

Yekutiel, D. (ed.) 1991: *Raptors in Israel: Passage and Wintering Populations.* IBCE, Eilat.

Zuppke, U. 1987: Beobachtungen zum Verhalten und zur Grossgefiedermauser einer in Gefangenschaft gehaltenen Rohrweihe (*Circus aeruginosus*). *Zool. Abh.* 42:169–180.

SPECIES INDEX